Critical and Cultural

One of the longest standing traditions in sociology, interactionism is concerned with studying human interaction and showing how society to a large part is constituted by patterns of interaction. In spite of the work of figures such as Robert E. Park, Everett C. Hughes, Erving Goffman, Herbert Blumer, Norman K. Denzin and Gary Alan Fine, interactionism – perhaps owing to its association with the perspective of symbolic interactionism – remains something of an odd man out in mainstream sociology. This book seeks to rectify this apparent neglect by bringing together critical social theories and microsociological approaches to research, thus revealing the critical and cultural potentials in interactionism – the chapters arguing that far from being oriented towards the status quo, interactionism in fact contains a critical and cultural edge. Presenting the latest work from some of the leading figures in interactionist thought to show recent developments in the field and offer an overview of some of the most potent and prominent ideas within critical and cultural criminology, *Critical and Cultural Interactionism* will appeal to scholars of sociology with interests in interactionism, social theory research methods and criminology.

Michael Hviid Jacobsen is Professor of Sociology at Aalborg University, Denmark. He is the co-author of *The Social Thought of Erving Goffman*, the editor of *Postmortal Society*; *Deconstructing Death*; *The Poetics of Crime*; and *Beyond Bauman: Creative Excursions and Critical Engagements*, and the co-editor of *The Sociology of Zygmunt Bauman; Encountering the Everyday*; *The Transformation of Modernity*; *Utopia: Social Theory and the Future*; *Imaginative Methodologies: The Poetic Imagination in the Social Sciences*; and *Liquid Criminology*.

Classical and Contemporary Social Theory
Stjepan G. Mestrovic
Texas A&M University, USA

Classical and Contemporary Social Theory publishes rigorous scholarly work that re-discovers the relevance of social theory for contemporary times, demonstrating the enduring importance of theory for modern social issues. The series covers social theory in a broad sense, inviting contributions on both 'classical' and modern theory, thus encompassing sociology, without being confined to a single discipline. As such, work from across the social sciences is welcome, provided that volumes address the social context of particular issues, subjects, or figures and offer new understandings of social reality and the contribution of a theorist or school to our understanding of it.

The series considers significant new appraisals of established thinkers or schools, comparative works or contributions that discuss a particular social issue or phenomenon in relation to the work of specific theorists or theoretical approaches. Contributions are welcome that assess broad strands of thought within certain schools or across the work of a number of thinkers, but always with an eye toward contributing to contemporary understandings of social issues and contexts.

Titles in this series

Updating Charles H. Cooley
Contemporary Perspectives on a Sociological Classic
Edited by Natalia Ruiz-Junco and Baptiste Brossard

Freud as a Social and Cultural Theorist
On Human Nature and the Civilizing Process
Howard L. Kaye

From the Peaceable to the Barbaric
Thorstein Veblen and the Charro Cowboy
Beatriz Aldana Marquez

Morality Made Visible
Edward Westermarck's Moral and Social Theory
Otto Pipatti

Critical and Cultural Interactionism
Insights from Sociology and Criminology
Michael Hviid Jacobsen

For more information about this series, please visit: https://www.routledge.com/sociology/series/ASHSER1383

Critical and Cultural Interactionism

Insights from Sociology and Criminology

Edited by
Michael Hviid Jacobsen

LONDON AND NEW YORK

First published 2019
by Routledge
2 Park Square, Milton Park, Abingdon, Oxon OX14 4RN

and by Routledge
52 Vanderbilt Avenue, New York, NY 10017

First issued in paperback 2020

Routledge is an imprint of the Taylor & Francis Group, an informa business

British Library Cataloguing-in-Publication Data
A catalogue record for this book is available from the British Library

Library of Congress Cataloging-in-Publication Data
Names: Jacobsen, Michael Hviid, 1971- author.
Title: Critical and cultural interactionism: insights from sociology and criminology/Michael Hviid Jacobsen.
Description: Abingdon, Oxon; New York, NY: Routledge, 2019. |
Identifiers: LCCN 2018056216 (print) | LCCN 2018060784 (ebook) |
ISBN 9781315141640 (Ebook) | ISBN 9781138306233 (hardback)
Subjects: LCSH: Symbolic interactionism. | Social interaction. |
Sociology. | Criminology.
Classification: LCC HM499 (ebook) | LCC HM499 .J33 2019 (print) |
DDC 302—dc23
LC record available at https://lccn.loc.gov/2018056216

ISBN 13: 978-0-367-67142-6 (pbk)
ISBN 13: 978-1-138-30623-3 (hbk)

Typeset in Times New Roman
by Deanta Global Publishing Services, Chennai, India

Contents

List of contributors   vii
Preface and acknowledgements   ix

Introduction: the coming of critical and cultural interactionisms   1
MICHAEL HVIID JACOBSEN

1 **Misgivings about Goffman: social structure, power
   and politics in the work of Erving Goffman**   12
   GREG SMITH AND MICHAEL HVIID JACOBSEN

2 **Upscaling Goffman: four principles of neostructural
   interactionism**   30
   MICHAEL L. SCHWALBE

3 **A call to a critical interpretive interactionism**   45
   NORMAN K. DENZIN

4 **Dramaturgical interactionism: ideas of self-presentation,
   impression management and the staging of social life as a
   catapult for critique**   61
   MICHAEL HVIID JACOBSEN AND SØREN KRISTIANSEN

5 **Critical interactionism: a theoretical bridge for
   understanding complex human conditions**   79
   PATRICIA M. BURBANK AND DIANE C. MARTINS

6 **Pacifism, gender and symbolic interactionism**   99
   MARY JO DEEGAN

7 **Towards a feminist symbolic interactionism**   119
   SHERRYL KLEINMAN AND EMILY R. CABANISS

8 **An invitation to 'radical interactionism':**
   towards a reorientation of interactionist sociology?   138
   MICHAEL HVIID JACOBSEN AND CAROLINE JOAN S. PICART

9 **Symbolic interactionism and the Frankfurt School:**
   a critical appraisal   164
   LAUREN LANGMAN

10 **Situational analysis as a critical interactionist method**   189
    ADELE E. CLARKE

11 **Cultural criminology and its incitement for symbolic**
    interactionism: transgression, marginalisation, resistance
    and media in the wider context of power and culture of
    late modernity   210
    THADDEUS MÜLLER

    Index   229

Contributors

Patricia M. Burbank is Professor of Nursing at the College of Nursing, University of Rhode Island, Kingston, United States. Her research interests include the following topics: nutrition and exercise behaviour change, fall prevention, correlates of gait parameters, testing technological innovations, prevention and reversal of diabetes, and health of LGBT older adults.

Emily R. Cabaniss is Assistant Professor at the Department of Sociology, Sam Houston State University, Huntsville, Texas, United States. She studies the social psychology of migration, inequality and social change.

Adele E. Clarke is Professor Emerita of Sociology & History of Health Sciences at the University of California, San Francisco, United States. Her research interests include qualitative inquiry; and science, technology and medicine studies.

Mary Jo Deegan is the founding director of the Jane Addams Research Center and Emeritus Professor of Sociology at the University of Nebraska-Lincoln, United States. She has published over 200 articles, essays and reviews, and written or edited 22 books. She is an international lecturer on nonviolence, feminism, pragmatism, education and democracy.

Norman K. Denzin is Distinguished Professor of Communications and Research Professor of Communications, Cinema Studies, Sociology, Criticism and Interpretive Theory at the Sociology Department, University of Illinois, United States. His academic interests include interpretive theory; performance studies; qualitative research methodology; and the study of media, culture and society.

Michael Hviid Jacobsen is Professor of Sociology at the Department of Sociology and Social Work, Aalborg University, Denmark. He has written, edited or co-edited more than 50 books. His research interest includes the following topics: crime, microsociology, social theory, qualitative research methodology and ethnography, death and dying, palliative care, deviance and utopia.

Sherryl Kleinman is Professor Emerita at the Department of Sociology, University of North Carolina, Chapel Hill, United States. She writes feminist sociology, memoir and poetry.

Søren Kristiansen is Professor of Sociology and Associate Dean at the Faculty of the Social Sciences at Aalborg University, Denmark. His current research projects focus on gambling with a special focus on online simulated gambling and the relationships between gambling behaviour and the role of social contexts. He has published widely on a range of issues, including deviance, research methods, research ethics, social problems and social policy.

Lauren Langman is Professor of Sociology at Loyola University of Chicago, United States. His primary interests are social structure and subjectivity, concerns pioneered by the Frankfurt School of Critical Theory. He has used this prospective to look at identity, alienation, national character, the body and various social movements left or right.

Diane C. Martins is Professor of Nursing at the College of Nursing, University of Rhode Island, Kingston, United States. Her research interests include the following topics: health care experiences of the homeless population, hunger and food insecurity for the homeless, social theory, experiences of older adults and immigration, and global health experiences for nurses.

Thaddeus Müller is Senior Lecturer at the Lancaster University Law School, Criminology, United Kingdom. His research interest includes the following topics: immigrant youth; urban sociology; the warm city; drugs and drug policy; qualitative research; academic fraud; resisting stigma; moral entrepreneurship; and transgression in sex, drugs and rock 'n' roll (from Lou Reed to Amy Winehouse).

Caroline Joan S. Picart is Attorney at Law and Adjunct Professor of Law, Florida A&M University, Orlando, United States. She is editor of the Fairleigh Dickinson University Press Series on Law, Culture & the Humanities. Her research interests include law and crime; terrorism; law, culture and the humanities; qualitative research methodology and ethnography; criminology and popular culture; sociology/rhetoric of science; and intellectual property law.

Michael L. Schwalbe is Professor of Sociology in the Department of Sociology and Anthropology, North Carolina State University, United States. His research interests include gender, life history, and the reproduction of inequality.

Greg Smith is Professor of Sociology in the School of Health & Society at the University of Salford, United Kingdom. He has published several dozen articles and chapters, and authored or edited six books. His main interests are in cultural and social theory, methods and methodology, restorative justice, sociologies of interaction, and visual sociology.

Preface and acknowledgements

This book is dedicated to furthering the continued development and relevance of interactionism in sociology and beyond. By now, interactionist sociology has been around for quite some time, fertilising the soil for multiple theoretical developments, methodological advances and empirical investigations into almost every nook and cranny of social life. One might provocatively claim that interactionism has itself now reached the status of one of the stalwart and longstanding perspectives of sociology. However, there is still need for interactionism to continue to engage in critical dialogue not only with its theoretical counterparts but also with itself.

This book is about what is called 'critical and cultural interactionism'. One could insist on creating the initialism of CCI in order to capture, specify and officially label this perspective (just as 'symbolic interactionism' is conventionally abbreviated as SI), was it not for the imminent risk of thereby reifying or formalising what this book covers. The concept of critical and cultural interactionism (CCI), just as the notion of symbolic interactionism is simply, in Herbert Blumer's memorable words, a 'somewhat barbaric neologism', and there is no point in trying to create a specific 'school of thought', 'paradigm' or 'research tradition' by the name of CCI. No attempt is therefore made with this book to monopolise or narrow down these terms, but the book offers some suggestions for some of the many variations and incarnations that such critically and culturally oriented interactionist ideas may take. The purpose of the book is therefore to open the treasure trove of interactionist ideas in order to facilitate a critical discussion of how interactionism may proceed from here, rather than narrowing or closing down the potential incarnations of interactionist sociology. All the contributions included in the book share a sympathetic devotion to interactionism, but they all also venture into critiquing, discussing, provoking and thereby expanding the interactionist imagination.

This book is the outcome of a relatively long and winding process of locating and persuading contributors who in one way or the other identify themselves with the notion of critical or cultural interactionism. I want to thank all those who eventually contributed to the book with thought-provoking ideas and perspectives. As always, I also want to extend my gratitude to my two editors at Routledge, Neil Jordan and Alice Salt, for supporting me in the endeavour to produce and publish this book with their pleasant, positive and professional editorial assistance. Without their understanding of the need for leeway, elbow space and deadline extensions in production plans, this book would not have surfaced. It is my hope that this book will qualify present and future discussions of critical and cultural interactionism.

Michael Hviid Jacobsen
Aalborg University, Denmark

Introduction

The coming of critical and cultural interactionisms

Michael Hviid Jacobsen

This book is an invitation to what is here termed 'critical and cultural interactionisms'. We shall in a bit more detail return to the purpose and content of this notion later. The book is a creative offspring from another volume I had the privilege and pleasure of editing a few years ago titled *The Interactionist Imagination* (Jacobsen 2017), which explored some of the many different roots and variations of interactionist sociology. When completing that volume, I came to consider the necessity of looking more detailed into some of the critical and cultural dimensions of interactionism. Obviously, I was neither the first nor perhaps even the most qualified to do so. However, it took me by surprise how many interactionists in writing as well as in conversation used the notions of 'critical' or 'cultural' interactionism without really qualifying, clarifying or specifying what was actually meant by the invocation of such wording.

For a long time, 'interactionism' has almost intuitively been seen as identical to the notion of 'symbolic interactionism', and for many outside the ranks of interactionist sociology, this may still be the case. This volume wants to rectify or at least challenge this view by exploring some of the critical and cultural potentials of interactionist sociology in a more general sense of the term. In many ways, such a volume is long overdue, especially since the idea of critical and cultural interactionism by now has long since lost its novelty and far predates my usage of the notion here. Interactionism probably always was and certainly still is a motley crew encompassing and embracing many different intellectual perspectives, schools of thought, research programs, and theoretical and methodological approaches. Moreover, interactionism, whether symbolic or otherwise, cannot be *solis sacerdotibus* – only for the initiated. There is something inherently anti-sectarian and anti-exclusionary in interactionism that prohibits it from turning into a church only for the chosen few. Even though conferences are held, journals are published and books are written intended for an interactionist audience, interactionism is not the property of any group of individuals or any organisation. In principle, everybody can study interaction as it takes place in everyday life. Simultaneously, it seems as if this fact in recent years has contributed to a certain intellectual influx from the outside as well as a compartmentalisation within interactionist sociology, to which we return, that by some is seen as a strength and a welcome development and by others as a problem. In this Introduction, we shall look briefly at this 'flaking' and accompanying proliferation of different versions of interactionism; we will deal with the notions of 'critical interactionism' and 'cultural interactionism'; and also, however briefly, discuss the 'politics' of interactionism, before at last describing what this book contains and aspires to achieve.

The implosion of interactionism

Until relatively recently it made some sense to claim that the mentioning of 'interactionism' to a large degree was almost synonymous with 'symbolic interactionism'. Although the notion of 'symbolic interactionism' dates as far back as 1937 when it was first coined by Herbert Blumer, it was not until the 1960s and 1970s that the perspective really started to gain ground as part of the wave of so-called creative sociologies – encompassing phenomenology, existentialism, ethnomethodology and symbolic interactionism (Morris 1977) – that swept across particularly the American sociological landscape. Symbolic interactionism was then seen as part of the opposition to the so-called orthodox consensus – the conglomerate of positivism, behaviourism, structural functionalism and modernisation theory – dominating the American sociological agenda during the postwar period. However, symbolic interactionism was also described at times as the 'loyal opposition' that despite its alternative understanding of a host of core sociological concepts, theories and methods did not really shake the foundation of the status quo, and it would thus eventually disappear again (Mullins 1973). As we know now, symbolic interactionism did not disappear, but rather seemed to gain strength and potency over the following decades. Due to the general proliferation of theoretical inventions, novel perspectives and new hyphenated sociological fields of research, today there are many other, more or less loyal or disloyal, oppositions around (even though we may now seriously question the existence of any 'orthodox consensus' or centre of gravity within sociology) that each in their way voices their critique of what they regard as mainstream and convention, and symbolic interactionism is thus now just one among many other voices (Maines 2003:5). Symbolic interactionism, or more broadly interactionism, has perhaps in this process lost some of the mysterious allure that surrounded it in the early heydays of creative sociology. Consequently, in its coming of age, interactionism is now no longer the odd man out within sociology.

Moreover, it is increasingly difficult to talk about 'interactionism' in the singular as there are nowadays so many different strands, camps, stances, variants and schools around. Obviously, 'interactionism' is the generic term for the study of interaction (at times also called 'social interaction'), but apparently today there is nothing to be called 'pure interactionism' or what was once called a 'simply interactionist approach unadorned with adjectives or hyphens' (McCall and Simmons 1978:11). Interactionism is now many different things at the same time. As Ken Plummer once observed: 'In the future ... it will probably be better to talk of 'interactionist sociologies', in the plural, and to acknowledge these diverse stances' (Plummer cited in Reynolds and Herman-Kinney 2003:85). Well, the future, it seems, is now. Since Plummer's prophecy, interactionism has imploded and is now splintering into a mosaic consisting of a multitude of colourful yet internally different pieces. In the early days (the 'good old days') of symbolic interactionism, there was apparently no strong need to specify one's interactionist sympathies. In fact, many young adepts in interactionism did not even consider their own symbolic interactionist approach to be something special. As Anselm L. Strauss thus famously stated: 'We didn't think symbolic interaction was a perspective in sociology; we thought it was sociology' (Strauss cited in Gusfield 1995:ix). Today, as mentioned, interactionism can be found in many different guises within sociology and its neighbouring disciplines: Marxist interactionism, existential interactionism, critical interactionism, interpretive interactionism, phenomenological interactionism, cognitive interactionism, semiotic interactionism, cultural interactionism, dramaturgical interactionism, structural interactionism, postmodern interactionism, radical interactionism, neostructural interactionism, feminist interactionism, poststructuralist interactionism, queer interactionism, pacifist interactionism, intersectional interactionism, ecological interactionism and so on. The list of interactionisms with a specifying prefix seems to be constantly growing. In fact, even long before this development began to take shape, interactionism was bifurcated between a 'Chicago School' and an 'Iowa School' (at times called a 'non-positivist' and a 'positivist' school) that each in their distinctive way – together with ethnomethodologists and dramaturgists – interpreted and used the basic tenets of symbolic interactionism as their defining trademark (see, e.g., Meltzer and Petras 1970; Petras and Meltzer 1973).

This development with the emergence of many new special branches of interactionism does not, however, signal that 'symbolic interactionism' as the volcanic epicentre of interactionist sociology itself has disappeared. In fact, it seems as alive and kicking as ever before, not least because many of the towering problems and challenges confronting contemporary society – such as the globalisation of crime and terrorism, immigration and integration, changing sexual identities and practices (and the rise and consequences of the #MeToo campaign), radicalisation concerns among young people, perceptions of and reactions to climate change, fake news and populist politics, and the like – not only call for but would greatly benefit from an interactionist sensitivity and understanding (Atkinson and Housley 2003:175). However, the diffusion of interactionism does perhaps challenge the comprehension that all types of interactionism necessarily have symbolic interactionism as their most obvious or sole birthplace. As Thomas DeGloma, former President of the Society for the Study of Symbolic Interaction (SSSI), stated on the state of symbolic interactionism in a speech delivered at the Couch-Stone conference in Lancaster in the summer of 2018:

> Over the past decade, we have witnessed a renewed interest in symbolic interactionism, and in pragmatist theory and methods more generally. Along with this renewed interested, we have seen a remarkable diffusion of interactionism into multiple areas of sociological research. This expansion of interest, coupled with theoretical and methodological diffusion into different substantive areas, has presented us with certain opportunities and challenges … Interactionism

is undeniably one of the most influential theoretical and empirical perspectives in the field. Yet, I think we are also simultaneously seeing a bit of a liquidation effect in our organisations (at least in the United States) – where the tenets of symbolic interactionism have been so widely accepted as the cultural microsociology of our day that those who engage in this work sometimes do not even think of themselves as symbolic interactionists. This diffuse influence presents a great challenge: how do we organize and acknowledge interactionists as an intellectual community given the broad influence of our ideas across different sub-groups and areas of research?

This diffusion and diversification (and to some undoubtedly also dilution) of many different kinds of interactionism particularly over the past two decades has perhaps exacerbated the challenge to interactionism as such an internally coherent intellectual community. Another challenge may be the many attempts to mix interactionism with outside influences. Today, one will often see interactionists refer to or draw equally on a multitude of 'external' theoretical influences when studying topics such as, for example, power (e.g., Michel Foucault), class and inequality (e.g., Pierre Bourdieu) or gender (e.g., Judith Butler). One can be in favour of such import or inculcation of external ideas, or one can be opposed to it. It is evident, however, that interactionism in itself already contains important and original core ideas about these topics – power (e.g., Dennis and Martin 2005; Prus 1999), class and inequality (e.g., Fields, Copp and Kleinman 2006; Schwalbe et al. 2000), or gender (e.g., Cahill 1980; Zimmermann and West 1987) – and that some of them are in fact just as useful and analytically potent as those imported or clipped from other theoretical schools. This is not to say that interactionists should not read, draw on or learn from other theoretical perspectives, but sometimes we seem to look elsewhere for that which we already have in our own possession.

'Critical' and 'cultural' interactionism

As a consequence of the aforementioned implosion of interactionism, today there are multiple interactionisms around and many new 'emerging voices' (Sandstrom and Fine 2003) that each in their way testify to the continued attraction and relevance of interactionism. Some of them still rely on the ballast of classic and core symbolic interactionist ideas, whereas others seem to share the ambition of shifting the centre of theoretical and analytical gravity towards more critical, cultural, structural or macro-oriented positions. The arrival of some of these new inventions or syntheses is, as hinted at earlier, perhaps partly a result of what has been regarded as a reluctance or inability of conventional symbolic interactionism to deal adequately or systematically with topics of power, inequality, social structure, domination and macrosociological issues. Perhaps this perceived reluctance or inability can be traced back to Blumer's aversion towards the use of seemingly abstract theoretical notions lacking empirical substantiation and his serious reservations about ridiculously refined statistical analyses (Blumer 1969:26–27). For example, Arlie R. Hochschild recalls from one of Blumer's courses how he would pressure and tease the students with questions such as: 'What is a social system? What is a social class? It is like a wall? No? Why do you call it a structure? ... What is the unconscious? Can you see it? Touch it? What is it you know when you know it is there?' (Blumer cited in Hochschild 1987:ii). However, associating interactionism merely with microsociology or social psychology (see, e.g., Carter and Fuller 2015) or idiographic naturalistic inquiry for that matter has also meant that its potential for providing a critical study of or commentary on structural or cultural conditions of constraint for a long time has been largely overlooked, which has been noted within as well as outside the ranks of interactionism (see, e.g., Coser 1976; Gouldner 1970; Musolf 1992; Hall 2003). Hence many of the 'emerging voices' of more recent interactionist inventions have been preoccupied with either upscaling, tilting or reframing the symbolic interactionist perspective into more critical and cultural directions.

What, then, is meant by the epithets of 'critical' or 'cultural' interactionism as invoked in the title of this book? It has once been suggested that it 'is problematic for interactionists to stake any claim to a domain called 'critical interactionism'' (Sandstrom, Martin and Fine 2001:226). This is indeed true as would a similar claim stating that it has conventionally been problematic for interactionists to stake a claim to a domain called 'cultural interactionism'. Most of the time, we almost instinctively do not connect interactionism with neither the critical nor the cultural. Back in the 1970s, Michael A. Overington stated that he was 'sad to say' that 'a critical vision, a reflection on the relation of what is to what could be ... is lacking in contemporary symbolic interactionism' (Overington 1976:243, original emphasis). Since then things have changed and different stances of critical inter-actionism have now slowly started to emerge. For example, Wayne M. Mellinger (2008) suggested that his own version of critical interactionism 'seeks to offer an alternative to seemingly procapitalist analyses of the present by focusing on the everyday practices which constitute sites of oppression and domination'. By trying to twist interactionism in a more critical direction, scholars have often thus aspired to move beyond the merely descriptive level and to provide their analyses with a sharper edge aimed at providing food not only for thought but also for action and the development of alternatives. For example, it has been noted how

> scholars have combined interactionist theory with critical theory to move beyond merely describing social worlds to a critical approach of consider-ing how activities can, and should, be organized to better meet the needs of participants ... [and how this] critical interactionist theory affords us an understanding of how identities are not fixed.
>
> (Pike and Weinstock 2013:126)

So despite its apparently long-lasting use, there is still an untapped potential for working more systematically with developing a 'critical interactionism'.

The longstanding reluctance surrounding the notion of the 'critical' has almost been matched by a similar distancing to the 'cultural' within interactionist ranks – perhaps seeking to steer clear of the functionalist preoccupation with culture, perhaps wanting to avoid association with 'cultural studies' and 'cultural theory' traditions, or perhaps because 'culture' could be seen as one prominent example of those 'definitive concepts' that Blumer (1969:140–153) so strongly warned against. Even though 'culture' (or 'subculture' for that sake) by no means is a no-go word in interactionist studies, it is often treated less lovingly and systematically as notions of 'self', 'identity', 'role', 'interaction', 'situation', 'meaning' and so on. As proposed by, for example, Norman K. Denzin (1992), James A. Forte (2001), Paul R. Lichterman (2007) and others, there is however an important and fruitful link between interactionism and cultural approaches. Although 'cultural interactionism' comes in many different shapes and forms, a common feature seems to be the stress on culture as a living and changing aspect of human and social life. The reason for this common ground is quite obvious: interaction is on the one hand circumscribed and shaped by what McCall and Simmons (1966: 23–25) once called 'cultural boundaries', meaning all those preferred 'whos', 'whats', 'whens' and 'wheres' that are dictated by cultural factors (and learned during socialisation), but on the other hand culture itself is also continuously explored, shared, consumed, constituted, challenged, contested and changed by interaction. Interaction and culture are therefore not two separate or opposed domains; they are rather interwoven in the complex process of human meaning-making in the world that is exactly one of the core concerns of interactionist sociology. There are thus many good reasons to start considering and making use of the critical and cultural strands of contemporary interactionism.

The 'politics' of interactionism

The question of the role of values, ideology, personal convictions and political opinions in social research is almost as ancient as social research itself. It is also a question that one needs to treat cautiously as there are many sore toes around just waiting to be trodden on. Also within interactionist sociology, it remains a delicate question, and when one is invoking notions of 'critical' and 'cultural' interactionism, this almost inevitably begets the question of politics. As mentioned earlier, interactionism is by many predominantly regarded as a microsociological perspective that is concerned with the in-depth study of face-to-face interaction and identity-construction and meaning-making on the level of everyday life. Thus, the question of politics (understood as the political system or 'Politics' with a capital P) has often been seen at best as secondary to such mundane concerns and mostly as irrelevant. As mentioned earlier, symbolic interactionism was once labelled the 'loyal opposition' to the existing and dominant theoretical positions – a loyal opposition that was perhaps a minor nuisance but posed no real threat to neither the status quo within sociology nor to society at large. During the 1970s, there was a certain discussion about the politics of symbolic interactionism (which at certain intervals has resurfaced since), and the general opinion seemed to be that interactionism (together with most other creative sociologies), despite its progressive research agenda and its concern with micro-issues of power and deviance, on the overall was a rather apolitical or conservative and even reactionary enterprise (see, e.g., Gouldner 1970; McNall and Johnson 1975; Morris 1975). Today, this seems to have changed. Attending interactionist conferences, reading interaction-ist studies and listening to interactionists talk, one is rarely in doubt that political indignation or moral sentiment are important motivation factors behind a lot of interactionist research.

Do we then with this book, by opting for a critical and cultural interactionism, open the floodgates for all sorts of political, ideological and value-laden outpour-ings? This has certainly not been the purpose behind the production of this book. Whether we want to use our social research for ideological or normative purpose is, at the end of the day, a matter of personal taste and preference. May every-one find and cultivate their own path within the realm of interactionism. In this respect, however, my own personal as well as professional conviction is very similar to that hinted at many years ago by Everett C. Hughes:

> Some say that sociology is a normative science. If they mean that social norms are one of its main objects of study, I agree. If they mean anything else, I do not agree. Many branches of human learning have suffered from taking norms too seriously. Departments of language in universities are often so normative that they kill and pin up their delicate moth of poetry and stuff their beasts of powerful living profess before letting students examine them.
> (Hughes 1971/1984:xviii)

It is my conviction that we would be doing a great disservice to interactionism (and to social science in general) if we – either openly or more subtly – conflate it with or mistake it for our personal and political opinions. It is also my con-viction that interactionism, at heart, is neither right wing nor left wing, neither ideologically conservative nor liberal or socialist for that matter. The community of interactionists comprises a broad range of positions, ideas, approaches, life-styles and personal predilections, but although many interactionists undoubtedly regard themselves as progressive and liberal-minded people (which is also why they study the topics they do), this progressiveness – at the end of the day – can-not be attributed to or explained by their interactionism or vice versa. So even though we, me and my colleagues in this book, argue for the importance of a critical and cultural interactionism, this does not necessarily entail the support for a political agenda of interactionism. I am, however, aware that not all of us in this volume agree on this topic. In my view, by allowing our interactionism to serve a political purpose or normative cause, we run the risk that not only does our work become tediously predictable but also inappropriately one-sided, and in neither case would this be beneficial for promoting an understanding and recognition of that which we claim to study.

To conclude here on perhaps a somewhat controversial note, it is my convic-tion (or opinion if you want) that no scientific enterprise can claim to be *political* without at the same time calling the very nature of what *science* is into question. A science, a scientific sub-discipline or a scientific school of thought, can and obviously should be *critical* – it can and indeed should investigate critical aspects of society and even of science itself – but it cannot admit or pretend to be a politically driven endeavour and still retain the claim to be a science. If this was the case, we would simply risk starting out with the answers and then be looking for appropriate or interesting questions instead of the other way around. Hence our finest ambition as interactionists (critical, cultural and otherwise) lies, I believe, first and foremost in incessantly studying, searching, rummaging, dissecting, investigating, questioning and understanding the wonderful world of interaction, not in parading as protagonists or defenders of political agendas or ideological stances. Others are obviously welcome (and not least destined) to disagree. I find at least some support for my perspective in Erving Goffman's famous last written testimony before his death:

> I've heard it said that we [the sociologists] should be glad to trade what we've so far produced for a few really good conceptual distinctions and a cold beer. But there's nothing in the world we should trade for what we do have: the bent to sustain in regard to all elements of social life a spirit of *unfettered, unsponsored inquiry*, and the wisdom not to look elsewhere but ourselves and our discipline for this mandate. That is our inheritance and that so far is what we have to bequeath.
>
> (Goffman 1983:17, italics added)

About this book

This book is about critical and cultural interactionism without patenting any of these notions. Thus, no one can claim any monopoly over the notions of 'critical interactionism' or 'cultural interactionism' (just as no one can rightfully insist that there is only one real way of doing interactionist research). There are now simply so many different varieties of interactionism around and they all contain different understandings of what it is all about. Consequently, this book does not claim to hold neither the first nor the last word about critical or cultural interactionism. It does not provide an authoritative reading or rendition of what should and should not be counted among critical or cultural versions of interactionism. Rather, the book wants to qualify our discussions about what critical or cultural interactionism might be by providing a series of different suggestions. This book will thus give voice to some of those who have contemplated or practiced critical and cultural aspects of interactionism in their own work.

The purpose of the book is to shed some light on different perspectives on interactionism that each in their way may warrant the epithets of 'critical' or 'cultural' contributions. In Chapter 1 by Greg Smith and Michael Hviid Jacobsen, we are invited back to the work of Erving Goffman in order to reconsider some of the objections to or 'misgivings' about his work for being micro-oriented, apolitical and thus noncritical, the authors concluding that one will, in fact, find snippets for critical analysis in Goffman's ideas. Chapter 2 by Michael L. Schwalbe also concerns itself with Goffman's work and here the author uses Goffman's ideas as a lever to develop what is called a 'neostructural interactionism'. In Chapter 3, Norman K. Denzin shows how a critical 'interpretive interactionism' to culture can be developed based on insights from performative ideas, activism and agendas of social justice. Chapter 4 by Michael Hviid Jacobsen and Søren Kristiansen revolves around the notion of 'dramaturgical interactionism' and it shows how there is an often overlooked critical potential in different varieties of the dramaturgical perspective such as the 'sociology of the absurd' and 'critical dramaturgy'. Patricia Burbank and Diane C. Martins in Chapter 5 discuss how a 'critical interactionism' can be developed by bridging ideas from symbolic interactionism and critical social theory, and how such a perspective can be applied to studies of social problems. Chapter 6 by Mary Joe Deegan is concerned with tracing the pacifist roots in the classic works of Jane Addams, John Dewey and George Herbert Mead, and in this way, the chapter provides some ideas into the politics of the early interactionist and pragmatist community in the United States. In Chapter 7, Sherryl Kleinman and Emily R. Cabaniss deal with 'feminist interactionism' as a fertile perspective to theorise and study topics such as heterosexism, racism and class inequality. Chapter 8 by Michael Hviid Jacobsen and Caroline Joan S. Picart introduces the perspective of 'radical interactionism' as developed by Lonnie H. Athens and discusses whether its proposed 'radical break' with symbolic interactionism calls for a reorientation of interactionist sociology. The topic of Chapter 9 by Lauren Langman is the relationship between symbolic interactionism and the critical theory of the Frankfurt School, and the author shows how our understanding of themes such as subjectivity, domination and normativity could benefit from a more fruitful dialogue between the two theoretical positions. Chapter 10 by Adele E. Clarke unfolds the perspective of 'situational analysis' as a critical 'theory-methods package' that can be used in shedding light on and critically analysing a multitude of different social phenomena by taking the situation as the unit of analysis. In Chapter 11, written by Thaddeus Müller, the author discusses some of the many important but often overlooked connecting points between cultural criminology and symbolic interactionism, and he shows how topics such as transgression, marginalisation, resistance and the media are obvious sites for making and developing such connections.

To conclude, despite its theoretical width and diversity, this book does far from provide an exhaustive account of the many possible forms of critical and cultural interactionism, but it takes us some of the way. It is therefore important to stress that with this book, the last word has not been said about critical or cultural interactionism; however, this may nevertheless be a good place to start out.

References

Atkinson, Paul and William Housley (2003): *Interactionism*. London: Sage Publications.

Blumer, Herbert (1969): *Symbolic Interactionism: Perspective and Method*. Englewood Cliffs, NJ: Prentice-Hall.

Cahill, Spencer E. (1980): 'Directions for an Interactionist Study of Gender Development'. *Symbolic Interaction*, 3 (1):123–138.

Carter, Michael J. and Celine Fuller (2015): 'Symbolic Interactionism'. *Sociopedia.isa*. Available online at: http://www.academia.edu/16545413/Symbolic_Interactionism.

Coser, Lewis A. (1976): 'Sociological Theory from the Chicago Dominance to 1965'. *Annual Review of Sociology*, 2:145–160.

Dennis, Alex and Peter J. Martin (2005): 'Symbolic Interactionism and the Concept of Power'. *British Journal of Sociology*, 56 (2):191–213.

Denzin, Norman K. (1992): *Symbolic Interactionism and Cultural Studies*. New York: Blackwell.

Fields, Jessica, Martha Copp and Sherryl Kleinman (2006): 'Symbolic Interactionism, Inequality and Emotions', in Jan E. Stets and Jonathan H. Turner (eds.): *Handbook of the Sociology of Emotions*. New York: Springer, pp. 155–178.

Forte, James A. (2001): *Theories for Practice – Symbolic Interactionist Translations*. New York: University Press of America.

Goffman, Erving (1983): 'The Interaction Order'. *American Sociological Review*, 48 (1):1–17.

Gouldner, Alvin W. (1970): 'Other Symptoms of the Crisis: Goffman's Dramaturgy and Other New Theories', in *The Coming Crisis of Western Sociology*. London: Heinemann, pp. 378–390.

Gusfield, Joseph R. (1995): 'Preface: A Second Chicago School?', in Gary Alan Fine (ed.): *A Second Chicago School? – The Development of a Postwar American Sociology*. Chicago: University of Chicago Press, pp. vii–xvi.

Hall, Peter M. (2003): 'Social Organization and Social Processes: Looking Back and Moving Ahead'. *Symbolic Interaction*, 26 (1):33–55.

Hochschild, Arlie R. (1987): 'Memorium for Herbert Blumer'. *Berkeley Journal of Sociology*, 32:i–iii.

Hughes, Everett C. (1971/1984): *The Sociological Eye: Selected Papers*. New Brunswick, NJ: Transaction Publishers.

Jacobsen, Michael Hviid (ed.) (2017): *The Interactionist Imagination: Studying Meaning, Situation and Micro-Social Order*. London: Palgrave/Macmillan.

Lichterman, Paul R. (2007): 'Invitation to Practical Cultural Sociology', in Isaac Reed and Jeffrey C. Alexander (eds.): *Culture, Society and Democracy – The Interpretive Approach*. Boulder, CO: Paradigm Publishers, pp. 19–54.

Maines, David R. (2003): 'Interactionism's Place'. *Symbolic Interaction*, 26 (1):5–18.

McCall, George and Jerry L. Simmons (1978): *Identities and Interactions* (Revised Edition). New York: Free Press.

McNall, Scott G. and James C. M. Johnson (1975): 'The New Conservatives: Ethno-methodologists, Phenomenologists and Symbolic Interactionists'. *Critical Sociology*, 5 (4):49–65.

Mellinger, Wayne M. (2008): 'Critical Interactionism: The Microsociology of Domination'. Available online at: http://criticalinteractionism.blogspot.dk/2008/08/critical-interactionism-microsociology.html.

Meltzer, Bernard N. and John W. Petras (1970): 'The Chicago and Iowa Schools of Symbolic Interactionism', in Tamotsu Shibutani (ed.): *Human Nature and Collective Behavior*. New Brunswick, NJ: Transaction Books, pp. 3–17.

Morris, Monica B. (1975): '"Creative Sociology": Conservative or Revolutionary?'. *American Sociologist*, 10:168–178.

Morris, Monica B. (1977): *An Excursion into Creative Sociologies*. New York: Columbia University Press.

Mullins, Nicholas (1973): *Theory and Theory Groups in Contemporary American Sociology*. New York: Harper & Row.

Musolf, Gil R. (1992): 'Structures, Institutions, Power and Ideology: New Directions within Symbolic Interactionism'. *Sociological Quarterly*, 33 (2):171–189.

Overington, Michael A. (1976): 'Policy Research and the Future: An Exemplar for a Critical Symbolic Interactionism'. *Sociological Focus*, 9 (3):239–250.

Petras, John W. and Bernard N. Meltzer (1973): 'Theoretical and Ideological Variations in Contemporary Interactionism'. *Catalyst*, 7:1–8.

Pike, Elizabeth C. J. and Johnny Weinstock (2013): 'Identity Politics in the Outdoor Adventure Environment', in Elizabeth C. J. Pike and Simon Beames (eds.): *Outdoor Adventure and Social Theory*. London: Routledge, pp. 125–134.

Prus, Robert C. (1999): *Beyond the Power Mystique: Power as an Intersubjective Accomplishment*. New York: State University of New York Press.

Reynolds, Larry T. and Nancy J. Herman-Kinney (eds.) (2003): *Handbook of Symbolic Interactionism*. Walnut Creek, CA: Altamira.

Sandstrom, Kent L. and Gary Alan Fine (2003): 'Triumphs, Emerging Voices and the Future', in Larry T. Reynolds and Nancy J. Herman-Kinney (eds.): *Handbook of Symbolic Interactionism*. Walnut Creek, CA: Altamira, pp. 1041–1058.

Sandstrom, Kent L., Daniel D. Martin and Gary Alan Fine (2001): 'Symbolic Interactionism at the End of the Century', in George Ritzer and Barry Smart (eds.): *Handbook of Social Theory*. Thousand Oaks, CA: Sage Publications, pp. 217–231.

Schwalbe, Michael L., Sandra Goodwin, Daphne Holden, Douglas Schrock, Shealy Thompson and Michele Wolkomir (2000): 'Generic Processes in the Reproduction of Inequality: An Interactionist Analysis'. *Social Forces*, 79 (2):419–452.

Zimmermann, Don H. and Candace West (1987): 'Doing Gender'. *Gender & Society*, 1 (2):125–151.

1 Misgivings about Goffman

Social structure, power and politics in the work of Erving Goffman

Greg Smith and Michael Hviid Jacobsen

Introduction

Erving Goffman is generally regarded as one of the most prominent representatives of interactionism in sociology during the 20th century. Throughout his career, he wrote a number of seminal books and coined numerous important concepts now considered essential constituents of the working vocabulary of the interactionist community. Goffman primarily regarded his own analysis of what he termed the 'interaction order' as a contribution to microsociology, which was concerned with studying and understanding the realm of face-to-face interaction in everyday life settings (Goffman 1983). In this chapter, we discuss some of the criticisms raised against Goffman's microsociological account for apparently neglecting many core concerns in much of sociology such as power, social stratification, social change, culture and social systems, and for providing a so-called 'nice guy' (Billig 2001) and consensual picture of the social world that overlooked issues of social conflict, contestation and dissonance. Often, the overall drift of these lines of criticism is to situate Goffman's sociology as naïve or incomplete or as lacking an adequate sociological awareness. Misgivings about Goffman are those flaws or omissions or oversights that, state the critics, if rectified would provide a much more satisfactory basis for the sociology linked to his name.

We suggest that while Goffman may indeed deliberately have neglected some of these dimensions in his writings, part of that neglect was justifiable in light of his ambitions to establish the sociology of the interaction order. We contend that Goffman provided an important analytical platform that in combination with other theoretical perspectives spawned a multitude of useful and valuable ideas for addressing the lacunae identified by critics. Reading Goffman on the surface level as well as between the lines, we suggest that his sociology provides a key microsociological resource for many macrosociological concerns.

In this chapter, we thus aim to demonstrate that (1) many of the misgivings about Goffman's sociology are in fact anticipated in various ways in Goffman's own writings and do not have the fatal status that some critics often seem to assume; and (2) that attention to various comments scattered across the corpus of Goffman's writings, together with some of Goffman's own analyses of social life, offers a basis for claiming Goffman as a kind of critical theorist and public sociologist. We end the chapter by briefly noting some of the ways in which

Goffman's ideas are being taken forward in contemporary sociological work that indicate the often overlooked critical dimensions and possibilities of the sociology of the interaction order he proposed.

Gouldner's misgivings about Goffman

It was particularly Alvin W. Gouldner's (1970) critique that first gave significant expression to many of the reservations about Goffman's sociology that up until that point had only circulated in seminar rooms and at academic conferences. Certainly, it was one of the earliest and most influential critical commentaries to express the 'misgivings' examined in this chapter. Gouldner's brilliant examination of 'Goffman's dramaturgy' saw it as a 'symptom' of an imminent 'crisis of Western sociology'. In a forceful yet subtle examination, Gouldner's 12-page essay offered a multitude of provocative interpretations of Goffman. Gouldner noted how dramaturgy refused to buy into conventional distinctions and valuations and thus exhibited 'no metaphysics of hierarchy', how Goffman presented a world whose social cement was 'tact', and which seem to articulate the experiences of middle-class workers in the new service occupations whose numbers had grown significantly since the end of World War II. Gouldner characterised the micro-world described by Goffman as a 'new bourgeois world of "impression management" … inhabited by anxious other-directed men with sweaty palms, who live in constant fear of exposure by others and of inadvertent self-betrayal' (Gouldner 1970:382).

More important for Gouldner, Goffman's dramaturgy 'has no metaphysics of hierarchy … the conventional cultural hierarchies are shattered' – the behaviour of children illuminates that of adults, mental patients manipulate psychiatrists – 'there is no higher and no lower' (Gouldner 1970:379). But the absence of hierarchy is ambiguous: it can imply that Goffman's dramaturgy is against existing hierarchies or it can imply an avoidance of or accommodation to the power differences implied by current stratification arrangements. Gouldner's core objections are thus set out the following way:

> Goffman's is a sociology of 'co-presence' … it is a social theory that dwells on the episodic and sees life only as it is lived in a narrow interpersonal circumference, ahistorical and noninstitutional, an existence beyond history and society, and one which comes alive only in the fluid, transient 'encounter' … Goffman's image of social life is not of firm, well-bounded social structures, but rather of a loosely stranded, criss-crossing, swaying catwalk along which men dart precariously … People are acrobatic actors and gamesmen who have, somehow, become disengaged from social structures and who are growing detached even from culturally standardized roles. They are … individuals 'working the system' for the enhancement of self. Although disengaged or partly alienated from the system, they are not, however rebels against it.
>
> (Gouldner 1970:379)

To Gouldner, then, Goffman's work oozed of a certain power-blind 'status quoism' since his 'rejection of hierarchy often expresses itself as an avoidance of social stratification and of the importance of power differences, even for concerns that are central to him; thus, it entails an accommodation to existent power arrangements' (Gouldner 1970:379). Some critics, for example T. R. Young (1971), considered this reading of Goffman too pessimistic and suggested that more radical and even liberatory messages could be gleaned from Goffman's work. Others, like Charles Edgley and Ronny E. Turner (1984), considered such complaints about Goffman's 'status quoism' to mistakenly malign an ally of progressive causes. Edgley and Turner thus regard much of Gouldner's and post-Gouldnerian critical commentary to be based on a shoot the messenger fallacy in which Goffman is blamed for the features of society he describes and analyses. Edgley and Turner claim that Goffman's sociology does not give political comfort to the status quo. On the contrary, Goffman's analyses 'simmer with politically astute criticism of the status quo' (Edgley and Turner 1984:36). Structural questions about power and status are transformed into more 'existentially accurate' forms. Goffman (1959:75) early reminded us that 'a status, a position, a social place is not a material thing, to be possessed and then displayed; it is a pattern of appropriate conduct, coherent, embellished, and well-articulated'. His sociology seeks to understand how such coherent, articulated conduct works in interaction. In that way, he can easily be read as transforming old questions about power and inequality 'in a revolutionary way which places people, rather than institutions at the apex of social and political change' (Edgley and Turner 1984:31). Goffman himself refused to address the issues directly, preferring an oblique and humorous response that acknowledged that his sociology 'does not catch at the differences between the advantaged and disadvantaged classes and can be said to direct attention away from such matters … He who would combat false consciousness and awaken people to their true interests has much to do, because the sleep is very deep. And I do not intend here to provide a lullaby but merely to sneak in and watch the way the people snore' (Goffman 1974:14).

Much of the early debate on Goffman's lack of critical edge was thus inspired by Gouldner's analysis that is infused with a late 1960s political rhetoric that now has lost much of its previous force. More than any other leading sociologist of his generation, Gouldner forged an approach to sociology that saw it as a form of political activism (Chriss 2015). Apparently, Goffman and Gouldner were friends; Gouldner spent parts of the summer of 1964 living in Goffman's house in Berkeley (Chriss 2015:16). In 1974, when Gouldner founded the journal *Theory and Society* (strapline: 'Renewal and Critique in Social Theory'), Goffman served on its advisory board and a little later published his 'institutional reflexivity' theory of gender relations there (Goffman 1977). James J. Chriss (2015) suggests that political differences lay at the heart of Gouldner's critique of Goffman and other interactionist sociologists. Certainly, Goffman found humour a useful device to distance himself from taking Gouldner's criticisms too seriously. These misgivings first articulated by Gouldner have shaped many of the subsequent debates and provide the main themes for our chapter's discussion of some of the major criticisms of Goffman's enterprise.

Goffman's 'microsociology': what about the macro social structure?

Unlike, say, some positions associated with ethnomethodology, Goffman never explicitly queries the existence or reality of conventional conceptions of culture and social structure. However, he does insist on the distinctiveness of his concerns with the interaction order and the ways in which these concerns differ from much of accepted sociology. Often the imagery Goffman uses is of the interaction order as a relatively closed system. Undoubtedly, some of his substantial stints of field-work – in the Shetland Islands, at St. Elizabeth's Hospital in Washington DC and in the casinos of Las Vegas – were research sites ('social establishments') with clear physical boundaries that marked off the social actions they contained from wider society. Especially in Goffman's publications in the late 1950s and early 1960s, there is a tendency for him to write of society's influence on interactional conduct in a strongly Durkheimian manner.

Sociology is conventionally and somewhat artificially divided between those who study large-scale social phenomena (such as the origins of capitalist society; the major economic, social and political institutions of entire societies; or the development of world systems), who are often called the 'macrosociologists', and then those who study social life as it is directly experienced by persons (such as the workings of small groups, the display and recognition of identities, or the structures of conversational interaction), who are often called the 'microsociologists'. Scale seemingly distinguishes microsociology from macrosociology. A fleeting exchange between two persons is of interest to microsociology, whereas macrosociology, as Arthur Stinchcombe (1985:572) once memorably put it, 'is sociology about millions of people'. The sociological tradition has tended to identify with the macrosociological. Microsociological concerns are often dismissed as 'social psychology'. So it is perhaps no surprise that Goffman's single-minded pursuit of a microsociology of the interaction order (Goffman 1953, 1983) could sometimes provoke exasperation from critics unable to see its point. For example, in a 1972 review in *The Sunday Times*, Goffman's then-newest book was greeted as 'a tome about "the realm of activity that is generated by face-to-face interaction and organized by norms of co-mingling" – such as what goes into saying "Excuse me!" to a stranger on the sidewalk – is a stupefying example of, while Rome's burning, fiddling on one string, on one note' (Cooper 1972). A topic, interactional minutiae, combined with a determination to concentrate on interaction's social organisation and only that, was a focus that puzzled and sometimes infuriated critics.

Faced with complaints about such situational limitations of his sociology, Goffman acknowledged its marginal position. As he once provocatively stated about the nature of his own work: 'I make no claim whatsoever to be talking about the core matters of sociology – social organization and social structure' (Goffman 1974:14). Indeed, Goffman's work – no matter how it is twisted and turned by either epigones or critics – *is* primarily microsociological. Although Norman K. Denzin has once claimed that 'those who are preoccupied with turning

[Goffman's] theory into another micro-model perhaps do the discipline a dis-service' (Denzin 2002:111), Goffman's ideas *were* indeed microsociological and have predominantly found use in microsociological contexts. This, however, does not mean that his ideas cannot be used for other analytical purposes, but their groundwork *is* microsociology. In fact, Goffman did have generalising ambitions, but he felt that theories and models of a general kind were still premature. Anthony Giddens thus rightly observed how Goffman 'deliberately avoided any sort of engagement with issues concerning the large scale or the long term' (Giddens 1988:251). In his more critical review, Gouldner stated that Goffman's work is 'a social theory that dwells on the episodic and sees life only as it is lived in a narrow interpersonal circumference, ahistorical and noninstitutional, an existence beyond history and society' (Gouldner 1970:379). Goffman himself also willingly admitted the limitations of his own micro-perspective when he – in one of his few interviews – remarked:

> If you take a substantial institution like a mental hospital you could say that my treatment of the hospital was not seated in a historical perspective, nor, more damaging, did it deal much with the relationship between the mental hospital and the system of institutions of which it is an interdependent part ... That failure is a characteristic of what I do and a weakness of it, although that is not to say that anybody is doing it well ... I defend with no apology treating 'small entities' as my subject matter.
>
> (Goffman in David 1980:7)

However, as mentioned, from this does not necessarily follow that Goffman's work might not have important implications for macro-scale theorising. Many contemporary social theorists – perhaps particularly those concerned with grand theory-building projects – have drawn on and actively used parts of Goffman's ideas as important building blocks in their own abstract theorising about modernity, society, class, communication, social change, gender, social order, and other predominantly macro-scale phenomena (think of Anthony Giddens, Jürgen Habermas, Richard Sennett, Niklas Luhmann, Pierre Bourdieu and others).

We thus suggest that Goffman's work might fruitfully be played against or integrated with more macrosociological concerns. Let us provide an illustrative example. Few have addressed Goffman's implicit vision of social change – and the question remains if Goffman's largely situational microsociology is at all suitable for shedding light on the impact of some of the major social and cultural transformations. While some seem to point out that Goffman's stressing of the art of 'impression management' in encounters and meetings supports the thesis of the rise of an 'other-directed' personality type in modern society (Riesman, Glazer and Denney 1953/2001) obsessively concerned with the validation of self from others (Zussman 2001), others have rather seen Goffman as a protagonist of the rise of recognition claims and reciprocal courtesies in contemporary polite society (Jacobsen 2010b; Jacobsen and Kristiansen 2009). Yet others, Marshall Berman for one in his review of *Relations in Public* published in *The New York Times* in 1972, attempted to look beyond Goffman's somewhat stationary view and saw some disturbing signs for the future of society in his depictions of social relations:

> If this is so, it forces us to face some disturbing questions about the breakthroughs of the sixties. For so many Americans these were years of unprecedented personal expression and political confrontation. In every sphere, we 'refused to keep our place', we broke boundaries, tore down walls, acted out what we felt, encouraged others to do the same. And where are we now? Goffman's final vision seems unrelievedly bleak. Life in the streets appears as a Hobbesian nightmare, life in the family an existential battleground. It seems terrifying both to go out and to stay in. And social life turns out to be far more fragile, more vulnerable than we thought.
>
> (Berman 1972/2000:276)

Later, Lauren Langman followed Berman's lead and has suggested that

> Goffman's analyses of self-presentations and interaction rituals of everyday life, strategies of winning interpersonal and material games in the context of a culture of consumption, inform the nature of modern alienation ... Commodified self-presentations and interaction rituals often can be seen as expressions of alienated selfhood, characteristic of today.
>
> (Langman 1991:108–109)

The question thus arises if these sinister views of a 'commodified' and 'alienated' life and the 'Hobbesian nightmare', which Langman and Berman spotted in Goffman's microsociological writings, can be substantiated by real-life, macro-scale events. Some signs point in a direction that may support Berman's and Langman's bleak readings of Goffman – for example, how we apparently and increasingly have come to live in a society of the spectacle obsessed with surface identities, staged impressions and shallow images (e.g., on Facebook, Twitter and reality-TV shows), how 'life in the streets' may appear more dangerous than ever before (e.g., due to increasing crime rates, the threat of terrorism and a concomitant tendency to become part of moral panics), and how many of the certainties and securities that guided generations before have now been either demolished or diluted (e.g., due to globalisation and financial crises), while many other developments admittedly point in quite the opposite direction.

Despite several attempts to read into Goffman's writings hidden political statements, critical potentials or diagnostical tendencies of a more general or macro-scale nature, it is, however, important to recognise that Goffman never ventured into presenting a timeless or universal model of social life, nor did he want to present a diagnosis of the times or a critical social theory. His aspirations were – some would say more modestly, others more ambitiously – to provide the discipline of sociology with a rich conceptual apparatus and a focused gaze with which to capture and comprehend those micro-aspects of social life, which until then had seemed either unimportant or incomprehensible. So contrary to, for example, Michel Foucault, who, armed with his archaeology of knowledge and genealogy, studied institutions – the prison and the clinic and indeed society as such as a 'generalized prison' – in a historical context focusing on changing power relations, discourses, games of truth and regimes of knowledge, Goffman was content to provide a much more situational, inside view of the 'interaction order' existing *within* the mental hospital without turning it into a grand narrative of modernity or civilisation (Hacking 2004) – although he did, in fact, insist that these traits of the 'total institution' might also be found in as diversified settings as schools, army barracks and concentration camps.

What Goffman thus perhaps lacked in regard to analysing macrosocial change and structural transformations he more than compensated for with his well-developed sense for descriptive detail and colourful and catching concepts when analysing the intricacies and minutiae of microsocial settings. Thus, as Robin Williams boldly observed in an obituary tribute to Goffman, his work met 'the most important requirements of modern social theory – to be self-conscious about the meaning of what it is to know' (Williams 1983:102). What Goffman wanted to investigate and obtain knowledge about was as mentioned the 'interaction order' and its contours, components and content as an analytical micro-domain in its own right.

The connections between the interaction order and other large-scale social orders were first sketched in the two essays making up *Encounters* (Goffman 1961b). Essentially Goffman here suggested that there is a kind of sifting and sorting of externally based attributes of the person (wealth, skills and knowledge, gender, ethnicity, age, etc.) that allows only some to figure in face-to-face interaction. Other characteristics may be screened out or excluded. A metaphorical membrane surrounds the face-to-face situation. Goffman argued that we take interaction roles in addition to regular social roles. In classic functionalist theory, institutions are composed of social statuses and roles involve the enactment of the norms (expectations and obligations) associated with the status. Role is thus the key term linking the individual to the relevant institutional framework. The interaction order exists 'below' the institutional framework. Some interactional roles, such as those linked to service queues, seem almost entirely creatures of the interaction order. Sometimes interactional roles overlap with institutional ones, where a parent talks to a child while a meal is prepared. On other occasions, people may use interactional roles to take 'role distance' from institutional roles, as when a member of a surgical team runs a line of banter with another surgeon during surgery. The idea Goffman develops is that people who engage in role distancing behaviours are not expressing their innate 'human' qualities, rather they are mobilising a role and identity alternative to the official ones.

In the posthumously published Presidential Address 'The Interaction Order', Goffman (1983) made a number of further suggestions about the interface between encounters and social structures, and builds a more coherent model of how micro and macro are related, adopting the metaphor of 'loose coupling' to describe the link between social structures and interactional practices. Externally relevant characteristics may or may not be relevant to how actions are managed within the encounter. They cannot be assumed in advance. That means that the only general relation between the micro and macro levels of sociological analysis is one of 'loose coupling'. Unlike Tom Burns (1992:55), who reads Goffman's proposal as a claim that the macro–micro relation either does not exist or is 'unfathomable', we consider this model a positive formulation. It is *not* a theory of the macro–micro relation because Goffman regards the precise nature of the link to be a question that in specific instances requires empirical investigation. In specific cases, the relevance of ethnicity, class, gender, etc., has to be demonstrated and treated 'as a matter for discovery' (Goffman 1983:12). In this way, Goffman admittedly did not provide us with an elaborated view of how micro and macro connects, although he did indicate that the intricate links between the interaction order and other large-scale social orders needed our careful attention in our studies.

Goffman's 'interaction rituals': what about power?

It has been suggested that Goffman's concentration on the ritual aspects of the interaction order has meant he 'missed the other crucial dimension of social relationships, namely power, and therefore spun a lopsided and incomplete account of social behavior' (Kemper 2011:5). And true, large parts of Goffman's work on the interaction order consisted of teasing out its expansive network of micro-rules and micro-rituals (e.g., Cheal 1988). To call Goffman a 'major theorist of power' (Jenkins 2008), we believe, would therefore be an exaggerated characterisation. Certainly, Goffman was not a class-theorist in any conventional sense of the term (Gonos 1980), although a recognition of the significance of class is signalled by his first paper on class status symbols (Goffman 1951) and in the extensive mention of occupational status that is a conspicuous feature of *The Presentation of Self in Everyday Life* (Boltanski 1973).

Power, it is often said, is a neglected feature of Goffman's sociology. This is not a new criticism, having been made as long ago as 1970 (Gouldner 1970), and it is a complaint that continues to be made by critics both unsympathetic (e.g., Tylor 2018) and sympathetic (e.g., Giddens 2009) to Goffman's enterprise. The term 'power' is, however, not entirely absent from Goffman's writings. Although it is indeed not a core element of his conceptual vocabulary, he does, for example, mention the notion explicitly in *The Presentation of Self in Everyday Life* (1959), his first book. In his discussion of 'teams' and 'teamwork', Goffman distinguishes between 'directive dominance', where someone in the team controls and directs the action, and 'dramatic dominance', where one team member can become the centre of attention or star (see Goffman 1959:97–104). For example, at a wedding a minister will exercise directive dominance while the bride enjoys dramatic dominance:

> The conceptions of dramatic and directive dominance, as contrasting types of power in a performance, can be applied, *mutatis mutandis*, to an interaction as a whole, where it will be possible to point out which of the two teams has more of which of the two types of power and which performers, taking the participants of both teams all together, lead in these two regards.
>
> (Goffman 1959:101)

However, Goffman did take an interest in power, albeit in a less than explicit manner. Clearly, power does not feature as a leading term in Goffman's lexicon, yet many of the key notions associated with it are embedded in his sociology. This much was noticed by Mary Rogers over 40 years ago (Rogers 1977, 1980). Goffman's writings, Rogers shows, contain the elements of a coherent conception of power, influence and control that gainsay any simple criticism that his sociology ignores forms of power and hierarchy. Power, influence and control stem from Goffman's emphasis on the capacity for intentionality. An emphasis on the designed or calculative aspects of human action (in contrast to 'unmeant' or 'unwitting' forms) can be found throughout his work but is especially conspicuous in books like *Strategic Interaction* (1969) and *Frame Analysis* (1974). Goffman's theory of power is largely implicit, centring upon 'instrumental resources' such as social position and interpersonal skills (character, composure and the like) and also 'infra-resources' concerned with perceptions, information and access (Rogers 1980:102–106). Influence is built into Goffman's (1959:15) conception of face-to-face interaction as the 'reciprocal influence of individuals upon one another's actions when in one another's immediate presence'. Control for Goffman is both a process (e.g., the remedial cycle) and an effect (where control of people stems from control of perceptions and definitions of the situation). Perhaps more contentiously, Rogers (1980:123) also argued that Goffman's claim that many expectations and obligations are shaped by 'habitual conventionality' points to a recognition of a nascent conception of false consciousness in his thinking. The deconstruction of that habitual conventionality that his sociology accomplishes might then be framed as a critical enterprise. The implied theory of power that Rogers identifies sets Goffman apart from Blumerian forms of symbolic interactionism and serves to neutralise blunter criticism about the neglect of power. Furthermore, Rogers' work begins to indicate the ways in which power works in ordinary interaction and also the ways in which interactional manifestations of power and influence can challenge and work against institutionalised forms of power. One could perhaps even argue that Goffman provides us with a sociological specification of Foucault's concept of power and that Rogers' reconstruction of the elements of Goffman's thinking about power shows how Foucault's ideas can be translated into a sociologically workable set of concepts (Hacking 2004; Leib 2017).

Contrary to many critics, Richard Jenkins (2008) argues that Goffman does, in fact, have a coherent theory of power embedded in his sociology. Building on Rogers's ideas about Goffman's view of power as the mobilisation of differential access to resources, Jenkins suggests that information, territory and capacity to enact procedural forms are central to how Goffman conceives the exercise of power. What Jenkins disputes is what he sees as Goffman's limited general conception of how these resources are mobilised by interactants in encounters. The point at issue is Goffman's claim that there is a potential disconnection between the interaction order and larger social structures: that social structures are not simple aggregates of interaction, and that what transpires interactionally is not a simple or direct reflection of social structures. As Goffman starkly claimed:

> I do not believe that one can learn about the shape of the commodities market, or the distribution of a city's land values, or the ethnic succession in munici- pal administrations, or the structure of kinship systems, or the systematic phonological shifts within the dialects of a speech by extrapolating or aggre- gating from particular social encounters among the persons involved in any one of these patterns.
>
> (Goffman 1983:9)

Although, as Jenkins notes, this statement is true, he suggests that this stance leads to Goffman underselling his sociology by insulating it from its relevance for understanding a society's larger structural features. If one undertakes microa- nalysis of job selection interviews, for example, Jenkins claims we can arrive at an understanding of 'something significant about how the macro "shape" of the labour market is produced and reproduced' (Jenkins 2008:166). Goffman would doubtless concur but insists upon observing the distinction between the situa- tional (the encounter's procedural forms) and the merely situated (the encoun- ter's effects). Indeed, in discussing 'people processing encounters', Goffman (1983:8) acknowledged how officially irrelevant structural attributes (race, class, gender and age are mentioned) can introduce a 'micro-dot of mystification' into the proceedings. It is the encounter's effects, merely situated matters such as the categories of person appointed to a job, that produce and reproduce the labour market, not the situational matters concerning, for example, how interviewers interpret the interviewee's demeanour in answering specific questions. In a sense, both Jenkins' and Goffman's points stand. If we want to understand how cer- tain categories of people succeed in getting certain jobs, then attention to pre- ferred forms of interview demeanour may provide part of the explanation. But Goffman's equally telling point is that not *all* the features of a macrosociological phenomenon like a labour market can be derived inductively by aggregating what transpires in the actual job selection interview. There are some features of what transpires, for example, the extended relationship between buyer and seller of labour, or the right of the buyer of labour to set the wage for the job, which are not interactional effects but are set in law. What looks like defensiveness or undersell- ing (Burns 1992; Jenkins 2008) could just as readily be regarded as Goffman's considered analytical caution.

Goffman made the further suggestion that the effects of structure on inter- actional practices, or the effects of interactional practices on macrosociological phenomena, cannot be assumed or asserted by theoretical fiat but need to be dem- onstrated by empirical research of actual cases. As he stated: 'one is encouraged to treat as a matter for discovery just who it is that does what to whom' (Goffman 1983:10). This is a refreshing take on the micro–macro question because it implies that it is a mistake to seek generalised solutions to this question, in the manner say of Pierre Bourdieu or Anthony Giddens. Through these formulations we suggest that the wider theoretical problem that Goffman is addressing is the phenomenon of 'emergence': how social forms arise out of meaningful social practices (e.g., McHugh 1968). The solution he sketches is not one of a smooth and uniform process, but rather a formulation marked by discontinuity and rupture, and motivated by a wish to take a tough and sceptical look at what is actually happening in society's institutionalised structures. For Goffman, business dress may have become more casual, but the business world is much as it was; blacks and women have breached segregated public places, thereby changing access rules, but the structural or hierarchical situation of these categories of persons are not much changed.

Goffman's 'analytic attitude': what about politics?

As we mentioned earlier, Goffman, in his own words, was far more concerned with 'watching the snorers' than with awakening them from their apparently deep sleep (Goffman 1974:14), and he was also more interested in finding out if Marxists brushed their teeth in the morning than in providing dry wood for their ideological pyres (Ledger 1982:42). Although Goffman never framed his sociology in political terms, it is worth considering aspects of his political attitudes prior to discussing wider questions about the critical potential of his sociology.

Not surprisingly, given Goffman's well-known efforts to preserve his incognito, data are scarce on this subject. One source of puzzlement about locating Goffman in the ideological universe stems from his early reputation as a novel and indeed radical thinker who – in particular through the impact of *Asylums* (1961a) and *Stigma* (1963) on audiences outside of sociology – cast fresh light on many overlooked features of everyday life and did so in a manner sensitive to the iniquities and injustices manifested in and through the interaction order. Just as Goffman's standing as a major contemporary sociologist grew through the 1960s, so too did he acquire a reputation of tending towards the apolitical if not conservative in outlook. In those tumultuous times, he often appeared to go out of his way to avoid direct political involvement. Goffman resisted pressures from colleagues to take anti-government positions by reminding them that he was a Canadian citizen (Taylor 1968:835). When the University of California at Berkeley became a major centre of student rebellion in the mid-sixties, Goffman had become a full professor. The Free Speech Movement ran a protest through the 1964–1965 academic year that soon became linked to the civil rights and anti-Vietnam War struggles. Goffman avoided any involvement in campus political activism and seemed less supportive of student demands than other faculty members such as Herbert Blumer. When asked about his position during one crisis at Berkeley, he replied: 'When they start shooting students from the steps of Sproul Hall I guess I'll get involved, but not until then' (Marx 1984:658). Goffman was advertised as a speaker at 'The Dialectics of Liberation' conference held in London in 1967 (reported in *The New Statesman*, June 16, 1967, p. 850), along with such notable radical activists and thinkers as Lucien Goldmann, Paul Goodman, R. D. Laing, Herbert Marcuse and Paul Sweezy (Cooper 1968). It was a significant event, suffused with the late 1960s zeitgeist. There were even rumours that Jean-Paul Sartre would be making an appearance. However, Goffman did not attend, apparently withdrawing – according to Gary T. Marx (1984) – when he heard that the conference organisers invited the Black Power activist Stokely Carmichael to speak. Whatever the reasons for Goffman's own withdrawal, his name on the posters indicated how many radicals situated his work, which they saw as in keeping with their concerns. Marx also recalls an exchange with a student quizzing Goffman about 'what's the use of it for chang-ing the conditions you describe?'. Goffman responded: 'I'm not in that business' and quickly stormed out of the room (Marx 1984:657).

It is important to ask, Was Goffman correct in this instant assessment, and more broadly, if not changing social conditions, what business was Goffman then in? He saw himself primarily as a sociologist with a conception of the critical task centred on changing people's thinking rather than any more openly engaged conceptions of the sociologist's social role. Against this image of the sociolo-gist reluctant to become publicly involved in political action must be set some facts that seem to lead in the opposite direction. Goffman's intellectual networks included sociologists like Gouldner, who, as mentioned earlier, invited Goffman to join the editorial board of *Theory and Society* when it was founded. In his dispute with the publisher about the cover image of the UK edition of the book *Gender Advertisements* (1979), Goffman was proud to remind the publisher of his sympathy for the social justice credentials of the advisory editorial team (notably Paul Walton, whom he counted as a colleague and a friend) in whose series the book appeared. While Goffman's default position was to steer clear of any politi-cal involvements, he did give active support in 1970 for Thomas Szasz's initiative American Association for the Abolition of Involuntary Mental Hospitalization (AAAIMH), which was one of the reasons why Goffman – together with the likes of Laing, Foucault and Szasz – was often described as an 'anti-institutionalist'.

However, Goffman's general pessimism and scepticism about social arrange-ments are sharply evident in an address he gave to graduating students on the occasion he was awarded an honorary doctorate at the University of Manitoba in 1976. According to a newspaper report, Goffman was reported as speaking of a world 'somewhat governed by aging idiots', observing that 'not even today have we learned how to make democracy safe for the world'. Student rebels were right about the institutions they criticised and the adults who staffed them, but they did not appreciate the 'strength of their weaknesses' and the rebellion fizzled out, ending 'not with a bang but in a boutique' as the demands of making a living were felt. The world was not better in the past – there were no 'good old days': 'every generation has whistled in the dark … but these are remorselessly informed times. More than your forebears you will have to forego whistling'. The decline of the 'prestige of class distinction' meant that social ambition was not the attractive goal it once seemed and with the fading of the prestige of class standing, people were now 'socially left to teeter'. Looking to his audience's futures, Goffman was downbeat. He told them: 'The only worlds left free for you to explore are those of the mind'. He recommended remaining clearheaded and curious. With that emphasis on the cultivation of their rational faculties, Goffman recommended students to quietly and tolerantly make do with the ills and imperfections of the society they faced. Small wonder the headline reporting his talk in the local newspaper glossed it as 'gloomy world forecast for grads' (Anon 1976).

The hope of ever reaching some conclusive and once-and-for-all assessment of Goffman's politics thus seems a doomed task, particularly, as Judith Posner once proposed, 'some view him as a political radical, others view him as a middle-class conservative; while others, like myself, view him as apolitical' (Posner 1978:71). Trying to establish Goffman's 'real' political position is, at the end of the day, a rather futile endeavour. Goffman would probably concur with the relativity of Sherri Cavan's statement: 'To people who were radical, he appeared quite conservative. To people who were conservative, he appeared to be radical, a rule breaker, an interpersonal anarchist' (Cavan 2014:65). With the passage of time and the shifts in the meaning of these political labels, questions of Goffman's politics seem of diminishing relevance to the assessment of his contribution and legacy. It seems true, though, that Goffman's political impact came through his words more than his deeds. His critical task is sometimes described under the heading of a Burkean 'perspective by incongruity'. The arresting comparisons, the compelling metaphors, the sentences that provoke that 'look again' experience are all important textual dimensions of Goffman's critical practice together with his frequent use of sarcasm, humour, powerful metaphors and an insincere self-effacement suggesting to his readers that what he is saying is really not all that important (Smith and Jacobsen 512010). The writings convey clear underdog sympathies – for hospitalised mental patients (in *Asylums*) as well as for those similarly troubled 'in the community' (in 'The Insanity of Place'). Kindred readings are often made of *Stigma* (Goffman 1963). Moreover, in the 1970s Goffman's 'low-burning feminism' (Gonos 1980:168n) turned into stronger support for feminist agendas, fuelled in part by the feminist interests of his students at the University of Pennsylvania.

In the last of the words Goffman knew would be published, his aforementioned undelivered Presidential Address to the American Sociological Association, he urged sociologists who needed to justify their work in terms of social needs to study those occupying positions of authority of all kinds who 'give official imprint to versions of reality' (Goffman 1983:17). Goffman's underdog sympathies were achieved not by the imposition of an explicit moral agenda or an already formulated partisan position but through careful observation of the ordinary situations people face and a command of language that Goffman carefully cultivated to express what he saw. Importantly, in his Presidential Address, Goffman prefaced the statement just cited about 'studying up' those who give official imprint to reality with a remark that makes it clear that sociology can exist without calls to uphold particular values such as social needs or social justice. So there is a second message to add to the one about studying up, and it runs in the opposite direction to the first. As sociologists, Goffman believes we are entitled to study society 'because it is there' and because historically, 'only in modern times have university students been systematically trained to examine all levels of social life meticulously', without reference to the demands of religion or tradition. Some may think that sociology has not achieved a great deal so far as a discipline, but it has achieved something historically important, namely 'the bent to sustain in regard to all elements of social life a spirit of unfettered, unsponsored inquiry, and the wisdom not to look elsewhere but ourselves and our discipline for this mandate. That is our inheritance and that so far is what we have to bequeath' (Goffman 1983:17).

If Goffman's sociology in certain respects seems apolitical, it was a robust, considered position, rooted in a conception of sociology suspicious of all forms of partisanship. While not openly oppositional, it embraced the critical use of irony, a key part of the 'Chicago habitus' (Winkin 1999:34–35) that Goffman absorbed as a graduate student in the late 1940s and early 1950s. The key idea was not to be co-opted – either by sociological theory or by the group under study. In the exploration of these ideas, we can find the basis of Goffman's analytic attitude and critical theory. Goffman was the classic example of the sociologist as a 'licensed voyeur' (Taylor 1968:865) in thrall to the act of observation. But as Berger (1973:354) suggested in writing of Goffman's 'demonic detachment', his descriptions express a 'strong sense of decency and propriety' and are 'least compromised by moral posturings, knowing leers or other vulgar ego trips'. Goffman's skill at articulating the taken for granted aspects of interactants' intuitions is remarkable. It rests in part on the absence of partisanship in Goffman's analyses – as T. R. Young stated: 'Goffman neither celebrates the priest nor castigates the prostitute'. Agreeing with Gouldner that Goffman's sociology lacks a 'metaphysics of hierarchy', Young (1971:276) insists, however, that 'the points of view of psychiatrists, salesmen, professors and police have no prior moral claim on the loyalty of the sociologist than do the points of view of the patient, the customer, the student or the criminal'. Goffman thus anticipated the notion of ethnomethodological indifference and kindred interpretive stances that seek to preserve the interactant's perspective (Jacobsen 2010a:12).

However, Goffman was not only a great observer of social life. Another feature of his analytic attitude was the capacity to mobilise his own everyday experience into his writings in a sociologically effective way. Observation was the gold standard for Goffman, and it might include not only formally organised stints of fieldwork but also observations and reflections made in the course of the daily round. Philip M. Strong (1983) expressed this idea as a neat slogan: 'you too can treat your own life as data'. Goffman thus led the way in the 1960s and 1970s towards new methods for the collection of sociological data that nowadays travel under the colourful headings of 'autoethnography', 'innovative methods' and 'self-analysis'.

Conclusion

Erving Goffman was an enigmatic and iconoclastic sociologist, a 'crossover writer' (Menand 2009:296). Like all good crossover writers, Goffman can be set in many contexts and framed in many different ways. Indeed, Goffman did not merely make a virtue out of this chameleon-like feature of his work – he turned it into a theory of the social organisation of experience (Goffman 1974). In this chapter, we have explored aspects of the doubts frequently expressed about

Goffman's sociology in order to better understand the diversity of his sociological contribution and the directions his ideas have inspired.

The purpose of this chapter has thus been to excavate and explore some of the critical potential in the work of Goffman. Even though Goffman is most often read and depicted as an apolitical microsociologist with no genuine understanding of power or social conflict, this chapter has critically engaged with some of these 'misgivings' about Goffman. This has been done by outlining his perspective on the topics of social structure, power and politics. It was shown that Goffman, in fact, does touch upon these issues in his work on the 'interaction order' either explicitly or more implicitly. We can then conclude that although Goffman did not pay any particular or sustained attention to such topics (at least not compared to many other sociologists writing during his time), he nevertheless provided the discipline of sociology with some insights into the themes of social structure, power and politics that subsequent interpreters and users of his work have been able to elaborate and expand on.

This also means that new generations of sociologists can find and indeed have found in the work of Goffman suggestions and leads for a critical understanding of the interaction order and of how subordination, domination and power work interactionally. Here we could mention some of the work done recently on stigma and disability studies (e.g., Link and Phelan 2014; Brune and Garland-Thomson 2013), on gender differences (West and Zimmerman 1987, 2009; West 1996) or on race and so-called racialised interaction orders (Rawls 2000; Rawls and Duck 2017; Rosino 2017). Although we are here unable to address all these studies and the many others around, we think that their very presence, in itself, testifies to Goffman's critical potential. With this chapter, the last word has obviously not been said about Erving Goffman's view on social structure, power or politics, as we are sure the interest in and investigation of these topics will continue unabated in years to come.

References

Anon (1976): '"Aging Idiots": Gloomy World Forecast for Grads'. *Winnipeg Free Press*, May 27, p. 83.

Berman, Marshall (1972/2000): 'Weird and Brilliant Light on the Way We Live Now'. *The New York Times*, February 27. (Reprinted in: Gary Alan Fine and Gregory W. H. Smith (eds.) (2000): *Erving Goffman*. 4 volumes. London: Sage Publications.)

Berger, Bennett M. (1973): 'A Fan Letter on Erving Goffman'. *Dissent*, 20:353–361.

Billig, Michael (2001): 'Humour and Embarrassment: Limits of "Nice-Guy" Theories of Social Life'. *Theory, Culture & Society*, 18 (5):23–43.

Boltanski Luc (1973): 'Erving Goffman et le Temps du Soupçon'. *Social Science Information*, 12 (3):127–147.

Brune, Jeffrey A. and Rosemarie Garland-Thomson (2013): 'Forum Introduction: Reflections on the Fiftieth Anniversary of Erving Goffman's *Stigma*'. *Disability Studies Quarterly*, available online at: http://dsq-sds.org/article/view/4014/3539.

Burns, Tom (1992): *Erving Goffman*. London: Routledge.

Cavan, Sherri (2014): 'When Erving Goffman Was a Boy: The Formative Years of a Sociological Giant'. *Symbolic Interaction*, 37 (1):41–70.

Cheal, David (1988): 'The Postmodern Origin of Ritual'. *Journal for the Theory of Social Behavior*, 18 (3):269–289.

Chriss, James J. (2015): *Confronting Gouldner: Sociology and Political Activism*. Leiden: Brill.

Cooper, David (ed.) (1968): *The Dialectics of Liberation*. Harmondsworth: Penguin Books.

Cooper, William (1972): 'Review of *Relations in Public*'. *The Sunday Times Weekly Review*, January 23.

David, Peter (1980): 'The Reluctant Self-Presentation of Erving Goffman'. *The Times Higher Education Supplement*, September 19.

Denzin, Norman K. (2002): 'Much Ado about Goffman'. *American Sociologist*, 33 (2):105–117.

Edgley, Charles and Ronny E. Turner (1984): 'Goffman as Critical Theorist: Some Notes on the Maligning of an Ally'. *Quarterly Journal of Ideology*, 8 (3):26–39.

Giddens, Anthony (1988): 'Goffman as a Systematic Social Theorist', in Paul Drew and Anthony Wootton (eds.): *Erving Goffman: Exploring the Interaction Order*. Cambridge: Polity Press, pp. 201–279.

Giddens, Anthony (2009): 'On Rereading *The Presentation of Self*: Some Reflections'. *Social Psychology Quarterly*, 72 (4):290–295.

Goffman, Erving (1951): 'Symbols of Class Status'. *British Journal of Sociology*, 2:294–304.

Goffman, Erving (1953): *Communication Conduct in an Island Community*. Unpublished PhD dissertation, Department of Sociology, University of Chicago.

Goffman, Erving (1959): *The Presentation of Self in Everyday Life*. New York: Doubleday/Anchor Books.

Goffman, Erving (1961a): *Asylums: Essays on the Social Situation of Mental Patients and Other Inmates*. New York: Doubleday/Anchor Books.

Goffman, Erving (1961b): *Encounters: Two Studies in the Sociology of Interaction*. Indianapolis: Bobbs-Merrill.

Goffman, Erving (1963): *Stigma: Notes on the Management of Spoiled Identity*. Englewood Cliffs, NJ: Prentice-Hall.

Goffman, Erving (1969): *Strategic Interaction*. Oxford: Basil Blackwell.

Goffman, Erving (1974): *Frame Analysis: An Essay on the Organization of Experience*. New York: Harper & Row.

Goffman, Erving (1977): 'The Arrangement Between the Sexes'. *Theory and Society*, 4:301–331.

Goffman, Erving (1979): *Gender Advertisements*. London: Macmillan.

Goffman, Erving (1983): 'The Interaction Order'. *American Sociological Review*, 48 (1):1–17.

Gonos, George (1980): 'The Class Position of Goffman's Sociology: Social Origins of an American Structuralism', in Jason Ditton (ed.): *The View from Goffman*. London: Macmillan, pp. 134–169.

Gouldner, Alvin W. (1970): *The Coming Crisis of Western Sociology*. London: Heinemann.

Hacking, Ian (2004): 'Between Michel Foucault and Erving Goffman: Between Discourse in the Abstract and Face-to-Face Interaction'. *Economy and Society*, 33 (3):277–302.

Jacobsen, Michael Hviid (2010a): 'Goffman Through the Looking Glass – From "Classical" to Contemporary Goffman', in Michael Hviid Jacobsen (ed.): *The Contemporary Goffman*. London: Routledge, pp. 1–47.

Jacobsen, Michael Hviid (2010b): 'Recognition as Ritualized Reciprocation – The Interaction Order as a Realm of Recognition', in Michael Hviid Jacobsen (ed.): *The Contemporary Goffman*. London: Routledge, pp. 199–231.

Jacobsen, Michael Hviid and Søren Kristiansen (2009): 'Micro-Recognition – Erving Goffman as Recognition Thinker'. *Sosiologisk Årbok/Yearbook of Sociology*, 14 (3–4):47–76.

Jenkins, Richard (2008): 'Erving Goffman: A Major Theorist of Power?' *Journal of Power*, 1:157–168.

Kemper, Theodore D. (2011): *Status, Power and Ritual Interaction: A Relational Reading of Durkheim, Goffman and Collins*. London: Ashgate Publishing.

Langman, Lauren (1991): 'Alienation and Everyday Life: Goffman Meets Marx at the Shopping Mall'. *International Journal of Sociology and Social Policy*, 11:107–124.

Ledger, Marshall (1982): 'The Observer'. *Pennsylvania Gazette*, February 28:36–42.

Leib, Robert S. (2017): 'Spaces of the Self: Foucault and Goffman on the Micro-Physics of Discipline'. *Philosophy Today*, 61 (1):189–210.

Link, Bruce G. and Jo Phelan (2014): 'Stigma Power'. *Social Science & Medicine*, 103:24–32.

Marx, Gary T. (1984): 'Role Models and Role Distance: A Remembrance of Erving Goffman'. *Theory and Society*, 13:649–662.

McHugh, Peter (1968): *Defining the Situation: The Organization of Meaning in Social Interaction*. Indianapolis: Bobbs-Merrill.

Menand, Louis (2009): 'Some Frames for Goffman'. *Social Psychology Quarterly*, 72 (4): 296–299.

Posner, Judith (1978): 'Erving Goffman: His Presentation of Self'. *Philosophy of the Social Sciences*, 8:67–78.

Rawls, Anne Warfield (2000): '"Race" as an Interaction Order Phenomenon: W. E. B. Du Bois's "Double Consciousness" Thesis Revisited'. *Sociological Theory*, 18 (2): 241–274.

Rawls, Anne Warfield and Waverley Duck (2017): '"Fractured Reflections" of High-Status Black Male Presentations of Self: Nonrecognition of Identity as a "Tacit" Form of Institutional Racism'. *Sociological Focus*, 50 (1):36–51.

Riesman, David, Nathan Glazer and Reuel Denney (1953/2001): *The Lonely Crowd: A Study of the Changing American Character*. New Haven: Yale University Press.

Rogers, Mary (1977): 'Goffman on Power'. *American Sociologist*, 12 (2):88–95.

Rogers, Mary F. (1980): 'Goffman on Power, Hierarchy and Status', in Jason Ditton (ed.): *The View from Goffman*. London: Macmillan, pp. 100–133.

Rosino, Michael L. (2017): 'Dramaturgical Domination: The Genesis and Evolution of the Racialized Interaction Order'. *Humanity & Society*, 41 (2):158–181.

Smith, Greg and Michael Hviid Jacobsen (2010): 'Goffman's Textuality – Literary Sensibilities and Sociological Rhetorics', in Michael Hviid Jacobsen (ed.): *The Contemporary Goffman*. London: Routledge, pp. 119–146.

Stinchcombe, Arthur L. (1985): 'Macrosociology is Sociology about Millions of People'. *Contemporary Sociology*, 14 (5):572–575.

Strong, Philip M. (1983): 'The Importance of Being Erving'. *Sociology of Health and Illness*, 5 (3):345–355.

Taylor, Laurie (1968): 'Erving Goffman'. *New Society*, December 5:835–837.

Tylor, Imogen (2018): 'Resituating Erving Goffman: From Stigma Power to Black Power'. *Sociological Review*, 66 (4):744–765.

West, Candace (1996): 'Goffman in Feminist Perspective'. *Sociological Perspectives*, 39 (3):353–369.

West, Candace and Don H. Zimmerman (1987): 'Doing Gender'. *Gender & Society*, 1 (2):125–151.

West, Candace and Don H. Zimmerman (2009): 'Accounting for Doing Gender'. *Gender & Society*, 23 (1):112–122.

Williams, Robin (1983): 'Sociological Tropes: A Tribute to Erving Goffman'. *Theory, Culture and Society*, 2:99–102.

Winkin, Yves (1999). 'Erving Goffman: What is a Life? The Uneasy Making of an Intellectual Biography', in Greg Smith (ed.): *Goffman and Social Organization: Studies in a Sociological Legacy*. London: Routledge, pp. 19–41.

Young, T. R. (1971): 'The Politics of Sociology: Gouldner, Goffman and Garfinkel'. *American Sociologist*, 6:276–281.

Zussman, Robert (2001): 'Review: Still Lonely After All These Years'. *Sociological Forum*, 16 (1):157–166.

2 Upscaling Goffman

Four principles of neostructural interactionism

Michael L. Schwalbe

Introduction

Unicorns are impossible to see because they do not exist. Universities exist but are no less impossible to see. We can of course see buildings, classrooms, laboratories, books, manicured lawns, people and so on. But such things can be found in many places that do not count as universities, and even in sum such things do not, by themselves, constitute a university. This is because a university is not a set of physical things but a form of collective doing. 'University' is simply a term we use to refer to a form of recurrent joint action. No action, no university.

The same principle applies to all organisations and institutions. Banks, corporations, hospitals, armies, unions, families, cities, governments, economies and world systems exist only as forms of collective doing; they consist of people engaged in patterned joint action on a regular basis. We use the terms 'bank', 'corporation', 'army', 'hospital' and so on to label and distinguish these patterns. The collective doing that constitutes a *bank* is different from the collective doing that constitutes an *army* (and it is good to know the difference). It is, in any case, the patterned joint action that constitutes the entity of which we speak and the entity with which we imagine ourselves interacting – as in 'the bank offered me a loan at a low interest rate'. And, again, if there is no action, there is, as with unicorns, no entity outside the imagination.

Sociologists talk about these patterns of joint action using the metaphor of 'social structure'. This metaphor reminds us that the patterns are real and do not exist only in imagination; we cannot wish them away any more than we can wish away the walls of a building. Just as a building has a solid structure that we must contend with, recurrent patterns of joint action exhibit a kind of solidity because we cannot easily alter them to suit our desires. The people whose actions constitute the pattern will cooperate with us only to the extent that we adjust our action to theirs. If we do not, it can feel like we have run into the proverbial brick wall.

The metaphor of social structure underscores the objective reality of the phenomena we sociologists claim as our domain of study. Structures evoke an impulse to dissect, to discern internal workings, to describe contours and to measure 'impacts'. Talk of structures not only implies that we have much work to do but gives us a shorthand way of referring to it. Instead of saying 'to understand what's going on in the social world, we need to look at how people organize themselves to do X, Y and Z, and how these forms of organization are related', we can say 'we need to look at the structural arrangements here', and know roughly what we mean.

Unfortunately, the structure metaphor invites confusion by leading us to attribute agency to the patterns themselves. This is the problem of reification (Berger and Luckmann 1966). In casual speech, this is usually harmless. We might say, for example, that a bank gave us a loan, or a fire department rescued a cat – and know, well enough, what we mean to say happened. But if the goal is to explain how the social world works, it is not enough to say 'the structure of a capitalist economy negatively impacts the democratic functioning of government', and leave it at that. Such talk obscures the people, interests and actions that should be studied directly if we hope to learn what is really going on.

To put it another way, the problem with the social structure metaphor is that it inclines us to think we have found something – aha! structure! – that can be invoked to explain patterns of joint action. The problem is that the patterns *are* the structure. Thus to invoke structure as a cause is to march in a circle. It is to say, in effect, that what causes people to do things together in regularised ways is people doing things together in regularised ways, which amounts to saying nothing insightful about the nature, origins and consequences of patterned joint action.

Defining social structure as recurrent patterns of joint action dissolves the false problem of trying to figure out how structure causes behaviour or affects interaction. It is a false problem, as I have argued, because it amounts to puzzling over how patterned joint action causes or affects patterned joint action. With a reified notion of structure out of the way, and a more direct focus on action thereby made possible, we can tackle more fruitful questions. For example: What is the basis of constraint? If action is everything, why is not every action possible? How are patterns of joint action generated and stabilised? How do small-scale patterns relate to larger ones? How does joint action in one place affect action in another place? Dispensing with a faulty notion of structure gives us a better shot at coming up with good answers.

In this chapter, I want to address the problems created by a reified conception of structure by outlining a perspective I call 'neostructural interactionism'. I begin by showing how large-scale forms of social organisation can be understood as interaction orders in Erving Goffman's sense. I then argue that these macrostructures can be analysed using the same concepts Goffman used to analyse order in face-to-face interaction. This is followed by discussion of four principles of neostructural interactionism: (1) constraint is pragmatic, ideological and affective; (2) macrostructures are multi-sited interaction orders; (3) interaction orders are enmeshed ontologically, culturally and materially; and (4) nets of accountability link action across sites. Neostructural interactionism, I conclude, offers a way to gain analytic purchase on features of the social world that are often seen as beyond the reach of interactionist sociology.

Interaction orders all the way up

A way out of the mire can be found in Erving Goffman's analysis of interaction orders. In mainstream sociology, Goffman is not usually thought of as an analyst of structure, at least not beyond the scale of the face-to-face encounter. He is generally seen as concerned mainly with strategic self-presentation. In the standard textbook rendering, Goffman's contribution to sociology is said to be an extended theatre metaphor with which to understand how people craft impressions of themselves in the eyes of others, much in the manner of stage actors – hence the label 'dramaturgy' attached to his work and to that of others who use his ideas (Brissett and Edgley 1991). Goffman offered this, yes. But his analysis of the presentation of self was, as he noted, scaffolding erected to aid the building of something else (Goffman 1959:254).

Goffman's real contribution to sociology was not the theatre metaphor, which pre-dated him by centuries, but the idea that the orderliness of interaction is generated by reliance on shared cognitive presuppositions, normative and procedural rules, and standard procedural forms – what he called, in sum, a 'system of enabling conventions' (Goffman 1983a:5). What Goffman observed is that interaction exhibits an orderliness, a regularity; it begins, unfolds and concludes in patterned ways. This occurs, he argued, because interactants share a set of background understandings and draw on a shared set of rules – usually existing as tacit knowledge – that make moves and countermoves predictable, sensible and meaningful. Interaction, in this view, is not so much like theatre as it is like a game (Goffman 1952; 1961a:34–37; 1967:149–270; 1969).

By acting on shared cognitive presuppositions, by using the same normative and procedural rules, and by recycling standard procedural forms, people can nearly always coordinate action successfully, and do so with minimal emotional risk. They can, in other words, get things done together without constant fear of damage to the feelings attached to images of themselves (Goffman 1959:243; 1961a:103–104; 1961b:23, 67; 1967:6, 31, 43). What is thereby created, Goffman said, is an *interaction order*: an orderly and stable way of carrying on life together in a particular place. This could be called a recurrent or stable pattern of joint action. It could also be called, consistent with the terms I have used here, a social structure.

A game is a paradigm example of an interaction order. A game – be it chess, baseball, poker, World of Warcraft or whatever – exhibits orderliness; it unfolds as a series of moves and countermoves made permissible and sensible by a set of commonly understood background rules. Any given episode of play can unfold differently depending on which moves and countermoves are made, but the rules establish the parameters of the action; some moves must be made, others cannot be made. As long as players share the same assumptions about what is going on (i.e., frame the action in the same way) and draw on the same set of rules, the game can be played in a sensible, predictable and orderly way. Without drawing upon shared rules about what is procedurally and morally prescribed and proscribed, no coordinated action – no game – is possible.

Given adequate opportunity to observe, we can describe the rule-guided action that constitutes a game: the moves and countermoves that are made again and again. We can identify standard procedural forms: readymade and recycled bits of action (e.g., punting on fourth down, shooting a free throw after a foul, opening with the queen's gambit). We can infer the underlying normative and procedural rules upon which players draw to fashion moves and to make sense of what other players do. We can probe the cognitive presuppositions of players – the unspoken, unquestioned assumptions upon which they act when engaged in the game. We can also look at outcomes. What changes as a result of the game? What stays the same? How does one episode of play create new starting conditions for the next episode of play? These are some of the questions that we can try to answer when analysing a game as an interaction order (see DiCicco-Bloom and Gibson 2010).

Such an analysis would not get far if all we did was to point to players, to a venue where the action occurs and to the physical objects used in the course of play. This might look like solid, 'structural' stuff, but it would tell us nothing about the game itself. Until the action begins, there is no game, no interaction order, to analyse. The object of analysis comes into being only when the action – a series of moves and countermoves – begins to unfold. When this joint action begins, there comes into being a 'structure' that can be described and analysed. But as soon as the action stops, the structure ceases to exist (see Giddens 1979:61–62; 1984:24).[1] Fortunately, as I have suggested, the impermanence of structure is no obstacle to sociological analysis.

Upscaling Goffman

What I have been suggesting here is a different way to think about what structure is and how to approach its analysis.[2] If structure is patterned joint action, then it must be studied as such, which means examining moves and countermoves, standard procedural forms, underlying normative and procedural rules, and the cognitive presuppositions of actors. This is, in essence, the form of sociological analysis bequeathed to us by Erving Goffman. For him, this was an approach to analysing the orderliness of face-to-face interaction. I am proposing that it can be used to analyse the orderliness of social life on larger scales.

This is not a huge leap. Once we recognise that these larger scales of social life do not consist of mysterious 'structures' but of patterned joint action, then it makes sense to use the best tools we have for analysing patterned joint action – no matter the scale. Just as we can analyse an interaction order that manifests at the level of face-to-face interaction, we can analyse an interaction order that manifests as what we call a university, a bank, an army or a corporation. And just as we can analyse an interaction order that manifests as what we call an organisation, we can analyse one that manifests as what we call an economy, a government, or a world system. In each case, we would look for and at similar things: the rules of the game, moves and countermoves, standard procedural forms, cognitive presuppositions. We would also look at the conditions and consequences of play, recognising that the 'play' in question can be deadly serious.

My use of the term *neostructural* to describe this perspective might suggest to some readers that what I am doing is not upscaling Goffman but updating Sheldon Stryker. Despite the terminological echo, Stryker's (1980) 'structural symbolic interactionism' is not my point of departure. Although Stryker describes

(2008:18–19) his version of interactionism as founded on George Herbert Mead's view of social life as process and says that it 'takes as its starting point sociology's sense of social structures as patterned interactions and relationships', Stryker's interactionism is not dedicated to the study of interaction as process but to the study of identity.

Stryker's epistemological commitments, following the work of Manford Kuhn (see Kuhn and McPartland 1954), are to methodological individualism. His focus is not on how people do things together in everyday life but on how social doings affect individual psychology. Stryker's interactionism thus focuses mainly on individual-level variables: identity salience, psychological centrality (of identities), commitment (to identities). Despite invoking process and the idea that structures are patterned interactions and relationships, Stryker's interest in measurable outcomes leads him to re-reify structure – that is, turn it back into an independent variable that produces impacts and effects. As he says in one of his last published explications of structural interactionism:

> This [perspective] … suggests that greater significance should be placed on the impact of social structures on social interaction than Mead's frame allows … In this view, social structures on various levels and of various kinds operate as facilitators of and constraints on entrance into and departures from networks of interpersonal relationships … Finally, structural interactionism sees the effect of social structures as a process by which large-scale structures such as class, age, gender, and ethnicity operate through more intermediate structures … to affect relationships in social networks.
>
> (Stryker 2008:19–20)

In the end, Stryker's structural interactionism is not much concerned with interaction at all. Its main concern, rather, is with how people are affected by membership in social categories, groups and organisations. Although this is a venerable project, it is not one devoted to understanding how patterns of joint action are created, maintained, altered and superseded. The latter project, which de-reifies structure and re-centres joint action, is the one being advanced here.

Defining structure *as* patterned joint action, analysing this action in the way that Goffman analysed interaction orders and treating so-called macrostructures as large-scale interaction orders, is what I am calling a neostructural view. Admittedly, this view is *neo* only against the background of prevailing reifications of structure and the doctrine that macrostructures must be analysed in a non-interactionist way. The view I am proposing could even be called *retro* in that it affirms basic symbolic interactionist ideas that society *is* symbolic interaction (Blumer 1969:6, 35, 38) and that social life consists of people doing things together (Becker 1986). But what is new, or marginally so, is an approach to overcoming the limitations of interactionisms that have struggled to understand how joint action is stabilised, how action in one situation affects action in another and the nature of constraint. From a neostructural view, four principles of which are spelt out next, these are surmountable problems.

Four principles

Statements of core principles risk loss of nuance and complexity. Statements of principles are also likely to evoke thoughts of exceptions, demands for definitions, and charges of oversimplification (charges of presumptuousness might not be far behind). On the other hand, statements of principles can sharpen ideas as targets for critique and, presuming the critique is not fatal, as tools for use and further development. Submitted for consideration, then, are four principles that constitute the heart of neostructural interactionism.

Constraint is pragmatic, ideological and affective

At the university where I teach, one cannot get a PhD in art history. A student who sought this outcome would be thwarted, as there is no art history department, no graduate program in art history, nor sufficient personnel with the requisite expertise to confer such a degree. It could thus be said that the would-be art historian is constrained by the structure of the university; what she or he wants cannot be gotten here. By unpacking this seemingly simple case of 'structural' constraint, we can see how constraint is simultaneously pragmatic, ideological and affective.

Constraint, in this case, is pragmatic in the sense that there are no people organised in a way that would make it possible to accommodate the student's desire to pursue a graduate degree in art history (given what this is conventionally understood to entail). The game of granting graduate degrees in art history is not being played, and one student's request will not get that game started, given the lack of personnel and other resources. In general terms, if the kind of collective doing into which one wants to enter is not going on, action is blocked until others, able and willing to go along, can be found. This need for the cooperation of others is what keeps us from being able to do whatever comes to mind. We might imagine a novel line of action and even take initial steps. But such imaginings and nascent undertakings can go no further than the cooperation of others will allow.

Constraint, in this case, is also ideological. It is not that the game of granting graduate degrees in art history could not be played at my university. In fact, it would mesh nicely with the other academic goings-on here. The problem is that the people who disburse resources do not believe that the game of granting graduate degrees in art history would be worth its cost. Other organisational actors – perhaps faculty who teach other types of history – might also be ideologically opposed to devoting scarce resources to a program in art history. Yet another possibility is that no one, student or faculty member, has ever thought of creating such a program. Ideology can thus constrain action by undermining cooperation or by precluding consideration of a line of action (see Lukes 2005).

How might constraint also be affective or emotional in this case? Imagine that the student who wants to pursue a PhD in art history is told by a beloved professor 'that's the stupidest thing you could do'. Imagine a faculty member who wanted to create a program of some kind to accommodate the student being told by a respected colleague 'that's an idiotic idea'. These obstructive sentiments might be conveyed more subtly, in keeping with the rules of interaction in academia. Yet selves could be damaged nonetheless. What would be damaged, more precisely, are the feelings attached to self-images. Proposing lines of action that others are likely to see as foolish puts such feelings at risk, perhaps even courts serious emotional damage. Awareness of this possibility puts another brake – another constraint – on action.

The art history example I have been unpacking is not unique or odd. Its features are common. Any time we want to get things done with others we face pragmatic, ideological and affective constraints. Our attempts at coordinating action can be daunted, most obviously, by others' refusal to cooperate; if others will not go along with our plans, our plans go nowhere. We can be daunted by ideologies that induce others to resist, make our actions appear insensible or that limit our ability to formulate options. We can also be daunted by anticipation of emotional damage if we persist in violating normative and procedural rules, and thereby discredit ourselves.

By de-reifying structure – by putting people and action back into a conceptualisation of what structure is – it becomes possible to see more clearly what it is that creates constraint in social life: the practical needs for coordination and cooperation to get things done together; the beliefs that make lines of action imaginable or unimaginable, morally acceptable or unacceptable; and the emotions at stake when selves are presented in interaction, as they inevitably are. It also becomes possible to see how action is not only constrained by structure but enabled by it (see Giddens 1984:16–25). In some places, it is possible to get a PhD in art history, because the game of granting such degrees is underway and, in accord with local rules, new players are allowed to enter. In this case, structure makes possible a line of action in one place that is impossible in another.

Macrostructures are multi-sited interaction orders

Interaction orders, as Goffman conceived them, manifest in face-to-face encounters. It is in such encounters that orderliness and regularity are evident. It is in encounters that we see (or can infer) that people draw on cognitive presuppositions, tacit knowledge of normative and procedural rules, and standard procedural forms to coordinate interaction in patterned, orderly ways. Goffman gave us example after example of this kind of orderliness in situated interaction. But if interaction orders are merely situational, and thus seemingly fleeting – as the term 'encounter' implies – then how does this perspective help us get a sociological grip on the more durable macrostructures of the social world?

Again, it is important to keep in mind that so-called macrostructures – organisations, governments, economies or world systems – consist of recurrent patterns of joint action: people doing things together in regular ways on a daily basis. What we as sociologists are thus doing, when we use the term 'macrostructure', is stepping back (or zooming out, to use a photographic metaphor) and looking at a large set of actors and actions that are coordinated in a consistent fashion across space and time. It is this consistent manner of coordination that gives the impression that a 'structure' exists – and indeed it does, as a complex pattern of action, not as a fixed configuration of stuff. What it amounts to, in the terms of my argument, is a multi-sited interaction order (see Goffman 1961a:37; 1983a:4).

If we once more think of a university as a game, it is clear that not all players ever engage in one grand face-to-face encounter at one time. Different parts of the game – budgeting, facilities maintenance, records keeping, teaching, researching and so on – are played by different personnel in different places at different times. Interaction in each situation exhibits an orderliness, and each type of situation can be thought of as constituting an interaction order in itself. But no one of these component situations or interaction orders is a university. Rather, it is all of these situations, *when the action within them is coordinated across them*, that amounts to the game of university. This is the sense in which a university is a large-scale, or multi-sited, interaction order. It is just that to see the order that warrants the label 'university' we must step further back, analytically, than when looking at a single face-to-face encounter.

My point is not just that macrostructures can be defined as multi-sited interaction orders. Rather, my point is that macrostructures exist *only because* they are multi-sited interaction orders. Just as the orderliness that is evident in face-to-face interaction is generated by use of systems of enabling conventions, so too is the orderliness we observe on larger scales. The same interactional dynamics, the same processes and resources, are at the root of things, generating the durable patterns of joint action to which we give conventional names (e.g., 'university') and sometimes mistakenly endow with independent agency.

Interaction orders are enmeshed ontologically, culturally and materially

On election day, interaction in polling places exhibits an orderliness that is generated by the shared cognitive presuppositions, normative and procedural rules, and standard procedural forms that voters and election officials use to coordinate action. The patterns of joint action evident in these venues constitute an interaction order. When voters show up to vote and align their actions with the established pattern, they participate in and reproduce this situated or 'micro' interaction order. At the same time, they also participate in and reproduce the macro interaction order called an electoral democracy. These two interaction orders – one micro and one macro – are ontologically enmeshed; the larger order is constituted by what happens in many smaller ones.

This principle of ontological enmeshment was suggested earlier in discussing the game of university. Interaction coordinated across multiple sites – offices, classrooms, laboratories, dormitories, cafés and coffee shops, libraries and so on – is what constitutes the university. Interaction in each venue exhibits an orderliness generated by actors' reliance on shared symbolic resources. The larger pattern of interaction we call a university does not exist apart from what occurs in these places of face-to-face interaction; it consists of them. The same principle applies to all macrostructures or macro interaction orders: what we think of as the larger structure – a multi-national corporation or a global economic system – exists only as a set of enmeshed micro orders.

Cultural enmeshment is different. This is not a matter of micro-orders constituting macro ones. It is a matter of the same symbolic resources being used to generate similar interaction orders in multiple, distant sites. Actors in these sites draw on the same cultural toolkit – the same cognitive presuppositions, normative and procedural rules as well as standard procedural forms – to generate orderly interaction. By implication, actors can move from one site to another – bodily or virtually – and successfully coordinate their action with previously unknown others in those sites. A faculty member or student who is culturally equipped to interact sensibly and competently at one modern Western university can probably do so, with minor adjustments, at any another.

A multi-national corporation provides another example of cultural enmeshment. Such a corporation might have many thousands of employees around the globe. Interaction in each constituent site, each physical space where face-to-face encounters occur on a regular basis, will exhibit orderliness. The patterns generated in these sites will arise in part from reliance on elements of the organisation's culture. Adjustments for variations in local ethnic, religious, and national cultures might be necessary, but normally it will possible for members of the organisation to move across sites and, by use of the same organisationally provided cultural toolkit, coordinate action with other members. The distant sites can be said to be enmeshed, or harmonised, by a shared culture.

A third form of enmeshment is created by flows of material resources. This can also be thought of as a kind of pragmatic enmeshment. For example, universities typically require physical equipment – desks, chairs, computers, books, lab benches and so on. Such equipment is typically acquired from manufacturing firms or through vendors. What is happening in these cases is that one kind of resource (i.e., physical equipment) is being exchanged for another kind (i.e., money in some form). Creating and sustaining these resource exchanges requires that some part of the interaction order that constitutes a university be suitably enmeshed with the interaction orders – the organisations – that make and deliver material goods.

In the case of material enmeshment, it is not only that one interaction order (a university) depends on others (manufacturing, selling, transporting), but that these interaction orders, or some parts of them, must be coordinated. Personnel in one interaction order must be able to coordinate their action with those of the correct personnel in the others, else the resources on which these orders depend will cease to flow. This requires a degree of cultural enmeshment as well; actors located in different places and in different interaction orders must come to share certain cognitive presuppositions, understand common normative and procedural rules, and be able to use standard procedural forms. It might thus be said that the need for large-scale interaction orders to import resources from other large-scale interaction orders is what generates new interaction orders at the points of intersection.

Nets of accountability link action across sites

Accountability refers to the condition of one's behaviour being subject to evaluation by others during interaction (Heritage 1984; Hollander 2013). To be 'accountable' in this sense is to face the prospect of having one's actions deemed appropriate or inappropriate by others in an encounter. One is usually held accountable as a member of a category or as a performer of a role. Acting in a way that others deem inappropriate for one's category or role is likely to elicit a signal – a raised eyebrow, a puzzled look, a question, a demand – that some kind of account is needed. If the implicit question *Why are you acting this way?* is not satisfactorily answered, one risks being seen as incompetent, immoral or insane. In which case, interaction is likely to break down (Goffman 1983b).

The concept of accountability helps us to understand why people generally do what is expected of them in face-to-face encounters. To do otherwise, and to be unable to account for the deviation, is to put at risk one's presumed social competence, even one's apparent sanity, and also to threaten the ability to smoothly coordinate action and get things done together. This is another reason situated interaction orders, once established, are relatively stable. Accountability mitigates against the revision of normative and procedural rules based on the whims of any single actor. To ignore a basic rule or make an insensible move, like trying to win a chess match by throwing the board into the air, usually brings the game to an abrupt end.

But accountability is more than a situational phenomenon; it also operates across situations. To see how this happens, the concept of *nets of accountability* (Schwalbe 2005, 2015) is helpful (see Collins 1981 on 'control chains'). These nets exist as both symbolic and practical realities and can be instantiated in either way or both ways, as might be necessary to keep actors in line. These nets link situations together and ensure that action in one setting will mesh with action in the other settings that together constitute a large-scale interaction order. Again to the university for an example.

Imagine that a student refuses to do an assignment (write a paper, take an exam). An instructor might try to hold the refusenik accountable as a student by saying, 'You should be glad to do this work, because it's a way to gain knowledge and skill, and that's presumably what you're seeking by being a student'. If this rhetorical tack fails, the instructor might say, 'Look, if you don't do the assignment, you'll fail the course and probably fail to graduate'. This might seem to be a simple person-to-person standoff, but it is much more than that. The instructor's first response implicitly invokes cultural ideologies about students, teachers, assignments, learning, universities, individual choice and personal enrichment. The second response invokes a net of accountability that extends beyond the classroom.

To tell the student that if the assignment is not completed satisfactorily she or he might fail the course and then fail to graduate implicates actors outside the situation. The instructor can make this threat stick because administrators and staff usually cooperate with instructors – according to a set of procedural and normative rules that generate the interaction order called a university – to decide who gets what grade, who completes which courses and who graduates with what degrees. Unless the student is willing to forgo passing the course, and possibly forgo getting a degree, she or he is effectively compelled to do the required work. The compulsion comes from a net of accountability that holds the university together as an interaction order. If all the actors whose joint action constitutes the university play by the agreed-upon rules, the student is caught in a virtual net.

At first, in the immediacy of the situation, the net is invoked symbolically. The instructor conjures it, calls it to mind and instantiates it, verbally. If the student understands the existence of this net, she or he will appreciate the potential force behind the instructor's demand, get back in line, and do the assignment. If symbolic invocation does not work, the net can be instantiated practically. All the instructor needs to do is submit a failing grade, and if other organisation actors play their parts, the student will indeed fail and perhaps not graduate. Those 'other actors' can be counted on to play their parts because they too are caught in a net of accountability; if they do not do their jobs they can be held accountable by organisation superiors and, possibly, deprived of employment.

Note, too, that the net of accountability, in this case, extends beyond the university. In the case of the student, parents (why aren't you graduating?) and future employers (no degree? sorry, no job) are potentially implicated. Likewise with instructors, staff and administrators. To ignore the established rules of the game would be to court unemployment and thereby incur other costs. All of these actors – entangled by the accountability demands they can impose on each other, inside and outside the university – are parts of the net. Each face-to-face encounter, each act of communication and coordination, is analogous to a place where the strands of a net are bound together.

What the concept of nets of accountability helps us to see is how patterns of joint action are linked across settings. Instructors and students interact as they do in classrooms not simply because of normative and procedural rules specific to classrooms. They interact as they do because of nets of accountability that extend beyond the classroom into other sites that constitute the university, the family, the economy and so on. Likewise, bosses and subordinate employees interact as they do in the workplace because of the wider nets of accountability in which they are caught and which they help to reproduce through their joint action. Most instances of situated action – indeed, all micro interaction orders – are tied to, ordered by and stabilised by the nets of accountability that surround them. Situations themselves are always situated (Strauss 1978; Maines 1982).

As argued earlier, large-scale interaction orders are held together by nets of accountability; conformity in one setting is compelled by consequences, real or imagined, potentially arising in linked settings. This linking is accomplished by communication. The student who resists doing a required assignment is not defeated by the instructor's charm but by the instructor's ability to communicate with and elicit the cooperation of other actors in the university. Likewise with bosses, vis-à-vis employees, in a capitalist workplace (Schwalbe 2015:193–205). In each case, the tools available to communicate beyond the immediate situation determine the extent and weave of the net. Today, digital surveillance, communication and information storage technologies can be used to fashion nets of accountability more invasive and far-reaching than anything Orwell imagined. Dissident acts at one time in one setting can now become part of a permanent, widely accessible digital record that produces negative repercussions for a lifetime (Schneier 2015).

A note on negotiation and improvisation

In laying out the aforementioned four principles, I have perhaps created the impression that most interaction is unproblematic, unfolding smoothly with little emotional risk, because people can draw on shared normative and procedural rules, shared cognitive presuppositions, and a common stock of standard procedural forms. But of course interaction does not always go smoothly; it can involve blunders, embarrassments, awkward moments and dead ends; it can go painfully awry or break down completely. Two questions thus arise: How do we account for these problems, and how do we account for the fact that they are usually overcome?

Even in games governed by an elaborate code of rules, joint action can break down. The possible causes are not mysterious: lack of knowledge of the rules, forgetting the rules, disagreement about the rules, disagreement about how a rule applies to a specific case (perhaps a rare or novel case), divergent cognitive presuppositions, inept enactment of a ritual form, disagreement about how or whether a particular ritual form should be used by whom, objection to the outcomes produced by following a rule. Each of these causes points back to what enables the generation of stable patterns of joint action – the game – in the first place: commitment to the use of a shared set of symbolic resources. Disruption occurs when these resources are less widely shared, or less widely accepted as appropriate to draw upon, than initially presumed. This account of the underlying causes of disruption offers a place to start when interaction breaks down, in games and in everyday life, and we want to know what has gone wrong.

When interaction is disrupted there also arises the problem of figuring out how to proceed. Interactants must first signal the emergence of a problem (see Goffman 1981:64), indicating a need for pause, reflection, negotiation and, possibly, improvisation. Depending on the seriousness of the breach in the action and on what is at stake, everything might be up for grabs: rules, cognitive presuppositions, standard procedural forms, the purpose of the action itself. It depends, as suggested earlier, on the source of the problem. What must then be negotiated is agreement about how to proceed. If no known rule or precedent can be invoked and accepted (at least tentatively) as a way to get action underway again, it may be necessary to improvise and invent a new rule. How these negotiations and improvisations occur, how they too are patterned, and how they shape future action are matters for empirical study (Lever 1976; DeLand 2013).

From the standpoint of neostructural interactionism, breakdowns in the smooth unfolding of games or everyday interaction are illuminating moments. As ethnomethodologists have taught us, a breach in the social order of a situation offers an opportunity to see how repair is done and, by implication, to learn something about how meaning and order are made more generally. Breakdowns in games or in everyday interaction thus do not challenge the principles articulated here. Rather, such occasions provide an opportunity to see these principles in operation. When negotiation and improvisation are necessary to put a game back on track, we can get a view to the interactional dynamics that are at the heart of social life, whether the game we are observing is literal or metaphorical.

Conclusion

In this chapter, I have argued that social structures should be thought of as recurrent patterns of joint action – the regularised ways that people do things together in social life. If there is no patterned joint action, no regularised doing, there is no structure. This view of structure rejects the notion that 'structures' are obscure forces that exist apart from observable human action and make people do things. Structures, rather, are *constituted by* people doing things together in regular ways. When we see such regularities in face-to-face encounters, we are seeing what Erving Goffman called an 'interaction order'. My attempt has been to adapt Goffman's analysis of regularity, of orderliness in face-to-face encounters, and turn it toward understanding the creation and reproduction of patterns on large scales, or what I have called macro interaction orders.

Goffman argued that the orderliness of face-to-face encounters is generated by shared cognitive presuppositions, shared normative and procedural rules, and a common stock of standard procedural forms. It is by drawing on these elements of shared symbolic culture that people can coordinate action smoothly, with minimal risk to the strong feelings attached to self-images. I have argued that the same analytic approach can help us understand how larger-scale interaction orders are generated and maintained. Whether we observe the orderliness of a casual, dyadic encounter, the orderliness of interaction in a government bureaucracy, or the orderliness of a capitalist corporation, we are seeing the outcome of – *the structure produced by* – the use of shared cognitive presuppositions, shared normative and procedural rules, and a common stock of standard procedural forms.

With a nod to its antecedents, I dubbed this approach to structure and its underlying basis *neostructural interactionism*. Proceeding from the conceptualisation of structure as patterned joint action, I laid out four core principles of the perspective: (1) constraint is pragmatic, ideological and affective; (2) macrostructures are multi-sited interaction orders; (3) interaction orders are enmeshed ontologically, culturally and materially; and (4) nets of accountability link action across sites. In articulating these principles my goal was to make the perspective a target for raiding, if anything it offers seems useful; and a target for critique, if it seems to warrant further development.

What advantages does neostructural interactionism offer? For one, as noted earlier, it demystifies the nature of social structure, transforming it from an invisible force or mere abstraction to something that can be observed. A second advantage – relative to interactionisms that are overly situational, treating orderly interaction as created anew in every encounter – is that it highlights the trans-situational elements of social life that generate orderliness: shared cognitive presuppositions, shared normative and procedural rules, and standard procedural forms.[3] As symbolic constructs, these elements of shared consciousness are not visible in the way that interacting bodies are visible, yet they too are amenable to empirical study. If we know what to look for, we can discern, as Goffman sought to do, the presuppositions, rules, and procedural forms that enable orderly and meaningful interaction in any locale. Finally, neostructural interactionism dissolves the artificial divide between micro and macro, avoiding the ontological mistake of treating situated interaction as constituting a different kind of reality than that of large-scale social structures. The social world, we might thus recognise, is all of a piece, and whether we see brush strokes, isolated scenes or the big picture is largely a matter of how closely we look.

Notes

1 My argument parallels that of Anthony Giddens (1984:16–25) in holding that the social world consists of patterned joint action created by drawing upon shared symbolic resources. There are, however, differences in terminology, and at least one important substantive difference. Giddens uses the term 'structure' to refer to the underlying codes – like the grammatical and syntactic codes of language – that are drawn upon, as elements of 'practical consciousness', to organise action. He uses the term 'systems' to refer to the visible patterns of joint action that result from the use of these codes. In language perhaps more familiar to American sociologists, I prefer to use the term 'structure' to refer to the latter, the visible patterns of joint action. The substantive difference is that, following Erving Goffman, I conceive of structuring resources more broadly, including not only normative and procedural rules but also shared cognitive presuppositions and standard procedural forms.

2 Others have tried to move sociological thinking about 'structure' in the same direction. See, for examples, Georges Gurvitch (1953) and Randall Collins (1981). With the understanding that he uses 'system' to mean what others would call structure, Anthony Giddens (1979, 1984) can be included here as well. Jeff Coulter (1982) takes a somewhat different approach, but likewise challenges the notion that social structures are fixed categories, roles or social arrangements. For a more recent attempt to turn sociological thinking in a processual direction, see Abbott (2016).

3 See George Gonos's (1977) critique of symbolic interactionism for its tendency to treat joint action as negotiated anew in every encounter. Gonos argued that, properly understood, Goffman's structural social psychology is one that stresses the importance of symbolic resources that are trans-situational and repeatedly drawn upon to organise what happens in encounters. As such, it is an antidote to implausible situationalism. Goffman seems to have agreed (see Goffman 1981).

References

Abbott, Andrew (2016): *Processual Sociology*. Chicago: University of Chicago Press.

Becker, Howard S. (1986): *Doing Things Together: Selected Papers*. Evanston, IL: Northwestern University Press.

Berger, Peter L. and Thomas Luckmann (1966): *The Social Construction of Reality*. Garden City, NY: Anchor Books.

Blumer, Herbert (1969): *Symbolic Interactionism*. Englewood Cliffs, NJ: Prentice-Hall.

Brissett, Dennis and Charles Edgley (eds.) (1991): *Life as Theater: A Dramaturgical Sourcebook* (2nd edition). Hawthorne, NY: Aldine.

Collins, Randall (1981): 'On the Microfoundations of Macrosociology'. *American Journal of Sociology*, 86 (5):984–1014.

Coulter, Jeff (1982): 'Remarks on the Conceptualization of Social Structure'. *Philosophy of the Social Sciences*, 12:33–46.

DeLand, Michael (2013): 'Disputing in the Key of Law: The Significance of Disputing in Pick-Up Basketball'. *Law & Society Review*, 47 (3):653–685.

DiCicco-Bloom, Benjamin and David R. Gibson (2010): 'More than a Game: Sociological Theory from the Theories of Games'. *Sociological Theory*, 28 (3):247–271.

Giddens, Anthony (1979): *Central Problems in Social Theory*. Berkeley, CA: University of California Press.

Giddens, Anthony (1984): *The Constitution of Society*. Berkeley, CA: University of California Press.

Goffman, Erving (1952): 'On Cooling the Mark Out: Some Aspects of Adaptation to Failure'. *Psychiatry*, 15 (4):451–463.

Goffman, Erving (1959): *The Presentation of Self in Everyday Life*. Garden City, NY: Anchor Books.

Goffman, Erving (1961a): *Encounters*. Indianapolis: Bobbs-Merrill.

Goffman, Erving (1961b): *Asylums*. Garden City, NY: Anchor Books.

Goffman, Erving (1967): *Interaction Ritual*. New York: Pantheon.

Goffman, Erving (1969): *Strategic Interaction*. Philadelphia: University of Pennsylvania Press.

Goffman, Erving (1981): 'A Reply to Denzin and Keller'. *Contemporary Sociology*, 10 (1): 60–68.

Goffman, Erving (1983a): 'The Interaction Order'. *American Sociological Review*, 48: 1–17.

Goffman, Erving (1983b): 'Felicity's Condition'. *American Journal of Sociology*, 89 (1): 1–53.

Gonos, George (1977): '"Situation" versus "Frame": The "Interactionist" and the "Structuralist" Analyses of Everyday Life'. *American Sociological Review*, 42:854–867.

Gurvitch, Georges (1955): 'On Some Deviations in the Interpretation of the Concept of Social Structure'. *Sociometry*, 18 (4):245–262.

Heritage, John (1984): *Garfinkel and Ethnomethodology*. Cambridge: Polity Press.

Hollander, Jocelyn (2013): 'I Demand More of People: Accountability, Interaction and Gender Change'. *Gender & Society*, 27 (1):5–29.

Kuhn, Manford H. and Thomas McPartland (1954): 'An Empirical Investigation of Self-Attitudes'. *American Sociological Review*, 19 (1):68–76.

Lever, Janet (1976): 'Sex Differences in the Games Children Play'. *Social Problems*, 23 (4):478–487.

Lukes, Steven (2005): *Power: A Radical View* (2nd edition). New York: Palgrave.

Maines, David R. (1982): 'In Search of Mesostructure: Studies in the Negotiated Order'. *Urban Life*, 11 (3):267–279.

Schneier, Bruce (2015): *Data and Goliath*. New York: Norton.

Schwalbe, Michael L. (2005): 'Identity Stakes, Manhood Acts and the Dynamics of Accountability'. *Studies in Symbolic Interaction*, 28:65–81.

Schwalbe, Michael L. (2015): *Rigging the Game: How Inequality Is Reproduced in Everyday Life* (2nd edition). New York: Oxford University Press.

Strauss, Anselm L. (1978): *Negotiations*. San Francisco, CA: Jossey-Bass.

Stryker, Sheldon (1980): *Symbolic Interactionism: A Social Structural Version*. Menlo Park, CA: Benjamin Cummings.

Stryker, Sheldon (2008): 'From Mead to a Structural Symbolic Interactionism and Beyond'. *Annual Review of Sociology*, 34:15–31.

3 A call to a critical interpretive interactionism

Norman K. Denzin

Introduction

Anticipating my conclusions, I will call for a critical, interpretive interactionism that resists containment by the disciplinary constraints of symbolic interactionism and standard American sociology. This is an inquiry committed to an ethically responsible social justice agenda. This is an inquiry that connects biography and history, joining the personal with the public through performative acts of activism. Critical interactionists change history by inserting themselves into it. The project is to change society, not just interpret or write about it.

I begin with performance. All the world is not, of course, a stage, but the crucial ways in which it isn't are not easy to specify (Goffman 1959:72). Critical interactionism must always start with a person, a body, a place and a historical moment. In performance, we reveal ourselves to ourselves (Turner 1985:187, paraphrase). I offer my performing body and my experiences as the raw material for cultural critique. My body carries the traces of my historical moment. I am the universal other. I am the performative. I am struggling to disrupt the status quo, resisting hegemonic systems of control and injustice (Spry 2011:20, paraphrase). This is about rethinking the formation of a critical performative cultural politics, about what happens when everything, as W. E. B. Du Bois (1926:134) observed, is already performative, when the dividing line between performativity and performance disappears. It is about discourse as moral critique, about using our interpretive practices for social justice purposes.

My discussion in this chapter unfolds in three parts: I begin with interactionist assumptions, then turn to key assumptions in the performance approach, and then towards the end of the chapter I address some issues of social justice and critical inquiry.

Critical interactionism

In its canonical form (Blumer 1969) critical interactionism rests on the following root assumptions. First, 'human beings act toward things on the basis of the meanings that the things have for them' (Blumer 1969:2). Second, the meanings of things arise out of the process of social interaction. Third, meanings are modified through an interpretive process, which involves self-reflective individuals symboli-cally interacting with one another (Blumer 1969:2). Fourth, human beings create the worlds of experience in which they live. Fifth, the meanings of these worlds come from interaction, and they are shaped by the self-reflections persons bring to their situations. Sixth, such self-interaction is 'interwoven with social interaction and influences that social interaction' (Blumer and Rhea 1981:153). Seventh, joint acts, their formation, dissolution, conflict and merger, constitute what Herbert Blumer calls the 'social life of a human society'. A society consists of the joint or social acts 'which are formed and carried out by [its] members' (Blumer and Rhea 1981:153). Eighth, a complex interpretive process shapes the meanings things have for human beings. This process is anchored in the cultural world, in the 'circuit of culture' (du Gay et al. 1997:3), where meanings are defined by the mass media, including adver-tising, cinema and television, and are shaped by a political economy that structures the production, distribution and consumption of wealth in a society.

The performance approach

In the beginning, there was interactionist *ethnography*, an inscriptive practice cap-tured in the phrase 'writing culture' (Clifford and Marcus 1986). Then there was *per-formance*, the understanding that people perform culture through their interpretive practices (Conquergood 1985). This implied that we could study persons as perform-ers and cultures as performative or ethnodramatic accomplishments (Saldana 2005). *Performance interactionist autoethnography* inserted itself in the picture when it was understood that all ethnographers reflexively (or unreflexively) write/perform them-selves into their ethnographies. The ethnographer's writing self cannot not be present, as there is no objective space outside the text. There are only ethnographic texts turned into performance events, into ethnodramas, into ethnotheatre, into narrative poems, scripts, short stories, texts with narrators, action, shifting points of view; dramaturgi-cal productions co-performed with audiences; life, narrative and melodrama under the auspices of late neo-liberal capitalism. As a critical interactionist, I seek stories of love, loss, pain, resistance, stories of hope, stories that dig beneath ideology, stories that contest how history goes on behind our backs.

The essence of theatre, as Augusto Boal reminds us, is the human being observing itself. *'The human being not only "makes" theatre: it is theatre'* (Boal 1995:13, italics in original). What does performing mean? Is all of social life a performance? Are we all performers presenting and performing selves to one another in everyday life, putting on first one mask and then another, engaging in endless rounds of impression management, as Erving Goffman (1959) proposed? Are we only the characters we play? Is everything an illusion, pretence? Are we confined to studying the metaphysics, the fundamental nature of performance itself? But performance is a contested concept; no single definition can contain it. D. Soyini Madison reminds us:

> If we accept the notion of human beings as *homo performans* and therefore as a performing species, performance becomes necessary for our survival.

That is we recognize and create ourselves as Others through performance …
In this process culture and performance become inextricably interconnected
and performance is a constant presence in our daily lives.

(Madison 2012:166, paraphrase)

There is only performance and performance matters.

Boal says we became human when we invented the theatre (Boal 1995:14).
As *homo performans* I engage with the world as a performative-I, as an embodied, moving reflective being. I establish my presence as a universal singular, an
embodied self interacting with culture/history/society in the lived present (Spry
2011:53). Performer, moral agent, actor; everybody is a universal singular, known
only through their performances.

Interactionist autoethnographer as performer

Performance matters for critical interactionist ethnography. Ethnographers
become methodological actors who creatively play, improvise, interpret and
re-present roles and enact scripts in concrete field settings. The (auto)ethnographer
is a co-performer in a social drama, a participant in rhetorically framed cultural
performances, enacting rituals, writing field notes, recording interviews, vide-
otaping, observing, talking, doing the things ethnographers do, turning research
into performative inquiry (Conquergood 2006:360).

Performance matters. Richard Schechner clarifies. The 'relationship between
studying performance and doing performance is integral. One performs fieldwork,
which is subject to the "rehearsal process" of improvising, testing and revising
and no position is neutral. The performance scholar is actively involved in advocacy' (Schechner 2013:4, paraphrase).

A performance-centred ethnographic approach is participatory, intimate, precarious, embodied, grounded in circumstance, situational identities and historical
process. The (auto)ethnographer body is anchored in time and place. The ethnographer engages in face-work that is 'part of the intricate and nuanced dramaturgy
of everyday life' (Conquergood 2006:359; see also Goffman 1959). The power
dynamic of inquiry moves from the gaze of the detached observer to the interactions, the give-and-take between situated actors. Performance-sensitive ethnography strains to produce situated understandings, ethnodramas, performance events
that make the injustices in the world socially visible. Through cultural performances persons participate in public life, in vital discussions central to their communities (Conquergood 2006:360). The performance (auto)ethnographer works
in those dialogic spaces where bodies, selves and emotions interact.

The performance (auto)ethnographer is not studying the other per se. She is
reflexively writing herself into her performance text, into those spaces where she
intersects with the other. Her primary interests are showing, not telling, social justice, critical reflexivity, interpretation, and ethically responsible inquiry (Madison
2012:x). She makes this world visible through her performative acts. Little boys
playing cowboys and Indians.

The world as performance

Performance is many things at the same time. It is a contested term. It is a verb, a noun, a form of being, an action, a form of doing, a form of mimicry, of minstrelsy, showing, a way of knowing, a way of making the world visible, an incitement to action, an entanglement (Madison and Hamera 2006:xi–xii; Schechner 2013:28; Spry 2016). There are multiple forms of acting which frame performances: realistic (Konstantin Stanislavski), oppositional-alienation (Bertolt Brecht), spec-actor (Augusto Boal), highly codified (ballet, opera), etc. (Schechner 2013:174–185). Clearly, performance operates at three levels and in three different discourses at the same time: *human being* as *homo performans*, *ethnographer* as *homo performans*, and *ethnographer* as *homo politicans*. Performance, the word, the noun, performs differently in performance studies (Schechner 2013), in the theatre (Dolan 2001), and in (auto)ethnography and communication studies.

Performance is dramaturgical, theatrical. It is about 'putting the body on the page, lifting it to the stage, understanding that body and paper and stage are one another' (Spry 2011:26). Performance is always embodied, involving feeling, thinking, acting bodies moving through time and space. The stage actor pretends to have the emotions of the character she is playing. She may even become the emotion, like the singer who acts out the sad lyrics in the song she is singing (see Dylan 2016; Love 2015).

Every performance is unique, even when it is a form of repetition (Phelan 1993:148). It reminds us that there are no original performances or identities, no 'preexisting identity by which an act or attribute might be measured' (Phelan 1993:141). Every performance is an imitation, a before and an after, a form of mimesis, so 'if heterosexuality is an impossible imitation of itself, an imitation that performatively constitutes itself as the original, then the imitative parody of "heterosexuality" … is always and only an imitation, a copy of a copy, for which there is no original' (Phelan 1993:644).

Every performance is an original and an imitation. But, as Augusto Boal argues (1979/1985:xiv), moved to the aesthetic space, the goal of performance is to change the world, not to imitate it; 'change starts in the theatre itself. Theatre is action' (Boal 1979/1985:155; 1995:xviii).

Performance's temporality is utopic, always in the future, not the past or the present, rather the future that unfolds in the present, as a succession of what has just been (Munoz 2005:10). Utopian performatives help us re-write the past, uncover structures of oppression and imagine hopeful futures (Spry 2016:97). Performance is often a form of restored behaviour, or twice-behaved behaviour, 'performed actions people train for and rehearse and then perform' (Schechner 2013:28). Still, each twice-behaved performance is a unique event. Disappearance is the hallmark of performance, a representation without representation (Phelan 1993:148–149; see also Munoz 2005:10).

Performance can be a form of resistance, as when one refuses to comply with an order, or when Dolly speaks directly to the audience and says, shall we do this again? Performance can be a form of imitation or pretence or make-believe.

A child wears the costume of a witch on Halloween. Performance can be a form of storytelling, an event, a ritual. Performance stands between persons, their embodied presence in a situation and their presentation of self.

The triadic relationship between performance, performance ethnography and doing performance studies is crucial (Schechner 2013:2). Ethnography is always a performance, and always grounded in the self of the ethnographer. What people do is made visible in performance. The author as performer or as autoethnographer performs the very inquiry that produces the text that is performed. The performing material, the corporeal body, is read as a text; it is assigned words that give it meaning.

As Tami Spry (2011:27–28) observes, performance autoethnography becomes an engaged, critical, embodied pedagogy. This allows for critique, criticism, personal commentary and critical analysis. The writer-as-performer draws on personal experience and autobiography, and embraces vulnerability, hoping to create a critical relationship with the audience that moves persons to action (Jones, Adams and Ellis 2013, paraphrase).

C. Wright Mills (1959) reminds us that our project is to read each person into their historical moment, to grasp the relationship between history, biography, personal troubles and public issues; to see each human being as a universal singular. Critical interactionist autoethnography focuses on those moments, epiphanies in a person's life that define a crisis, a turning point that connects a personal trouble, a personal biography, with larger social, public issues. The sting of memory locates the moment, the beginning. Once located, this moment is dramatically described, fashioned into a text, or 'mystory' to be performed (Ulmer 1989:209). A mystory begins with those moments, those epiphanies that define a crisis in the person's life. This moment is then surrounded by those cultural representations and voices that define the experience in question. These representations are then contested and challenged.

The writer-as-ethnographer-as-performer is self-consciously present, morally and politically self-aware. She uses her own experiences in a culture 'reflexively to bend back on herself and look more deeply at self-other interactions' (Ellis and Bochner 2000:740). A key task of performance autoethnography is now apparent: it helps the writer 'make sense of the autobiographic past' (Alexander 1999:309). Autoethnography becomes a way of 'recreating and re-writing the biographic past, a way of making the past a part of the biographic present' (Pinar 1994:22; also cited in Alexander 1999:309). Here follows an extended example from a larger study, *Searching for Yellowstone* (Denzin 2008:57, 71):

Scene one: Memories, blankets and myths – narrator re-remembers the past: 1955

This is a short story within a larger story. I want to go back to the Spring and Summer of 1955. That spring my father sold me a $5000 life insurance policy from the Farm Bureau Life Insurance Company. I was 16 years-old, and a life insurance policy at that age seemed a stretch. But Dad was desperate. He said this sale would put him over his quota for the month and qualify him for a fishing trip to Ontario, Canada. On July 5, 1955 my father returned to our little house on Third Street in Indianola, Iowa from his company-sponsored fishing trip in Ontario, Canada. Mother greeted him at the door. Slightly drunk, Dad handed her a Hudson's Bay wool blanket as a present, and promptly left for the office. I still have that blanket. In this family we value these blankets and exchange them as gifts. This exchange system gives me a somewhat indirect history with Canada, Hudson's Bay Company blankets, the fur trade, nineteenth century British and French traders and Native Americans. This history takes me right into the myths about Yellowstone Park, Lewis and Clark, the Corps of Discovery, and Sacagawea. Lewis and Clark, it appears, also traded blankets and other gifts for good will on their expedition. But this was a tainted exchange, for many of these blankets were carriers of the small pox disease. Likewise, the blanket father gave to mother was embedded within a disease exchange system, in this case alcoholism. While father's alcoholism was not full-blown in 1955, it would be within two years of his return from this fishing trip. Today that blanket is in the blanket chest at the foot of our bed.

Scene two: Narrator remembers another version of the past: 1994

The Hudson's Bay blanket that my father bought for me and my wife at a farm auction in Kalona, Iowa in the winter of 1994 was expensive. He and his best friend bid against one another, driving the price up over $300.00. The price was fitting, for the blanket is marked with four black pelt or point lines, which defined the blanket's worth in that nineteenth century economy where pelts were traded for blankets. A four pelt blanket is indeed pricey. Today that four-pelt blanket is in the guest room in our cabin outside Red Lodge, Montana. As I said earlier, in this family we value these blankets and exchange them as gifts.

It's all here: memories; biographies; family histories; the salesman as an iconic American figure; crises; alcoholism; ritual, family performances; pretense; impression management; gift-exchange systems; fathers and sons; larger historical, cultural and economic structures and systems; life insurance companies; Lewis and Clark; Native Americans; 19th century American colonialism; Yellowstone Park; blankets; nature; wildlife; tourism. Buying that insurance policy from my father implicated me (and my family) in his dreams, connecting us to a global exchange system that is still in place today, making us complicit with Lewis and Clark's and Hudson's Bay's mistreatment of Native Americans.

When I reflect on the day my father sold me that life insurance policy and I signed that check, I feel flashes of anger, guilt, shame and pride. How could he have done this to me? Whose version of a father was he performing that day, and whose version of a son was I performing? What choices did we have?

Race and the call to performance

As the dividing line between performativity (doing) and performance (done) disappears, matters of gender and racial injustice remain. On this, W. E. B. Du Bois reminds us that 'modern democracy cannot succeed unless peoples of different races and religions are also integrated into the democratic whole' (Du Bois 1901/1978:281, 288). Du Bois addressed race from a performance standpoint. He understood that 'from the arrival of the first African slaves on American soil … the definitions and meanings of blackness, have been intricately linked to issues of theatre and performance' (Elam 2001:4).[1] Being black meant wearing and performing the masks of blackness. It meant wearing black skin. It meant hiding inside and behind blackness. As Bryant Alexander elaborates:

> I am interested in skin as performance;
> I am interested in skin on 'colored' bodies.
> I am interested in Skin as in a box checked.
> I am interested in skin – performing it, seeing it, dark, light skin,
> Skin as a marketing tool
>
> (Alexander 2012:154–155, paraphrase)

Race as performance, as skin, as mask, blackface, whiteface, a minstrel show. 'Black, white, red, yellow, is it about color, or something else?' (Diversi and Moreira 2009:90–91, paraphrase).

bell hooks has elaborated the need for a black political performance aesthetic. In another time, as a child, she and her sisters learned about race in America by watching

> the Ed Sullivan show on Sunday nights … seeing on that show the great Louis Armstrong, Daddy who was usually silent, would talk about the music, the way Armstrong was being treated, and the political implications of his appearance … responding to televised cultural production, black people could express rage about racism … unfortunately … black folks were not engaged in writing a body of critical cultural analysis.
>
> (hooks 1990:3–4)

But in America today, unarmed black male teenagers with their hands in the air can be shot by the police, and a 12-year-old black boy can be shot and killed by police in Cleveland because the officer mistook a toy gun for a real gun (Kelley 2014). It is no longer safe for black teenage males to even walk alongside, let alone cross over Du Bois's colour line.

I fold my project of critical interactionism into Du Bois's, Alexander's and hooks's by asking how a radical performative discourse can confront and transcend the problems surrounding the colour line in the second decade of the 21st century. Such a project will write and perform culture in new ways. It will connect reflexive autoethnography with critical pedagogy and critical race theory (see Donnor and Ladson-Billings 2017). It will call for acts of activism that insist on justice for all. Unarmed young black males can no longer just be shot down by police without recrimination. Robin Kelley reminds us that we know their names and how they died:

> We hold their names like recurring nightmares, accumulating the dead like ghoulish baseball cards. Except that there is no trading. No forgetting. Just a stack of dead bodies: Trayvon, Michael, Eleanor Bumpurs, Michael Stewart, Eula Love, Amadu Diallo, Oscar Grant, Patrick Dorismond, Malice Green, Tyisha Miller, Sean Bell, Aiyana Stanley-Jones, Margaret LaVerne Mitchell. Names attached to dead black bodies. Symbols of police violence and this does not even begin to count the harassed, the beaten, the humiliated, the stopped-and-frisked, the raped.
>
> (Kelley 2014, paraphrase)

There is no longer, but there never was, an age of innocence for persons of colour in America.

The goal is to undo official racial history and to create a space for marginalised voices, alternative histories, new ways of writing and performing the past so new futures can be imagined. This performative discourse imagines a politics of resistance, a new politics of possibility, new ways of re-imagining the future and the past. D. Soyini Madison, after Jill Dolan (2005), calls these re-imaginings 'utopian performatives'. They are akin to Paulo Freire's 'pedagogies of hope' (Madison 2010:26; 2012:182; Freire 1992/1999; Dolan 2005:5). Freire reminds us that without hope there is only tragic despair and hopelessness (Freire 1992/1999:8–9).

Hope and acts of activism[2]

Performances of possibility create spaces 'where unjust systems ... can be identified and interrogated' (Madison 2010:159). Persons can become radicalised when confronted with such performances. As Madison notes: 'one performance may or may not change someone's world ... but one performance can be revolutionary in enlightening citizens as to the possibilities that grate against injustice' (Madison 2010:159). Utopian performatives offer a reflexive what if, a utopian imagining of how a situation could be performed differently (Conquergood 2002/2013:29). It is a retooling, a redoing, a renewing (Spry 2016:96).

The utopic stages itself. It pushes and pulls us forward. It incites the imagination. It offers blueprints for hope and 'outlines of a world not quite here, a horizon of possibility, not a fixed scheme' (Munoz 2005:9). Utopia is flux, change, stasis, chaos, and disorganisation all jumbled together, a fluid 'moment when the here and now is transcended by a then, and a there that could be and indeed should be' (Munoz 2005:9). Utopia is always a critique of the here and now. It involves a politics of emotion, an insistence that something is missing from the present, hope, a dream, freedom. It involves the belief that things can be different, better; there can be social justice in a place called utopia where hope dwells.

A performative, pedagogical politics of hope imagines a radically free democratic society, a society where ideals of the ableist, ageist, indigenist, feminist, queer, environmental, green, civil rights and labour movements are realised. In their utopian forms, these movements offer 'alternative models of radical democratic culture rooted in social relations that take seriously the democratic ideals of freedom, liberty, and the pursuit of happiness' (Giroux 2000:9). Madison is quite explicit; critical, performative autoethnography begins 'with a duty and ethical responsibility to address suffering, unfairness and injustice within a particular historical moment. There is a commitment to perform acts of activism that advance the causes of human rights' (Madison 2010:1; 2012:5, paraphrase).

Accordingly, a radical performative discourse revolves around specific acts of resistance and activism, performances where persons put their bodies on the line, staged re-enactments which incite resistance. These acts are public interventions. That is performance is used subversively, as a strategy for awakening critical consciousness and moving persons to take human, democratic actions in the face of injustice, efforts that serve social justice, and that are expected to bring net gains in the lives of people (Madison 2010:1; Cohen-Cruz 2005:4). These explicit acts of activism imply an embodied epistemology, a poetic reflexive performing body moving through space, an ethical body taking responsibility for its action. Frederick C. Corey observes that the use of performance

> to initiate social change predates the theatres of Greece, where, by way of example, in Lysistrata, Aristophanes created a lead character who corals her friends to withhold sex from their husbands in order to stop the wars … Contemporary examples include Brecht's Epic Theatre, Boal's Theatre of the Oppressed, agit prop, and guerilla theatre.[3]
>
> (Corey 2015:1, paraphrase)

Gloria Anzaldua's (1987:2–3) writing performs its own acts of resistance. She speaks of border crossing, crossing the borders:

> I walk through the hole in the fence
> To the other side
> Beneath the iron sky
> Mexican children kick the soccer ball across,
> run after it, entering the U.S.
> 1,950- mile-long open wound …
> staking fence rods in my flesh …
> This is my home
> this thin edge of barbwire.
> This land was Indian always and is
> And will be again.

Changing the world[4]

Returning to the social justice theme, critical interactionist inquiry can contribute to social justice in the following ways. First, it can help identify different definitions of a problem, or a situation is being evaluated and there is some agreement that change is required. It can show, for example, how battered wives interpret the shelters, hotlines and public services that are made available to them by social welfare agencies. Through the use of personal experience narratives, the perspectives of women and workers can be compared and contrasted. Second, the assumptions that are held by various interested parties – policymakers, clients, welfare workers, online professionals – can be located and shown to be correct or incorrect. Third, strategic points of intervention into social situations can be identified. In such ways, the services of an agency and a program can be improved and evaluated. Fourth, it is possible to suggest 'alternative moral points of view from which the problem', the policy and the program can be interpreted and assessed (see Becker 1967:23–24). Because of its emphasis on experience and its meanings, the interpretive method suggests that programs must always be judged by and from the point of view of the persons most directly affected. Fifth, the limits of statistics and statistical evaluations can be exposed with the more qualitative, interpretive materials furnished by this approach. Its emphasis on the uniqueness of each life holds up the individual case as the measure of the effectiveness of all applied programs.

Interpretation and understanding are key features of social life. In social life, there is only interpretation. That is, everyday life revolves around persons interpreting and making judgments about their own and other's behaviours and experiences. Many times these interpretations and judgments are based on faulty or incorrect understandings. Persons, for instance, mistake their own experiences for the experiences of others. These interpretations are then formulated into social programs, which are intended to alter and shape the lives of troubled people, for example, community services for the mentally ill or the homeless, treatment centres for alcoholics, medical services for AIDS patients, and so on. But often the understandings that these programs are based upon bear little relationship to the meanings, interpretations and experience of the persons they are intended to serve. As a consequence, there is a gap or failure in understanding. The programs do not work because they are based on a failure to take the perspective and attitude of the person served.

Moral criticism and taking sides

As a cultural critic, the critical interactionist researcher speaks from an informed moral and ethical position. He or she is anchored in a specific community of moral discourse. The moral ethnographer takes a side. Taking sides is a complex process. Researchers must make their own value positions clear, including the so-called facts and ideological assumptions that they attach to these positions. Scholars must identify and analyse the values and claims to objective knowledge that organise positions that are contrary to their own. In so doing, they will show how these appeals to ideology and objective knowledge reflect a particular moral and historical standpoint. They show how this standpoint disadvantages and disempowers members of a specific group.

In a call to action, researchers engage in concrete steps that will change situations in the future. They may teach persons how to bring new value and meaning to identities or draw attention to cultural commodities and texts that are marginalised and stigmatised by the larger culture. They will demonstrate how particular definitions and meanings negatively affect the lives of specific people. They indicate how particular texts, directly and indirectly, misrepresent persons and reproduce prejudice and stereotypes.

Blurring interpretive genres

The current historical moment is characterised by a willingness to experiment with new representational forms. The move to performance has been accompanied by a shift in the meaning of ethnography and ethnographic writing. There are many different performance forms. These forms include not only performance autoethnography but also short stories, conversations, fiction, creative nonfiction, photographic essays, personal essays, personal narratives of the self, writing stories, self stories, fragmented, layered texts, critical autobiography, memoirs, personal histories, cultural criticism, co-constructed performance narratives, and performance writing,[5] which blur the edges between text, representation and criticism.

In each of these forms, the writer-as-performer is self-consciously present, morally and politically self-aware. She uses her own experiences in a culture 'reflexively to bend back on self and look more deeply at self-other interactions' (Ellis and Bochner 2000:740). The task of autoethnography is now apparent: it helps the writer 'make sense of the autobiographic past' (Alexander 1999:309). Autoethnography becomes a way of 'recreating and re-writing the biographic past, a way of making the past a part of the biographic present' (Pinar 1994:22).

The new writers treat facts as social constructions, blur writing genres, use the scenic method to show rather than tell, write about real people and create composite characters, use multiple points of view including third-person narration to establish authorial presence, and deploy multiple narrative strategies (flashbacks, foreshadowing, interior monologues, parallel plots and so on) to build dramatic tension and to position themselves as moral witnesses to the radical changes going in American society (Denzin 1997:131).

I have no desire to reproduce arguments that maintain some distinction between fictional (literary) and nonfictional (journalism, ethnography) texts. Nor do I distinguish literary, nonliterary, fictional and nonfictional textual forms. These are socially and politically constructed categories. They are too often used to police certain transgressive writing forms, for example fictional or literary ethnography, ethnodrama or ethnopoetry. There is only narrative, that is only different genre-defined ways of representing and writing about experiences and their multiple realities. The discourses of the postmodern world constantly intermingle literary, poetic, journalistic, fictional, cinematic, documentary, factual and ethnographic writing and representation. No form is privileged over another; each simply performs a different function for a writer and an interpretive community.

Performance pedagogy and the sociological imagination

C. Wright Mills (1959) anticipated and shaped the turn to critical qualitative inquiry and critical pedagogy in the human sciences. Indeed, a direct line can be drawn from Mills to Paulo Freire, and from Freire to contemporary versions of critical pedagogy (Kincheloe and McLaren 2000). It remained for the next generation of theorists to take the performance and autoethnographic turn; that is to link critical pedagogy with performance autoethnography. This was the missing step in Mills's formulations. Critical performance autoethnography forges a link between individual biography, history and social structure, the lynchpins of Mills's sociological imagination. Performance is a way of knowing, a way of creating and fostering understanding, a method that persons use to create and give meaning to everyday life.

Performances are grounded in the autoethnographic text, those sites where writers become ethnographers of their own lives, moving back and forth between self and other, self and history, self and social structure (Ellis and Bochner 2000:733). The autoethnographic text is a form of personal history, or what Gregory Ulmer (1989), as mentioned earlier, calls the 'mystory'. The mystory is anchored in epiphanies, major and minor turning-point moments that have left their marks on the person. The mystory is a performance narrative that critiques those social structures that have shaped and marked the person.

D. Soyini Madison and Judith Hamera remind us that today, in a globalised, post-9/11 world, performances, identities and personal histories have become the enactment of stories that literally bleed across national borders. Being a U.S. citizen is to be 'enmeshed in the facts of U.S. foreign policy, world trade, civil society and war' (Madison and Hamera 2006:xx). Garoian and Gaudelius (2008) extend Madison and Hamera, locating inquiry within a critical, post 9/11 spectacle pedagogy. Using performance as a method of investigation, they show how pedagogies of terror and fear have increasingly permeated everyday life.

Mills would agree with this focus. At one level, the most important events of the last decade follow from the 9/11 attacks, including the wars in Iraq and Afghanistan, the global war on terror, and the institutionalisation of a new surveillance regime that affects every travelling body entering or leaving the United States. A critical inquiry, in all its forms, must locate itself in these historical spaces. As Mills stated, 'all classic social scientists have been concerned with the salient characteristics of their time' (Mills 1959:165). This means they have been preoccupied with how history and human nature is being made within their historical moment. They have been concerned with the variety and types of individuals, men, women and children who have prevailed in their historical present (Mills 1959:165).

Interpretive inquiry in the contemporary period is committed to understanding how this historical moment universalises itself in the lives of interacting individuals. Each person and each relationship studied is assumed to be a universal singular, or a single instance of the universal themes that structure the postmodern period. Each person is touched by the mass media, by alienation, by the economy, by the new family and childcare systems, by the increasing technologising of the social world and by the threat of nuclear annihilation. Critical qualitative inquiry fits itself to the relation between the individual and society, to the nexus of biography and society. Interpretive inquiry attempts to show how individual troubles and problems become public issues. In the discovery of this nexus, it attempts to bring alive the existentially problematic, often hidden, and private experiences that give meaning to everyday life as it is lived in this moment in history.

To make the invisible more visible to others is, after all, a major goal of the interpreter. This means that we want to capture the stories of everyday persons as they tell about the pains, the agonies, the emotional experiences, the small and the large victories, the traumas, the fears, the anxieties, the dreams, fantasies and the hopes in their lives. We want to make those stories available to others. Our voice must speak to the terrible and magnificent world of human experience in the second decade of this new century.

The project is clear. Today we are called to change the world, and to change it in ways that resist injustice while celebrating freedom and full, inclusive, participatory democracy.

Conclusion

Critical interactionist research will be defined by the work that scholars do as they implement the assumptions presented in this chapter. These situations set the stage for critical inquiry's transformations in the 21st century. I have outlined some of the major assumptions underlying a performative, critical interactionist approach to cultural critique. This entailed treating the ethnographer as a performer while distinguishing different approaches to performance, theatre and critique. An extended example from my own biography illustrated the interrelationship between memories, biographies, family histories, and pedagogies and performance. This opened the way for a discussion of acts of activism, hope and the politics of resistance.

In moving from fieldwork and inquiry to page and then to stage and performance, autoethnographers as symbolic interactionists resist speaking for the other (Spry 2011). Rather they assist in the struggles of others, staging performance events, screening and re-presenting history, offering new versions of official history, performing counter-memories, exposing contradictions in official ideology, reflexively interrogating their own place in the performance thereby taking ethical responsibility for the consequences of their own acts and performances (Madison 2010:11). In these ways, staged ethnography, ethnodramas and performance autoethnographies do the work of advocacy (see Saldana 2005). The performance is not a mirror, it is, as D. Soyini Madison argues, after Bertolt Brecht, the hammer that breaks the mirror, shatters the glass and builds a new reality (Madison 2010:12). In their performances, autoethnographers incite transformations, cause trouble and act in unruly ways. They self-consciously become part of the performance itself, the instrument of change. Performance now becomes a moral, reflexive act, more than a method, an ethical act of advocacy.

Notes

1 Race and racism for Du Bois were social constructions, performances, minstrelsy, blackface, powerful devices that produce and reproduce the colour line. Du Bois believed that African Americans needed performance spaces where they could control how race was constructed. Consequently, as Harry J. Elam Jr. (2001:5–6) observes, African American theatre and performance have been central sites for the interrogation of race and the color line (also Elam and Krasner 2001). 'The inherent "constructedness" of performance and the malleability of the devices of the theatre serve to reinforce the theory that blackness ... and race ... are hybrid, fluid concepts' (Elam 2001:4–5).
2 I steal the phrase 'acts of activism' from Madison (2010, 2012).
3 Cohen-Cruz (2005:1) expands Corey's examples to include such community-based performances as public protests, skits at union halls, rallies, ritual, dance, music making and public theatre.
4 This section extends arguments in Denzin (2017).
5 Performance writing shows, rather than tells. It is writing that speaks performatively, enacting what it describes. Performance writing is evocative, reflexive, multi-vocal, citational, always incomplete (Pollock 1998:80–95).

References

Alexander, Bryant Keith (1999): 'Performing Culture in the Classroom: An Instructional (Auto) Ethnography'. *Text and Performance Quarterly*, 19 (4):307–331.
Alexander, Bryant Keith (2012): *The Performativity Sustainability of Race: Reflections on Black Culture and the Politics of Identity*. New York: Peter Lang.
Anzaldua, Gloria (1987): *Borderlands/La Frontera: The New Mestiza*. San Francisco, CA: Aunt Lute Books.
Becker, Howard S. (1967): 'Whose Side Are We On?' *Social Problems*, 14:239–247.
Blumer, Herbert (1969): *Symbolic Interactionism: Perspective and Method*. Englewood Cliffs, NJ: Prentice-Hall.
Blumer, Herbert (1981): 'George Herbert Mead', in Buford Rhea (ed.): *The Future of Sociological Classics*. London, Boston: Allen & Unwin, pp. 136–169.
Boal, Augusto (1979/1985): *The Theatre of the Oppressed*. New York: Theatre Communications Group.
Boal, Augusto (1995): *The Rainbow of Desire: The Boal Method of Theatre and Therapy*. London: Routledge.
Bochner, Arthur P. and Carolyn Ellis (2016): *Evocative Autoethnography: Writing Lives and Telling Stories*. New York: Routledge.
Clifford, James and George E. Marcus (1986): *Writing Culture: The Poetics and Politics of Ethnography*. Berkeley, CA: University of California Press.
Cohen-Cruz, Jan (2005): *Local Acts: Community-Based Performance in the United States*. New Brunswick: Rutgers University Press.
Conquergood, Dwight (1985): 'Performance as a Moral Act: Ethical Dimensions of the Ethnography of Performance'. *Literature in Performance*, 5 (2): 1–13.

Conquergood, Dwight (1992a): 'Ethnography, Rhetoric and Performance'. *Quarterly Journal of Speech*, 78:80–97.

Conquergood, Dwight (1992b): 'Life in Big Red: Struggles and Accommodations in a Chicago Polyethnic Tenement', in Louise Lamphere (ed.): *Structuring Diversity: Ethnographic Perspectives on the New Immigration*. Chicago: University of Chicago Press, pp. 95–144.

Conquergood, Dwight (2006): 'Rethinking Ethnography: Towards a Critical Cultural Politics', in D. Soyini Madison and Judith Hamera (eds.): *The Sage Handbook of Performance Studies*. Thousand Oaks, CA: Sage Publications, pp. 351–365.

Conquergood, Dwight (2002/2013): 'Performance Studies: Interventions and Radical Research', in *Cultural Struggles: Performance, Ethnography, Praxis: Dwight Conquergood* (edited and with an introduction by E. Patrick Johnson). Ann Arbor: University of Michigan Press, pp. 32–46.

Corey, Frederick C. (2015): 'Editor's Introduction: Performance and Social Change'. *Text and Performance Quarterly*, 35 (1):1–3.

Denzin, Norman K. (1997): *Interpretive Ethnography*. Thousand Oaks, CA: Sage Publications.

Denzin, Norman K. (2008): *Searching for Yellowstone: Race, Gender, Family and Memory in the Postmodern West*. Walnut Creek, CA: Left Coast Press.

Denzin, Norman K. (2017): *Performance (Auto)Ethnography: Critical Pedagogy and the Politics of Culture* (2nd edition). New York: Routledge.

Diversi, Marcelo and Claudio Moreira (2009): *Betweener Talk: Decolonizing Knowledge Production, Pedagogy and Praxis*. Walnut Creek, CA: Left Coast Press.

Dolan, Jill (2001): 'Performance, Utopia and the "Utopian Performative"'. *Theatre Journal*, 53 (3):455–479.

Dolan, Jill (2005): *Utopia in Performance: Finding Hope in the Theater*. Ann Arbor: University of Michigan Press.

Donnor, Jamel K. and Gloria Ladson-Billings (2017): 'Critical Race Theory and the Post-Racial Imaginary', in Norman K. Denzin and Yvonna S. Lincoln (eds.): *Handbook of Qualitative Research* (5th edition). Thousand Oaks, CA: Sage Publications.

Du Bois, W. E. B. (1901/1978): 'The Problem of the Twentieth Century is the Problem of the Color Line', in W. E. B. Du Bois: *On Sociology and the Black Community* (edited and with an introduction by Dan S. Green and Edward Driver). Chicago: University of Chicago Press, pp. 281–289.

Du Bois, W. E. B. (1926): 'Krigwa Players Little Negro Theatre: The Story of a Little Theatre Movement'. *Crisis*, 32 (July):134–136.

du Gay, Paul, Stuart Hall, Linda Janes, Hugh Mackay and Keith Negus (1997): *Doing Cultural Studies: The Story of the Sony Walkman*. London: Sage Publications.

Dylan, Bob (2016): 'The Banquet Speech, Nobel Prize in Literature'. Stockholm: The Nobel Foundation, 10 December. Available online at: https://www.nobelprize.org/nobel_prizes/literature/laureates/2016/dylan-speech.html.

Elam, Harry J. Jr., (2001): 'The Device of Race: An Introduction', in Harry J. Elam Jr. and David Krasner (eds.): *African American Performance and Theater History: A Critical Reader*. New York: Oxford University Press, pp. 3–16.

Elam, Harry J., Jr. and David Krasner (eds.) (2001): *African American Performance and Theater History: A Critical Reader*. New York: Oxford University Press.

Ellis, Carolyn and Arthur P. Bochner (2000): 'Autoethnography, Personal Narrative, Reflexivity: Researcher as Subject', in Norman K. Denzin and Yvonna S. Lincoln (eds.): *Handbook of Qualitative Research* (2nd edition). Thousand Oaks, CA: Sage Publications, pp. 733–768.

Freire, Paulo (1970/2000): *Pedagogy of the Oppressed* (30th anniversary edition with an introduction by Donaldo Macedo). New York: Continuum.

Freire, Paulo (1992/1999): *Pedagogy of Hope*. New York: Continuum.

Garoian, Charles R. and Yvonne M. Gaudelius (2008): *Spectacle Pedagogy: Art, Politics and Visual Culture*. Albany, NY: State University of New York Press.

Giroux, Henry (2000): *Stealing Innocence: Corporate Culture's War on Children*. New York: Palgrave.

Goffman, Erving (1959): *The Presentation of Self in Everyday Life*. New York: Doubleday.

hooks, bell (1990): *Yearning: Race, Gender and Cultural Politics*. Boston: South End Press.

Jones, Stacy Holman, Tony E. Adams and Carolyn Ellis (eds.) (2013): *Handbook of Autoethnography*. Walnut Creek, CA: Left Coast Press.

Kelley, Robin D. G. (2014): 'Why We Won't Wait'. *CounterPunch*, 25 November. Available online at: http://www.counterpunch.org/2014/11/25/75039/.

Kincheloe, Joe L. and Peter McLaren (2000): 'Rethinking Critical Theory and Qualitative Research', in Norman K. Denzin and Yvonna S. Lincoln (eds.): *Handbook of Qualitative Research* (2nd edition). Thousand Oaks, CA: Sage Publications, pp. 279–314.

Love, Robert (2015): 'Bob Dylan Does the American Standards His Way'. *AARP Magazine*, 22 January, pp. 4–16.

Madison, D. Soyini (2012): *Critical Ethnography* (2nd edition). Thousand Oaks, CA: Sage Publications.

Madison, D. Soyini (2010): *Acts of Activism: Human Rights as Radical Performance*. Cambridge: Cambridge University Press.

Madison, D. Soyini and Judith Hamera (2006): 'Introduction: Performance Studies at the Intersections', in D. Soyini Madison and Judith Hamera (eds.): *The Sage Handbook of Performance Studies*. Thousand Oaks, CA: Sage Publications, pp. xi–xxv.

Mills, C. Wright (1959): *The Sociological Imagination*. New York: Oxford University Press.

Munoz, Jose Esteban (2005): 'Stages: Queers, Punks, and the Utopian Performative', in D. Soyini Madison and Judith Hamera (eds.): *The Sage Handbook of Performance Studies*. Thousand Oaks, CA: Sage Publications, pp. 9–20.

Phelan, Peggy (1993): *Unmarked: The Politics of Performance*. London: Routledge.

Pinar, William (1994): *Autobiography, Politics and Sexuality*. New York: Peter Lang.

Pollack, Della (1998): 'Performing Writing', in Peggy Phelan (ed.): *The Ends of Performance*. New York: New York University Press, pp. 73–103.

Richardson, Laurel (2000): 'Writing: A Method of Inquiry', in Norman K. Denzin and Yvonna S. Lincoln (eds.): *Handbook of Qualitative Research* (2nd edition). Thousand Oaks, CA: Sage Publications, pp. 923–948.

Saldana, Johnny (2005): *Ethnotheatre*. Walnut Creek, CA: Let Coast Press.

Schechner, Richard (1998): 'What Is Performance Studies Anyway?', in Peggy Phelan and Jill Lane (eds.): *The Ends of Performance*. New York: New York University Press, pp. 357–362.

Schechner, Richard (2013): *Performance Studies: An Introduction*. New York: Routlege.

Spry, Tami (2011): *Body, Paper, Stage: Writing and Performing Autoethnography*. Walnut Creek, CA: Left Coast Press.

Spry, Tami (2016): *Autoethnography and the Other: Unsettling Power Through Utopian Performatives*. New York: Routledge.

Turner, Victor W. (1985): *On the Edge of the Bush: Anthropology as Experience*. Tucson: University of Arizona Press.

Ulmer, Gregory (1989): *Teletheory*. New York: Routledge.

4 Dramaturgical interactionism

Ideas of self-presentation, impression management and the staging of social life as a catapult for critique

Michael Hviid Jacobsen and Søren Kristiansen

Introduction

Interactionism is a broad church providing shelter to many different camps, sects and offshoots, each in their way providing width and substance to the perspective, often by privileging their own specific vocabularies, methods, theoretical understandings and worldviews. Counted among these, by now, many branches of interactionism is dramaturgy – the approach that takes the concepts and insights from theatrical life and applies them to shed light on social life. 'Dramaturgy' is a term most frequently used within the realm of the theatre and its artistic performances. It signifies a world of actors and actresses, audiences, roles, stage managers, performances, props, costumes, scripts, stages, prompters and rehearsals. Dramaturgical sociology is a sociology that applies these basic tenets of the theatre to the study and analysis of a variety of different aspects of life outside of the theatre. In its transfer of meaning from the artificial performative environment of the theatre to real-life events, dramaturgical sociology draws on the framework provided by dramaturgy. Dramaturgical sociology was particularly developed, embraced and utilised within the confines of interactionist sociology from the late 1950s and onwards, and was originally associated primarily with the work of Erving Goffman. Even though there are many other origins and variants of dramaturgical thinking within disciplines such as anthropology (e.g., Tambiah 1981; Turner 1982), social psychology/clinical psychology (e.g., Scheibe 2002; Steiner 1974), media studies (Postman 1985) and performance studies (e.g., Schechner 2013) (interestingly enough, an actual 'dramaturgical criminology' has still not materialised), Goffman remains a key referent in most of the research conducted, whether theoretical or empirical. Many of the introductions to and explications of dramaturgical sociology published post-Goffman – or at least in the wake of the publication of his dramaturgical manifesto in *The Presentation of Self in Everyday Life* (1959) – thus refer back to his by-now classic understandings (see, e.g., Brissett and Edgley 1990a; Burns 1972; Combs and Mansfield 1976; Edgley 2013; Hare and Blumberg 1988; Shulman 2017). In addition to this, empirical studies of various social sites and contexts such as presidential politics, gynaecological clinics, mental hospitals, prisons, hotel foyers, strip clubs and funeral parlours using dramaturgical ideas by drawing particularly on

Goffman continue to be conducted and published at a steady pace within sociology (see, e.g., Brown 2005; Henslin and Biggs 1978; Faccio and Costa 2013; Dillard et al. 2000; Sujiwade 1995; Turner and Edgley 1976), testifying to the continued relevance yet also much diversified use of the dramaturgical perspective. Moreover, Goffman's dramaturgical sociology has been a precursor to and an important source of inspiration for fields such as 'performance theory' and 'performance studies' (Schechner 2003; 2013) and the so-called scripting theory, which particularly rose to prominence within studies of sexuality (e.g., Gagnon and Simon 1973), clinical psychology (e.g., Steiner 1974) and in studies of everyday life (e.g., MacDonald 2005). In this way, dramaturgical perspectives continue to thrive, develop and proliferate within contemporary sociology.

'Dramaturgical interactionism' (here abbreviated as DI) is the term we in this chapter reserve to describing those ideas, approaches and theories that draw on dramaturgical notions and use these within an overall interactionist framework. The specific term of DI has been used before in the literature of symbolic interactionism, however often without much qualification or exhaustive elaboration. Even though used here in the singular, DI is *not*, as we will show, a single monolithic or solidified perspective. Rather, it is a notion that covers a range of different perspectives which view social life (and particularly social interaction) through the lens of a theatrical/dramaturgical metaphor with an accompanying focus on the embodied performances of the self (see, e.g., Waskul and Vannini 2006). It relies on the basic (symbolic) interactionist tenets as outlined, for example, by Herbert Blumer (1969) and couples these with the dramaturgical insights of, for example, Goffman. As already suggested by Elizabeth Burns (1972), the notion of drama can refer to factual as well as fictional aspects of life and there are thus many different ways in which to rely on dramaturgical-interactionist ideas ranging from the descriptive and analytical to the evaluative and critical. For example, whereas Goffman's notions of self-presentation and impression management primarily worked as descriptive and metaphorical tools (playing on the 'as if') for teasing out and interpreting overlooked aspects of social and life, others after him have rather relied on dramaturgical ideas in order to show how social (and political) life *in itself* is constituted by dramatic performances, yet others have used dramaturgy for explanatory or predictive purposes and yet others have used dramaturgical ideas as a means for advancing social critique or political viewpoints (see, e.g., Borreca 1993). There are thus many different ways in which dramaturgical ideas may influence and find use in social science studies.

In this chapter, we initially want to outline some of the main ideas of DI and then discuss their uses, their limitations and not least their potentials for providing a critical perspective on contemporary society. First, we start by delineating Goffman's dramaturgical sociology in which ideas about roles, performances, impression management and the like function as a metaphorical scaffold for understanding everyday life as drama. Following this, we briefly touch upon some of the main objections and criticisms raised against Goffman's dramaturgical perspective. This provides a platform for discussing in some detail some of the different ways in which the ideas of DI can work as a catalyst or catapult for social critique.

Goffman's dramaturgy as a metaphorical scaffold

There exists a conventional distinction in the human and social science literature between 'dramatism' and 'dramaturgy'. Roughly speaking, dramatism is rooted in the humanities and is inspired by the philosophy of Kenneth Burke (1955), whereas dramaturgy is often characterised by a more microsociological approach finding a major exponent in the works of Erving Goffman (Pushkala 2005:43), who himself relied on and expanded on a number of already existing dramaturgical understandings (see, e.g., Edgley 2003; Edgley and Turner 1975; Hopper 1981; Messinger et al. 1962).[1] While making use of different conceptual metaphors (theatre, game, ritual and frame) throughout his sociological scholarship, much of Goffman's early work was devoted to elaborations on and popularisation of dramaturgical lines of thinking. Although he drew on insights from Burke, significant inspiration came from the works of George Herbert Mead. Goffman's dramaturgy, therefore, takes its offspring and continues a symbolic interactionist line of thought focusing on social interaction and role-play. To state it short and with the risk of simplifying, Goffman proposed the dramaturgical perspective in order to provide (or, better perhaps, revitalise) a perspective stressing the similarities between theatre and everyday life with the potential to grasp the mechanics of staged and regionalised self-presentation within the boundaries of shared sets of meaning (or definitions of the situation). In his, perhaps, most famous book, *The Presentation of Self in Everyday Life*, Goffman (published originally in 1956 with a revised version appearing in 1959)[2] describes the perspective as 'that of the theatrical performance' and accordingly that the principles following from the analysis are 'dramaturgical ones'. The overall aim of his dramaturgical analysis was to provide a sociological understanding of how people in ordinary face-to-face interactions present themselves to others; how they manage the information that they respectively 'give' and 'give off' in situations of co-presence; and how such staged performances with audiences, scripts, cues and stages restrict and enable the maintenance of a shared definition of the situation. In short, then, Goffman provided a dramaturgical perspective conceptualising individuals' conduct as 'performances', often done or 'staged' collaboratively in 'teams' whose members must master the 'arts of impression management' (Goffman 1959).

The conceptual backbone of Goffman's dramaturgical reframing of everyday-life encounters is thus a number of dramaturgical elements, which, taken together, provide a framework for understanding the microsociological mechanisms underlying the mundane encounters and the role-play in modern social life. Goffman's analysis centres on performances, teams, regions and region behaviour; discrepant roles; communication out of character; and impression management, and we will here provide some brief 'snapshots' of selected ones. While the latter, 'impression management', is perhaps the most well known and frequently cited Goffmanian concept, the others, of course, shed light on important dramaturgical issues and contingencies concerning the collaborative role-play of everyday life. In Goffman's (1959:26) terms, a performance can 'be defined as all the activity of a given participant on a given occasion which serves to influence in any way any of the other participants'. Performances, then, are about making, sustaining and controlling the impressions others form of the immediate social situation and they entail efforts of asserting to others that the person is what and whom he pretends to be. Stagecraft and stage management involves certain sorts of equipment, and Goffman's dramaturgical analysis reveals how performers make use of certain expressive equipment such as clothes and gender to facilitate the expression of situational claims. Also, performances may be subject to 'idealisation' indicating that performers sometimes provide the audience with an impression that is not fully aligned with the objective reality. Characteristic of his style, the illustrative material in Goffman's dramaturgy comes from a variety of sources (what he called of 'mixed status'). Thus, processes of idealisation are exemplified by referring to tales of domestic Scottish performances, where 'the average laird and his family lived far more frugally in the ordinary way than they did when they were entertaining visitors. They would rise to a great occasion and serve dishes reminiscent of the banquets of the medieval nobility; but like those same nobles, between the festivities, they would "keep secret house", as the saying used to be, and live on the plainest of fare' (Goffman 1959:47). In addition to the idealisation aspect of performance, Goffman also talked about 'dramatisation' or 'dramatic realisation', by which he meant that while engaged in interaction, 'the individual typically infuses his activity with signs which dramatically highlight and portray confirmatory facts that might otherwise remain unapparent or obscure' (Goffman 1959:41). The purpose of idealisation and dramatisation is thus to ensure that one's desired image of self is displayed as well as accepted in the interaction without revealing that 'all too human' and fallible self that should be kept behind locks and bolts.

Another important aspect of the dramaturgical model is the notion of 'regions'. Dramaturgical activity, Goffman noted, is performed in different places that in one way or another is bounded by barriers of perception (Goffman 1959:109). In exploring the characteristics of these regions, Goffman distinguishes between the 'scene' or the 'front region' and the 'back region' (often referred to as 'frontstage' and 'backstage'). In the front region, actors present their performances before an audience, and they thus play their roles and adjust their performances according to the situation's normative structure. The back region is outside the immediate 'spotlight' and thus a place for the performer to rehearse and recharge. It may also be described as a realm of authenticity where people can be 'themselves' and prepare for their more public performance (Pushkala 2005:46). While these two regions in themselves may catalyse understandings of social life, situations of transitions from the front region to the back region may also reveal some general aspects of how self is presented in everyday life. By studying these transitions, Goffman explained, students may observe 'a wonderful putting on and taking off character'. Again, one of Goffman's illustrative examples is taken from a rather unconventional source, *in casu* the works of British novelist George Orwell who described, from the dishwasher's backstage point of view, how waiters change character by moving from the hotel kitchen to the dining room: 'As he passes the door, a sudden change comes over him. The set of his shoulders alters; all the dirt and hurry irritation have dropped off in an instant. He glides over the carpet with a solemn priest-like air' (Goffman 1959:123).

As it appears, performers engage themselves in processes of communication in order to sustain a certain definition of the situation. However, in Goffman's analysis, there are different forms of 'destructive information' or certain types of 'secrets' (dark, strategic, inside, entrusted and free) that may discredit or disrupt the impression that the performances, collaborative or individual, are designed to foster. The dramaturgical element of so-called discrepant roles is thus concerned with the fact that certain people may 'learn about the secrets of the team' and therefore may constitute 'threats to their privileged position' (Goffman 1959:143). In everyday life, as in staged theatrical performances, certain people (such as gumshoes or undercover field researchers) possess information that may undermine the reality that a performing team is engaged in sustaining and therefore people in such discrepant roles constitute a potential risk for the entire team and its information control

The final, and perhaps the most well-known dramaturgical element, 'impression management',[3] involves the participant's efforts to control the impressions made during the course of face-to-face interaction where individuals are in each other's continuous presence and are mutually exposed to the visual, audial, olfactory and physical presence of each other. As such, this concept entails many elements of the preceding analysis as it summarises many of the techniques and attributes involved in sustaining a definition of the situation or staging a specific character. The practices and techniques here involve 'dramaturgical loyalty', 'dramaturgical discipline' and 'dramaturgical circumspection'. Impression management, then, signifies how actors – through their utterances, body language, attire, etc. – seek to gain control of the impression formed by the audience and it also intimates the collaboration (or 'working consensus' as Goffman called it) expected on behalf of the audience, say, by ignoring or forgetting about a performer's slips and inadvertent self-contradictions (Jacobsen and Kristiansen 2015:72).

Viewed through the metaphor of dramaturgy, everyday life as face-to-face interaction between individuals emerges as a continuous series of staged negotiations or exchanges. In Goffman's dramaturgical analysis, everyday-life performers must offer something which fellow interactants will appreciate or reward. In other words, our presentations of self must be adapted to the situationally specific expectations formed by the participants and audiences being present at any given time. Different situations have different adherent audiences and thus different expectations, which is why the self-images presented by everyday-life performers need constantly to be adapted to the changing social situations. Thus, as pointed out by Richard Münch (1986:53), Goffman demonstrates, by using dramaturgy as a prism of interpretation, how the social interactions of everyday life should not only be construed as a game of masks where we deliberately seek to hoodwink each other, but also as a functional process where individuality and social order are united in an endless process of idealisation and dramatisation (Jacobsen and Kristiansen 2015:73).

While Goffman's dramaturgical analysis of people's self-presentations and impression management have outlined important principles underlying the face-to-face interactions in modern everyday life, he was quite explicit regarding the relationship between the dramaturgical model and real life. By the end of *The Presentation of Self in Everyday Life*, he thus stated that the dramaturgical framework, in part, was 'at rhetoric and a manoeuvre' and as such a kind of auxiliary tool enabling new insights into the micro-dimensions of social life. As he explained, 'scaffolds, after all, are meant to build other things with, and should be erected with an eye to taking them down' (Goffman 1959:246). In other words, Goffman used the dramaturgical perspective as a descriptive lens or analytical metaphor revealing new dimensions of social interactions and thus enabling more comprehensive understandings of the processes, structure and syntax of people's everyday face-to-face interactions. In the words of Consuelo Corradi, his use of the dramaturgical metaphor was constitutive

> in the sense that it creates the analogy by offering, through the metaphorizer, a set of rules of usage, a dictionary of expressions with which to describe a given social phenomenon that explores the latter from a new perspective: the individual is conceptualized as an actor, and those who observe him/her as an audience, his/her behaviour as a performance or masquerade, the place there it occurs as a setting or stage and so on.
>
> (Corradi 1990:166–167)

Goffman, then, employed the dramaturgical model as a form of perspectivism or 'as if' logic. Using a variety of illustrative materials, Goffman re-described everyday social interactions as if they were theatrical performances and thereby teasing out new layers of meaning and thereby sharpening the sociological understanding of the structuring of everyday-life encounters. Stage performance in a theatre before an audience is of course different to the character performance of everyday life, but as Goffman, rephrasing William Shakespeare, put it: 'All the world is not, of course, a stage, but the crucial ways in which it isn't are not easy to specify' (Goffman 1959:78).

Objections to Goffman's dramaturgy

Although Goffman's popularisation and sociologicalisation of the dramaturgical perspective have had a considerable impact on generations of scholars within the humanities and social sciences since the 1960s, it has not been without criticisms. Even from the early launch of his interactionist version of dramaturgy, Goffman himself presented some reservations regarding the dramaturgical framework and vocabulary. Thus, as Philip Manning (1992:44–48) has pointed out, in the revised and second edition of *The Presentation of Self in Everyday Life* published in 1959, Goffman downplayed the value of the dramaturgical perspective and especially the rather cynical view of the actor most explicitly apparent in the 1956 edition. In the concluding sections of the second edition, Goffman (1959:246) even stated that 'the language and mask of the stage will be dropped' indicating that the dramaturgical metaphor had now served its time as a vehicle for highlighting the theatre-like aspects of everyday-life encounters. In other words, Goffman abandoned the dramaturgical perspective as a descriptive model while emphasising its heuristic value (Manning 1992:48) alongside other analytical metaphors such as ritual, game and frame.[4]

Despite the revisions, self-criticism and qualifications provided by Goffman in the second edition of *The Presentation of Self in Everyday Life* (1959) and also in a section of *Frame Analysis* devoted to dramaturgy (Goffman 1974b), his dramaturgical ideas have been subject to some criticisms. Some scholars, such as Alvin W. Gouldner, have criticised the ahistorical perspective and the lack of critical potential in Goffman's dramaturgy as well as its apparently 'middle-class bias'. In a lengthy analysis, Gouldner characterised Goffman's dramaturgy as one (of many) symptoms of the so-called crisis in Western sociology:

> In Goffman's theory the conventional cultural hierarchies are shattered: for example, professional psychiatrists are manipulated by hospital inmates; doubt is cast upon the difference between the cynical and the sincere; the behavior of children becomes a model for understanding adults; the behavior of criminals becomes a standpoint for understanding respectable people; the theater's stage becomes a model for understanding life. Here there is no higher and no lower.
>
> (Gouldner 1970:378)

Gouldner reads Goffman's dramaturgical sociology as one of mere co-presence and thus as a social theory 'that wells upon the episodic and sees life only as it is lived in a narrow interpersonal circumference, ahistorical and noninstitutional, an existence beyond history and society' (Gouldner 1970:379). While sensing some critical potential in Goffman's dramaturgy (a potential for unmasking the dramaturgical society of serving the bourgeoisie), Gouldner found Goffman's perspective somewhat narrow-sighted and lacking historical and institutional sensitivity, and criticised it for its lack of potential as a theory of social change. Basically, then, Gouldner saw Goffman's dramaturgical model as a primarily conservative one that tended to commodify humans as actors within a societal frame that is taken for granted.

Other criticisms of Goffman's dramaturgy have emphasised that it presents a rather bleak and cynical view of the human actor as one of mere performance and manipulation that hides behind a variety of masks – the self is thus seen merely as a 'manager of impressions' (Cuzzort 1969:175). In their reading of Goffman, Stanford M. Lyman and Marvin B. Scott (1975:107) conclude that the Goffmanian dramaturgy gives the impression that 'a brooding and suspicious sense of inauthenticity is the basic condition of performative human existence'. In a somewhat similar vein, Jürgen Habermas (1984:93) claimed that 'Goffman's model of action does not provide for his [the actor's] behaving toward the social world in a norm-conformative attitude'. As we have touched upon earlier, such criticisms were, at least partly, addressed by Goffman himself in the revised edition of *The Presentation of Self in Everyday Life* and also in his later writings, such as *Interaction Ritual* (1967) and *Frame Analysis* (1974a), stressing the normative, ritual and moral underpinnings of everyday social interactions as well as the limitations of the theatre analogy. While these criticisms address the adequacy and applicability of Goffman's dramaturgical framework as a theory, there has also been some criticism of the methodological aspects of Goffman's dramaturgy. The thrust of these criticisms is that although Goffman's dramaturgy offers a new perspective for interpreting human life, it has no 'specific, systematic method of testing propositions about the world' (Hare 2001:3836). The question remains, however, if the provision of such a method was among Goffman's intentions. As pointed out by Manning, part of Goffman's dramaturgical work was not to prove or test the accuracy of the theatrical model, but to give it credibility as a tool that highlights the 'inherent cynicism that is accompanying our self-presentations' and it should thus be seen as a part of his 'spiralling strategy that explores the strengths and weaknesses of a variety of metaphors and perspectives' (Manning, 1992:54–55). As we have shown, the various criticisms of Goffman's version of DI touch upon different normative and methodological aspects of his ideas. After this presentation of some of these points of criticism, let us now consider a few examples of later developments of Goffman's dramaturgy that attempt to take it in a more critical direction.

Dramaturgy as a revolt against absurdity

Dramaturgy, as we have seen earlier, can be and has been used as a metaphor for analytically teasing out some hidden, overlooked or unacknowledged dimensions of social life. Whereas Goffman, as we saw earlier, primarily proposed dramaturgy as a metaphor (and one among many other metaphors) for understanding social life – as a conceptual scaffold to be dismantled again once the analytical task had been completed – others have used the dramaturgical metaphor in a much more literal sense. They claim that social life *is* drama and *is* dramatic. For example, looking at the somewhat unacknowledged 'sociology of the absurd' developed by the aforementioned Stanford M. Lyman and Marvin B. Scott in the late 1960s, it is evident that Goffman's ideas here are twisted in a much more existential and critical direction (see Greek and Jacobsen 2017; Jacobsen 2008). In their book *A Sociology of the Absurd* (1970), a book that was apparently written on Goffman's typewriter, Lyman and Scott sowed the seeds of a critical dramaturgical analysis by proposing an arsenal of concepts and analytical angles showing how people dramaturgically and strategically try to counter the inherent absurdity of life. By combining interactionist insights from Goffman with ideas from amongst others Niccolò Machiavelli, Georg Simmel, Jean-Paul Sartre and Luigi Pirandello (and the idea of the 'theatre of the absurd') as well as absurdist novelists, the sociologists of the absurd came up with a theoretical model of man and society that privileges experiences of conflict, struggle, strategy, power and deviance (Lyman and Scott 1970).

The sociology of the absurd used a dramaturgical model and combined this with what is called a 'game framework' in order to shed light on the way in which people – in order to create a sense of meaning in a sea of meaninglessness – strategically (just like Machiavelli's Prince) handle conflicts over definitions of situations, accounts, the use of territories, identities and time-tracks, and how they through acts of coolness seek to counter or control feelings of deviance, paranoia and stage fright in everyday situations. In this endeavour, strategy and dramaturgy become important instruments in order to carve out meaning and to obtain successful and desired outcomes of interaction. As Lyman and Scott (1970:20) stated, 'man's success arises not from the presence and absence of humanity, rather from the strategic employment of appearances', and – by quoting Peter L. Berger and Thomas Luckmann – they insisted that 'he who has the bigger stick has the better chance of imposing his definition of reality' (Lyman and Scott 1970:66). It is obvious from this that the sociology of the absurd, at least at a theoretical level, took topics of hierarchy, differential power and conflicting interests seriously. In a revised and expanded edition of the book published almost two decades later, Lyman and Scott (1989) also hinted at connecting their absurdist microanalysis with comments on politics and changes in the cultural and social order; however, it remained a somewhat sketchy and unfulfilled attempt.

Lyman and Scott thus made use of Goffman's main dramaturgical groundwork, but by mixing it with other philosophical and theoretical sources of inspiration they came up with a more existential and critical version of dramaturgical sociology, which, however, despite efforts to expand the perspective, largely remained at the microsociological level. In this way, they added some critical edge to Goffman's dramaturgy. As Mary Jo Deegan once concluded in her comparison of the dramaturgical theories of Goffman and Victor W. Turner: 'Because Goffman portrays a world without anti-structure, he is making a political statement on alienation. He makes a further political statement in his lack of condemnation of such an order or world. It is almost as if he said, "this is an absurd world and here is how we live it"' (Deegan 1978:43). To provide arms for a revolt against this absurd world was therefore not Goffman's ambition, but his ideas were, as we have seen here, adopted and developed in such a direction by some of his colleagues.

Dramaturgy as critique/unmasking

Besides serving as a comment on or framework for understanding the inherent absurdity of life in modern society as in the sociology of the absurd, DI may also be used for critiquing aspects of contemporary society thus providing grounds for social change. There has been some intellectual debate as to whether dramaturgy as an analytic perspective holds potential for unravelling the shallowness, superficiality and inauthentic manner of contemporary social life in advanced capitalist and consumerist societies. In his essayistic monograph *The Drama of Social Life*, T. R. Young (1990) outlined and described the potentials of a 'critical dramaturgy' (a synthesis of interactionist dramaturgy, critical theory, ethnomethodology and cultural hermeneutics). In this work, he used the concept of 'colonisation of desire' to designate the process by which dramaturgy and mass media (one might in contemporary society add also social media) colonise the individual's desires in the direction of self-presentation, display and ownership on the behalf of important interpersonal relations such as friendship, marriage and community. Young's monograph thus serves as an invitation to combine the emancipatory dimensions of dramaturgy (micro level) with critical theory (macro level) in order to provide a framework for critiquing contemporary monopoly capitalism. In a similar vein, John F. Welsh (1990:400) has offered a critical dramaturgy 'that allows the reader to understand and challenge the fraudulent legitimation of political power', and by using American politics as an example, he has shown the dramaturgical processes involved in transforming political power into authority, while mystifying or masking the social relations of class and power (Welsh 1985). Writers like Young and Welsh – equally inspired by critical theory and dramaturgy – directed attention towards what they saw as signs of the rise of the so-called dramaturgical society, which is characterised by

> organizations controlled by class and political elites [that] utilize the technologies of behavioral science, mass communication, marketing, advertising and the theater. With these technologies, state and business elites manage consciousness and behavior of the population for the purposes of maximizing profit and political control.
>
> (Welsh 1990:1)

According to Young, Welsh and other like-minded critical theorists, dramaturgical sociology as developed by, for example, Goffman (described by them as a 'politically neutral observer') was not fully equipped to capture 'these exploitative and dehumanizing processes' (Welsh 1990:2), and was in fact itself part and parcel of the dramaturgical society's manipulation of sociological knowledge.

In addition to these critical dramaturgical ideas, attempts have also been made to connect dramaturgical ideas to postmodern and critical sociology (see Boje et al. 2004; Paolucci and Richardson 2006a, 2006b). Finally, some commentators, such as Lauren Langman, have emphasised how Goffman's dramaturgy offers a view into the alienation processes in contemporary society:

> Goffman's analyses of self-presentations and interaction rituals of everyday life, strategies of winning interpersonal and material games in the context of a culture of consumption, inform the nature of modern alienation ... Commodified self-presentations and interaction rituals often can be seen as expressions of alienated selfhood, characteristic of today.
>
> (Langman 1992:108–109)

Dramaturgy is thus not only to be considered a tool for microsociological analysis. It can also provide a framework for more macrosociological insights and structural critiques (Young and Massey 1978). In his groundbreaking monograph,

The Society of the Spectacle, situationist philosopher Guy Debord (1970) argued how capitalist mass society was increasingly mesmerised by superficial images and performances that pacified the onlookers and made them alienated from important aspects of human existence. With its focus on the theatrical and performative aspects of modern social life, the dramaturgical tradition in sociology, then, holds some potential to dig beneath the surface and unmask such superficiality and alienated aspects of contemporary society.

As shown here, DI can work as a catalyst for critiquing what David Riesman and colleagues (1950/2001) famously – and well before Goffman – called the spread of the 'other-directed' personality type: the superficial and potentially manipulative, fraudulent and cynical con-man actor engaged in the game of impression management and incessantly craving validation from others. Most of the subsequent developments of Goffman's dramaturgy mentioned earlier were conceived well before the invention of the Internet. Today, the consolidation of such an other-directed personality type has been aided and abetted by the tireless use of Facebook, YouTube, Twitter, Snapchat, Instagram, Tinder, Happn, Grindr, Tumblr, Flickr and all the other types of social media platforms now available for communication, expression and self-presentation (see, e.g., Bullingham and Vasconcelos 2013; Hogan 2010). The Internet, as well as all the other information and communication technologies available, has provided us with ever new avenues and vehicles for connecting and engaging with others. Today, all the web's truly a stage, and Goffman's sedentary notions of frontstage and backstage have collapsed into one gigantic dramaturgical arena in desperate need of critical commentary.

But what, then, are the guidelines for scholars working within the dramaturgical traditions aiming at exploring the concealment and frontstage, backstage processes in contemporary social life? Drawing on Robert D. Benford and Scott A. Hunt's (1992) dramaturgical study of social movements and their communications of power, and Benford and Hunt's identification of four dramatic techniques associated with such communicative processes, Prasad Pushkala (2005:49–50) suggests that we must pay attention to three common techniques used to influence audience reception, namely the techniques of scripting, staging and performing: '*Scripting* refers to the development of a set of directions that define the scene, identify actors and outline expected behaviour' (Benford and Hunt 1992:38, italics added). Scripts, then, are not to be thought of as rigid and formalised guidelines for behaviour; rather they should be seen as guides for action that emerge through the course of interaction, typically backstage, and thus involve some level of flexibility and openness to improvisations. Scripts are valuable analytic tools as they lead the researcher to search for, explore and describe the situationally appropriate actions and vocabularies. And while some scripts may be produced through collaborate conscious reflection, 'implicit scripts can be found in virtually any social situation be it the planning of office parties, the design of professional training programs, the agenda of meetings' (Pushkala 2005:49). While scripting designates the interactionally created guides for action, *staging* 'refers to appropriating, managing and directing materials, audiences and performing regions'

(Benford and Hunt 1992:43). It designates, then, the process by which individuals and groups of individuals manage and control materials and members in order to make a certain impression on an audience. Basically, this process is a kind of role-play and performance-preparation during which actors learn how to perform their roles and important symbols are collected and made ready for use. This may involve cognitive and emotional rehearsal. and some organisations even have 'formally designated staging areas where employees or cast members learn their roles in training sessions' (Pushkala 2005:50). The third technique, *performing*, 'involves the demonstration and enactment of power. It concretises ideas regarding the struggle between protagonists and antagonists and reveals to audiences ways they can achieve or preserve desirable power relations' (Benford and Hunt 1992:45). This technique has to do with the actual way individuals play out their roles. It involves focusing on how actors, individually and/or collectively, address and attempt to influence the audience, their improvisations and internal competitions in terms of audience attention. Taken together, these techniques may serve as tools for digging beneath the surface of the existing social order, for unmasking the orchestration of organisational performances and the emotional labour carried out in formal organisations. Thus, by zooming in on 'the scripts, rehearsals, and performances of everyday life, dramaturgy destroys their innocence and forces an awareness of the hidden dynamics behind the seemingly smooth fabric of the social world' (Pushkala 2005:50).

Potentials and limitations of DI

As should be obvious from the preceding discussion, DI has certain potentials and limitations, which have been discussed vividly in the reception of particularly Goffman's work. A major potential of Goffman's version of DI is that it offers a perspective that allows us to see how meaning is socially produced among parties involved in an interactive and communicative process. The perspective has emphasised the emergent and dynamic nature of this expressively created meaning, and how the process and social reality of creating and sustaining these meanings was 'fragile, impermanent, full of unexpected holes and in constant need of repair' (Burns 1992:26). By alerting attention towards the expressive and communicative dimensions of social interactions, DI illustrates the value of a social behavioural approach in order to tease out the patterns and complexities of human interaction. In the beginning of *The Presentation of Self in Everyday Life*, Goffman gave a rather clear description of his focus on two specific streams of human expressiveness:

> The expressiveness of the individual (and therefore his capacity to give impressions) appears to involve two radically different kinds of sign activity: The expression of what he *gives*, and the expression of what he *gives off*. The first involves verbal symbols or their substitutes which he uses admittedly and solely to convey the information that he and the others are known to attach to these symbols. This is communication in the traditional and narrow

sense. The second involves a wide range of action that others can treat as symptomatic of the actor, the expectation being that the action was performed for reasons other than the information conveyed in this way.

(Goffman 1959:14)

By focusing on how people express themselves and orient their actions toward other expressive parties, Goffman's perspective also emphasised and illustrated the dramaturgical side of the self. The self, in Goffman's dramaturgy, is not then an entity that is possessed once and for all and that resides inside a human being. It is a dramaturgical product of various dramaturgical arrangements (regions, teams, audience, etc.); it is a dramaturgical construct or a 'dramatic effect arising diffusely from the scene that is presented, and the characteristic issue, the crucial concern, is whether it will be credited or discredited' (Goffman 1959:245). By paying attention to and providing a framework for systematising the often overlooked myriads of verbal and non-verbal signs and objects that people use interactively to present themselves and to create meaning in their everyday life, DI thus underscores the communicative nature of the self. This interactionist version of dramaturgy, and especially the work of Goffman, thus provides scholars with a perspective that

> goes beyond the surface interactions of everyday life in order to uncover the hidden dynamics behind work, home, professional, and community performances. It is therefore one of the few scholarly traditions that systematically explores the complex but enduring relationships between self-presentation, trust, and social tact ... looking at how individuals figure out their own roles in social situations and assess audience responses to them while simultaneously preparing public performances that would have a desired effect on these audiences.
>
> (Pushkala 2005:47)

As for limitations, there have been some critiques of interactionist dramaturgy (see, e.g., Ryan 1978; Psathas 1977; Miller 1984; Wilshire 1982). In their *Dramaturgical Sourcebook*, Dennis Brissett and Charles Edgley (1990b:23–36) have synthesised some of the theoretical and methodological reservations that have been made. First, dramaturgy has been criticised for being a 'pedestrian, non-systematic form of inquiry'. The core of this criticism, with which we partly agree, is that dramaturgy is not to be considered an adequate and testable theory since it lacks a systematic set of interrelated concepts and propositions bound together in a coherent conceptual framework. Second, dramaturgy has been criticised for its presumed inability to produce 'universal statements about human behaviour' and that the insights gained from it are specific for Western societies and not applicable to other times and places. While acknowledging this critique, Brissett and Edgley, rightly we think, contend that being able to understand how individuals behave in modern Western societies is no small achievement. Third, there has been some critique of the methodology of dramaturgy. According to

Brissett and Edgley, 'it is said to have no specific, systematic method of testing its propositions about the world'. However, while this may be true, it may not necessarily be a problem. We agree with Brissett and Edgley that, in principle, there is nothing special that sets dramaturgy aside from other strands of qualitative and interpretive research. Like any other social scientist, scholars working within DI must pursue their research with rigour in a systematic and transparent way. Fourth, critics have pointed out that dramaturgy to some extent ignores the impact of larger social arrangement and institutions of human behaviour on the micro level (Brissett and Edgley 1990b:27). While this criticism is partly true, some versions of dramaturgy (such of those of T. R. Young and John F. Welsh mentioned earlier) have recognised the crucial links between macro-structural conditions and micro-level contexts. Finally, the very nature of the dramaturgical metaphor has been subject to reservations as critics have pointed to the fundamental differences between theatre and real life: after all, theatre is a realm of pretence and make-believe, social life is reality (Brissett and Edgley 1990b:30). While this is, obviously, the case, DI does not suggest that social life is similar to the theatre, rather (as Goffman indicated in the revised version of *The Presentation of Self in Everyday Life*) the utility of the dramaturgical metaphor lies in its heuristic capacity as it directs attention to the theatre-like qualities of modern human life.

Conclusion

In this chapter, we have introduced, outlined and discussed some of the main limitations and potentials of a dramaturgical interactionist (DI) perspective on social life with a specific focus on the ideas developed by Erving Goffman and some of those writing in his slipstream. Dramaturgy is an important perspective that shows us how social life can either be seen through or analysed within a theatrical framework. Even though the ending of 'urgy' in dramaturgy – similar to that of 'metallurgy', 'liturgy' or 'chemurgy' as observed by Bruce E. Gronbeck (1980:315) – makes it sound as an almost magical or alchemical process, dramaturgy as used in and by DI scholars is nevertheless a very tangible and potent perspective that directs our attention towards and sharpens our understanding of social life as drama. Whether (and to what extent) life actually imitates the theatre or vice versa is obviously difficult to determine once and for all, and it has not been the purpose of this chapter to position itself within such a debate.

Instead, we have argued that despite its theoretical limitations and methodological pitfalls, DI can in fact function as a useful catalyst for advancing social critique. It has been pointed out that DI in general and Goffman's dramaturgical ideas in particular contain important seeds for critiquing, for example, the contemporary culture of narcissistic self-awareness and self-performance as well as the world of commodified existence (see, e.g., Edgley and Turner 1984; Kivisto and Pittman 2007; Rogers 1984). As we have shown, there is indeed such a potential for critical commentary also on a more macrosociological or structural scale even in Goffman's own seemingly apolitical and primarily interpretative use of the dramaturgical metaphor and not least in some of his dramaturgical successors – e.g. the sociology of the absurd and critical dramaturgy – who have taken his ideas further. As T. R. Young commenting on Gouldner's previously mentioned critique of Goffman once stated: 'It is Goffmanian analysis that permits Gouldner and others to understand the world as it has come to be and to begin to take political action to transform it' (Young 1971:276). In the end, even though Erving Goffman himself did neither operate the swing arm nor fire the payload of a dramaturgical critique of society, he surely did provide the catapult from which to do so.

Notes

1 It should be noted that dramaturgy, as theatrical theory and practice, in itself is a much diversified and comprehensive field with many different positions and perspectives (see, e.g., Turner and Behrndt 2008).
2 See Manning (1991) for an exploration of Goffman's changing use of the dramaturgical metaphor in the two editions of *The Presentation of Self in Everyday Life* from 1956 and 1959.
3 Even though some have argued that there is a difference between dramaturgical and impression management positions (see Tseëlon 1992), this is not a position we adopt in this chapter.
4 It has also been argued that Goffman's extensive use of the dramaturgical perspective resonated well with his preference for naturalistic participant observation as a data collection method (Pettit 2011).

References

Benford, Robert D. and Scott A. Hunt (1992): 'Dramaturgy and Social Movements: The Social Construction and Communication of Power'. *Sociological Inquiry*, 62:36–55.
Blumer, Herbert (1969): *Symbolic Interactionism: Perspective and Method*. Englewood Cliffs, NJ: Prentice-Hall.
Boje, David M., Grace A. Rosile, Rita A. Durant and John T. Luhman (2004): 'Enron Spectacle: A Critical Dramaturgical Analysis'. *Organization Studies*, 25 (5):751–774.
Borreca, Art (1993): 'Political Dramaturgy: A Dramaturg's (Re)View'. *The Drama Review*, 37 (2):56–79.
Brissett, Dennis and Charles Edgley (eds.) (1990a): *Life as Theater: A Dramaturgical Sourcebook* (2nd edition). New York: Aldine de Gruyter.
Brissett, Dennis and Charles Edgley (1990b): 'The Dramaturgical Perspective', in Dennis Brisset and Charles Edgley (eds.): *Life as Theater: A Dramaturgical Sourcebook* (2nd edition). New York: Aldine de Gruyter, pp. 1–46.
Brown, Robert E. (2005): 'Acting President: The Dramaturgy of Bush Versus Kerry'. *American Behavioral Scientist*, 49 (1):78–91.
Bullingham, Liam and Ana C. Vasconcelos (2013): 'The Presentation of Self in the Online World: Goffman and the Study of Online Identities'. *Journal of Information Science*, 39 (1):101–111.
Burke, Kenneth (1955): *A Grammar of Motives*. New York: Prentice-Hall.
Burns, Elizabeth (1972): *Theatricality: A Study of Convention in the Theatre and in Social Life*. New York: Harper Torchbooks.
Burns, Tom (1992): *Erving Goffman*. New York: Routledge.
Combs, James E. and Michael W. Mansfield (eds.) (1976): *Drama in Life*. New York: Hastings House.

Corradi, Consuelo (1990): 'The Metaphoric Structure of Scientific Explanation'. *Philosophy and Social Criticism*, 16 (3):161–178.

Cuzzort, Raymond P. (1969): *Humanity and Modern Sociological Thought*. New York: Holt, Rinehart & Winston.

Debord, Guy (1970): *The Society of the Spectacle*. Detroit: Black & Red.

Deegan, Mary Jo (1978): 'Interaction, Drama and Freedom: The Social Theories of Erving Goffman and Victor Turner'. *Humanity and Society*, 2 (1):33–46.

Dillard, Courtney, Larry D. Browning, Sim B. Sitkin and Kathleen M. Sutcliffe (2000): 'Impression Management and the Use of Procedures at the Ritz-Carlton: Moral Standards and Dramaturgical Discipline'. *Communication Studies*, 51 (4):404–414.

Edgley, Charles (2003): 'The Dramaturgical Genre', in Larry T. Reynolds and Nancy Herman-Kinney (eds.): *The Handbook of Symbolic Interactionism*. Walnut Creek, CA: AltaMira Press, pp. 141–172.

Edgley, Charles (ed.) (2013): *The Drama of Social Life: A Dramaturgical Handbook*. London: Routledge.

Edgley, Charles and Ronny E. Turner (1975): 'Masks and Social Relations: An Essay on the Sources and Assumptions of Dramaturgical Social Psychology'. *Humboldt Journal of Social Relations*, 3 (1):5–12.

Edgley, Charles and Ronny E. Turner (1984): 'Goffman as Critical Theorist: Some Notes on the Maligning of an Ally'. *Quarterly Journal of Ideology*, 8 (3):26–39.

Faccio, Elena and Noberto Costa (2013): 'The Presentation of Self in Everyday Prison Life: Reading Interactions in Prison from a Dramaturgic Point of View'. *Global Crime*, 14 (4): 386–403.

Gagnon, John H. and William Simon (1973): *Sexual Conduct: The Social Sources of Human Sexuality*. London: Hutchinson.

Goffman, Erving (1959): *The Presentation of Self in Everyday Life*. Harmondsworth: Penguin Books.

Goffman, Erving (1967): *Interaction Ritual: Essays on Face-to-Face Behaviour*. New York: Anchor Books.

Goffman, Erving (1974a): *Frame Analysis – An Essay on the Organization of Human Experience*. Boston: Northeastern University Press.

Goffman, Erving (1974b): 'The Theatrical Frame', in *Frame Analysis – An Essay on the Organization of Human Experience*. Boston: Northeastern University Press, pp. 123–155.

Gouldner, Alvin W. (1970): 'Other Symptoms of the Crisis: Goffman's Dramaturgy and Other New Theories', in *The Coming Crisis of Western Sociology*. London: Heinemann, pp. 378–390.

Greek, Cecil and Michael Hviid Jacobsen (2017): 'Stanford M. Lyman – A Sociology of the Absurd and Beyond', in Michael Hviid Jacobsen (ed.): *The Interactionist Imagination – Studying Meaning, Situation and Micro-Social Order*. London: Palgrave/Macmillan, pp. 341–374.

Gronbeck, Bruce E. (1980): 'Dramaturgical Theory and Criticism: The State of the Art (or Science?)'. *Western Journal of Speech Communication*, 44:315–330.

Habermas, Jürgen (1984): *The Theory of Communicative Action*. Volume 1, *Reason and the Rationalization of Society*. Boston: Beacon Press.

Hare, Paul A. (2001): 'Dramaturgical Analysis: Sociological', in Neil J. Smelser and Paul T. Baltes (eds.): *International Encyclopedia of the Social & Behavioral Sciences*. New York: Elsevier (online version).

Hare, Paul A. and Herbert H. Blumberg (1988): *Dramaturgical Analysis of Social Interaction*. New York: Praeger.

Henslin, James M. and Mae A. Biggs (1978): 'Dramaturgical Desexualization: The Sociology of Vaginal Examination', in James M. Henslin and Edward Sagarin (eds.): *The Sociology of Sex: An Introductory Reader.* New York: Schoken Books, pp. 243–272.

Hogan, Bernie (2010): 'The Presentation of Self in the Age of Social Media: Distinguishing Performances and Exhibitions Online'. *Bulletin of Science, Technology & Society*, 30 (6):377–386.

Hopper, Marianne (1981): 'Five Key Concepts of the Dramaturgical Perspective'. *Free Inquiry in Creative Sociology*, 9 (1):47–52.

Jacobsen, Michael Hviid (2008): 'The Sociology of the Absurd: An Absurd Man in an Absurd World', in Michael Hviid Jacobsen (ed.): *Encountering the Everyday – An Introduction to the Sociologies of the Unnoticed.* London: Palgrave/Macmillan, pp. 279–303.

Jacobsen, Michael Hviid and Søren Kristiansen (2015): *The Social Thought of Erving Goffman.* Newbury Park, CA: Pine Forge Press/Sage Publications.

Kivisto, Peter and Dan Pittman (2007): 'Goffman's Dramaturgical Sociology – Personal Sales and Service in a Commodified World', in Peter Kivisto (ed.): *Illuminating Social Life: Classical and Contemporary Theory Revisited.* London: Sage Publications, pp. 271–290.

Langman, Lauren (1992): 'Alienation and Everyday Life: Goffman Meets Marx at the Shopping Mall', in Felix Geyer and Walter Heinz (eds.): *Alienation, Society and the Individual: Continuity and Change in Theory and Research.* New Brunswick, NJ: Transaction, pp. 107–124.

Lyman, Stanford M. and Marvin B. Scott (1970): *The Sociology of the Absurd.* Pacific Palisades, CA: Goodyear.

Lyman, Stanford M. and Marvin B. Scott (1975): *The Drama of Social Reality.* New York: Oxford University Press.

Lyman, Stanford M. and Marvin B. Scott (1989): *A Sociology of Everyday Life* (2nd edition). Dix Hills, NY: General Hall Inc.

MacDonald, Richard (2005): *Thinking Sociologically: Social Scripts and Everyday Life.* Dubuque: Kendall Hunt Publishing.

Manning, Philip (1991): 'Drama as Life: The Significance of Goffman's Changing Use of the Theatrical Metaphor'. *Sociological Theory*, 9 (1):70–86.

Manning, Philip (1992): *Erving Goffman and Modern Sociology.* Stanford, CA: Stanford University Press.

Messinger, Sheldon L., Harold Sampson and Robert D. Towne. (1962): 'Life as Theater: Notes on the Dramaturgic Approach to Social Reality'. *Sociometry*, 25 (1):98–110.

Miller, Thomas (1984): 'Goffman, Social Action and Moral Behavior'. *Journal for the Theory of Social Behavior*, 14, 141–163.

Münch, Richard (1986): 'The American Creed in Sociological Theory: Exchange, Negotiated Order, Accommodated Individualism and Contingency'. *Sociological Theory*, 4: 41–60.

Paolucci, Paul and Margaret Richardson (2006a): 'Dramaturgy, Humor and Criticism: How Goffman Reveals *Seinfeld's* Critique of American Culture'. *Humor: International Journal of Humor Research*, 19 (1):27–52.

Paolucci, Paul and Margaret Richardson (2006b): 'Sociology of Humor and a Critical Dramaturgy'. *Symbolic Interaction*, 29 (3):331–348.

Pettit, Michael (2011): 'The Con Man as Model Organism: The Methodological Roots of Erving Goffman's Dramaturgical Self'. *History of the Human Sciences*, 24 (2): 138–154.

Postman, Neil (1985): *Amusing Ourselves to Death: Public Discourse in the Age of Show Business*. London: Meuthen.

Psathas, George (1977): 'Goffman's Image of Man'. *Humanity and Society*, 1:84–94.

Pushkala, Prasad (2005): *Crafting Qualitative Research: Working in the Postpositivist Tradition*. New York: Taylor & Francis.

Riesman, David, Nathan Glazer and Reuel Denney (1950/2001): *The Lonely Crowd: A Study of the Changing American Character*. New Haven: Yale University Press.

Rogers, Mary F. (1984): 'Watching the Snores: Erving Goffman and the Ideology of Narcissistic Awareness'. *Quarterly Journal of Ideology*, 8 (3):13–25.

Ryan, Alan (1978): 'Maximising, Minimising, Moralising', in Christopher Hookway and Philip Pettit (eds.): *Action and Interpretation*. Cambridge: Cambridge University Press, pp. 65–82.

Schechner, Richard (2003): *Performance Theory*. London: Routledge.

Schechner, Richard (2013): *Performance Studies: An Introduction* (3rd edition). London: Routledge.

Scheibe, Karl E. (2002): *The Drama of Everyday Life*. Cambridge, MA: Harvard University Press.

Shulman, David (2017): *The Presentation of Self in Contemporary Social Life*. Thousand Oaks, CA: Sage Publications.

Steiner, Claude M. (1974): *Scripts People Live: Transactional Analysis of Life Scripts*. New York: Bantam Books.

Sujiwade, Philip O. (1995): 'Counterfeit Intimacy: A Dramaturgical Analysis of Erotic Performance'. *Social Behavior and Personality*, 23:369–376.

Tambiah, Stanley (1981): *A Performative Approach to Ritual*. London: British Academy.

Tseëlon, Efrat (1992): 'Self Presentation Through Appearance: A Manipulative vs. a Dramaturgical Approach'. *Symbolic Interaction*, 15 (4):501–513.

Turner, Cathy and Synne K. Behrndt (2008): 'What Is Dramaturgy?', in Cathy Turner (ed.): *Dramaturgy and Performance*. London: Palgrave/Macmillan, pp. 17–37.

Turner, Ronny E. and Charles Edgley (1976): 'Death as Theater: A Dramaturgical Analysis of the American Funeral'. *Sociology and Social Research*, 60 (4):377–392.

Turner, Victor W. (1982): *From Ritual to Theatre: The Human Seriousness of Play*. New York: PAJ Publications.

Waskul, Dennis and Philip Vannini (2006): *Body/Embodiment: Symbolic Interactionism and the Sociology of the Body*. Aldershot: Ashgate Publishing.

Welsh, John F. (1985): 'Dramaturgy and Political Mystification: Political Life in the United States'. *Mid-American Review of Sociology*, 10 (2):3–28.

Welsh, John F. (1990): 'Dramaturgical Analysis and Societal Critique'. Essex, MI: The Red Feather Institute.

Wilshire, Bruce (1982): 'The Dramaturgical Model of Behavior: Its Strengths and Weaknesses'. *Symbolic Interaction*, 5 (2):287–298.

Young, T. R. (1971): 'The Politics of Sociology: Gouldner, Goffman and Garfinkel'. *American Sociologist*, 6 (4):276–281.

Young, T. R. (1990): *The Drama of Social Life: Essays in Post-Modern Social Psychology*. New Brunswick, NJ: Transaction Publishers.

Young, T. R. and Garth Massey (1978): 'The Dramaturgical Society: A Macro-Analytic Approach to Dramaturgical Analysis'. *Qualitative Sociology*, 1:78–98.

5 Critical interactionism

A theoretical bridge for understanding complex human conditions

Patricia M. Burbank and Diane C. Martins

Introduction

Two diverse theoretical perspectives, symbolic interactionism and critical social theory, have each been used effectively to understand complex issues, guide research and interpret results. Symbolic interactionism is a broad perspective within social psychology that is useful for understanding human beings and their behaviour in their social worlds. It is credited to George Herbert Mead and focuses on meaning derived from interactions. Symbolic interactionism has been used as a theoretical framework for research and knowledge development in a variety of disciplines, focusing on symbols, language and meaning at an individual level. Other concepts such as stigma and labelling emerge when the focus is broadened to the societal level. Critical social theory, also called critical perspective or critical theory, emerged from the Frankfurt School and Marxism and focuses on understanding concepts such as class, domination, ideology and social inequalities. Critical social theory has also been used in knowledge development in sociology, anthropology, education, gender studies and health care especially through the work of Paulo Freire (1971), Jürgen Habermas and critical feminist theory. When critical social theory is used, dominant hegemonic influences are analysed at a societal level and may be brought to the individual level through Habermas's theory of communicative action. Both perspectives are broad and complex and have become very diverse since their inception, with different authors emphasising various aspects of the perspective, sometimes resulting in changes in the core concepts themselves and divergent theoretical developments (Sandstrom and Fine 2003).

Despite their areas of divergence, symbolic interactionism and critical social theory have been combined into *critical interactionism*, a broad new theoretical perspective, capable of providing a theoretical base for addressing complex issues at both micro and macro levels. While the major foci, concepts, premises and goals of the two perspectives are divergent, there are areas within each perspective that may be seen as complementary. The philosophical underpinnings provide two different views of reality and knowledge development, however, they are not necessarily contradictory. The goal in critical interactionism is to understand and intervene at both downstream and upstream levels through understanding value-laden meanings at the individual/group level and repressive structures at the organisational and societal levels. It is argued that complex human conditions can best be addressed by this new theoretical perspective, critical interactionism, that combines symbolic interactionism and critical social theory (Martins and Burbank 2011).

This chapter will present an overview of the historical and philosophical origins of symbolic interactionism and the critical social theory perspective, briefly review the central themes of the two theoretical perspectives, relate them to studies of the medical and health care system, and describe their main points of divergence and synergism. Then critical interactionism will be described as a framework for viewing both micro and macro perspectives and moving across systems levels. Applications to people experiencing incarceration and homelessness will be discussed. By viewing complex human conditions with a critical interactionist lens, both micro and macro perspectives can be studied and innovative strategies for change across individual and larger system levels can be developed.

Symbolic interactionism: historical and philosophical origins

George Herbert Mead, a social psychologist, is often thought of as the father of symbolic interactionism. Mead's academic career began at the University of Michigan where he met and established a close friendship with John Dewey. When Dewey was appointed head of the philosophy department at the newly founded University of Chicago in 1894, he brought the 31-year-old Mead in as an assistant professor of philosophy. Together with other faculty, they formed a core group of what was called the 'Chicago school of pragmatism' (Baldwin 1986:10). One of Mead's students, Herbert Blumer, continued Mead's work in symbolic interactionism at the University of Chicago after Mead became ill. Blumer integrated much of Mead's work with others, whose ideas were foundational in symbolic interactionism such as William James, Charles Saunders Peirce, John Dewey, William I. Thomas and Charles Horton Cooley.

At the University of Iowa, from 1946 to 1953, Manford H. Kuhn developed his ideas of symbolic interaction in a different direction. The development of the two schools resulted in two varieties of symbolic interactionism, the 'Chicago School' and the 'Iowa School', both remaining within the pragmatist tradition but each with a different philosophy of science. (A third dramaturgical approach by Erving Goffman [1959] is beyond the scope of this chapter.) The Chicago School and Herbert Blumer emphasised a relativist philosophy of science, an idiographic approach to concept development with the goal of understanding and discovery of ideas. They viewed the self as a spontaneous active creator with behaviour driven by inner impulse and thus indeterminate. The Iowa School and Manford H. Kuhn used a quasi-realist philosophical base and a nomothetic approach, and worked to define and operationalise concepts, with the goal of precise analysis and knowledge testing. They defined the self as more structured and having a stable core across individuals. Behaviour was seen as more socially determined and thus at least potentially predictable (Meltzer, Petras and Reynolds 1975).

Both varieties of symbolic interactionism consider reality to be social, developed in interaction with others. Most symbolic interactionists believe a physical reality does indeed exist independently of the individual's social definition of it and that social definitions do develop, at least in part, in relation to something 'real' or physical. People do not respond to this reality directly, however; they define situations as they exist 'out there'. People therefore live in a physical objective reality and in a social reality, as well as in a third reality, created out of the social reality – a unique, private interpretation of the reality that is shown to the person by others.

Symbolic interactionism: some central ideas

Symbolic interactionism views human beings as social, thinking beings who do not simply respond to events and situations but give meanings to these. Individuals and society are created through social interactions and are inseparable from each other. Behaviour is a reflective, socially derived interpretation of the internal and external stimuli that are present (Meltzer, Petras and Reynolds 1975). Thus, a person's actions are based on the meanings situations have for him or her rather than in direct response to the event or situation. Human action is caused by interaction among individuals and within the individual. The continuous active process of thinking and conversing with one's self during interaction with others is key to understanding action (Charon 2009). According to Blumer (1969), human beings through the process of social interaction learn meanings. He outlined three basic premises underlying symbolic interactionism:

- People act toward things based on the meaning those things have for them.
- Meanings are derived from social interaction.
- Meanings are modified through interpretation.

Meaning thus emerges out of the ways in which other people act toward the person in relation to the thing for which meaning is developing. The actions of other people serve to define the things for the person. Within the symbolic interactionist perspective, the self is dynamic as a result of continuous social interaction throughout life (Mead 1934). One characteristic of the self is that the individual is able to view the self as object, to step outside and imagine viewing one's self as others would. Cooley called this the 'looking glass self' (Cooley 1972).

The 'definition of the situation' is a sub-theory within symbolic interactionism that purports that people do not sense their environment directly but instead define the situations they are in. An environment may actually exist, but it is the definition of it that is important (Melzer, Petras and Reynolds 1972). The definition of the situation emerges through interaction where an individual has taken the role of the other or has adopted a group standpoint (McHugh 1968).

Symbols, such as words, are a central concept of the symbolic interactionist perspective. They are social objects, have meaning and are used with the intention to represent and to communicate. Interaction occurs through the use of symbols.

The processes of symbolic interaction begin with interaction with self and other in one's reference group. This results in the formation of a perspective that guides the person in defining the situation at hand. The person then bases his or her action on this perspective and defines the situation. After the action, the effects of this action are interpreted or given meaning, and then alter the person's perspective and definition of the situation. This changed perspective and definition of the situation then influences future actions (Charon 2009).

Symbolic interactionism has often been concerned with examining the interaction between the different role players in the health and illness situation as well as health care. The focus is often on how the subjective experience of health and illness is constructed through the health care professional–patient exchange. The argument here is that illness is a social phenomenon among actors rather than just a matter of physiological malfunction (Bilton et al. 2002). In nursing, symbolic interactionism has been widely used as a theoretical foundation for grounded theory or dramaturgical interviewing methods as well as a framework for diverse works including conceptualisation of care with families (e.g., Meiers and Brauer 2008), describing the nurse's role in perinatal safety (e.g., Lyndon and Kennedy 2010), the effects of nurses' use of traditional Chinese medicine on professional identity (e.g., Bertrand 2010), and to study nurse–mother communication in the neonatal ICU (e.g., Cleveland 2009).

In symbolic interactionism, people are viewed as active beings in relation to their environment. Words like

> conditioning, responding, controlled, imprisoned, and formed are not used to describe the human being. Humans are not passive, but actively involved in what they do. To a great extent, we control what we do. Symbolic interactionism examines the preconditions necessary for human freedom and normally tries to explain an active being that is able to overcome whatever forces that the environment pushes on us. We ultimately form our own action rather than responding to the physical environment. Never is self control complete.
>
> (Charon 2007:30)

Critical social theory perspective: historical and philosophical origins

The critical social theory perspective represents sociological thought based on the work of Karl Marx and has its intellectual origins in the radical humanist paradigm. According to Gibson Burrell and Gareth Morgan (1979), this paradigm comprises the subjective and objective idealist strains of thought, both of which have their origins in German idealism. Radical humanists focus on the alienated state of humans. Marx argued that there was no absolute above man and that religion and the state were creations of man rather than any 'absolute spirit' (Marx 1975). All objectifications in the social world were created by humans, and he suggested an emancipatory philosophy where humans create and change the society in which they live. Marx saw humans as alienated with society holding domination over them. He demonstrated how capitalism was the centre of human alienation and thus an attack on the status quo.

The critical social theory perspective has its origin in the Frankfurt School of critical social theory. It is also based on the work of György Lukács, Antonio Gramsci and Louis Althusser. Lukács (1923/1971) sought to develop a theory of revolution, which had strong emphasis on the role of class-consciousness and the proletariat in overthrowing capitalism. Lukács was one of the earliest theorists to develop the idea and use of bourgeois hegemony to refer to the dominance of the ideas of the ruling class. These ideas come to be seen as the norm and to benefit everyone, although they in fact only benefit the ruling class. Bourgeois hegemony was further developed by Gramsci, the Italian political activist who strongly influenced the development of the critical theoretical perspective. His 'philosophy of praxis' represented a worldview and a political methodology for the working class.

Critical social theory: some central ideas

Critical social theory is derived from the belief that social meanings structure life through oppression and domination (Martins 2019). Domination refers to the power influenced over another, while oppression refers to the unjust exercise of authority or power. Emancipation describes the effort to be set free or obtain social justice and is the goal of critical perspective, where a society is transformed by personal and collective power.

Gramsci's *Prison Notebooks* (1971) presented critical theoretical perspective as a fusion of structure and consciousness. According to Gramsci, the capitalist class uses ideological hegemony where the relationships of domination and exploitation are embedded in the dominant ideas of society. For Gramsci, ideological hegemony permeated our schools, churches, mass media and family to influence values, beliefs, attitudes and morality that permeate society. This ideological system supports the established order and class interests of the ruling class and those with power or with domination.

The dominant ideology of society also permeates the face-to-face interactions of individuals since ideology is present in interpersonal interactions where elements of ideology appear in every communication (Habermas 1984). For example, according to Howard Waitzkin (1989), medical encounters are 'micro-level' processes that involve interaction with individual patients. Medical ideology, similar to the dominant ideology discussed by Gramsci, helps to maintain and reproduce class structure and social domination within health care. Medical ideology has several premises: (1) disturbance in biological homeostasis similar to a machine rather than multifactorial; (2) disease is the problem of the individual; (3) science can control the human being; (4) medicine can offer a social control function; and (5) medical knowledge creates professional dominance over others (Waitzkin 1983, 1989). At the macro-level structure of society, ideology impinges on patients and health care providers as part of the social context of medical encounters. At the micro-level of interpersonal interaction, ideology is evident in patient–health care provider communication (Waitzkin 1986, 1989; Waitzkin, Britt and Williams 1994). The interactions between client and health care provider reinforce broader social structures and have been described as medical discourse (Waitzkin 1989, 1991). Waitzkin suggested this pattern in health care sheds light on professional–client discourse in exploring connections between personal and social issues and the social context of medicine. Critical social theory in nursing augments understanding of how dominant ideology impacts the health care professions and the health care delivery system.

Vincente Navarro (1976) also argued that the health care system mirrors the class structure of the broader society. The 'upstream' medical–industrial complex in the United States and other industrialised countries exploits illness for profit in pharmaceutical and medical equipment industries, which play a prominent role in promoting expensive therapeutic interventions such as critical care and specialised interventions (Ehrenreich and Ehrenreich 1971; Stevens and Glatstein 1996; Waitzkin 1979, 2001). An example of this tendency for older adults is the polypharmacy that has resulted in approximately one-third of older adults using at least five prescription medications concurrently (Qato et al. 2008) and up to 10% of hospital admissions due to adverse drug reactions (Kane, Ouslander and Abrass 2004).

An example of ideological hegemony is the pervasive negative view of ageing and older adults in the United States. This view has fostered a billion dollar anti-ageing industry of hair dyes, cosmetics, treatments and plastic surgery (*USA Today* 2011). Additionally, it can be seen in the low levels of clinical specialisation in gerontology in medicine and nursing with less than 1% of U.S. medical school graduates pursuing gerontology at the fellowship level (Hazzard 2004). Older people as a group have little social power in relationships and the internalised effects of ideological hegemony result in negative views of themselves.

The sub-theory of communicative action

Jürgen Habermas's (1973) theory of communicative action emerged from the critical social perspective. Habermas criticised the tendency to idealise the role of communication. He argues that the proponents of hermeneutics do not take into consideration that communicative interaction also is 'a medium of domination of social power' which 'serves to legitimate relationship of organized force' (Habermas 1988:172). Inger Holter has argued that critical social perspective must show what constitutes a communicative interaction in which the domination of power is eliminated and in what ways distorted communication can be explained (Holter 1993).

Communicative action refers to the interaction of at least two persons who are capable of speech and action. For Habermas, speech is a vehicle of rationality. He outlined communicative competence and applied the concept of linguistic expression from Noam Chomsky (1968). Habermas's (1979, 1984) normative dimension of discourse proposed that anyone acting communicatively must raise universal validity claims. Four validity claims were developed: truth, rightness, truthfulness and comprehensibility, which are contained in the speech acts. *Truth* statements indicate the speaker must have the intention of communicating a true proposition (Habermas 1979). *Rightness* refers to the speech acts that are right normatively within the context of action producing legitimisation. *Truthfulness* is the representative speech act where a truthful expression of one's beliefs, intentions, feelings and desires suggests credibility. The *comprehensibility* validity claim refers to interpretations that are mutually agreeable. Thus, truth is comparable to veracity, rightness is to justice or fairness, and truthfulness to meaning. Ideally, the speech acts ideally should take place with reciprocity conditions where participants have an equal chance to express their views, feelings and wishes with an equal chance to resist, allow or forbid, and make and retract a promise, to be accountable and to owe an explanation (Habermas 1984).

Some areas of divergence

So far, we have reviewed some of the central ideas of symbolic interactionism and critical social theory and some of their sub-theories. Symbolic interactionism and critical perspective have consistently been thought of as divergent theoretical perspectives within sociology and are often considered to belong to different disciplines. Symbolic interactionism is generally thought to be a social psychological perspective, while the critical social theory perspective is solidly within the discipline of sociology. As stated earlier, their underlying philosophies of science are divergent as well as their level of focus with symbolic interaction having primarily a micro perspective and critical perspective using a macro perspective. This micro/macro difference is reflected in the differences in their major concepts and propositions as well as their major goals and concerns. Each of these areas will be explored further here.

Authors of the critical perspective are generally thought to hold a critical realist ontology, which is based on the belief that there is a reality 'out there' but that it may not ever be completely known or understood. Evidence of this critical realist position can be found in the goal of critical theory of liberation of people who are oppressed, including their movement from 'false consciousness' to 'true consciousness' (Guba 1990). Epistemologically, critical social theorists espouse a subjectivist view based on their belief that objective observation is impossible. The process of inquiry is always coloured by the values of the observer, so not even a modified objectivist viewpoint is possible (Guba 1990).

Symbolic interactionism, on the other hand, is grounded in the American philosophy of pragmatism originally attributed to William James and Charles Saunders Peirce. In Mead's view, the scientific method could be extended to all areas of intellectual inquiry including psychology, sociology and philosophy, testing hypotheses for their ability to solve problems and provide useful knowledge. He believed that any idea, including ethical and aesthetic ones, could be evaluated in light of the consequences that resulted from it (Baldwin 1986). The world as experienced is thought of as natural events sensed by observers. These events are a property of the observer as much as they are a property of the things observed. Charles Morris (1962:xix) called this an 'objective relativism' where 'qualities of the object may yet be relative to a conditioning organism. A certain portion of the world, as experienced, is private; but a portion is social or common, as science formulates it'.

A second major area of divergence is in the level of focus and the concepts, premises and goals of the perspectives in relation to that focus. Symbolic interactionism generally holds a micro perspective, most often focusing on individuals or small groups of individuals. Major concepts and premises of symbolic interactionism include the self, meaning-making through interaction, the use of symbols and individual behaviour. Society is considered, but usually only in relation to the construction of meaning and aiding in formation of individuals' definitions of situations. The goal is to understand and explain behaviour, the creation of meaning, and the self through interaction.

Symbolic interactionism has been criticised because of its lack of ability to address issues of power (Stryker 1980; Athens 2013). Alex Dennis and Peter J. Martin (2005) disagree, instead arguing that the interactionist tradition demonstrates a fundamental concern with power. They cited examples in the fields of deviance and education where social processes were studied in terms of power enacted and institutionalised in real situations. Yves Laberge (2015) pointed out that Mead did not oppose the inclusion of critical perspective concepts in symbolic interactionism, but he simply did not pay much attention to them in his unfinished thinking cut short by his illness. There are areas where symbolic interactionism may seem to include power, however, they do not suggest how to rebalance power inequity through social change, or work toward emancipation of those with little power.

Within the critical social theory perspective, the main focus is looking first to the macro level of society to understand power structures within social systems. Major concepts include social class, ideology, power and oppression, with the goal of rebalancing power relationships through emancipation. Habermas, in his aforementioned theory of communicative action, brought the critical perspective to the individual level and argued that all the power inequities that can be seen in society at large are mirrored in interactions between people as well. Other than Habermas and Waitzkin and others building on their work, however, the critical perspective maintains a macro perspective.

A final area of divergence involves the symbolic interactionist view of human freedom where people are thought of as free to make meaning of their social worlds and to choose their responses to situations. Michel Foucault and other critical social theorists disagree, denying the existence of an authentic subject who is free to choose their responses. Instead, humans are seen as socially constructed, the result of the power relations that constrain their responses and even shape who they may or may not be (Sundin and Fahy 2008).

Some areas of convergence

While the underlying philosophies, major foci, most concepts, premises and goals of the two perspectives presented in this chapter are different, there are areas within each perspective that may be seen as complementary or synergistic.

The underlying philosophies, while providing two different views of reality and knowledge development, are not contradictory. Critical realists are not usually thought of as subjectivists, however, this ontology/epistemology combination leads to the idea that there is a reality 'out there', although it is unable to be truly known because objective, value-free observation is impossible. Pragmatists do not answer the question about whether or not there really is a reality 'out there', but instead aim to develop knowledge that is useful for solving problems. Mead believed that qualities of objects were relative to the observer; events were a combination of the properties of the events along with the properties of those who observed them (Morris 1962). This relativist position on knowledge development is similar to the subjectivist position of critical perspective without the added attribution of subjectivity to value-laden observation (Burbank and Martins 2010).

The symbolic interactionist concepts of 'reference groups' and 'looking glass self' and 'ideological hegemony' within the critical social theory perspective can also be seen as complementary. Tamotsu Shibutani (1955:564) described a perspective as 'an ordered view of one's world – what is taken for granted about the attributes of various objects, events, and human nature'. Reference groups in symbolic interactionism are the groups with whom the individual communicates and whose perspective is used to define reality. They can be any groups to which the individual belongs such as social class, ethnic groups, community or society. In the critical social theory perspective, the dominant ideology is believed to be transmitted within a society so that all social classes and the entire society reflect the ideology of the ruling classes. The symbolic interactionist concept of reference groups may explain this transmission mechanism. The dominant ideology may also be communicated through the looking glass self, a symbolic interactionist concept where a person can step outside themselves and imagine seeing themselves as others see them.

The goal in the critical social theory perspective is emancipation through balancing power inequities. One premise of definition of the situation in symbolic interactionism indicates that through interaction with others, situations may be re-defined. Perhaps a group with little power may organise and increase its own power base within the social structure, thus redefining the situation for itself. A grassroots movement may gain power and voice by redefining the situation for those in power and be successful in getting the resources it needs to increase its power base.

Critical interactionism: a theoretical bridge

To date, most of the theoretical perspectives and approaches used in psychology and health care are focused at the individual, micro or 'downstream level'. In health care and psychology, symbolic interactionism has been used at the individual level to understand meanings. It provides the theoretical basis for grounded theory and is a framework for understanding perceptions and interactions and the 'definition of situation' primarily among individuals and families at the micro level. Critical social theory is the theoretical perspective that has often been utilised to address the structural, macro or 'upstream level', and provide a framework for analysis and interventions at this level (McKinlay 2008). Habermas (1984) and Waitzkin (1989) have applied critical social theory to understanding health inequities and oppression at the individual level, while suggesting refocusing on larger system issues to address inequities. This new theoretical approach is needed to provide a guide for examining complex human conditions best understood by a multifaceted perspective that considers underlying factors at the individual, organisational, cultural and societal level (both macro and micro perspectives). Critical interactionism combines symbolic interactionism and critical social theory to provide this framework (Burbank and Martins 2010; Martins and Burbank 2011).

Other authors have suggested the combination of symbolic interactionism and critical social theory in theoretical discussions and in research studies. Kent Sandstrom and Gary Alan Fine (2003) suggested the term 'critical interactionism' to describe this convergence of the two perspectives. They discussed Peter M. Hall's (1972, 1987, 1997) work in developing a framework for a critical interactionist analysis of politics, power and policy formation and Michael L. Schwalbe's (1986) synthesis of Marx's and Mead's theories, making linkages between local actions and extra-local inequalities. Interactionists have also contributed to an analysis of ideology (Fine and Sandstrom, 1993). Norman K. Denzin (1997) suggested an emancipatory critical interpretive interactionism with attention to language and behaviour that considered gender, biography and class. Larry T. Reynolds also blended critical theory with an interactionist perspective stating that 'a skillful welding of the radical sociology of Karl Marx with the liberal social psychology of George Herbert Mead is where to start; it holds the key to a viable future for our discipline [sociology]' (Reynolds 1998:35).

Deborah Sundin and Kathleen Fahy (2008) critiqued Denzin's interpretive interactionism in light of critical and postmodern thought and developed a new methodology called critical, post-structural, interpretive interactionism. They identified areas of divergence between symbolic interactionism and the critical social theory perspective and then modified the symbolic interactionist premises to include critical perspective. The method was used to study end-of-life decision-making in the critical care unit. Change was added as a new step to the research as they incorporated the 'imperative that critical research is designed to bring about change in the social world' (Sundin and Fahy 2008:20).

'Radical interactionism' is the term coined by Lonnie H. Athens (2007, 2013) in his critique of Mead's symbolic interactionism (see Chapter 8 on radical interactionism). In radical interactionism, the master principle behind society's operation is domination rather than sociality, with domination providing a much more accurate account of the origins and daily operations of societal institutions. The impact of domination extends to every institution in society, language, family, economics, religion and science as well as the polity (Athens 2007). Anthony Puddephatt used Athens's radical interactionism and Pierre Bourdieu's ideas of power asymmetries to explore the role of domination and power in science. Changing fundamental assumptions about social action leads to asking new questions about the micro and macro processes explored in research (Puddephatt 2013).

All of the authors mentioned here recognised the importance of combining symbolic interactionism with the critical social theoretical perspective to provide a more complete understanding of individual social actions as well as those of larger groups, institutions and society as a whole. In many of these efforts to join symbolic interactionism and critical social theory; however, the critical social theoretical perspective emerges as the primary lens through which all other concepts are viewed. In this approach to critical interactionism (Martins and Burbank 2011), the perspectives still maintain their individuality; however, they are used together to increase understanding of phenomena and guide interventions with both macro and micro directions to obtain the best possible outcomes. Table 5.1 compares parameters across the three theoretical perspectives: symbolic interactionism, critical social theory and critical interactionism.

In critical interactionism, the richness of each individual perspective of symbolic interactionism and critical social theory is maintained while strengthening their areas of mutuality. The concepts of meaning from symbolic interactionism and emancipation from critical social theory move across system levels to address complex human conditions. The concepts of reference groups and the looking glass self from symbolic interactionism and ideological hegemony from critical social theory are used together to facilitate understanding of how the dominant ideology may be transmitted to all social classes within society. Critical interactionism is a powerful, dynamic theoretical tool for addressing complex human conditions, moving back and forth between the downstream and upstream approaches. It allows for movement not only between upstream and downstream but between macro and micro levels as well. It is proposed that both perspectives in their entirety need to be applied in a fluid motion, moving back and forth among levels. In this way, we can generate new knowledge and transform the human condition both at the individual and larger system levels making positive and enduring changes.

Theoretical applications to populations identified as homeless and criminals

In this section, homelessness and criminal behaviour will be used as examples to illustrate the difference in the application of symbolic interactionism, critical social theory and critical interactionism. The factors contributing to homelessness have been discussed extensively in the literature ranging from personal to socio-structural factors. Personal factors have included mental illness, substance misuse and lack of personal resiliency. Structural factors such as lack of housing, unemployment and poverty have also been listed. Interestingly, Malcolm Williams (2001:1) suggested that 'there is no such thing as homelessness, but instead a range of heterogeneous characteristics that give rise to the wide range of symptoms that we term homelessness'. Factors contributing to criminal behaviour have also been attributed to individual characteristics or risk factors and socio-structural factors. Individual factors include mental illness and substance misuse. Socio-structural factors neighbourhoods with high crime rates and gang activity,

Table 5.1 Summary of symbolic interactionism, critical social theory and critical interactionism

	Symbolic interactionism	Critical social theory	Critical interactionism
Discipline	Social psychology	Sociology	Cross-disciplinary
Level of focus	Downstream and micro	Upstream and macro	Upstream and downstream, macro and micro
Ontology	Pragmatism (originally) Relativism	Critical realism	Pragmatism
Epistemology	Subjective, relative to those who observe them (Mead) Reality is socially constructed (interpretivism) Objective relativism (Morris)	Subjectivism Value-laden observation	Subjectivism Interpretivism
Goal	Understand human actions based on definitions and meanings they have of world around them	Emancipation, interventions to promote egalitarian balance of power	Understanding and intervening at both downstream and upstream levels examining both meanings, and organisational and societal repressive structures
Major concepts	Meaning, self, interaction, symbols, acts, perspectives	Power, social class, ideology, oppression, emancipation	Meaning and power Upstream – social class, ideology, oppression, emancipation Downstream – self, interaction, symbols, acts, perspectives
Perspectives	Derived from reference groups and orientational others Looking glass self – viewing ourselves as others see us	Ideological hegemony – pervasive dominant thinking that permeates society at all levels	Derived from reference groups and orientational others who perpetuate pervasive dominant thinking
View of human beings	I and me, socially constructed, free to make meaning of social world and to choose responses	Socially constructed, limited freedom to choose response and result of power relations that constrain their responses	I and me, socially constructed, with varying degrees of socially constrained freedom to make meaning of their worlds and choose responses

Health/health care	Focuses on individual's experiences of health, illness and health care, and the meanings surrounding them	Focuses on power inequities that manufacture and perpetuate illness and its treatments	Focuses jointly on the individual's and society's contributions to and responsibility for health and illness
Actions/ interventions	Defining and reinterpreting situations for more healthy outcomes, individual behaviour change	Balancing power inequities Re-structure manufacturers of illness to promote health	Changing societal constraints on re-defining situations and supporting positive individual behaviour change while working to change manufacturers of illness

Source: Martins, Diane C. and Patricia Burbank (2011), *Advances in Nursing Science*, 34 (4):315–329.

availability of drugs and alcohol, and high poverty rates. A youth growing up in a disadvantaged area may therefore be at increased risk for delinquency (Murray and Farrington 2010). It is apparent from the literature on contributing factors that both individual characteristics (micro) and socio-structural factors (macro) act together to produce homelessness and criminal behaviour. This underscores the need for a dual theoretical approach that can address both micro and macro levels to address these complex problems.

A symbolic interactionist perspective

A symbolic interactionist's perspective on people experiencing homelessness addresses the meaning of the situation they are experiencing. They focus on the ways individuals interact with each other in relationship to their 'homelessness'. The symbolic interactionist focuses on understanding the meaning (symbols) of 'homelessness' and the homeless experience. Several researchers have used the symbolic interactionist perspective with the homeless population including Laura Blankertz et al. (1990); Katherine Boydell, Paula Goering and Tammy Morrell-Bellai (2000); and Anne Rochelle and Peter Kaufman (2004). The lens of symbolic interactionism was used by the authors to analyse their findings. They identified components of the self, the need to understand the subjective meaning of the experience or the need to gain trust with the population by using shared symbols.

Many other studies have used the symbolic interactionist perspective to view people identified as criminals. Lonnie H. Athens (1980) and Leanne Alarid and Ofelia Vega (2010) suggested that interactionism explains action through the criminal's self-image and judgement of the situation. David Brownfield and Kevin Thompson (2005) reported that the self-concept is about as highly correlated with delinquency as is peer delinquency. JoAnn Lee, Emiko Tajima, Todd Herrenkohl and Seunghye Hong (2017); and Jonathan Caudill, Brie Diamond, Stephanie Karas and Matt DeLisi (2017) used labelling theory and concluded that labels become the lens through which all future behavioural expectations are created.

A critical social theory perspective

A critical social theoretical perspective views homelessness as a condition related to an imbalance of power secondary to capitalism. This results in exploitation of housing markets and regulations to control those who are labelled and marginalised. The people experiencing homelessness are the lumpen proletariats in the oppressive class system. The 'social problem' of homelessness has been addressed using a critical social perspective by Christopher Dum, Robert Norris and Kevin Weng (2017:1336). Suzanne Fitzpatrick (2005) suggested that poverty, spatial concentrations of the disadvantage and domestic violence are examples of inter-related causes of homelessness. David Snow and Leon Anderson (1993) studied homeless street people and argued that 'congregated at the bottom of every social order is an aggregation of demeaned and stigmatized individuals variously referred to historically as the lumpen proletariat, untouchables, the underclass, or superfluous people'.

From a critical social theory perspective, controlling undesirable behaviour has been associated with incarceration for centuries. For example, Michel Foucault (1975) sought to analyse punishment in its social context and examine how changing power relations affected punishment. He believed that society portrays fairness and social justice in its effort to control deviant/unwanted behaviour through its institutions of discipline and punishment (the prison system). Steven Spitzer (1975) addressed deviance from a Marxian perspective. Controlling deviant/unwanted behaviour through medicalisation has also been discussed by Peter Conrad (1975), and Conrad and Joseph Schneider (1992).

Antonio Gramsci (1971) addressed dominance and control in *Prison Notebooks* while incarcerated for his anti-Mussolini behaviour. He identified the role of 'cultural hegemony', used to support the ruling class. Ideological hegemony permeates society to maintain the status quo. If hegemonic forces do not work, the ruling party uses coercive power in the form of repressive state apparatuses including military, police, courts and prison systems (Althusser 1972). The lens of domination, oppression and control informs the critical social theoretical perspective.

A critical interactionist approach

A critical interactionist approach utilises both a symbolic interactionist and critical social theory perspective. Together they address the full range of potential contributing factors of those identified as homeless or as criminals. Micro-level factors, as well as the macro-level factors and their interrelationships, would be identified. Suzanne Fitzpatrick (2005) suggested that personal factors could be susceptible to structural causes. These personal factors can be contributing factors in conjunction with structural conditions.

Examples of critical interactionist interventions at the micro level include assessment of individuals using definition of the situation. For instance, a systematic approach is necessary to assess meaning for individuals with mental illness or misusing substances. Behaviour can be changed through redefining the situation and one's self-image and can be improved through positive interaction with reference groups. Habermas's analysis of communicative action can be applied, recognising that power imbalances are reflected in each face-to-face interaction. Individual strategies would focus on addressing the 'immediate problem' such as shelter, food or water for survival. It may also include treatment related to substance misuse. Recognising the strengths of the person experiencing homelessness or incarceration is essential. The people experiencing incarceration and homelessness need to be empowered to rise, resist and have a voice in their lives, while considering the meaning that these changes would have for them.

Macro-level approaches would include the need for changes in policies and legislation that punish and label the population experiencing homelessness or incarceration. David Farrugia and Jessica Gerrard (2016) suggested that if research is being done 'on' this population, it should result in policy changes on behalf of the population. This would include working to change town and city ordinances that incarcerate people for 'loitering' when there is no place to stay. Laws in New York and other cities across the United States demanded removal of 'questionable' people from outside public shared space to emergency departments or prisons. Another example would be advocacy work to address antidiscrimination policies related to education, housing, jobs and health care. Critical interactionism at the macro level requires changes in organisation structures and practices that would also fully address the social determinants of health (Marmot and Wilkinson 2006). This would provide a social justice lens for the social factors that result in human inequality.

Conclusion

As shown in this chapter, by using a pragmatic approach and combining symbolic interactionism and the critical social theory perspectives into critical interactionism, both micro and macro levels come into focus, and strategies for change across individual and societal levels can be developed and applied. Theory can be used as a guide for both practice and research. Application of critical interactionism is especially useful as a theoretical lens to view complex human conditions. These are best understood by a multifaceted perspective that considers underlying factors at the individual, organisational, cultural and societal level. For practitioners, developing strategies to change oppressive human conditions using a critical interactionist perspective can address the immediate problems at the individual level while also initiating socio-structural strategies including empowerment, advocacy and social change. It is difficult to intervene at both of these levels at the same time and as a single practitioner, however. Teams of practitioners are more effective in working collaboratively with individuals and across systems levels to impact complex problems.

In the research arena, participatory action research is one method that is useful to study questions utilising a critical interactionist perspective. Mixed methods can also be used to further understanding of large data sets of socio-structural factors by seeking individuals' voices in a qualitative component. Again, team science with researchers who are skilled at these methodological approaches may bring the best results.

The landscape is rich with new research questions emerging from this expanded theoretical perspective, new possibilities for continued theory development, and the potential for new strategies that can address individual and larger system problems through empowerment of clients and nurses. Perhaps social inequities can be brought into more balance through a creative, persistent application of critical interactionism in research, education and practice.

References

Alarid, Leanne and Ofelia Vega (2010): 'Identity Construction, Self-Perceptions and Criminal Behaviour of Incarcerated Women'. *Deviant Behaviour*, 31:704–728.

Althusser, Louis (1972): *Lenin and Philosophy and Other Essays*. New York: Monthly Review Press.

Athens, Lonnie H. (1980): 'Violent Criminal Acts and Actors – A Symbolic Interactionist Study'. *National Criminal Justice Reference Service.* Available online at: https://www.ncjrs.gov/App/Publications/abstract.aspx?ID=64262.

Athens, Lonnie H. (2007): 'Radical Interactionism: Going beyond Mead'. *Journal for the Theory of Social Behavior*, 32 (2):137–165.

Athens, Lonnie H. (2013): 'Radical and Symbolic Interactionism: Demarcating Their Borders', in Lonnie H. Athens (ed.): *Radical Interactionism on the Rise* (Studies in Symbolic Interaction, Volume 41). Bingley: Emerald Group Publishing, pp. 1–24.

Baldwin, John D. (1986): *George Herbert Mead: A Unifying Theory for Sociology*. Thousand Oaks, CA: Sage Publications.

Bertrand, Sharon (2010): 'Inroads to Integrative Health Care: Registered Nurses' Personal Use of Traditional Chinese Medicine Affects Professional Identity and Nursing Practice'. *Complementary Health Practice Review*, 15 (1):14–30.

Bilton, Tony, Kevin Bonnet, Pip Jones, Tony Lawson, David Skinner, Michelle Stanworth and Andrew Webster (2002): *Health, Illness and Medicine: Introductory Sociology* (4th edition). New York: Palgrave/Macmillan.

Blankertz, Laura, Ram A. Canaan, Kalma White, Jima Fox and Karlyn Messinger (1990): 'Outreach Efforts with Dually Diagnosed Homeless Persons'. *Families in Society*, 71 (7):387–397.

Blumer, Herbert (1969): *Symbolic Interactionism: Perspective and Method*. Englewood Cliffs, NJ: Prentice-Hall

Boydell, Katherine, Paula Goering and Tammy Morrell-Bellai (2000): 'Narratives of Identity: Re-Presentation of Self in People Who are Homeless'. *Qualitative Health Research*, 10 (1):26–38.

Brownfield, David and Kevin Thompson (2005): 'Self-Concept and Delinquency: The Effects of Reflected Appraisals by Parent and Peers'. *Western Criminology Review*, 6 (1):22–29.

Burbank, Patricia and Diane C. Martins (2010): 'Symbolic Interactionism and Critical Perspective: Divergent or Synergistic?' *Nursing Philosophy*, 11 (1):25–41.

Burrell, Gibson and Gareth Morgan (1979): *Sociological Paradigms and Organizational Analysis*. London: Heinemann Publishing.
Caudill, Jonathan, Brie Diamond, Stephanie Karas and Matt DeLisi (2017): 'Decoupling the Labeling Tradition: Exploring Gang Affiliation and the Application of Law'. *Youth Violence and Juvenile Justice*, 15 (4):343–358.
Charon, Joel M. (2007): *Symbolic Interactionism: An Introduction, An Interpretation, An Integration* (9th edition). Upper Saddle River, NJ: Pearson Prentice Hall.
Charon Joel M. (2009): *Symbolic Interactionism: An Introduction, An Interpretation, An Integration* (10th edition). Upper Saddle River, NJ: Pearson Prentice Hall.
Chomsky, Noam (1968): *Language and Mind*. New York: Harcourt, Brace & World.
Cleveland, Lisa M. (2009): 'Symbolic Interactionism and Nurse-Mother Communication in the Neonatal Intensive Care Unit'. *Research and Theory for Nursing Practice: An International Journal*, 23 (3):216–229.
Conrad, Peter (1975): 'The Discovery of Hyperkinesis: Notes on the Medicalization of Deviant Behaviour'. *Social Problems*, 23 (1):12–21.
Conrad, Peter and Joseph Schneider (1992): *Deviance and Medicalization: From Badness to Sickness*. Philadelphia: Temple University Press.
Cooley, Charles Horton (1972): 'Looking Glass Self', in Jerome G. Manis and Bernard N. Meltzer (ed.): *Symbolic Interaction: A Reader in Social Psychology* (2nd edition). Boston: Allyn & Bacon, pp. 231–233.
Dennis, Alex and Peter J. Martin (2005): 'Symbolic Interactionism and the Concept of Power'. *British Journal of Sociology*, 56 (2):191–213.
Denzin, Norman K. (1997): *Interpretive Ethnography: Ethnographic Practices for the 21st Century*. Thousand Oaks, CA: Sage Publications.
Dum, Christopher, Robert Norris and Kevin Weng (2017): 'Punishing Benevolence: The Criminalization of Homeless Feeding as an Act of State Harm'. *Critical Criminology*, 25 (4):483–506.
Ehrenreich, Barbara and John Ehrenreich (eds.) (1971): *The American Health Empire: Power, Profit and Politics*. New York: Vintage Books.
Farrugia, David and Jessica Gerrard (2016): 'Academic Knowledge and Contemporary Poverty: The Politics of Homelessness Research'. *Sociology*, 50 (2):267–284.
Fine, Gary Alan and Kent Sandstrom (1993): 'Ideology in Action: A Pragmatic Approach to a Contested Concept'. *Sociological Theory*, 11:21–38.
Fitzpatrick, Suzanne (2005): 'Explaining Homelessness: A Critical Realist Perspective'. *Housing, Theory and Society*, 22 (1):1–17.
Foucault, Michel (1975): *Discipline and Punishment: The Birth of the Prison*. New York: Pantheon Books.
Freire, Paulo (1971): *Pedagogy of the Oppressed*. New York: Herder and Herder.
Goffman, Erving (1959): *The Presentation of Self in Everyday Life*. Garden City, NY: Doubleday/Anchor.
Gramsci, Antonio (1971): *Selections from the Prison Notebooks*. London: Lawrence and Wishart.
Guba, Egon (1990): *The Paradigm Dialogue*. Newbury Park, CA: Sage Publications.
Habermas, Jürgen (1973): *Theory and Practice*. Boston, MA: Beacon Press.
Habermas, Jürgen (1979): *Communication and the Evolution of Society*. Boston, MA: Beacon Press.
Habermas, Jürgen (1984): *Theory of Communicative Action*. Volume 1, *Reason and the Rationalization of Society*. Boston, MA: Beacon Press.
Habermas, Jürgen (1988): *On the Logic of the Social Sciences*. Cambridge, MA: Polity Press.

Hall, Peter M. (1972): 'A Symbolic Interactionist Analysis of Politics'. *Sociological Inquiry*, 42:35–75.

Hall, Peter M. (1987): 'Interactionism and the Study of Social Organization'. *Sociological Quarterly*, 28 (1):283–305.

Hall, Peter M. (1997): 'Meta-Power, Social Organization and the Shaping of Social Action'. *Symbolic Interaction*, 20 (4):397–418.

Hazzard, William R. (2004): 'Commentary: Geriatrics: Specialty, Subspecialty or Supraspecialty?' *Journals of Gerontology, Series A: Biological Sciences and Medical Sciences*, 59 (11):1161–1162.

Holter, Inger (1993): 'Critical Action Research and the Changing Role of Nurse Executives: A Case Study'. Unpublished doctoral dissertation, University of Rhode Island, Kingston.

Kane, Robert L., Joseph Ouslander and Itmar Abrass (2004): *Essentials of Clinical Geriatrics* (5th edition). New York: McGraw-Hill.

Laberge, Yves (2015): 'Against the Symbolic Interactionism Dogma? Radical Inter-actionism Enters into Force'. *Symbolic Interaction*, 38 (3):442–444.

Lee, Jo Ann, Emiko Tajima, Todd Herrenkohl and Seunghye Hong (2017): 'Effects of Formal and Informal Deviant Labels in Adolescence on Crime in Adulthood'. *Social Work Research*, 41 (2):97–109.

Lukács, György (1923/1971): *History and Class Consciousness*. London: Merlin Press.

Lyndon, Audrey and Holly Powel Kennedy (2010): 'Perinatal Safety: From Concept to Nursing Practice'. *Journal of Perinatal & Neonatal Nursing*, 24 (1):22–31.

Marmot, Michael and Richard Wilkinson (2006): *Social Determinants of Health*. Oxford: University Press.

Martins, Diane C. (2019): 'Thinking Upstream: Nursing Theories and Population-Focused Nursing Practice', in Mary Nies and Melanie McEwen (eds.): *Community/Public Health Nursing: Promoting the Health of Populations* (7th edition). St Louis, MO: Elsevier.

Martins, Diane C. and Patricia Burbank (2011): 'Critical Interactionism: An Upstream-Downstream Approach to Health Care Reform'. *Advances in Nursing Science*, 34 (4): 315–329.

Marx, Karl (1975): *Early Writings*. Harmondsworth: Penguin Books.

Matsueda, Ross (1992): 'Reflected Appraisals, Parental Labeling and Delinquency: Specifying a Symbolic Interactionist Theory'. *American Journal of Sociology*, 97 (6): 1577–1611.

McHugh, Peter (1968): *Defining the Situation: The Organization of Meaning in Social Interaction*. New York: Bobbs-Merrill.

McKinlay, John B. (2008): 'A Case for Refocusing Upstream: The Political Economy of Illness', in Peter Conrad (ed.): *The Sociology of Health and Illness: Critical Perspectives*. New York: Worth Publishing, pp. 578–591.

Mead, George Herbert (1934): *Mind, Self and Society* (edited by Charles W. Morris). Chicago: University of Chicago Press.

Meiers, Sonja and Donna Brauer (2008): 'Existential Caring in the Family Health Experience: A Proposed Conceptualization'. *Scandinavian Journal of Caring Sciences*, 22 (1):110–117.

Meltzer, Bernard N., John W. Petras and Larry T. Reynolds (1975): *Symbolic Interactionism: Genesis, Varieties and Criticism*. Boston: Routledge and Kegan Paul.

Morris, Charles W. (ed.) (1962): *Mind, Self, and Society: The Works of George Herbert Mead*. Chicago: University of Chicago Press.

Murray, Joseph and David P. Farrington (2010): 'Risk Factors for Conduct Disorder and Delinquency: Key Findings from Longitudinal Studies'. *Canadian Journal of Psychiatry*, 55 (10):633–642.

Navarro, Vincente (1976): *Medicine Under Capitalism*. New York: Prodist.

Puddephatt, Anthony (2013): 'Toward a Radical Interactionist Account of Science', in Lonnie H. Athens (ed.): *Radical Interactionism on the Rise* (Studies in Symbolic Interaction, Volume 41). Bingley: Emerald Group Publishing, pp. 53–82.

Qato, Dima M., G. Caleb Alexander, Rena M. Conti, Michael Johnson, Phil Schumm and Stacy Tessler Lindau. (2008): 'Use of Prescription and Over-the-Counter Medications and Dietary Supplements among Older Adults in the United States'. *Journal of the American Medical Association*, 300 (24):2867–2878.

Reynolds, Larry T. (1998): *Interactionism: Exposition and Critique* (3rd edition). Dix Hills, NY: General Hall.

Roschelle, Anne and Peter Kaufman (2004): 'Fitting In and Fighting Back: Stigma Management Strategies among Homeless Kids'. *Symbolic Interaction*, 27 (1):23–46.

Sandstrom, Kent L. and Gary Alan Fine (2003): 'Triumphs, Emerging Voices and the Future', in Larry T. Reynolds and Nancy J. Herman-Kinney (eds.): *Handbook of Symbolic Interactionism*. New York: AltaMira Press, pp. 1041–1057.

Schwalbe, Michael L. (1986): *The Psychosocial Consequences of Natural and Alienated Labor*. Albany, NY: State University of New York Press.

Shibutani, Tamotsu (1955): ''Reference Groups as Perspectives.' *American Journal of Sociology*, 60 (6): 562–569.

Shibutani, Tamotsu (1986): *Social Processes*. Berkeley, CA: University of California Press.

Snow, David and Leon Anderson (1993): *Down on Their Luck: A Study of Homeless Street People*. Berkeley, CA: University of California Press.

Spitzer, Steven (1975): 'Toward a Marxian Theory of Deviance'. *Social Problems*, 22 (5): 638–651.

Stevens Craig and Eli Glatstein (1996): 'Beware of the Medical-Industrial Complex'. *The Oncologist*, 1 (4):190iv–190v.

Stryker, Sheldon (1980): *Symbolic Interactionism: A Social Structural Version*. Reading, MA: Benjamin Cummings Publishing Company.

Sundin, Deborah and Kathleen Fahy (2008): 'Critical, Post-Structural, Interpretive Interactionism: An Update on Denzin's Methodology'. *Nurse Researcher*, 16 (1):7–23.

USA Today (2011): 'Boomers Spending Billions to Counter Aging'. Available online at: http://usatoday30.usatoday.com/news/health/story/healty/story/2011/08/anti-aging-industry-grows-with-boomer-demand/50087672/1.

Waitzkin, Howard (1979): 'A Marxian Interpretation of the Growth and Development of Coronary Care Technology'. *American Journal of Public Health*, 69:1260–1268.

Waitzkin, Howard (1983): *The Second Sickness: Contradictions of Capitalist Health Care*. New York: Collier Macmillan.

Waitzkin, Howard (1986): 'Micropolitics of Medicine: Theoretical Issues'. *Medical Anthropology Quarterly*, 17:134–136.

Waitzkin, Howard (1989): 'A Critical Theory of Medical Discourse: Ideology, Social Control and the Processing of Social Context in Medical Encounters'. *Journal of Health and Social Behavior*, 30:220–239.

Waitzkin, Howard (1991): *The Politics of Medical Encounters: How Patients and Doctors Deal with Social Problems.* New Haven, CT: Yale University Press.

Waitzkin, Howard (2001): *At the Front Lines of Medicine.* Langham, MD: Rowman & Littlefield Publishers.

Waitzkin, Howard, Theron Britt and Constance Williams (1994): 'Narratives of Aging and Social Problems in Medical Encounters with Older Persons'. *Journal of Health and Social Behavior*, 35:322–348.

Williams, Malcolm (2001): 'Complexity, Probability and Causation: Implications for Homelessness Research'. *Journal of Social Issues.* Available online at: http://www.whb.co.uk/socialissues/mw.htm.

6   Pacifism, gender and symbolic interactionism

Mary Jo Deegan

Introduction

George Herbert Mead, John Dewey and Jane Addams created a profound and unique American theory that analysed society and the individual as social objects. Both society and the individual emerged from cooperative, democratic processes between the self, the other and the community. These patterns and behaviours were socially generated, rational and learned. Intelligence, the mind, problem solving and reflection were part of the socialisation of children and the emergence of the self and the ability to take the role of the other (e.g., Addams 1909; Dewey 1899; Mead 1910, 1913). Before World War I (hereafter referred to as WWI), there was a different emphasis on gender and political action by the men and Addams, but the fundamental definitions of the self, the other, democracy and education were held in common (Deegan 1999).

During the war, however, their commonality was fractured and strained. Mead and Dewey became noted speakers and authors in defence of the war: they supported the power of the state to use violence. This male perspective differed from the female one. Addams became an infamous speaker and author in opposition to the war: she repeatedly challenged the power and wisdom of the state to use violence. She actively resisted the war and advocated non-violence, arbitration and cooperation between nations. She became the most famous, international leader of women who opposed the war. She based this activity on a number of American positions: on William Lloyd Garrison's (1904/1924) non-resistance, her family's heritage as Hicksite Quakers, and, most important, women's values and culture. In the 1920s, and the cool aftermath of a return to rational thought, Mead and Dewey came to accept Addams's position, but only after a deep and painful struggle to understand war's impact on their thought and practices (Deegan 1988a, 1991, 1999, 2001; Rucker 1969; Seigfried 1998). The commitment to pacifism was downplayed, if not erased, after Herbert Blumer (1937, 1969) institutionalised the men's ideas in the perspective he named 'symbolic interactionism'.

The argument advanced in this chapter begins with the joint work of the three theorists. Next, the men's perspective on war and peace before, during, and after WWI is described. Both Mead and Dewey were 'international pacifists' before the war started in Europe in 1914. Dewey's adoption of a pro-war stance in 1915, therefore, startled and dismayed several of his students and colleagues in New York City. Mead continued his pacifist position, however, until the United States entered the fighting in 1917. Mead's male students and colleagues in Chicago tended to be pro-WWI, too, after 1917. After the war ended in 1918, Mead and Dewey returned to their original, pacifist theory. Meanwhile, Addams led a large group of colleagues and allies in her increasingly sophisticated theory of feminist symbolic interactionism where pacifism was explicit, even during wartime, and women led the non-violent battle to end war. Dozens of women in Chicago developed lifelong, intense friendships with other women, which helped them resist the war fever of many Americans. A brief overview on the role of pacifism and symbolic interaction after the war is presented next in two stages. First, the immediate period after the war in 1918 until Dewey's intellectual support of Addams in 1945 is documented. This is followed by an analysis of the era of symbolic interactionism led by Herbert Blumer between 1937 and today. The conclusion points to some possible future research.

The birth of theory and practice

Jane Addams founded Hull-House, a social settlement, in 1889 and established her 'experiment in democracy' in Chicago (Deegan 2008:22–23). Meanwhile, in 1891 Mead joined Dewey at the University of Michigan in Ann Arbor, where they taught philosophy. Three years later, in 1894, Dewey was offered a position at the University of Chicago. Before accepting the new job, Dewey visited Addams and Hull-House, which had already become a centre of innovation in education and sociology (Deegan 1999:xxxvii). Dewey liked what he saw at the university and at the social settlement. When Dewey accepted the Chicago invitation, he brought his colleague Mead with him to elaborate on their joint interests in philosophy, education and social science. They both believed in the unity of theory and application. The two men quickly became part of life at Hull-House, delivering lectures, meeting neighbours and befriending the residents, especially Addams. In 1897, Dewey joined the board at Hull-House, a position he held until he left the city in 1904. In 1902, Addams founded the Labor Museum after talking with Dewey about the problems of intergenerational misunderstanding between formerly rural immigrant parents and their urban offspring who worked in factories. Mead became part of the board at the University of Chicago Settlement, headed by a former Hull-House resident and Chicago sociologist Mary E. McDowell, and spent considerable time there and at Hull-House developing an expertise in applied social change (Mead 1929a, 1999).

The three colleagues and professionals developed their ideas on community, the other, education, democracy, play, interaction, and the unity of theory and practice during these years. The men's work at the university was identified as a unique perspective, 'the Chicago School', by William James, the Harvard pragmatist and symbolic interactionist, in 1904 (James 1904).

The male perspective on war and peace before, during and after World War I

Although Addams was the most feminist, radical, pacifist and political actor of the three friends before WWI, they all shared a cooperative, global worldview called 'international pacifism' or 'progressive internationalism' (Kloppenberg 1998). They drew others into their work and created a unique American theory and praxis. Although Addams, Mead and Dewey shared an international pacifism, the men's more restricted approaches to peace and social activism did not limit their friendships. The three scholars and friends, for example, were invited 'To Act As Correspondents of the Neutral Conference for Continuous Mediation' in 1915 (see JAP, reel 10, frame 0017) before the United States entered the war.

During the war, a gendered position on pacifism developed: the male symbolic interactionists changed their concepts and politics, and became more conflict-oriented and supported war, while Addams and her female allies did not. Ultimately the women elaborated on and extended their pacifism and linked it to expanded areas of influence, widening their differences with the men.

Mead and Dewey as international pacifists, 1894–1914

Dewey and Mead helped train students in their perspective in their own department at the University of Chicago and in sociology, too. This intellectual approach became the basis for a social psychology of human behaviour that emphasised human cooperation, shared symbols and meanings that emerged through cooperation between the self and the other. This global process generated and maintained society. These internationalists argued that all societies functioned at their best when they engaged in cooperative processes. Dewey left Chicago in 1904 and continued to teach and develop his ideas at Columbia University in New York City. Although the two men worked in different cities and universities after 1904, they kept a close friendship and intellectual relationship the rest of their lives.

Between 1904 and 1914 the men expanded their theory of international, cooperative societies. Addams became increasingly recognised as a pacifist, especially after she published *Newer Ideals of Peace* in 1907. Mead (1907) reviewed her book in *The American Journal of Sociology*, demonstrating their shared interest in the subject. Her increasing understanding of immigrants, urban problems and role in founding the Juvenile Court was matched by Mead's growing interest in each topic, too.

Chicago symbolic interactionism, the University of Chicago and World War I, 1914–1921

The global conflagration began on 28 June 1914 with the assassination of Archduke Franz Ferdinand of Austria-Hungary in Sarajevo, but the United States did not enter the war until 6 April 1917. Between 1914 and 1918, the years of the Great War, the University of Chicago became a centre for research, expertise and teaching about both this specific war and wars in general (Boyer 2004). Mead was part of this campus-wide expertise. Before the United States entered the war in 1917, however, Mead maintained his pacifism. After 1917 he helped organise and support public lectures on war and peace in Chicago. He developed a sophisti-cated, albeit flawed, critique of Marxist conflict theory to explain the class unrest in Germany and not in the United States. He became a popular spokesperson in support of the war by publishing his ideas in the newspapers (e.g., Mead 1917a, 1917b, 1917c, 1917d, 1917e, 1917f). He then developed an analysis and critique of aggressive instincts and impulses. He supported Fabian socialism or extensive government programs to guarantee minimum standards of living for the disabled, unemployed, ill, homeless and poor. He helped establish the American welfare state in his role as a pragmatist, citizen and leader of social change, including his understanding of social reconstruction emerging from wartime (Deegan 2008).

Mead taught an entire course on 'The Intellectual Background to the War' in the spring of 1918. His theory and practices emerged from his historical location, and as this changed, his work changed; during peacetime, he was an international pacifist, and during wartime, he was an advocate of 'the war to end wars'. Portions of his theory and practices remained stable, nonetheless, and he continued to support internationalism, anti-militarism and arbitration. His model of the self also displayed the same process of the child learning to become human through social interaction emerging from language and shared meanings. He changed his understanding of German values and ideas, however, from one of admiration to one of criticism. His theory and practices also changed in reference to the definitions of democracy; the dichotomisation of the enemy; and his understanding of hostility, both nationally and personally, and cooperation. In addition, he became more emotional in his observations of society. His theory and practices were shaken by his professional and personal definitions of democracy and cooperation during wartime (Deegan 2008; Mead 1917a, 1917b, 1917c, 1917d, 1917e, 1917f).

These professional issues were echoed in the work of his colleagues Dewey and W. I. Thomas, with the latter being another former student of Mead and Dewey in sociology. Mead's understanding of the nation-state, democracy and social justice combined with a new definition of Germany as the 'enemy' and an unreflexive trust in the American government's definitions of the need for self-defence. These changes reveal both weaknesses and strengths in Mead's theory, which he never exposed so dramatically again. The theory and praxis surrounding pacifism, conflict, cooperation and war demarcate a significant dividing line between the feminist symbolic interactionists (Deegan 2016) and the male-defined intellectuals.[1] As I examine in more depth later, the women decided in favour of cultural pluralism, pragmatism, feminism, pacifism and a cooperative model after 1915. The men, meanwhile, defined war as part of defending democracy; men needed to protect and obey the orders of the state and the military; and male values of competition, belligerence and violence were sometimes necessary and sometimes it was the basis of other values such as courage and community. The men often articulated sweeping generalisations about the enemy, particularly Germans, Germany and Germanic culture. The men, including Mead and Dewey, often built on the work of another founding figure in symbolic interactionism, William James (1910/1991) as he articulated it in 'The Moral Equivalent of War'. The men's worldview was less open, flexible, cooperative, pacifist and feminist than the women's (Schott 1993). The Great War massively challenged the ideas and work of both gendered groups.

During WWI, as noted earlier, Chicago became the centre for men at the University of Chicago to become experts on war, while many women in the city became worldwide leaders in the struggle for peace and opposition to war. Although New York City was also the home of war experts and pacifists, some of Dewey's former students publicly denounced him for abandoning international pacifism. In contrast, most of Mead's students and colleagues from the University of Chicago supported his war efforts (e.g., Small 1917).

Mead also maintained a position during the war that was closer to Addams than Dewey did. Thus Mead (e.g., 1917g, 1918b) tried to understand and reflect on the conscientious objector as more than a coward and traitor. Although Mead did not believe in minority rights to oppose the state, he did support pacifist communities, such as the Quakers, who suffered during wartime. He was committed to a peaceful arbitration process through the League to Enforce Peace, a group in which Addams briefly served as a vice president until she broke with them as too violent. There is no record of a break in the friendship of Mead and Addams, unlike the situation between Dewey and Addams (see Addams 1929, 1930; Dewey 1945a, 1945b). The men's evolution from international pacifists to war experts is examined in more detail next.

Mead and sociology

Although George Herbert Mead is recognised as the founder of symbolic inter-actionism, he was not trained as a sociologist and he did not work in the depart-ment of sociology. It is important to identify him as a sociologist, which is a complicated situation (see an in-depth discussion of this difficulty in Huebner 2014). To begin with, Mead was a 'classical theorist in sociology', who started publishing and teaching in the early 1890s. From his student days in the 1880s until approximately 1910 Mead continued many of the questions explored by one of his senior professors in Germany, Wilhelm Wundt, and the study of compara-tive psychology (Mead 2001), but he was also training sociology students such as William I. Thomas and Annie Marion MacLean as early as the 1890s (see Deegan 2014a; Huebner 2014). After 1910, Mead increasingly explored the importance of democracy, education and the American tradition of pragmatism, although he never abandoned his ties with Wundt (see Mead 1919, 1934). Mead's belief in rationality was rooted in Enlightenment values (Deegan 2014a:271–272) and in a Germanic emphasis on the mind over emotions (e.g., Weber 1947).

Until the United States entered the war, Mead continued to elaborate on his cooperative, scientific, rational model of the self and society. In his model, play, not war, held a central place (Mead 1999). International cooperation and life flourished in this perspective (Mead 1915). Mead's ideas were compatible with and strengthened by his ties to Addams, a Quaker and pacifist. Thus in 1915, before the United States entered the war, Addams (1915) invited Mead (1915) to participate in a major issue of *The Survey*, which both of them supported as associates of and authors of the magazine, on peaceful ends to the war in Europe.

Once the United States entered the fray, however, the two friends fundamen-tally parted. Mead abandoned his international pacifism: his ideas and world underwent a dramatic change. In terms of his family, Mead made pain-racking sacrifices during the war because his son and his beloved daughter-in-law were in the European war zones. His only child Henry served in the military and was wounded and his daughter-in-law Irene Tufts Mead served as a caretaker for French children orphaned by the violence ('5 Women Sent by Chicago Will Save War Babies' 1917).[2] In addition, his wife and several of his female relatives were active members of the Women's International League of Peace and Freedom (WILPF; originally called the International Congress of Women), founded by Addams and others in 1915 (Deegan 1999, 2003), that Mead did not support during the war.

Mead, moreover, experienced and loved Germany during his personally and intellectually formative years as a graduate student. Thus, he was drawn to Germany because he received postgraduate training there, was fluent in German and had German family members (Deegan 1999, 2001, 2008). Mead's writings on war and peace include his critiques of other theorists of the state, such as Thomas Hobbes, Jean-Jacques Rousseau and Karl Marx. Mead directly connects their analyses with his theory of democracy (Deegan 2008). Mead employed scientific theory in order to improve society through the generation of 'working hypotheses' (Mead 1899) or the more sweeping process of 'social reconstruction', which emerged as a major theme in Mead's writings on war (see also Dewey 1920). His writings, especially the essays published during his lifetime, are permeated with the development of theoretical concepts, such as the 'self' and the 'generalised other', which have direct impact on historically based, politically engaged, human behaviour (Mead 1910, 1913, 1934, 2001).

Most contemporary sociological textbooks categorise Mead as a 'microsociologist', a theorist definitively concerned with face-to-face and small group interactions. Mead's writings and political commitment that focused on the meaning of war, peace, citizenship, and democracy unequivocally refute such interpretations (see also Mead 1999, 2001). Mead is both a 'micro' and 'macro' sociologist, fundamentally committed to the avoidance of dichotomised analyses. Some sociologists (especially Deegan 1988a, 1992, 1999, 2001; Habermas 1984/1987; Shalin 2011) have long recognised Mead's large-scale, international approach, but this is a minority perspective within the discipline of sociology today.

Because of the posthumous publications of four of Mead's books in the 1930s (Mead 1932, 1934, 1936, and 1938), and sociologists' emphasis on *Mind, Self, and Society* published in 1934,[3] Mead is misclassified, again, as a theorist who emerged during that decade. He is labelled a 'contemporary theorist', therefore, and he is often compared to theorists of the 1930s or 1940s, such as Robert E. Merton, Talcott Parsons and Alfred Schutz who worked and taught in the generations after his death. Mead held his war positions between 1917 and 1921, during the classical era.

Dewey and Chicago symbolic interactionism, 1915–1918

John Dewey, like Mead, was based institutionally in philosophy and education, but Dewey also trained sociologists at the University of Chicago in the 1890s and even trained Robert E. Park at the University of Michigan before that. Dewey, Mead and Addams opposed Woodrow Wilson's war-like and aggressive policies prior to 1915 as part of a well-recognised group called 'internationalists' or 'progressive liberals' (Chatfield 1970). On 17 October 1916, however, Dewey joined a number of other 'progressive liberals', who published a statement reversing their former opposition to Wilson's pro-war statements. Their signed statement appeared in *The New York Times* (Knock 1992:94, 303 n31; Mead did not sign this document). After Wilson declared war in 1917, Dewey quickly became a national figure who represented a supportive war position among the internationalists.

By 1917, Mead shared the majority of Dewey's (1917a, 1917b) positions, and both men split with those opposing the war within this formerly united group. Thus, in July 1917, Dewey wrote: 'we are fighting for democracy ... It seems certain that the Allies will be victorious ... We are fighting to do away with the rule of kings and Kaisers. When we have finished the job we may find that we have done away with the rule of money and trade' (Dewey 1917c/1991:21). Dewey foretold positive changes in capitalism, marriage, the family and women's roles in society as a result of the violent conflict. A year later, Dewey (1918) was arguing that a victory was needed to secure America's liberal ideals. Mead (1918a) expected similar sweeping and positive social results, basing his argument on changes in the welfare state in England and the United States. At the University of Chicago, the male faculty, including the sociologists, became experts and leaders on war and state violence (Boyer 2004; see also Small 1917).

Scholarship on Mead and Dewey on war

Dewey's wartime arguments, usually shared with Mead, are the subject of great controversy (e.g., Bourne 1964; Chatfield 1970; Diggins 1981; Ryan 1995). This debate began with his former students in New York City, led by Randolph S. Bourne (1964). Mead's ideas on war and peace are unexamined in general (for the exception, see Deegan 2008). This is partially due to Blumer's (1969) definition of symbolic interactionism as contemporary, apolitical, micro-level and abstract. Thus, Deweyian scholars define his ideas on this topic as problematic, but most Meadian scholars do not consider Mead's ideas in this area at all. Deweyian scholarship must be, therefore, the focus of interest here, and Mead's work would be the subject of similar critiques.

John Patrick Diggins aptly noted that 'the outbreak of World War I confronted John Dewey's pragmatism with its greatest challenges'. Dewey abandoned his belief in rational intelligence and the scientific method. Dewey interpreted conflict and violence in a new way:

> The war was not only an instrument of integration and socialization; it also compelled the intellectual to reconsider the 'intelligent use of force' in international affairs. The war had dramatized the impotence and 'moral innocency' of the pacifists.
>
> (Diggins 1981:214)

Mead also shared these revised positions, too, and the separation from previous allies.

This reversal in ideas shocked many of Dewey's former students who had become public intellectuals. Thus, Randolph S. Bourne, Dewey's pre-war friend and a liberal pacifist, was shocked and betrayed by Dewey's militant pro-war positions. Bourne (1917) wrote in October 1917 a passionate, widely read article titled 'Twilight of Idols'. Here he articulated his disillusionment with Dewey and those who supported him. Dewey, according to Bourne, was worse than a hero with feet of clay; he was an immoral opportunist. Dewey and Bourne engaged in public debates in *The Nation* and *The New Republic*, and their differing views were widely considered and discussed. Bourne's rapid decline and death from the virulent flu epidemic in 1918 ended their personal confrontations (Bourne 1917, 1964), but not the debates about war and pragmatism in Dewey's corpus.

Alan Cywar (1969) analysed Dewey's combination of patriotism and international progressivism, and Cywar's work clarifies Mead's perspective, too. The male symbolic interactionists believed that good would emerge from the violence: they predicted that bureaucracy, rationality and efficiency would increase. Class conflict in Europe would result and be succeeded by socialist welfare states. The socialist goals would be accomplished as a result of WWI (Cywar 1969:580–581; Mead in Deegan 2008, see chapters 5 and 7). Dewey, however, underestimated the irrationality of war and the unintended consequences of efficiency serving the goals of war.

Both Dewey and Mead argued that German *Kultur* was dualistic. They supported its achievements in religion, music, and science, but not its nativism, sentimentality, arrogance, and domination (Cywar 1969:584). Both men favoured American ways and government, especially their commitment to democracy. They saw a new economic and pacifist international order, but they underestimated the forces of destruction, animosity and control that had been set in motion. Dewey's widely recognised and often-discussed position is echoed in the life and writings of Mead during wartime. For both men, their patriotic nativism broke with their ideas and practices both pre-war and post-war. This is especially true for Dewey who displayed personal and emotional upheavals. Dewey is portrayed frequently as an unusually even-tempered, somewhat boring, person in terms of his affect. He is analysed as an upright and repressed New Englander, especially in descriptions of his sleep-inducing lectures. During the war, however, Dewey's demeanour changed and he displayed a far from staid image. Two indicators of his emotional turmoil are his poetry and his emotional attraction to a talented and volatile Polish immigrant, Anzia Yezierska (1932). Dewey had written poetry privately for many years, but he captured his emotional upsets during the war in his now published poetry (Dearborn 1988). JoAnne Boydston in her introduction to a volume of his poems (Dewey 1977) ably recounts the bizarre stories of intrigue over collecting these poems that Dewey had discarded.

Dewey started pulling back from many of his wartime positions shortly before the end of the war in November 1918, but Mead did not. When Mead's son and daughter-in-law were in Europe, Mead was leading the Chicago City Club (CCC) as a wartime leader and teaching a course on war at the university. Mead gradually became less oriented to war and resumed his original positions on peace during the 1920s. Mead rarely explicitly discussed these changes although he did write in 1929 that Wilson misled Americans about the sinking of the Lusitania. Mead criticised America's perfidy in secretly carrying arms to the British while declaring the Germans as aggressors against innocent civilians on the ship (Mead 1929b). While Dewey and Mead had been affected by war fever, women in Chicago remained true to the vision of international pacifism.

The female world in Chicago during and after World War I

Addams and the female peace tradition emerged from a vibrant female world found in women's clubs, social settlements, the academy and families. Over a hundred women supported and developed international pacifism during and after the Great War.[4] This female world was rooted in gendered friendship patterns found in the 18th and 19th centuries in the United States and elaborated into more modern formats in the 20th century in Chicago and in pockets around the world, especially in cities.

In a previous study of the correspondence shared by two feminist symbolic interactionists, Marion Talbot and Sophonisba Breckinridge, I documented how their work emerged from 'the Chicago female world of love and ritual' and its union of activism, feminism, intellectual labour and emotions (Deegan 1996a). I drew upon the work of Carroll Smith-Rosenberg (1975:1) who studied 'the female friendship of the nineteenth century, the long-lived, intimate, loving friendship between two women … [these] deeply felt, same-sex friendship were casually accepted in American society … from at least the late eighteenth century through the mid-nineteenth century'. She called the pattern of such friendships 'the female world of love and ritual'. Supportive networks 'were institutionalized in social conventions or rituals which accompanied virtually every important event in a woman's life, from birth to death' (Smith-Rosenberg 1975:9). This world was emotionally dense and complex including devotion to and love of other women and traditional, cooperative female values.

Smith-Rosenberg's subjects led relatively obscure lives, married and lived in patriarchal families mainly in the Northeastern and Southern United States. In contrast, the female feminist symbolic interactionists typically (1) were unmarried; (2) lived in Chicago; (3) were long-time intimate friends; (4) lived together in female-headed homes, social settlements or in college/university dormitories; (5) were powerful political and intellectual leaders; and (6) were part of the world of Chicago pragmatism. The women supported the female values of nurturance and cooperation and stressed the importance of families and the home.

The Chicago women created a new model of friendship that creatively extended the earlier, much less public and less publicly powerful friendship patterns of the 18th and 19th centuries described by Smith-Rosenberg. The Chicago female world of love and ritual is a distinctive American ritual based on the liminal status of professional women from the 1890s to the 1930s (Deegan 1989, 1995, 1998).

It was based institutionally in the academy and social settlement and was integral to the formation of sociology as a profession in general and symbolic interactionism in particular.

This female world was not only gendered and associated with Chicago pragmatism, but it attracted international pacifists globally who were opposed to militarism. As a cooperative theory, strongly influenced by Quaker thought, especially through Addams, Kelley, the Abbott sisters Grace and Edith, and Emily Green Balch, the Chicago female world of love and ritual became the foundation for WILPF and the growing worldwide resistance to state violence (Addams 1907, 1922/1960, 1930, 1976; Addams, Balch and Hamilton 1915/2003; Deegan 2003; Schott 1993). Thus, Addams's pacifism was adopted outside of the academy by the hundreds of thousands of women in WILPF who were organised through the feminist symbolic interactionists allied with Hull-House. These members of WILPF have made pacifist symbolic interactionism a global force for social change for over a century.

The female perspective on international pacifism before and during World War I

Addams was an internationalist who stressed the need to develop newer ideals and world consciousness as an interconnected system (Addams 1907, 1930). Her constant campaigns against American belligerence and militarism appeared in her speeches, testimony before government hearings, and many essays and books. Some of her most significant writings discussed her belief in the newer ideals of peace (Addams 1907), her experiences as a 'pacifist in wartime' (Addams 1917a, 1922/1960, 1930), and her insightful analyses of the fundamental connections between 'peace and bread' (Addams 1922/1960) and a growing 'world consciousness' (Addams 1930). These ideas and texts are particularly important in the establishment of women's international pacifism.

Addams's (1928, 1931, 1976) work for peace was grounded in the non-violent theories of William Lloyd Garrison (1904/1924), Leo Tolstoy (1910/1928) and Mahatma Gandhi (1928/1954). Addams was part of the American tradition of 'non-resistance' articulated first by the abolitionist Garrison, and then adopted by the Russian pacifist Tolstoy (1904/1924), and then by the Indian pacifist and spiritual leader Gandhi. She followed these men's lives, practices, protests and implementation of non-violent, radical opposition to wrongs perpetuated by the community and the state. In addition to her focus on women, she was integral to the American tradition of non-resistance in race relations, drawing on her Quaker background; the domestic abolitionism of her family; and work for social justice for the poor, the immigrant, the child and the elderly (Deegan 2002).

Addams analysed worldwide traditions of peace. She understood the importance of working with one's hands and creating food: for example, she analysed 'bread labour', a concept developed by Russian intellectuals and practised by Tolstoy. Addams (1910, 1917b, 1928, 1931) read Tolstoy throughout her life, even using his writings in study groups at Hull-House. Because Addams has been rarely characterised as a scholar, and because Tolstoy's ideas were ones she struggled to understand, modified and at times criticised, the influence of his underlying vision on her has been greatly underestimated (for an exception to this statement, see Cracraft 2012). Addams extended her commitment to pacifism that she had shared with Mead and Dewey before 1914 and spent the remainder of her life from 1914 to 1935 with a primary focus on worldwide peace (Deegan 2016). By 1918, Addams and the men were repairing the damage to their joint work ruptured through global, state-sponsored violence.

Pacifism and symbolic interactionism post World War I, 1918–1945

At the end of the war, both Mead and Dewey regretted much of their wartime fervour and ultimately came closer to the view of the feminist symbolic interactionists. Mead had a shorter path to follow than Dewey did, but both men abandoned the vitriolic and aggressive rhetoric that they had adopted during wartime. Ironically, Dewey (1945a, 1945b, 1946) became a pacifist after the war and adopted this position even during World War II (Howlett 1977), but Mead never clarified this position on non-violence as clearly as Dewey did. The women's values, analyses and culture pointed to a new way to conceptualise cooperation, the unity of people around the world and the need for more peacemaking. In fact, the women's pre-war cultural feminism, a major theory and practice that interacted with the men's pre-war pragmatism, generated a new branch of thought, feminist pragmatism (e.g., Deegan 1987b, 1988a, 1991, 1996a, 1996b, 1999, 2007a, 2007b, 2014a, 2014b). This female perspective on symbolic interactionism emerged from a shared community based on the interaction of cultural feminism and pragmatism after a confrontation with global war and its aftermath.

By the 1920s, both Mead and Dewey had renewed their appreciation of the women's values, analyses and culture. Both Mead and Dewey reassessed their commitments to democracy; internationalism; world unity, especially with Germany and other former 'enemy states'; the role of war fever to rationalise state violence; and their understanding of human values and value-neutral science. Mead, in particular, wrote differently during the war about impulses, Marxism and social reconstruction, and this set of wartime ideas opposed his post-war theory and praxis. In many ways, he returned to his pre-war international pacifism. But he was shocked that the Versailles Treaty was harsh and unfair, a punitive pact that would never end war. WWI was not a war for democracy as he and Dewey had argued, and their behaviour during the war was neither wholly rational nor logical. Dewey changed his ideas and practices even before the war ended, but Mead continued to struggle with applying his wartime ideas until 1921.

In 1923 Dewey combined his pacifist ideas with children's education for peace and citizenship (Dewey 1923). He used many concepts of Mead, such as 'social consciousness' (Mead 1910), 'mind' and 'intelligence' to discuss the formation of a new way of thinking about cooperation and the school. Dewey wanted a worldwide, cultural revolution that rejected adherence to the single nation-state and advocated social connections with others as neighbours and friends, drawing on Addams's notions of neighbourliness as part of a community and social change.

After the war Dewey (e.g., 1945a, 1945b) became more radical politically and adopted a very strong pacifist commitment, especially aligning with Addams's feminist symbolic interactionism. Mead became more abstract, less oriented to political discussions, and less active in social settlement work. Dewey and Mead modified their support of war, with Dewey (Howlett and Cohen 2016) becoming an open pacifist and Mead (1929b) condemning the deceptive practices of President Woodrow Wilson. Mead regretted his war fever and succinctly concluded that 'warfare is an utterly stupid method of settling differences of interest between different nations' (Mead cited in Deegan 2008:290). Once again, he advocated for 'international-mindedness' to form a global society.

When Mead and Dewey split with the feminist pacifists during WWI, this fundamental division on a major issue strained their ties and friendship with Addams. Addams and Dewey needed to repair their significant, public break, while Mead and Addams quietly resumed joint interests such as feeding the hungry in Russia ('The Status of Russian Relief' 1920). Pacifism defined Addams's ideas and practices after the war ended in 1918 until her death in 1935. Addams and Mead supported the establishment of the League of Nations, although Dewey remained suspicious about its effectiveness. Dewey devoted himself to the Outlawry of War movement and to training young minds for peace and citizenship (Howlett and Cohen 2016).

Dewey publicly restored his friendship with Addams (1930), a move she gladly embraced at the fortieth anniversary of Hull-House. After Addams's death, Dewey (1945b) sponsored a symposium praising the 'realism' of Addams's non-violent resistance to war. Most of the symposiums' male scholars were more restrained in their evaluations than Dewey. Dewey (1946) pushed beyond this position when he endorsed the feminist pacifism of Emily Greene Balch, one of Addams's closest intellectual allies on non-violence (Deegan 1996b, 2003). Dewey (1946) became a leader in Balch's nomination for the Nobel Peace Prize, which she was awarded in 1946. Addams and Balch institutionalised their feminist symbolic interactionism through WILPF, which provides a continuing presence in the peace movement around the world.

Although the pacifist foundation for symbolic interaction was entrenched and affirmed after WWI through the largely female effort, the academic scholars and theorists who followed Mead and Dewey after 1937 generally ignored their predecessors' allegiance to peaceful negotiations and arbitration between nations. The 'new' perspective of a sociological pragmatism became more abstract and separated from its epistemology as a politically inspired commitment to liberal values and global work for peace. Addams's centrality to academic symbolic interactionism was erased.

Pacifism and symbolic interactionism, 1937–2018

Pacifism and feminism were integral to the work and political commitments of Addams, Dewey and Mead, but after the rise of 'symbolic interactionism' under the leadership of Herbert Blumer (1969) the white men's perspective was retained but stripped of its roots in social cooperation as a liberal and political enterprise. Even worse, the heritage of Addams and other Chicago women in sociology was buried. Blumer's strong support of Robert E. Park, moreover, brought with it an antipathy toward women as colleagues and a topic of analysis (Deegan 1988a, 1988b, 2006, 2017). The gendered nature of symbolic interactionism was not explored but forgotten. The 'public sociology' underlying symbolic interactionism was disconnected in contemporary practices (Deegan 2014b).

Global efforts towards peace have grown over time, but symbolic interactionists rarely connect with these activities and theories. For example, the most powerful pacifism of the last two decades is the 'pragmatic pacifism' of Gene Sharp (e.g., 1973, 2010) that inspired the revolutions behind the Arab Spring, which spread throughout the Middle East after 2011 (see Nepstad 2015:134–148). Understanding why this 'pragmatic pacifism' is similar to and different from the 'pacifism of pragmatism' is an important, yet unanswered, sociological question. Similarly, Charles F. Howlett and Audrey Cohen (2016) examine how Dewey's pacifist pragmatism can and should be applied in the classroom as a mechanism to change social consciousness and culture throughout the world. Dewey's emphasis on citizenship as a mechanism to learn about peaceful policies echoes that of Addams's (Deegan 2010). Howlett and Cohen's pedagogical article could be used by symbolic interactionists to restore these questions to the canon in sociology, if sociologists chose to do so.

Female symbolic interactionists (not necessarily feminists) were often active in this group, but they, unlike the men, rarely held offices in the American Sociological Association or become national leaders in the discipline. The female cohort at the University of Chicago that graduated between 1945 and 1960, for example, were treated often as 'the second sex' with few tenured faculty positions in powerful universities (Deegan 1995). The male symbolic interactionists, in contrast, held numerous significant positions in professional societies, as recipients of grants, and in prestigious academies. Pacifism was not a major topic for this post-World War II generation.

Feminist symbolic interactionism, nonetheless, has a long tradition after 1937, rising in visibility and influence after the feminist second wave began in the mid-1960s (Deegan and Hill 1987). Few of these feminists traced their ideas to Addams, although this is now occurring with increasing frequency (see Bibliography; Lengermann and Niebrugge-Brantley 1998; McDonald 1994a, 1994b, 1998).[5] Barbara Misztal (2009), for example, has noted the significance of pacifism and the female peace tradition in the work of Addams, Balch and Alva Myrdahl. The autobiography of Lemayah Gbowee (Peace Nobelist 2011; see Gbowee and Mithers 2011) points to her study of Addams and conflict resolution in her leadership of women peacemakers in Liberia and Ghana. Addams's

(1976, 2003), and Addams, Balch and Hamilton's (1915/2003) writings on peace, moreover, have been reprinted and become the focus of renewed study. More contemporary critiques are needed, nonetheless, as we see in this volume on critical and cultural approaches to symbolic interaction.

Conclusion

As this chapter has indicated, America's entry into the Great War (WWI) fundamentally challenged the founders of symbolic interactionism: George Herbert Mead, John Dewey and Jane Addams. Prior to the war, the three friends created an extraordinary American theory of human action and meaning. The men's ideas were called 'Chicago pragmatism' and became the foundation of symbolic interactionism, while Addams's approach became the foundation of feminist symbolic interactionism. Before the war, there was a different emphasis on gender and political action in these two approaches, but the fundamental definitions of the self, the other, democracy and education were held in common. This politically engaged macro- and micro-level theory was rooted in the American experience of democracy, emerging from the core documents of the US Constitution, Bill of Rights and Emancipation Proclamation. During the war, the men supported violence by the nation-state, while Addams developed an increasingly sophisticated theory of non-violence and pacifism, at least partially based on women's culture and values. Through time, Addams honed her ideas and commitment to peace drawing on an American heritage from the Civil War, found in the work of William Lloyd Garrison and Abraham Lincoln, and a global approach created by Leo Tolstoy and Mahatma Gandhi. She successfully institutionalised pacifist symbolic interactionism in the global work for peace anchored in WILPF and the women's peace tradition honoured in several Nobel Peace Prizes.

This chapter aspires to re-introduce the pacifist roots of symbolic interaction in today's contexts. Perhaps there are contemporary pacifist symbolic interactionists who are ready to write about contemporary issues such as nuclear war talk and the introduction of new, smaller, nuclear weapons by numerous nations. Another path to exploring this heritage would be the analysis of many pacifists' writings; for example, the speeches of Martin Luther King Jr. and the writings of Mahatma Gandhi, from a symbolic interactionist perspective. These male pacifists applied non-violence to specific conflicts and used a cooperative model of the self, the other and the nation-state.

The historical and gendered bases for pacifism and symbolic interactionism could be analysed in more depth, as well. Thus students and faculty at the University of Chicago and at Columbia University during and after World War II, for example, could be added to the present analysis. Dozens of female pacifists who adopted the work of Addams through WILPF could show us new connections and insights. The symbolic interactionist roots for work resulting in Nobel Peace Prizes, like that of Leymah Gbowee, could be a fruitful area for future researchers, as well. This chapter points to new areas for critical and political conflict resolutions.

Herbert Blumer's definition of symbolic interactionism moved his followers away from the international pacifism of Mead, Dewey and Addams. Blumer de-emphasised democracy and erased pacifism. Face-to-face, small-group behaviours became the subject of many ethnographies and case studies. New ethnographies of pacifist organisations and people could be combined with this literature to re-integrate pacifist symbolic interactionism into this corpus.

Despite the contemporary, generally apolitical focus of symbolic interactionism, the original vision of the founders of symbolic interactionism has been and remains a factor in a portion of contemporary scholarship, as this anthology and feminist scholars, in particular, document. Research into this alternate path is an exciting possibility for a very different understanding of pacifism, feminism and symbolic interactionism.

Notes

1 Ella Flagg Young was also part of Chicago pragmatism with an emphasis on education. Her work is usually ignored in symbolic interactionist literature.
2 Irene was the daughter of his friend and another Chicago symbolic interactionist James Hayden Tufts, an interconnection of personal and professional ties typical of this world (Deegan 1999).
3 Almost every introductory and theory textbook in sociology presents this view of Meadian thought. Herbert Blumer (1969) popularised this interpretation, and many sociologists who call themselves 'symbolic interactionists' support it. Many others, however, do not and their macrosociological interpretations are ignored systematically in textbooks and sociological journals. This latter analysis of Mead can be found in the work of Joe R. Feagin (2001), Feagin and Vera (2008), Kathy Ferguson (1980), Jürgen Habermas (1984/1987), Dimitri N. Shalin (2011), and my colleagues and myself (e.g., Deegan 1988a, 1999, 2002, 2007b, 2014b; Deegan and Hill 1987).
4 I analyse dozens of these women in a number of publications (e.g., Deegan 1987a, 1987b, 1996a, 1996b, 2002, 2017).
5 Charlene Haddock Seigfried (e.g., 1991, 1996, 2002) and her colleagues and former students are exploring feminism and pragmatism in philosophy.

References

Addams, Jane (1907): *Newer Ideals of Peace*. New York: Macmillan.
Addams, Jane (1909): *The Spirit of Youth and the City Streets*. New York: Macmillan.
Addams, Jane (1910): *Twenty Years at Hull-House*. New York: Macmillan.
Addams, Jane (1915): 'Foreword: War and Social Reconstruction'. *Survey*, 33:603.
Addams, Jane (1917a): 'Patriots and Pacifists in War Time'. *City Club Bulletin*, 10:184–190.
Addams, Jane (1917b): 'Tolstoy and the Russian Soldiers'. *The New Republic*, 12:240–242.
Addams, Jane (1922/1960): *Peace and Bread in Time of War* (introduction by John Dewey). Boston: Hall.
Addams, Jane (1928): 'Tolstoy, Prophet of Righteousness'. *Unity*, 102:11–12.
Addams, Jane (1929): 'A Toast to John Dewey'. *Survey*, 63:203–204.
Addams, Jane (1930): *The Second Twenty Years at Hull-House: With a Record of a Growing World Consciousness*. New York: Macmillan.
Addams, Jane (1931): 'Tolstoy and Gandhi'. *Christian Century*, 48:1485–1488.
Addams, Jane (1976): *Jane Addams on Peace, War and International Understanding, 1899–1932* (edited by Allen F. Davis). New York: Garland Press.

Addams, Jane (2003): *Jane Addams's Writings on Peace*, 4 volumes (edited and with introduction by Marilyn Fischer and Judy D. Whipps). Bristol: Thoemmes Press.

Addams, Jane, Emily G. Balch and Alice Hamilton (1915/2003): *Women at the Hague: The International Congress of Women and Its Results* (with an introduction by Mary Jo Deegan). Amherst, NY: Humanity Books.

Blumer, Herbert (1937): 'Social Psychology', in Emerson P. Schidt (ed.): *Man and Society*. New York: Prentice-Hall, pp. 148–198.

Blumer, Herbert (1969): *Symbolic Interactionism*. Englewood Cliffs, NJ: Prentice Hall.

Bourne, Randolph S. (1917): 'Twilight of Idols'. *Seven Arts*, 2:688–702.

Bourne, Randolph S. (1964): *War and the Intellectuals* (edited by Carl Resek). New York: Harper and Row.

Boyer, John W. (2004): 'Judson's War and Hutchins's Peace: The University of Chicago and War in the Twentieth Century'. *University of Chicago Record*, 38:2–14.

Chatfield, Charles (1970): 'World War I and the Liberal Pacifist in the United States'. *American Historical Review*, 75:1920–1937.

Cracraft, James (2012): *Two Shining Souls: Jane Addams, Leo Tolstoy, and the Quest for Global Peace*. Lanham, MD: Lexington Books.

Cywar, Alan (1969): 'John Dewey in World War I: Patriotism and International Progressivism'. *American Quarterly*, 21:578–594.

Dearborn, Mary V. (1988): *Love in the Promised Land: The Story of Anzia Yezierska and John Dewey*. New York: Free Press.

Deegan, Mary Jo (1987a): 'Women and Symbolic Interactionism', in Mary Jo Deegan and Michael R. Hill (eds.): *Women and Symbolic Interaction*. Winchester, MA: Allen and Unwin, pp. 3–15.

Deegan, Mary Jo (1987b): 'An American Dream: The Historical Connections Between Women, Humanism and Sociology, 1890–1920'. *Humanity and Society* 11:353–365.

Deegan, Mary Jo (1988a): *Jane Addams and the Men of the Chicago School, 1892–1918*. New Brunswick, NJ: Transaction Books.

Deegan, Mary Jo (1988b): 'The Sociology of Herbert Blumer'. North Central Sociological Association. Pittsburgh, Pennsylvania.

Deegan, Mary Jo (1989): *American Ritual Dramas: Social Rules and Cultural Meanings*. Westport, CT: Greenwood Press.

Deegan, Mary Jo (ed.) (1991): *Women in Sociology: A Bio-Bibliographical Sourcebook*. New York: Greenwood Press.

Deegan, Mary Jo (1992): 'The Genesis of the International Self', in Luigi Tomasi (ed.): *Non-European Youth and the Process of Immigration*. Trento: University of Trento, pp. 339–353.

Deegan, Mary Jo (1995): 'The Second Sex and the Chicago School: Women's Accounts, Knowledge and Work, 1945–1960', in Gary Alan Fine (ed.): *A Second Chicago School?* Chicago: University of Chicago Press, pp. 322–364.

Deegan, Mary Jo (1996a): '"Dear Love, Dear Love": Feminist Pragmatism and the Chicago Female World of Love and Ritual'. *Gender & Society*, 10:590–607.

Deegan, Mary Jo (1996b): 'A Very Different Vision of Jane Addams and Emily Greene Balch'. *Journal of Women's History*, 8:121–125.

Deegan, Mary Jo (1998): *American Ritual Tapestry: Social Rules and Cultural Meaning*. Greenwich, CT: Greenwood Press.

Deegan, Mary Jo (1999): 'Play from the Perspective of George Herbert Mead', in George Herbert Mead: *Play, School and Society* (edited by Mary Jo Deegan). New York: Peter Lang, pp. xix–cxii.

Deegan, Mary Jo (2001): 'Introduction: George Herbert Mead's First Book' in George Herbert Mead: *Essays in Social Psychology* (edited and introduction by Mary Jo Deegan). New Brunswick, NJ: Transaction Publishers, pp. xi–xliv.

Deegan, Mary Jo (2002): *Race, Hull-House, and the University of Chicago: A New Conscience Against Ancient Evil*. Westport, CT: Greenwood Press.

Deegan, Mary Jo (2003): 'Introduction', in Jane Addams, Emily Greene Balch and Alice Hamilton: *Women at the Hague: The International Congress of Women and Its Results*. Amherst, NY: Humanity Books, an imprint of Prometheus Press, pp. 11–34.

Deegan, Mary Jo (2006): 'The Human Drama Behind the Study of People as Potato Bugs: The Curious Marriage of Robert E. Park and Clara Cahill Park'. *Journal of Classical Sociology*, 6:101–122.

Deegan, Mary Jo (2007a): 'Jane Addams', in John Scott (ed.): *Fifty Key Sociologists: The Formative Theorists*. London: Routledge, pp. 3–8.

Deegan, Mary Jo (2007b): 'Jane Addams and The American Commission on Conditions in Ireland, 1920-1922'. *Sociological Origins*, 5:29–37.

Deegan, Mary Jo (2008): *Self, War and Society*. New Brunswick, NJ: Transaction Books.

Deegan, Mary Jo (2010): 'Jane Addams on Citizenship in a Democracy'. *Journal of Classical Sociology*, 10:217–238.

Deegan, Mary Jo (2014a): *Annie Marion MacLean and the Chicago Schools of Sociology, 1894–1934*. New Brunswick, NJ: Transaction Publishers.

Deegan, Mary Jo (2014b): 'Hull-House and the Chicago Schools of Sociology: Public and Liberation Sociology on Race, Class, Gender and Peace, 1892–1920', in Jacqueline Low and Gary Bowden (eds.): *The Chicago School Diaspora: Epistemology and Substance*. Montreal: McGill-Queens University Press, pp. 29–46.

Deegan, Mary Jo (2016): 'Jane Addams, the Chicago Schools of Sociology and the Emergence of Symbolic Interaction, 1889–1935', in Gil Richard Musolf (ed.): *The Astructural Bias Charge: Myth or Reality?* (Studies in Symbolic Interaction, Volume 46). Bingley: Emerald Publishing, pp. 57–76.

Deegan, Mary Jo (2017): 'A Twisted Path: Park, Gender, and Praxis', in Peter Kivisto (ed.): *The Anthem Companion to Robert Park*. Thousand Oaks, CA: Sage Publications, pp. 17–36.

Deegan, Mary Jo and Michael R. Hill (eds.) (1987): *Women and Symbolic Interaction*. Boston, MA: Allen and Unwin.

Dewey, John (1899): *School and Society*. Chicago: University of Chicago Press.

Dewey, John (1917a): 'Force, Violence and Law'. *New Republic*, 11. (Reprinted in Jo Ann Boydston (ed.): *John Dewey: Middle Works*, Volume 10 (1916–1917). Carbondale, IL: Southern Illinois University Press, 1980, pp. 211–215.)

Dewey, John (1917b): 'The Future of Pacifism'. *New Republic* 11:358–360. (Reprinted in Jo Ann Boydston (ed.): *John Dewey: Middle Works*, Volume 10 (1916–1917). Carbondale, IL: Southern Illinois University Press, 1980, pp. 265–270.)

Dewey, John (1917c): 'War's Social Results'. *New York World*, 29:1E. (Reprinted in Jo Ann Boydston (ed.): *John Dewey, The Later Works*, Volume 17 (Miscellaneous Writings). Carbondale, IL: Southern Illinois University Press, 1991, pp. 21–25.)

Dewey, John (1918): 'View on "What the War Means to America"'. *Columbia Alumni News*, 9:1002. (Reprinted in Jo Ann Boydston (ed.): *John Dewey, The Later Works*, Volume 17 (Miscellaneous Writings). Carbondale, IL: Southern Illinois University Press, 1991, p. 123.)

Dewey, John (1920): *Social Reconstruction*. New York: Hamilton Holt Co.

Dewey, John (1945a): 'Democratic Versus Coercive International Organization: The Realism of Jane Addams', in Jane Addams: *Peace and Bread in Time of War*. Boston: G. K. Hall & Co., 1922/1960, pp. ix–xx.

Dewey, John (1945b): 'The Theory of International Relations: A Discussion of the Theory of International Relations'. *Journal of Philosophy*, 42:477–478.

Dewey, John (1946): 'Emily Greene Balch – An Appraisal' (Pamphlet). New York: Women's International League of Peace and Freedom.

Dewey, John (1977): *The Poems of John Dewey* (edited and with an introduction by Jo Ann Boydston). Carbondale, IL: Southern Illinois University Press.

Diggins, John Patrick (1981): 'John Dewey in Peace and War'. *American Scholar*, 50:213–230.

Feagin, Joe R. and Hernan Vera (2008): *Liberation Sociology* (2nd edition). Boulder, CO: Paradigm Publishers.

Ferguson, Kathy E. (1980): *Self, Society and Womankind*. Westport, CT: Greenwood Press.

Gandhi, Mahatma (1928/1954): *Satyagraha in South Africa*. Stanford, CA: Academic Reprints.

Garrison, William Lloyd (1904/1924): *William Lloyd Garrison on Non-Resistance*. New York: Nation Press Printing.

Gbowee, Leymah with Carol Mithers (2011): *Mighty Be Our Powers: How Sisterhood, Prayer, and Sex Changed a Nation at War – A Memoir*. New York: Beast Books.

Habermas, Jürgen (1984/1987): *The Theory of Communicative Action*, Volume I–II. Boston: Beacon Press.

Howlett, Charles F. (1977): *Troubled Philosopher: John Dewey and the Struggle For World Peace*. Port Washington, NY: Kennikat Press.

Howlett, Charles F. and Audrey Cohen (2016): 'John Dewey: His Role in Public Scholarship to Educate For Peace'. *HSE – Social and Education History*, 5:203–222.

Huebner, Daniel R. (2014): *Becoming Mead: The Social Process of Academic Knowledge*. Chicago: University of Chicago Press.

JAP (Jane Addams Papers) edited by Mary Lynn McCree Bryan (1985). 82 Microfilm Reels. Microfilming Corporation of America and University Microfilms International.

James, William (1904): 'The Chicago School'. *Psychological Bulletin*, 1:1–5.

James, William (1910/1991): 'The Moral Equivalent of War', in John Whiteclay Chambers (ed.): *The Eagle and the Dove* (2nd edition). Syracuse, NY: University of Syracuse Press, pp. 14–17.

Kloppenberg, James T. (1998): 'Pragmatism', in Morris Dickstein (ed.): *The Revival of Pragmatism*. Durham, NC: Duke University Press, pp. 83–127.

Knock, Thomas J. (1992): *To End All Wars*. Princeton, NJ: Princeton University Press.

Lengermann, Patricia Madoo and Jill Niebrugge-Brantley (eds.) (1998): *The Women Founders: Sociology and Social Theory, 1830–1930*. New York: McGraw-Hill.

McDonald, Lynn (1994a): *The Early Origins of the Social Sciences*. Montreal: McGill-Queen's University Press.

McDonald, Lynn (1994b): *The Women Founders of the Social Sciences*. Ottawa: Carleton University Press.

McDonald, Lynn (1998): *Women Theorists on Society and Politics*. Waterloo: Wilfred Laurier University Press.

Mead, George Herbert (1899): 'The Working Hypothesis in Social Reform'. *American Journal of Sociology*, 5:367–371.

Mead, George Herbert (1907): 'Review of *The Newer Ideals of Peace*'. *American Journal of Sociology*, 13:121–128.

Mead, George Herbert (1910): 'Social Consciousness and the Consciousness of Meaning'. *Psychological Bulletin*, 7:397–405.

Mead, George Herbert 1913): 'The Social Self'. *Journal of Philosophy*, 10:374–380.

Mead, George Herbert (1915): 'The Psychological Bases for Internationalism'. *Survey*, 33:604–607.

Mead, George Herbert (1917a): 'Germany's Crisis – Its Effect on Labor: Part I'. *Chicago Herald* (26 July), p. 4, cols. 4–5.

Mead, George Herbert (1917b): 'Germany's Crisis – Its Effect on Labor: Part II'. *Chicago Herald* (27 July), p. 4, cols. 4–5.

Mead, George Herbert (1917c): 'War Issue to U.S. Forced by Kaiser'. *Chicago Herald* (2 August), p. 4, cols. 4–5.

Mead, George Herbert (1917d): 'America's Ideals and the War'. *Chicago Herald* (3 August), p. 4, cols. 4–5.

Mead, George Herbert (1917e): 'Democracy's Issues in the World War'. *Chicago Herald* (4 August), p. 4, cols. 4–5.

Mead, George Herbert (1917f): 'Camouflage of the Conscientious Objector'. *New York Times* (23 December), p. 56, cols. 1–4.

Mead, George Herbert (1918a): 'Social Work, Standards of Living and the War'. *Proceedings of the National Conference of Social Workers*, 45:637–644.

Mead, George Herbert (1918b): *The Conscientious Objector*. Pamphlet No. 33, Patriotism through Education Series. New York: The National Security League.

Mead George Herbert (1919): 'A Translation of Wundt's *Folk Psychology*'. *American Journal of Theology*, 23:533–536.

Mead George Herbert (1929a): 'Mary E. McDowell'. *Neighborhood*, 2:77–78.

Mead, George Herbert (1929b): 'National-Mindedness and International-Mindedness'. *International Journal of Ethics*, 39:385–407.

Mead, George Herbert (1932): *The Philosophy of the Present* (edited and with an introduction by Arthur E. Murphy). Chicago: University of Chicago Press.

Mead, George Herbert (1934): *Mind, Self and Society* (edited and with an introduction by Charles Morris). Chicago: University of Chicago Press.

Mead, George Herbert (1936): *Movements of Thought in the Nineteenth Century* (edited and with an introduction by Merritt H. Moore). Chicago: University of Chicago Press.

Mead, George Herbert (1938): *The Philosophy of the Act* (edited and with an introduction by Charles W. Morris). Chicago: University of Chicago Press.

Mead, George Herbert (1999): *Play, School and Society* (edited and with an introduction by Mary Jo Deegan). New York: Peter Lang.

Mead, George Herbert (2001): *Essays in Social Psychology* (edited and with an introduction by Mary Jo Deegan). New Brunswick, NJ: Transaction Publishers.

Misztal, Barbara A. (2009): 'A Nobel Trinity: Jane Addams, Emily Greene Balch and Alva Myrdal'. *American Sociologist*, 40:332–353.

Nepstad, Sharon Erickson (2015): *Nonviolent Struggle: Theories, Strategies, and Dynamics*. New York: Oxford University Press.

Rucker, Darnell (1969): *The Chicago Pragmatists*. Minneapolis: University of Minnesota Press.

Ryan, Alan (1995): *John Dewey and the High Tide of American Liberalism*. New York: W.W. Norton.

Schott, Linda (1993): 'Jane Addams and William James on Alternative to War'. *Journal of the History of Ideas*, 54:241–254.

Seigfried, Charlene Haddock (1991): 'Where Are All the Feminist Pragmatists?' *Hypatia*, 6:1–19.

Seigfried, Charlene Haddock (1996): *Pragmatism and Feminism: Reweaving the Social Fabric*. Chicago, IL: University of Chicago Press.

Seigfried, Charlene Haddock (1998): 'John Dewey's Pragmatist Feminism', in Larry Hickman (ed.): *Reading Dewey: Interpretations for a Postmodern Generation*, Bloomington, IN: Indiana University Press, pp. 187–216.

Seigfried, Charlene Haddock (ed.) (2002): *Feminist Interpretations of John Dewey*. University Park, PA: Pennsylvania State University Press.

Shalin, Dimitr N. (2011): *Pragmatism & Democracy*. New Brunswick, NJ: Transaction Publishers.

Sharp, Gene (1973): *The Politics of Nonviolent Action*, Volume 1–2. Boston: Porter-Sargent.

Sharp, Gene (2010): *From Dictatorship to Democracy* (4th edition). Boston: The Albert Einstein Institution.

Small, Albion W. (1917): 'Americans and the World Crisis'. *American Journal of Sociology*, 23:145–173.

Smith-Rosenberg, Carroll (1975): 'The Female World of Love and Ritual'. *Signs*, 1:1–29.

'The Status of Russian Relief' (1920). *Survey*, 44 (26 June), p. 431.

Tolstoy, Leo (1904/1924): 'What I Owe to Garrison', in *William Lloyd Garrison on Non-Resistance*. New York: Nation Press Printing, pp. 46–55.

Tolstoy, Leo (1910/1928): 'Letter Written by Tolstoy to Gandhi, Two Months Before His Death'. *Unity*, 102:21–22.

Weber, Max (1947): *The Theory of Social and Economic Organization* (edited and with an introduction by Talcott Parsons). New York: Free Press.

Yezierska, Anzia (1932): *All I Could Never Be*. New York: Brewer, Warren and Putnam.

7 Towards a feminist symbolic interactionism

Sherryl Kleinman and Emily R. Cabaniss

Introduction

American sociologists have caricatured symbolic interactionism (SI) as psychologistic or as having an astructural bias (see Musolf 2016). Perhaps it is the indeterminism in SI; every person is capable of responding rather than merely reacting to situations, others and ourselves, thereby undermining social scientific claims to prediction. Maybe it is because SI makes its social psychology explicit – how individuals develop selves through society – rather than hiding it. Or maybe it is because practitioners focus on social process and interaction rather than reify structure. But, as David R. Maines (1977:235) argues, 'there is nothing inherent in the perspective that precludes the analysis of social organization'. Symbolic interactionists do not evade the social, but look for patterns and social arrangements – what Herbert Blumer (1969) called 'obdurate reality'. SI analyses what people do together (Becker 1986) as members of groups, settings or social categories.

Our purpose in this chapter is not so much to critique SI but to see what a feminist SI (FSI) would add to understanding social phenomena. As the first author noted elsewhere, becoming a feminist fieldworker did not lead her to abandon interactionist concerns; instead, she linked them to 'the reproduction of inequality, including sexism, racism, heterosexism and class inequality' (Kleinman 2007:2). The feminist perspective we are talking about is grounded in the ideas of feminist philosopher Marilyn Frye, who uses the metaphor of a birdcage to describe the systematic oppression of women:

> Consider a birdcage. If you look very closely at just one wire in a birdcage, you cannot see the other wires … There is no physical property of any one wire, nothing that the closest scrutiny could discover, that will reveal how a bird could be inhibited or harmed by it except in the most accidental way. It is only when you step back, stop looking at the wires one by one, microscopically, and take a macroscopic view of the whole cage, that you can see why the bird does not go anywhere; and then you see it in a moment … [T]he bird is surrounded by a network of systematically related barriers, no one of which would be the least hindrance to its flight, but which, by their relations to each other, are as confining as the solid walls of a dungeon.

(Frye 1983:4–5)

And there are multiple birdcages (all the *-isms*); feminist symbolic interactionists have studied how people reproduce two or more of those systems at the same time.

Frye's birdcage metaphor points to what an older generation of feminists called 'patriarchy' (Lerner 1986; Walby 1990). Allan Johnson (2014:41) defines patriarchy as 'a system of inequality organized around culturally created gender categories'. Under patriarchy, men hold most positions of power and authority (male-domination); men and manhood are associated with core cultural values about what is normal, standard or good (male-identification); and attention is paid throughout the society to men and what men are doing (male-centeredness). For Johnson, patriarchy is not an antiquated concept but a necessary one for understanding contemporary societies (see also Enloe 2017). FSI would study patriarchy as both condition and process.

There are multiple feminisms (Johnson 2014:92–124). Some of these streams of feminist thought reflect a narrow, sometimes superficial view of gender inequality, while others are more radical, in that they problematise fundamental aspects of social reality. Liberal feminism, for example, tends to restrict its attention to legal barriers to women's political, civic and economic equality with men, while leaving capitalism and white supremacy unexamined. Likewise, cultural feminism tends to focus on how women are disadvantaged by the lower value placed on emotion, nurturing, child raising and peacemaking – practices historically associated with women and 'femininity'. In this chapter, we embrace a more radical feminist view.

Just as there is no single feminism, there is no single radical feminism. Marxist feminism, materialist feminism, socialist feminism and black feminism can all be called radical feminisms. What characterises these perspectives is attention to domination based not only on gender but also race and class. Understanding women's subordination, each of these perspectives holds, requires looking at multiple systems of inequality simultaneously. Radical feminism is, in a word, intersectional. It is also concerned not only with laws and cultural values but with how those laws and values are created and reproduced through everyday practices that have the intended and unintended consequences of subordinating women in multiple domains of social life. These practices are the wires of Frye's birdcage.

FSI has a clear affinity for radical feminism, though without implying a commitment to analytically privileging capitalism, economic exploitation, or race/racism. The affinity derives from SI's focus on everyday practices, taken-for-granted meanings, and the consequences of face-to-face encounters for reinforcing privilege and oppression, including radical feminism's focus on the pervasiveness and multi-dimensionality of gender inequality. FSI also suits the goals of intersectional analysis, potentially yielding insight into how economic exploitation is tied to subordination based on gender and race – and vice versa. As other symbolic interactionists have argued (e.g., Schwalbe 2016), the big 'structures' of social life – patriarchy, capitalism, white supremacy, etc. – must be understood as rooted in the practices of everyday life. This analytic focus on getting-to-the-root-of-things makes FSI radical and makes a generic radical feminism a suitable partner for symbolic interactionists seeking to analyse gender inequality.

We begin the chapter by distinguishing between conventional symbolic interactionist and feminist symbolic interactionist analyses of *meaning and mundane reality, agency* and *emotions.* We then discuss *intersectionality* (Crenshaw 1991; Hill Collins 2000) in more detail, pointing out how the concept has been used in other studies and how FSI can deepen our understanding of how systems of inequality are linked. Some of these studies, we argue, have made use of symbolic interactionist principles without claiming the interactionist label (see Fine 1993). We conclude with a discussion of our scepticism about previous symbolic interactionist work that has been called feminist.

From symbolic interactionism to feminist interactionism

Meaning and mundane reality

SI posits that 'every action, mundane or dramatic, has meaning for those who engage in it' (Kleinman 1996:10). To understand how members of groups or social categories feel, think, and act, we must learn their perspective (Blumer 1969; Thomas and Thomas 1928). Which objects – including people – are significant to them? What do those objects mean? How did those meanings come to be? Answering these questions requires paying attention to mundane reality, 'observing what goes on in social life under one's nose' (Blumer 1969:50).

For interactionists, meanings are not personal or unique, but social; symbols are necessarily shared and realised in interaction. Even the monk on the mountaintop has learned what 'monk' conveys to members of the in-group and those outside it. The individual has learned to find a way, through interaction with others and the symbols associated with 'monkhood', to become that person. Some may try to dissuade the individual from taking on that identity or have different ideas about how to live as a monk. The monk-to-be thinks and responds, but thinking is only possible with language (symbols), and what one responds to is other people, whether in interaction, reading, anticipating others' responses and so on. In the public imagination as well as in practice, 'monk' signifies an ascetic man, not a woman. The social is there in every step.

Symbolic interactionists also study how social arrangements and beliefs (meanings) make it difficult for people to imagine that things could be otherwise. Fieldworkers pay attention to such phrases as 'it has always been this way' or 'it's tradition'. These reifications become clear when a newcomer breaks a rule and others in the setting have a bad reaction to it. Only then do we hear participants say 'this isn't how things are done around here'. What kinds of problems do people face in their position or setting for which their perspective provides a solution? For example, Howard S. Becker (1993) found that medical students used the word 'crock' to refer to patients who presented a lot of symptoms, but from which students felt they could learn little.

In addition, stasis and change are not assumptions, but *empirical questions* for SI: What are the conditions under which change becomes possible? One can study the 'mundanity' of what people do together to keep things the same or work on effecting change, including what participants consider success or failure.

FSI recognises that gender inequality is part of mundane reality and occurs when people take the path of least resistance. Despite having choices, however limited, 'all of these paths vary in how much social resistance we'd run into if we followed them, with the odds loaded toward those paths with the *least*' (Johnson 2018:69). Men often discover, for instance, that it is easier to go along with a male friend's sexist remarks than risk ostracism, thereby sustaining men's dominance through inaction. Men who bond by talking about harassing or assaulting women may later trivialise it as 'locker-room' talk, bravado or joking around.

Like all systems of inequality, patriarchy is continually lived out as people interact in patterned ways in everyday life. For example, in a patriarchal gender order, electoral politics is accepted as the proper purview of men. To maintain that view, men (and some women) have long claimed that women are not tough or decisive enough to be good leaders. At the same time, men have used the ambitions of women who seek political power as evidence that they are not proper women. During the 2008 American presidential campaign, for instance, Sarah Palin and Hilary Clinton were popularly characterised as 'the ditz' and 'the bitch' respectively (Fortini 2008). Whether studying sexist language that makes women invisible (e.g., 'you guys', 'freshmen', 'chairman') (Kleinman 2002), male temp workers whose bosses and co-workers treat as deserving of full-time 'real jobs' when compared to female temps (Henson and Rogers 2001), men's sexual harassment of women in the streets or workplace (Benard and Schlaffer 1997; Giuffre and Williams 1994; Quinn 2002), fraternities and rape on campuses (Boswell and Spade 1996), middle-class student volunteers' efforts to see themselves as 'doing good' while enforcing rules at a homeless shelter (Holden 1997; see also Rogers 2017), or parents' approval of their 'tomboyish' daughters breaking gender norms by engaging in 'rough and tumble' play but disapproval of their young sons acting in any way 'like a girl' (Kane 2006:157), feminist interactionists examine how privilege and subordination play out in everyday life.

Feminists, like interactionists, treat meaning as social, but we have an explicit interest in understanding how meanings and organisational arrangements reproduce or challenge power relations (McIntosh 1988; Hill Collins 2000). For example, in their meta-analysis of qualitative articles on the reproduction of inequality, Michael L. Schwalbe and his colleagues (2000) identified four generic processes: othering, boundary maintenance, emotion management and subordinate adaptation. Members of dominant groups seek to hold onto their power by defining into existence an inferior group – usually for the purposes of exploiting or excluding them ('othering'); maintaining control over valued resources (material and symbolic) and keeping subordinates from accessing them ('boundary maintenance'); and by 'conditioning emotional subjectivit[ies]' (Schwalbe et al. 2000:426) that reinforce inequality and discourage dissent ('emotion management'). Subordinates may respond to oppression by developing subcultures (Fine and Kleinman 1979) that support the principles of equality for all, or adapt in ways that undermine solidarity, create internal divisions and obscure inequality.

Using the strategy of 'subordinate adaptation', members of oppressed groups distance themselves from the social category to which they belong by insisting, 'there are indeed Others to whom this [negative stereotype] applies, but it does not apply to me' (Schwalbe et al. 2000:425). Women who enjoy being 'one of the guys' will laugh at men's sexist jokes, believing that the jokes refer to *other* women, not them. The person in the subordinate category becomes an exception, giving tacit legitimacy to the stigma of the group as a whole. Similarly, when subordinates 'trade power for patronage' (Schwalbe et al. 2000:426), they give up the fight for equality and settle for the perks that come from accommodating the dominant group's desires. A member of an oppressed group may benefit individually from these adaptive responses, but she or he simultaneously reinforces the ideology that casts their group as inferior. The individual gain is also a collective loss (see Copp and Kleinman 2008).

Feminist interactionists study internalised oppression – how oppressed people come to see themselves from the perspective of dominants: 'All systems of oppression not thoroughly coerced through brute force and overt repression involve the dominant group's ability to win consent of the oppressed' (Pyke 2010:556). As feminist philosopher Sandra Bartky (1990:23) wrote, when psychological oppression has become institutionalised and systematic, 'it serves to make the work of domination easier by breaking the spirit of the dominated and by rendering them incapable of understanding the nature of those agencies responsible for their subjugation'. A key way hierarchy is maintained is through the use of 'controlling images' that ideologically ensnare subordinates in narrow stereotypes and mask the exploitative activities of dominants (Hill Collins 2000:69). Some Asian Americans, for instance, embrace the 'model minority' stereotype – an image created and disseminated by white elites to deflect attention from systemic racism – because it implies that they are morally upstanding, smart and hard-working, unlike other racially oppressed groups, especially blacks. Asian Americans who refuse to challenge the connection between this image and racism may be treated as 'honorary whites' (Chou and Feagin 2016), but they will still be demoted when it is in the interest of white elites: The United States government's internment of Japanese Americans during WWII is a case in point.

When subordinates internalise mainstream (sexist, racist or classist) messages/meanings about oppressed groups, they – often unintentionally – reinforce that oppression (Hill Collins 2000; Pyke 2010). With internalised sexism, women unconsciously reinforce their subordinate position *as women* (women can, of course, be privileged or oppressed by class, race, sexual orientation and so on). 'The positionings of the subjugated', Donna Haraway asserts, 'are not exempt from critical reexamination' (Haraway 1988:584). FSI, then, does not simply give voice to oppressed groups. It asks how subordinated groups come to interpret things as they do and what their joint actions reproduce or challenge. Matthew Ezzell (2009), for example, found that female college rugby players responded to their subordinated status as women and the stigma tied to their violation of conventional gender norms by resisting *and* accommodating those norms. By playing rugby, one of the few collegiate sports with the same rules for male and female teams, female players challenged the belief that women cannot compete in an aggressive sport. At the same time, they adopted defensive othering strategies that distanced them from 'typical' college women (considered too weak to play) and emphasised their similarities with men (the dominant group). Yet because the women identified as heterosexual and wanted men to desire them, they over-played a sexualised presentation of self off the field, especially in relation to male rugby players, their main dating pool.

Feminists not only seek to study the sense-making strategies of oppressed groups. To understand social harm (Kleinman and Copp 2009), we also examine how groups whose privileges and power shield them from scrutiny operate. Gatekeepers make it difficult to 'study up', but fieldworkers should keep trying. To that end, feminist interactionists study the conscious and unconscious sexist behaviours of men. How, for instance, do men who espouse egalitarian values unwittingly reinforce inequal-ity? Kris Macomber (2018) found that men involved in the movement to end men's violence against women received more praise and public attention than female pio-neers. Although the men spoke publicly about the need to defer to feminist women, especially those who started the movement, behind the scenes they rarely addressed male privilege or held each other accountable for sexist practices in the movement. Under patriarchy, even well-intentioned, pro-feminist men have a vested interest in maintaining the privileges of manhood (Schwalbe 2014).

Agency

In symbolic interactionism, agency is a given. As George Herbert Mead (1934) and Herbert Blumer (1969) argued, becoming human is a movement toward self-reflexivity: a child learns, through interaction, to see herself as an object that she can reflect on and respond to. That process involves 'play' (perspective-taking of one child at a time); 'game' (organised play in which children learn how play-ers in multiple positions cooperate, as in softball); and developing a conscience through taking the perspective of the community (the 'generalised other') (Mead 1934). Socialised beings also have an 'I' – the individual can respond to what she is thinking about, what is going on around her, and can anticipate others' reac-tions. Inner conversations between the 'I' (individual sense-making) and the 'me' (social expectations) can lead to conformity, change or resignation. But without primary socialisation (childhood) and secondary (adult) socialisation (Berger and Luckmann 1966), the person would have nothing to reflect on and respond to and thus no basis for the self. Self and society, then, are two sides of the same coin, and the ability for self-reflexivity constitutes agency.

As Mary Jo Deegan (1987:6) has argued, Mead's pragmatism was 'an optimis-tic, and very American, view of the world'. Mead construed the generalised other as positive, with the internalised community keeping individuals from engaging in untoward behaviours. FSI, however, recognises that the generalised other is patriarchal and that gendered beings' agency is shaped by power relations. Instead of accepting agency as an assumption and moving on, feminist symbolic interactionists study how unequal social arrangements, especially patriarchy, constrain and shape thoughts, words, and actions. How is our subjectivity conditioned by patriarchal expectations? In what ways do women and men respond to unequal social circumstances? And what are the consequences – for systems of privilege and oppression – of those responses?

Under conditions of inequality, subordinates learn to see themselves as dominants see them. If subordinates internalise (rather than reject) these images, they experience not only self-doubt but false power – enjoying practices that fit with dominants' expectations (Kleinman, Copp and Sandstrom 2006). This is especially so for women (under patriarchy), given the denial of sexism in the broader culture (Johnson 2014) and the presence of compulsory heterosexuality (Rich 1980). Seen through a patriarchal lens, 'women are either fuckable or invisible' (Gail Dines quoted in Tarrant 2010). Being invisible is existentially threatening, so it is not surprising that so many women acquiesce to gendered expectations about appearance, speech patterns and more. Women learn to buy products (varying by class) that keep us attractive to men while also learning we can never measure up (Bartky 1990). We learn to 'put on our faces', wear high heels, smile at men and put other women down. Yes, women exercise agency by engaging in these behaviours, but what are the consequences of putting agency to this use for *women as a group*? A feminist analysis would show us that making these choices impedes solidarity among women and masks patriarchy.

As bell hooks (1989:130) taught us, sexism is the only form of oppression in which subordinates are meant to *love* their oppressors. Patriarchy persists, in part, because women are conditioned to enjoy and go along with practices that subordinate them, even at times when they favour sexual relations with women. Our female college students tell us they like receiving free drinks on 'Ladies Night', though the real offer is for *men* looking for sex with women; the drunker she is, the easier to manipulate. Women are taught to feel flattered by men's acts of 'chivalry', and depending on the circumstances, 'cat calls', though such acts reinforce the idea that women need men to protect or affirm them. Women learn to feel special when men initiate dates, drive and pay for expenses – even though these practices put the man in control (making it seem 'natural' for men to direct women), imply that women need not have money to pay for themselves (indirectly reinforcing the wage gap), make it harder for a woman to exit the date (he drove) and may lead men to expect sexual rewards in return. Challenging inequality is more difficult if subordinates have been conditioned to believe practices such as these make them happy (see Ahmed 2010).

Men's assertions of agency are also conditioned by patriarchy; they learn to interrupt women, to expect sexual access to them, and that it is natural to dominate women and lower-status men (Schwalbe 2014). Engaging in manhood acts or resisting 'being a man' (Jensen 2017) are both agentic. For FSI, the key question is: What are people using their agency *for*?

Eroticising domination and subordination also keeps relations of inequality in place (Bindel 2017) – even when those relations are 'reversed'. For example, in her research on a BDSM community, Danielle Lindemann (2012) found that 'dominatrices' (women who assume a dominant sexual role), often experienced a heightened sense of power in their immediate interactions with male submissives. Those *feelings* of empowerment, however, did not lead to higher status or respect outside the BDSM subcommunity. Similarly, Bernadette Barton's (2017) research on strip clubs in the United States showed that men who pay women to strip or lapdance gave women a temporary feeling of control over men; disempowerment in the rest of their lives continued. Even on the scene, women became depressed, feeling unattractive if men chose other women for lap dancing. Strippers also worried about men following them home, highlighting the difference between false power and real power. The much smaller pool of men who strip for women rarely have such problems; a man who strips to get through college is unlikely to suffer if the interviewer for admission to medical school recognises him. It might be amusing, but not damaging. Men, after all, become players, not sluts.

Recognising false power is quite different from symbolic interactionists who adopt, as 'analysis', whatever participants tell them about inequality ('I enjoy being sexually submissive'; 'we share the housework') (e.g., Newmahr 2006, 2011; Harris 2001). In FSI, accounts are treated as data (Kleinman and Kolb 2011), grist for critical analysis. Some have argued (Avishai, Gerber and Randles 2013; Harris 2001) that analysing rather than accepting the desires, accounts and practices of oppressed people denies or insults their agency. What, then, might an FSI approach to agency look like? Feminist interactionists 'can examine whether we are accepting the culturally common way of construing agency as 'personal choice'' (Kleinman 2007:80). We should instead examine 'where those choices come from as well as what they reinforce' (Kleinman 2007:80). For instance, young women in a 'goth' community said they found their uninhibited sexuality and non-monogamy 'empowering' and egalitarian (Wilkins 2008). Yet the women's investment in romance made it hard for them to recognise a sexual double standard among goths that benefited the men and devalued women's sexual agency. If a goth man's female partner had sex with a woman, he found it acceptable or exciting; if she became sexually involved with another man, he often baulked. As Shira Lipkin (2013) wrote: 'Girls don't count'.

For members of subordinate groups, asserting agency also requires navigating double binds. Any action has negative consequences:

> Women are caught ... by networks of forces and barriers that expose one to penalty, loss or contempt whether one works outside the home or not, is on welfare or not, bears children or not, raises children or not, marries or not, stays married or not, is heterosexual, lesbian, both or neither.
>
> (Frye 1983:140–141)

Women's clothing is deemed overly sexualised or dowdy and unfeminine, our actions as aggressive (unwomanly) or ladylike (too delicate for work). In 'hookup culture' on American college campuses, students often treat sex as a game (Wade 2017), one that women lose whether they play or opt out (i.e., however they use their capacity for agency). Women who reject pressure to have casual sex – by refusing to have sex at all – lose the opportunity to explore their sexuality; yet women in hookups earn bad reputations, particularly among heterosexual men.

In sum, an FSI perspective on agency examines what people do or fail to do that reinforces or challenges patriarchy and other systems of privilege and oppression. Women may feel empowered by engaging in practices associated with femininity (complimenting or criticising each other as they dress for going out) or acting in subordinate or dominant ways in sexual relations with men or women. But, 'patriarchal complicity', Cynthia Enloe (2017:164) reminds us, 'is not the same as patriarchal power'. Men may feel disempowered if they do not live up to expectations for manhood, but they still retain male privilege and may engage in compensatory manhood or critique manhood and become pro-feminist. For FSI, examining how women and men learn to engage in practices that sustain or challenge hierarchy is the goal. That subordinates experience some practices as celebrations of 'agency' constitutes data for examination rather than an FSI analysis. And if people work on living out feminist ideals – pushing against hierarchy – an FSI analysis would study the conditions that make it easier or harder to maintain egalitarian practices.

Emotions

For SI, emotions are social rather than spontaneous, physiological responses to stimuli; people note a sensation, consider whether it is a feeling, and then apply a social label (e.g., sad, mad). Our feelings are shaped by rules that tell us how we should feel in a situation and how to express those feelings – 'feeling rules' and 'display rules' (Hochschild 1979). In mainstream American culture, for instance, one is expected to feel sad (and tearful) at a funeral, happy (and smiling) at a birthday party, angry (and fist-pumping) at injustice. People whose emotional expressions deviate from convention typically face sanctions. We do emotion work, learning to suppress or change socially inappropriate emotional expressions to avoid interactional trouble, save face or maintain a cherished identity. Children figure out that it is better to stifle the urge to giggle during a church sermon or feign interest in a lecture than face punishment. Emotions, then, are more than socially constructed; they are tools of social control.

FSI studies what happens to emotion work (interpersonal), emotional labour (workforce) and emotion management (organisations/teamwork regarding emotions) under conditions of inequality. Arlie Russell Hochschild (1983) studied how emotions manifest under late capitalism, sexism and racism. Women are expected not only to do the emotion work in intimate relationships with men and children (the third shift, after the work shift and the second shift of housework/childcare) but also the kind of labour that uplifts others. Our female students report that male customers and employers ask them to smile in their jobs as baristas, servers and receptionists. They also hear, 'Hey, baby, smile', while walking down the street. If a woman has a neutral expression, she may be accused, in the United States, of having RBF (resting bitch face) (Bennett 2015). There is no equivalent label for men.

Hochschild (1983) observed that customers typically treated male flight attendants respectfully while treating women as 'open persons' (Goffman 1963:126) who could be dumped on. Because 'man' is equated with competence and authority, it provides a status shield that helps men avoid demands for emotional labour. For immigrant caregivers from privileged class backgrounds, social class has a similar shielding effect. Pei-Chia Lan (2003), for instance, found that young, middle-class Taiwanese couples sought middle-class, English-speaking Filipinas to work as nanny–housekeepers because they thought that having a 'classy' worker showed their peers that they were 'classy' employers. As resources for their employers' identity work, the Filipina workers sometimes traded domestic duties for higher status tasks that required less care-work. Employers asked Filipinas to tutor the children in English or help them with their own work, such as making phone calls to English-speaking business associates. These tasks represented a step up in status for the Filipinas, thereby reducing their need to manage emotions related to feelings of class/status inconsistency. It also gave them a reprieve from what many nannies experience: ongoing demands for emotional labour (see Hondagneu-Sotelo 2007; Parreñas 2015).

Women working in high-level positions at American corporations whose bosses and co-workers (men, mostly) complain about their 'aggressiveness' may be sent to the 'Bully Broads' program (Banerjee 2001) to learn how to add 'ums' to their speech, cry and play nice. When employers expect men to do emotional labour it is typically to *demote* others – creating discomfort or pushing people to pay up (e.g., bill collectors, insurance agents, criminal attorneys or detectives). As a consequence, men learn to suppress empathy and women learn to suppress anger (Hochschild 1983). Men also learn to act stoic in the face of stress or conflict to convince other men at work that they are in control (Sattel 1976) and to maintain invulnerability in intimate relationships with women.

Because emotions can reflect and reinforce status inequalities, the first author encourages ethnographers to pay attention to the 'oppressive consequences of desire for the disadvantaged group' (Kleinman 2007:80). Love, guilt, fear or resignation can be used by dominants – and internalised by subordinates – to encourage the latter to control themselves. These 'role-taking emotions' (Shott 1979) may lead women to feel guilty if they do not please a partner (Bartky 1990:99–119). Similarly, in the workplace, nannies have a harder time negotiating better wages and working conditions when they see themselves as working for love rather than money (Parreñas 2015).

Candace Clark (1990) elaborated on the asymmetrical power dynamics at work in the expression of role-taking emotions. She observed that sympathy often flows downward, from the powerful to the powerless, thereby *marking* the place of each interactant. Subordinates might try to invert this power relationship by expressing sympathy for the stresses experienced by those in higher status positions, but dominants have the power to reject subordinates' 'sympathy gifts' to avoid appearing weak (Clark 1987). In relationships of inequality, subordinates are far better at understanding the powerful than the reverse (Thomas, Franks and Calonicos 1972); subordinates have a lot more to lose, materially and emotionally, if they fail to correctly anticipate or interpret the dominant's mind and mood.

Victims of domestic and sexual violence, for example, walk an emotional tightrope to convince authorities that they deserve protection (Dunn 2002). In court, women victimised by men are expected to demonstrate that they consistently resisted their abusers, yet not come across as aggressive – or risk attacks by attorneys (if she is so tough, how could she be a victim?). At the same time, female victims who appear helpless or too passive will be seen as complicit in their victimisation or as wallowing in their victimhood. One misstep in their emotional performance at a critical moment may lead police, victim advocates, attorneys, judges and juries to dismiss their calls for help. The result can be deadly.

Feminist interactionists also study those who use emotions to make change (Polletta and Jasper 2001). The second author, for instance, examined how undocumented youth activists involved in the DREAM Act Movement in the United States used gripping stories to elicit sympathy and support for their cause (Cabaniss 2018). She found that gender expectations – and the stigma of victimisation – complicated their efforts. The activists believed that the best stories made audiences feel what it is like to be undocumented; but this tactic created problems for men in the movement who resisted appearing vulnerable and women who worried about appearing weak if they showed *too much* vulnerability. Nevertheless, they maintained a gendered division of emotional labour in which women made tearful appeals for sympathy while men expressed righteous indignation over the unfairness of being undocumented. In so doing, they equated women with vulnerability, men with strength – implying that men are more deserving of the privileges of the documented.

Feminist researchers also seek to understand the role of emotions through ongoing critical *self*-reflection. It is not enough to acknowledge our feelings in the field; we *use* our reactions – and those of research participants – as analytic tools to inform and deepen our analyses (Kleinman and Copp 1993). We are not calling for a catalogue of our positions (e.g., women/white people/middle class). Instead, we seek to understand how our positions and perspectives in social hierarchies shape our interpretations and our ability to empathise with *and* maintain analytic distance from participants (see also Kleinman and Kolb 2011).

Intersectionality

Feminists conceptualise oppression as systematic, multidimensional and relational; so, we study not only the resilience of patriarchy but its relationship to other systems of inequality. As Frye (1992:70) wrote about sexism, women experience 'a common (but not homogeneous) oppression'. By extension, men experience a common, but not homogeneous experience of privilege. For example, Devon Carbado (1999), a black man, wrote that he is unlikely to be accused of sleeping his way to the top at work, but whites may assume he got the high-level job only because of Affirmative Action (which, in the United States, popularly connotes incompetence and 'reverse racism').

Feminist interactionists approach intersectionality in two main ways. Using conventional social categories of race, class and gender, scholars compare the experiences of women from different social categories who share a common identity or characteristic (e.g., student, activist). Laura Hamilton and Elizabeth Armstrong (2009), for example, found that white middle-class and working-class heterosexual college women faced different kinds of dilemmas in campus hookups. Class-privileged women 'struggled to be both "good girls" who limited their sexual activity to relationships and "good students" who did not allow relational commitments to derail their educational and career development' (Hamilton and Armstrong 2009:604; see also Wilkins and Dalessandro 2013). Their solution was to occasionally participate in hookups, finding it preferable to having committed relationships with men. Working-class women, on the other hand, viewed college as an opportunity to build their careers *and* relationships. They avoided hookups to maintain 'good' reputations with the middle-class men they hoped to marry.

Alternately, researchers conceptualise race, class and gender as 'categories [of] meanings' we use to make sense of ourselves and others (Kleinman 2007:96). Our words, behaviours and appearance are treated 'as if they were indicative of some underlying state', for instance, of our maleness/femaleness (West and Fenstermaker 1995:23). By 'doing difference' (West and Fenstermaker 1995) in our interactions with others, we may challenge some inequalities while reproducing others. For example, in her study of two lesbian- and gay-affirming congregations, Krista McQueeney (2009) showed that the consequences of racial oppression made it hard for leaders and members of a *black* church to show unconditional support and compassion for gay members of their congregation while still claiming status as a real church. To make up for the class, race and gender privileges they lacked as a working class, black and increasingly female congregation, the leader (a black lesbian) and members of the congregation privileged gay men and put them centre stage. Fighting heterosexism was undermined at least in part by an acceptance and even idealisation of the gender hierarchy. The *white* church faced no challenges to its claims of legitimacy in the broader community.

Similarly, in her article on Puerto Rican wannabes, Amy Wilkins (2008) found that young, white, middle-class women who wanted to date only black and Puerto Rican men failed to recognise that they unwittingly reinforced racial stereotypes while relying on whiteness to win favour with these men. The women's efforts paid off in some ways – sexual relationships with men, recognition as transgressing gendered expectations for white women – but also incurred costs. To make themselves attractive to men of colour, the women spent time and energy managing their sexual reputations and competing with other 'wannabes', rather than forging friendships with them. The men used the white women for sex but did not consider them long-term partners. So, the wannabes crossed race and class boundaries by subordinating themselves to men and distancing themselves from other women. Their strategies not only reinscribed their own marginalisation – accepted neither by whites nor blacks – but also reinforced negative images of working-class Puerto Rican and black cultures.

Yen Le Espiritu (2001) found that young Filipina/o Americans responded to the stigma of racism by constructing opposing images of Filipina sexual virtue and white female promiscuity and using those images to assert their superiority over white women. They fashioned an image of Filipinas as chaste to represent the moral integrity of their ethnic community as a whole. By complying with male-defined criteria for signalling ideal feminine virtue ('sexual purity'), Filipinas could claim a positive identity in their community. But doing so required them to submit to constant monitoring of their sexuality by other Filipinas/os. Women who refused to conform were subject to community members' criticism.

Matthew Ezzell (2012) found that impoverished black and Latino participants in a men's drug treatment program engaged in compensatory manhood acts in response to lacking upper-middle-class markers of successful men (good jobs and money). Many of the men had been imprisoned, and the court made them choose between incarceration and treatment. Despite their subordinated status in racial and class hierarchies, the men used displays of aggression and emotion management strategies to assert control, using sexist and homophobic taunts to elevate themselves above women and nonconventional men.

In a study of the mythopoetic men's movement, Michael L. Schwalbe (1996) found that middle-class white men who lacked physical prowess and upper-middle-class jobs appropriated 'womanly' displays of emotion (i.e., crying, open expressions of vulnerability) but redefined these as signs of *masculine* virtue ('deep masculinity'). They showed that they were sensitive (good guys) without giving up their privileges as men.

Conclusion

In this chapter, we have outlined how a feminist orientation, in the ways we define it, can inform and deepen symbolic interactionism. Feminist symbolic interactionism (FSI) examines how inequality manifests in the mundane realities all of us participate in. It is in this realm of the ordinary that we encounter, create and respond to meanings and behaviours. Feminism teaches that through our thoughts, feelings and actions, we assert, affirm and sometimes resist the ideology of superiority and inferiority that justifies and defends inequality. We also make choices as we interact, but as feminist symbolic interactionists, we understand that those choices are not made outside of society. Social conditions and positions constrain people within hierarchies, including through the anticipation of what may befall us if we resist. Yet, choosing between actions that reinforce inequality or those that challenge it has different consequences and thus unequal benefits for social change. And because people are interdependent, what the 'I' says or does, or fails to say or do, has consequences for power relations, even if we are not conscious of those impacts.

Without a feminist analysis, symbolic interactionists might fail to see how meanings are shaped by our positions in unequal social relations, and how assertions of agency reflect back on the groups to which we belong. It might lead researchers to take subordinates' accounts at face value, such as those who say: 'I don't *feel* oppressed' or 'I feel empowered'. Yet as Marilyn Frye (1983) asserts, oppression is an objective state. Years of sociological research support the existence of the 'wires' of the sexist birdcage (Frye 1983): the second shift, the wage gap, the sexualisation of women in every sphere, the threat of men's violence in public and private (we could go on). Many of these wires are dismissed or not experienced *as* oppression by women. That's part of how the system works. But as Allan Johnson (2018) reminds us, oppression and privilege exist in relationship to each other; they reflect systemic inequalities *between* groups, rather than residing in an individual's feeling.

For FSI, any analysis of agency must include an analysis of power. Under what conditions do women (and other subordinates) make choices, especially in relation to men (or to members of other dominant groups)? Under conditions of inequality, why do women at times settle for false power? What do we believe we might lose if we gave up particular practices or worked with other women in solidarity against patriarchy? How do men understand their assertions of agency when they objectify and (sometimes) dominate women sexually? What are the consequences of men's 'choices' for other women?

Some work that goes by FSI takes the current pop view of feminism: women just need more choices and anything a woman chooses and enjoys must be feminist, especially if she says so. For example, Staci Newmahr (2006, 2011) argues that if a woman enjoys enacting or receiving 'discipline', then BDSM becomes a feminist choice. Yet such practices sustain *hierarchy*, reinforcing the idea that equality is unsexy and inequality is natural. Examining the conditions that give rise to domination, subordination, and internalised oppression, as well as the consequences for reinforcing or challenging patriarchy and other systems of inequality, constitute the start and end of feminist analysis.

Some who claim to practice 'feminist ethnography' take the moral imperative out of feminism and reflect the beliefs of anti-feminists who equate feminist researchers with ideologues: 'Feminism can operate as a blinder, limiting our ability to see and interpret empirical realities that do not conform with feminist expectations' (Avishai, Gerber and Randles 2013:394). Yet the opposite is true. One cannot maintain feminist consciousness without paying close attention to social patterns that reflect and reproduce inequality.

An FSI analysis does more than help us understand how systems of inequality work; it also provides directions for dismantling them and creating conditions that make collective, feminist change possible. The birdcage of oppression makes it hard for women to give up the few benefits we get from going along with practices that sustain patriarchy. FSI, though, suggests what we might gain from refusing to take the path of least resistance. Exercising *critical* agency – making decisions in light of sexist programming and the consequences for women as a group – opens the possibility for authentic relationships with other women (and men) and for creating 'culture[s] of resistance' (Hill Collins 2000:101). What do men gain by resisting sexist conditioning? No less than their humanity.

What kind of world do we want to live in? As feminist symbolic interaction-ists, we ask that question first, and then examine human practices in light of those ideals. A feminist commitment to social change demands that we use the best analytic tools, examining our investments in privilege and oppression in research and everywhere else. Too much is at stake to do less.

References

Ahmed, Sara (2010): 'Feminist Killjoys (and Other Willful Subjects)'. *Polyphonic Feminisms*, 8 (3):50–87.

Avishai, Orit, Lynne Gerber and Jennifer Randles (2013): 'The Feminist Ethnographer's Dilemma: Reconciling Progressive Research Agendas with Fieldwork Realities'. *Journal of Contemporary Ethnography*, 42 (4):394–426.

Banerjee, Neela (2001): 'Some 'Bullies' Seek Ways to Soften Up: Toughness Has Risks for Women Executives'. *The New York Times*. Available online at: http://www.nytimes.com/2001/08/10/business/media-business-some-bullies-seek-ways-soften-up-toughness-has-risks-for-women.html.

Bartky, Sandra (1990): *Femininity and Domination: Studies in the Phenomenology of Oppression*. New York: Routledge.

Barton, Bernadette (2017): *Stripped: More Stories from Exotic Dancers* (2nd edition). New York: New York University Press.

Becker, Howard S. (1986): *Doing Things Together: Selected Papers*. Evanston, IL: Northwestern University Press.

Becker, Howard S. (1993): 'How I Learned What a Crock Was'. *Journal of Contemporary Ethnography*, 22 (1):28–35.

Benard, Cheryl and Edit Schlaffer (1997): 'The Man in the Street: Why He Harasses', in Laurel Richardson, Verta Taylor and Nancy Whittier (eds.): *Feminist Frontiers IV*. New York: McGraw-Hill, pp. 395–398.

Bennett, Jessica (2015): 'I'm Not Mad, That's Just My RBF'. *The New York Times*. Available online at: https://www.nytimes.com/2015/08/02/fashion/im-not-mad-thats-just-my-resting-b-face.html?smid=tw-nytstyles.

Berger Peter L. and Thomas Luckmann (1966): *The Social Construction of Reality: A Treatise in the Sociology of Knowledge*. Garden City, NY: Anchor Books.

Bindel, Julie (2017): *The Pimping of Prostitution: Abolishing the Sex Work Myth*. London: Palgrave/MacMillan.

Blumer, Herbert (1969): *Symbolic Interactionism: Perspective and Method*. Englewood Cliffs, NJ: Prentice-Hall.

Boswell, A. Ayres and Joan Spade (1996): 'Fraternities and Collegiate Rape Culture: Why Are Some Fraternities More Dangerous Places for Women?' *Gender & Society*, 10 (2):133–147.

Cabaniss, Emily (2018): 'Pulling Back the Curtain: Examining the Backstage Gendered Dynamics of Storytelling in the Undocumented Youth Movement'. *Journal of Contemporary Ethnography*, 47 (2):199–225.

Carbado, Devon (1999): 'Epilogue: Straight out of the Closet: Men, Feminism, and Male Heterosexual Privilege', in Devon Carbado (ed.): *Black Men on Race, Gender and Sexuality: A Critical Reader*. New York: New York University Press, pp. 417–447.

Chou, Rosalind and Joe Feagin (2016): *Myth of the Model Minority: Asian Americans Facing Racism* (2nd edition). New York: Routledge.

Clark, Candace (1987): 'Sympathy Biography and Sympathy Margin'. *American Journal of Sociology*, 93:290–321.

Clark, Candace (1990): 'Emotions and Micropolitics in Everyday Life: Some Patterns and Paradoxes of 'Place'', in Theodore D. Kemper (ed.): *Research Agendas in the Sociology of Emotions*. Stony Brook, NY: State University of New York Press, pp. 305–333.

Copp, Martha and Sherryl Kleinman (2008): 'Practicing What We Teach: Feminist Strategies for Teaching about Sexism'. *Feminist Teacher*, 18 (2):101–124.

Crenshaw, Kimberle (1991): 'Mapping the Margins: Intersectionality, Identity Politics, and Violence against Women of Color'. *Stanford Law Review*, 43 (6):1241–1299.

Deegan, Mary Jo (1987): 'Symbolic Interaction and the Study of Women: An Introduction', in Mary Jo Deegan and Michael Hall (eds.): *Women and Symbolic Interaction*. Boston: Allen & Unwin, pp. 3–15.

Dunn, Jennifer (2002): *Courting Disaster: Intimate Stalking, Culture and Criminal Justice*. New Brunswick, NJ: Transaction Publishers.

Enloe, Cynthia (2017): *The Big Push: Exposing and Challenging the Persistence of Patriarchy*. Oakland, CA: University of California Press.

Espiritu, Yen Le (2001): '"We Don't Sleep Around like White Girls Do": Family, Culture and Gender in Filipina American Life'. *Signs*, 26 (2):415–440.

Ezzell, Matthew (2009): '"Barbie Dolls" on the Pitch: Identity Work, Defensive Othering and Inequality in Women's Rugby'. *Social Problems*, 56 (1):111–131.

Ezzell, Matthew (2012): '"I'm in Control": Compensatory Manhood in a Therapeutic Community'. *Gender & Society*, 26 (2):190–215.

Fine, Gary Alan (1993): 'The Sad Demise, Mysterious Disappearance and Glorious Triumph of Symbolic Interactionism'. *Annual Review of Sociology*, 19:61–87.

Fine, Gary Alan and Sherryl Kleinman (1979): 'Rethinking Subculture: An Interactionist Analysis'. *American Journal of Sociology*, 85 (1):1–20.

Fortini, Amanda (2008): 'The "Bitch" and the "Ditz": How the Year of the Woman Reinforced the Two Most Pernicious Sexist Stereotypes and Actually Set Women Back'. *New York Magazine*. Available online at: http://nymag.com/news/politics/nationalinterest/52184/.

Frye, Marilyn (1983): *The Politics of Reality: Essays in Feminist Theory*. Freedom, CA: The Crossing Press.

Frye, Marilyn (1992): *Willful Virgin: Essays in Feminism*. Trumansburg, NY: Crossing Press.

Goffman, Erving (1963): *Stigma: Notes on the Management of Spoiled Identity*. Englewood Cliffs, NJ: Prentice-Hall.

Giuffre, Patti and Christine Williams (1994): 'Boundary Lines: Labeling Sexual Harassment in Restaurants'. *Gender & Society*, 8 (3):378–401.

Hamilton, Laura and Elizabeth Armstrong (2009): 'Gendered Sexuality in Young Adulthood: Double Binds and Flawed Options'. *Gender & Society*, 23 (5):589–616.

Haraway, Donna (1988): 'Situated Knowledges: The Science Question in Feminism and the Privilege of Partial Perspective'. *Feminist Studies*, 14 (3):575–599.

Harris, Scott (2001): 'What Can Interactionism Contribute to the Study of Inequality? The Case of Marriage and Beyond'. *Symbolic Interaction*, 24:455–480.

Henson, Kevin and Jackie Krasas Rogers (2001): '"Why Marcia You've Changed!" Male Clerical Temporary Workers Doing Masculinity in a Feminized Occupation'. *Gender & Society*, 15 (2):218–238.

Hill Collins, Patricia (2000): *Black Feminist Thought: Knowledge, Consciousness and the Politics of Empowerment* (2nd edition). New York: Routledge.

Hochschild, Arlie Russell (1979): 'Emotion Work, Feeling Rules and Social Structures'. *American Journal of Sociology*, 85 (3):551–575.

Hochschild, Arlie Russell (1983): *The Managed Heart: Commercialization of Human Feeling*. Berkeley, CA: University of California Press.

Holden, Daphne (1997): '"On Equal Ground": Sustaining Virtue among Volunteers in a Homeless Shelter'. *Journal of Contemporary Ethnography*, 26 (2):117–145.

Hondagneu-Sotelo, Pierrette (2007): *Doméstica: Immigrant Workers Cleaning and Caring in the Shadows of Affluence* (2nd edition). Berkeley, CA: University of California Press.

hooks, bell (1989): *Talking Back: Thinking Feminist, Thinking Black*. Cambridge, MA: South End Press.

Jensen, Robert (2017): *The End of Patriarchy: Radical Feminism for Men*. North Melbourne: Spinifex Press.

Johnson, Allan (2014): *The Gender Knot: Unraveling our Patriarchal Legacy* (3rd edition). Philadelphia: Temple University Press.

Johnson, Allan (2018): *Privilege, Power, and Difference* (3rd edition). Boston: McGraw-Hill.

Kane, Emily (2006): '"No Way My Boys Are Going to Be like That!" Parents' Responses to Children's Gender Nonconformity'. *Gender & Society*, 20 (2):149–176.

Kleinman, Sherryl (1996): *Opposing Ambitions: Gender and Identity in an Alternative Organization*. Chicago: University of Chicago Press.

Kleinman, Sherryl (2002): 'Why Sexist Language Matters.' *Qualitative Sociology*, 25 (2): 299–304.

Kleinman, Sherryl (2007): *Feminist Fieldwork Analysis*. Thousand Oaks, CA: Sage Publications.

Kleinman, Sherryl and Martha Copp (1993): *Emotions and Fieldwork*. Thousand Oaks, CA: Sage Publications.

Kleinman, Sherryl and Martha Copp (2009): 'Denying Social Harm: Students' Resistance to Lessons about Inequality'. *Teaching Sociology*, 37 (3):283–293.

Kleinman, Sherryl, Martha Copp and Kent Sandstrom (2006): 'Making Sexism Visible: Birdcages, Martians and Pregnant Men'. *Teaching Sociology*, 34 (2):126–142.

Kleinman, Sherryl and Kenneth Kolb (2011): 'Traps on the Path of Analysis'. *Symbolic Interaction*, 34 (4):425–446.

Lan, Pei-Chia (2003): 'Maid or Madam? Filipina Migrant Workers and the Continuity of Domestic Labor'. *Gender & Society*, 17 (2):187–208.

Lerner, Gerda (1986): *The Creation of Patriarchy*. New York: Oxford University Press.

Lindemann, Danielle (2012): *Dominatrix: Gender, Eroticism and Control in the Dungeon*. Chicago: University of Chicago Press.

Lipkin, Shira (2013): 'Girls Don't Count'. Available online at: http://shiralipkin.tumblr.com/post/43647177973/girls-dont-count.

Macomber, Kris (2018): '"I'm Sure as Hell Not Putting Any Man on a Pedestal": Male Privilege and Accountability in Domestic and Sexual Violence Work'. *Journal of Interpersonal Violence*, 33 (9):1491–1518.

Maines, David R. (1977): 'Social Organization and Social Structure in Symbolic Interactionist Thought'. *Annual Review of Sociology*, 3 (1):235–259.

McIntosh, Peggy (1988): 'White Privilege and Male Privilege: A Personal Account of Coming to See Correspondences through Work in Women's Studies'. Working Paper 189. Wellesley, MA: Wellesley College Center for Research on Women.

McQueeney, Krista (2009): '"We Are God's Children, Y'all:" Race, Gender, and Sexuality in Lesbian- and Gay-Affirming Congregations'. *Social Problems*, 56 (1):151–173.

Mead, George Herbert (1934): *Mind, Self and Society: From the Standpoint of a Social Behaviorist*. Chicago: University of Chicago Press.

Musolf, Gil Richard (2016): 'The Astructural Bias Charge: Myth or Reality?', in Gil Richard Musolf (ed.): *Studies in Symbolic Interaction* (Volume 46). Somerville, MA: Emerald, pp. iii.

Newmahr, Staci (2006): 'Experiences of Power in SM: A Challenge to Power Theory'. *Berkeley Journal of Sociology*, 50:37–60.

Newmahr, Staci (2011): *Playing on the Edge: Sadomasochism, Risk and Intimacy*. Bloomington, IN: Indiana University Press.

Parreñas, Rhacel Salazar (2015): *Servants of Globalization: Migration and Domestic Work* (2nd edition). Stanford, CA: Stanford University Press.

Polletta, Francesca and James Jasper (2001): 'Collective Identity and Social Movements'. *Annual Review of Sociology*, 27 (1):283–305.

Pyke, Karen (2010): 'What Is Internalized Racial Oppression and Why Don't We Study It? Acknowledging Racism's Hidden Injuries'. *Sociological Perspectives*, 53 (4):551–572.

Quinn, Beth (2002): 'Sexual Harassment and Masculinity: The Power and Meaning of "Girl Watching"'. *Gender & Society*, 16 (3):386–402.

Rich, Adrienne (1980): 'Compulsory Heterosexuality and Lesbian Existence'. *Signs*, 5 (4):631–660.

Rogers, Laura E. (2017): '"Helping the Helpless Help Themselves": How Volunteers and Employees Create a Moral Identity While Sustaining Symbolic Boundaries within a Homeless Shelter'. *Journal of Contemporary Ethnography*, 46 (2):230–260.

Sattel, Jack (1976): 'The Inexpressive Male: Tragedy or Sexual Politics?'. *Social Problems*, 23 (4):469–477.

Schwalbe, Michael L. (1996): *Unlocking the Iron Cage: The Men's Movement, Gender Politics and American Culture*. New York: Oxford University Press.

Schwalbe, Michael L. (2014): *Manhood Acts: Gender and the Practices of Domination*. New York: Routledge.

Schwalbe, Michael L. (2016): 'Overcoming Aprocessual Bias in the Study of Inequality: Parsing the Capitalist Interaction Order', in Gil Richard Musolf (ed.): *Studies in Symbolic Interaction* (Volume 46). Somerville, MA: Emerald, pp. 95–122.

Schwalbe, Michael L., Sandra Goodwin, Daphne Holden, Douglas Schrock, Shealy Thompson and Michele Wolkomir (2000): 'Generic Processes in the Reproduction of Inequality: An Interactionist Analysis'. *Social Forces*, 79:419–452.

Shott, Susan (1979): 'Emotions and Social Life: A Symbolic Interactionist Analysis'. *American Journal of Sociology*, 84:1317–1334.

Tarrant, Shira (2010): 'Porn: Pleasure or Profit? An Interview with Gail Dines, Part I'. *Ms. Magazine*. Available online at: http://gaildines.com/2010/07/ms-magazine/.

Thomas, Darwin, David Franks and James Calonicos (1972): 'Role-Taking and Power in Social Psychology'. *American Sociological Review*, 37 (5):605–614.

Thomas, William I. and Dorothy Thomas (1928): *The Child in America: Behavior Problems and Programs*. New York: Knopf.

Wade, Lisa (2017): *American Hookup: The New Culture of Sex on Campus*. New York: W.W. Norton & Company.

Walby, Sylvia (1990): *Theorizing Patriarchy*. Oxford: Basil Blackwell.

West, Candace and Sarah Fenstermaker (1995): 'Doing Difference'. *Gender & Society*, 9 (1):8–37.

Wilkins, Amy (2008): *Wannabes, Goths and Christians: The Boundaries of Sex, Style and Status*. Chicago: University of Chicago Press.

Wilkins, Amy and Cristen Dalessandro (2013): 'Monogamy Lite: Cheating, College and Women'. *Gender & Society*, 27 (5):728–751.

8 An invitation to 'radical interactionism'

Towards a reorientation of interactionist sociology?

Michael Hviid Jacobsen and
Caroline Joan S. Picart

Introduction

Many core sociological concepts such as 'power', 'inequality', 'conflict', 'oppression', 'stratification', 'alienation', 'domination' or 'subjugation' are not those most commonly associated with interactionist studies. Instead, less conflict-laden notions of 'self', 'roles', 'performance', 'identity', 'impression management', 'meaning', 'negotiation' and the like seem to be more in line with what one expects to find when opening a book on interactionist sociology. In fact, interactionism/symbolic interactionism has conventionally been accused of lacking a theoretical as well as empirical sensitivity towards the understanding of topics such as conflict and power (see, e.g., Athens 2013b; McNall and Johnson 1975; Musolf 1992). Contrary to this, others have insisted that symbolic interactionism is not only compatible with but in fact particularly suitable for the study of power, conflict and inequality in everyday life (see, e.g., Anderson and Snow 2001; Dennis and Martin 2005; Denzin 1992). Reading through the many studies conducted by interactionists (of whatever observance or conviction), one will in fact often find descriptions and depictions of social life in which for example conflict, power or domination is a most prominent feature. As already some of the founding figures of interactionist sociology such as Robert E. Park and Georg Simmel hinted at, social life is indeed characterised by conflict relations and experiences that relate to culture, race and webs of subordination and superordination (Park 1931/1950, 1937/1950; Simmel 1955). Also others within interactionist sociology have later argued for the importance of understanding conflict and power as pivotal topics in studies of society such as, for example, Stanford M. Lyman, Jack D. Douglas, Norman K. Denzin, Arlie R. Hochschild and not least among many deviance scholars and feminist interactionists. Despite their important insights, it has been a recurring critique raised against interactionists that they lack a substantial conflict perspective and that they are promoting a status quo and situationally oriented understanding of social life, which neglects social structure, social change and social power. Radical interactionism (RI) is an attempt seeking to rectify this situation by proposing a perspective that pays particular attention to the themes of conflict, domination and subjugation.

Although it is not uncommon that schools of thought or theoretical perspectives – also within interactionism – are associated with specific spearheading individuals (for example, the very concept of 'symbolic interactionism' was invented by Herbert Blumer, the 'Iowa School' was founded and for many years personified by Manford H. Kuhn, and the so-called sociology of the absurd was almost exclusively advanced by Stanford M. Lyman and Marvin B. Scott), radical interactionism has so far been invented and promoted almost singlehandedly by American criminologist Lonnie H. Athens. Admittedly, radical interactionism is thus perhaps not the hottest topic within interactionist sociology. In fact, if you confront many interactionist scholars with the notion of 'radical interactionism', quite a few would necessarily not know what you were talking about. However, despite its somewhat subdued or shadowy existence, this does not detract from the importance of what RI proposes. Although a few volumes (edited or written by Athens himself) have now been published (Athens 2013a, 2015), searching databases for journal articles or books devoted to RI reveals that this is indeed still a rather limited perspective when it comes to proliferation and application. Even though a growing number of studies have drawn on some of the ideas behind RI (see, e.g., Gougherty and Hallett 2013; Picart 2013; Puddephatt 2013), we are still waiting to see the full potential of the perspective. In this respect, Athens has so far almost been a one-man army in outlining and advancing RI. Thus, we do not present and discuss RI here because it is a widely used or intensely debated perspective or position within interactionist circles, but rather because it is still a relatively overlooked yet also very *promising development within* and an *alternative to* the more conventional perspective of symbolic interactionism (SI).

This chapter initially introduces and then discusses the interactionist contribution of Lonnie H. Athens and his notion of 'radical interactionism'. Abbreviations used in the chapter will be SI for 'symbolic interactionism' and RI for 'radical interactionism'. First, we will delineate the background for and the development of the perspective of RI and then subsequently discuss if and how RI does, in fact, inaugurate a reorientation of interactionism.

A maverick's perspective

Within almost every scientific perspective one will find so-called core-representatives and periphery-perspectives. The core-perspectives refer to those thinkers or texts that are most frequently quoted and which are regarded as constituting the orthodoxy. In the periphery, one often finds those thinkers who challenge the mainstream and who are concerned with developing perspectives or niches that are regarded as heterodox or who critically revise the canonical ideas developed in the core. Lonnie H. Athens' development of RI has in many ways been a project conceived at the outskirts of interactionist orthodoxy. In his work, it is obvious that Athens over the years has grown increasingly critical of conventional symbolic interactionism and in a book devoted to his work, he is fittingly described as a 'maverick criminologist' (Rhodes 2000). Let us look a bit at the personal background of this maverick because it constitutes an important impetus for understanding the development of RI.

Thanks to Pulitzer Prize-winning historian Richard Rhodes, the facts of Athens' life are generally well known. Rhodes' *Why They Kill: The Discoveries of a Maverick Criminologist* (2000) traces, in vivid and compelling prose, the genesis and evolution of Athens' early criminological frameworks by grounding these frameworks in crucial influences and events that shaped Athens' personal life and professional development. Rhodes describes Athens' father, Petros Athens or 'Pete the Greek', as the son of a Pennsylvanian 'brickyard worker and a professional wrestler – a brutal, hardcore, hand-to-mouth peasant from Sparta, and an unnamed woman whose only portraiture is that of dying in Pete's arms, after being decapitated in a car' (Rhodes 2000:9). Rhodes' description of Athens' mother also locates her predominantly in the background; he characterises Irene Zaharias as a 'sheltered daughter' of the third prominent figure during Athens' early years: Athens' grandfather, Lombros Zaharias, the business-savvy owner of a 'slop joint', The Manchester Café, in Richmond (Rhodes 2000:7–8). Lonnie's name was Irene's 'transliteration' of her father's Greek name, 'Lombros', into English and constituted an attempt to shield the boy from the ridicule and racism that plagued Greeks in an environment where being neither black nor white meant, in Athens' words, that he was a 'strange foreigner caught between two groups and marginalized [by both]' (Rhodes 2000:7, 9). Rhodes also briefly introduced Athens' older brother, Rico, born four years before Lonnie. Although there are other siblings (sisters born before and after Lonnie, and a baby brother), 'the two older boys and their mother carried the burden of Pete's domination' (Rhodes 2000:9). Athens' earlier years were principally characterised by first-hand experiences of violence from his father, who did not hesitate to use violence (and humiliation) to exert his will over him, Rico and their mother.

Nevertheless, Pete the Greek's propensity for violence was also an essential survival skill when located within the rough, working-class neighbourhood in which the family worked and resided as Pete kept an unlicensed gun in a holster underneath the counter, close to the cash register of a diner he later bought from one of Irene's uncles, which he used to ward off potential robbers (Rhodes 2000:10–11). However, there were cases where the option for violence was closed off, and instead Pete strategically deployed his 'gift of gab', for example, to dissuade a black gunman, who issued diatribes against all whites, while he held Pete at gunpoint, from shooting him; Pete pleaded that he was not white, but Greek, and thus was blameless for all the injustices the gunman recounted, resulting in the second gunman convincing his companion to stand down (Rhodes 2000:15). Pete was also a 'one stop salesman' selling an endless variety of wares inclusive of alleged aphrodisiacs, 'rubbers, vibrators, nude pictures, penis extensions', among others, to diverse consumers, often exploiting racial tensions, as by selling nude pictures of black women at white redneck bars, and selling nude pictures of white women at black bars (Rhodes 2000:19). As a counterpoint, it was Athens' grandfather, Lombros Zaharias, or Pop Zaharias, who was the stabilising counterpart to Pete the Greek. Despite the peasant origin he shared with Pete, Pop Zaharias was, in contrast, 'shrewd and pragmatically antimacho' and constantly counselled the young Lonnie not to follow Pete's example. In addition to this,

Father Dombalis, a pragmatic Greek Orthodox priest, who described himself, in confidence to the young boy, as a 'Robin Hood' who stole from the rich to give to the poor, was another steadying force (Rhodes 2000:21–22).

Against this backdrop, the young Athens learned quickly. Despite his size, according Rhodes (2000:21) 'barely five feet three inches and 120 pounds', he developed a reputation for ferocity; in his eighth grade, Athens threatened his father with a chair when his father grabbed him by the throat, and in a separate incident, mounted an arrow on a bow he pointed at his father, threatening to kill him if Pete ever abused him again. Thereafter, although Pete continued to beat Rico and their mother, Pete did not touch Lonnie again (Rhodes 2000:19). Although Rhodes' book systematically traces Athens' interactions with his key academic mentors – Marshall B. Clinard and Herbert Blumer (in fact he was one of only a few sociologists mentored directly by Blumer) – it is clear that as Athens moved through the educational and cultural challenges of becoming a professional criminologist, achieving his bachelor's degree from Virginia Polytechnic in 1970; his master's degree from the University of Wisconsin at Madison in 1972, both in sociology; and his doctorate in criminology at the University of California at Berkeley in 1975 (James 1999:3–4), the kernel from which his sustained and dedicated study of why some individuals act violently would spring, and the core of what would make Athens a 'maverick criminologist', were already in place.

Rhodes recounts episodes of the young Athens at graduate school either being accused of being a thief, because of the manner in which he dressed (with his hair in a ponytail, wearing jeans and boots) or being laughed at because of Athens' Virginian accent at a seminar (Rhodes 2000:31). Nevertheless, it is precisely that deviation from the stereotypical expectations regarding academics, alongside an untiring persistence, that granted him access, and credibility, to the prisoners who provided him with the raw data from which he eventually forged his first theoretical framework. Athens' two books, *Violent Criminal Acts and Actors* (originally published in 1980) and *The Creation of Dangerous Violent Criminals* (originally published in 1989), drew high praise from renowned figures in criminology and sociology, including his mentor, Herbert Blumer, but were dismissed by many of his peers (James 1999:4).

The study of violence as a precursor to RI

At a time when criminology's and sociology's intellectual elite regarded a quantitative (and especially positivist) approach as the *summum bonum* of sociological inquiry, and in defiance of his then-mentor's (Clinard) advice to take the 'easy route' to finishing the requirements for his master's degree (Rhodes 2000:39), Athens independently arrived at the conclusion that the question of how violent individuals become violent required a qualitative approach, which allowed each individual narratively to reconstruct his or her life's stories leading up to the incident(s) that led to their eventual incarceration. To arrive at his conclusions in both of his earlier books, Athens, in cumulation, conducted in-depth interviews of more than 100 violent felons, including murderers and rapists in prisons in Virginia, Iowa and California (James 1999:3).

Briefly summarised, Athens' theory of what he calls 'violentisation' – coined from the coupling of 'violence' and 'socialisation' – (Rhodes 2000:103) – begins with a negation of the then-popular compunction theory: that acts of violence are mindless compulsive acts, devoid of active reflection or decision-making. Rather, Athens posits that becoming violent entails an active interpretive and decision-making process (Athens 1997:32), and it is the quality of the interpretive frame and the act of decision-making that often separates victims from perpetrators: '[T]he data reveal that violent people consciously construct violent plans of action before they commit violent criminal acts' (Athens 1997:32). Athens thus concluded that there were four violent interpretations: (1) *physically defensive* (in which 'the victim makes a gesture that the perpetrator designates to himself as foreshadowing or constituting a physical attack, generating a grave sense of fear for his own or an intimate's safety'); (2) *frustrative* (in which 'the perpetrator becomes angry after designating to himself the direction along which the larger act is heading and his desire for the act not to follow that course'); (3) *malefic* (in which 'the perpetrator judges the victim to be extremely evil or malicious, which in turn ignites his hatred for the victim'); and (4) *frustrative-malefic* (which is a hybrid of items 2 and 3, in that it first starts out as motivated by anger, but then turns into hatred, because of the perpetrator's interpretation of the victim as evil, malicious or loathsome, as the perpetrator mounts his attack) (Athens 1997:34–40). Athens cautions that variable outcomes result from these interpretations, depending on whether the perpetrators 'stay in a fixed line of indication or form a restraining or overriding judgment' (Athens 1997:98).

In the study, Athens also concluded that there were three types of self-images among individuals who commit violent criminal acts, which were *always congruent* (Athens 1997:98, original emphasis) with the aforementioned types of interpretations. First, those with non-violent self-images would commit violent acts only when they formed physically defensive interpretations. Second, those with incipiently violent self-images engaged in violent acts only when they formed defensive or frustrative-malefic interpretations. Third, those with violent self-images would commit violent criminal acts when they formed any of the four interpretations outlined earlier. Athens identified three 'careers' of violent individuals: (1) *stable*, in which the violent individuals' self-image, and the quality and quantity of the violent acts in which the individuals engage, remain constant; (2) *escalating*, in which the individuals' self-images become increasingly more violent, corresponding with an increase in the amount and severity of their violent acts; and (3) *de-escalating*, in which the individuals' self-images become increasingly less violent, corresponding with a decrease in the amount and severity of their violent acts (Athens 1997:98–99).

In his early work, Athens relied heavily on George Herbert Mead's model of self-interaction, although he already then had strong doubts about Mead's notion of a 'generalised other', which Mead postulated was the source of where an individual acquired a sense of their community's collective attitude (Rhodes 2000:80). However, in Athens' retrospective review of his initial work, he replaced Mead's 'generalized other' with the notion of a 'phantom community'

(Athens 1994:525–526), which, in contrast to Mead's 'generalised other', is derived, not from the community, but from '[individuals'] past significant social experiences, which may be different from those of [their] present corporal community members' (Athens 1997:139, citing Athens 1994:529–530). Consequently, one of Athens' major conclusions at the end of *Violent Criminal Acts and Actors* is retrospectively recast in the following manner:

> [P]eople who commit substantially violent acts have different [phantom communities] ... Those who hold violent self-images have an *unmitigated* [phantom community] ... providing them with pronounced and categorical moral support for acting violently towards other people. Those who hold incipiently violent self-images have a *mitigated* [phantom community] ... providing them with pronounced, but *limited*, categorical moral support for acting violently toward other people. Finally, those who hold nonviolent self-images have a *nonviolent* [phantom community] ... that does not provide them with any pronounced, categorical moral support for acting violently toward other people, *except* in the case of defending themselves or intimates from physical attack.
>
> (Athens 1997:99, 139; original emphasis)

Athens' other revision of his initial study is that individuals may change their phantom communities, and it is these changes that determine the type of 'career' the violent individual develops. What transforms the phantom community (and the type of 'career' they develop, whether escalating or de-escalating) appears to be the violent actor's success in conflictive situations, leading others to consider him more violent than they had initially thought and to treat him with greater deference; if the individual accepts that new, more violent 'definition' of him, and enjoys the new, more deferential treatment of him, then the individual becomes more violent and may even change his corporal community to include more violent individuals (Athens 1997:140). Thus, with success in conflictive situations, those with formerly non-violent self-images, develop incipiently violent self-images and a mitigated phantom community, which now spur them to take violent action more readily in response to frustrative-malefic interpretations, where formerly they would act violently only in response to situations where they formed physically defensive interpretations. Those with incipiently violent self-images, with success in performing violent acts, metamorphose into individuals with violent self-images and unmitigated phantom communities, leading them to interpret all conflictive situations as requiring unmitigated violence. The converse, the de-escalating career, results when individuals with unmitigated violent phantom communities 'develop mitigated violent communities and then finally nonviolent ones' (Athens 1997:140). What causes the change in the phantom community is either failure in conflictive situations or the development of a 'restraining judgment' (Athens 1997:140–141).

In *The Creation of Violent, Dangerous Criminals* (originally published in 1989), Athens proposed his initial theory of the four-stage violentisation process, which he viewed as the underlying social dynamic that creates violent individuals. The first phase, *brutalisation*, is the stage in which the individual is forced into subjugation by a member of the individual's primary group. Brutalisation is characterised by violent subjugation (in which the individual feels helpless in the face of the assault and submits), 'personal horrification' (because it is exacted by an intimate), and violent coaching, in which the brutaliser assumes the role of coach, insisting that it is the sole personal responsibility of the brutalised to defend himself or herself using violence. Methods of coaching include vainglorification (the narrative glorification of violence), ridicule (which promotes violence through belittling and derision) and coercion (where coaches threaten novices with psychological or physical punishment) (Athens 2017c:25–53). The second phase, *belligerency* (later renamed the 'defiance' phase; Athens 2017c:110), which is highly emotionally laden, occurs when the brutalised subject takes personal responsibility for stopping the brutalisation, as if only now comprehending his violent coach's message. However, the brutalised subject's violent response is mitigated by provocation and precaution: he decides that he will resort to serious violence only if he is seriously provoked and if he perceives the situation to be one in which he can prevail. The formation of the first mitigated violent resolution is what ends the second phase (Athens 2017c:55–60). The third phase, *violent performances* (later renamed the 'dominant engagement' phase; Athens 2017c:111) involves violent performances, in which the individual gradually develops confidence in the success of his or her violent performance, in response to the highest levels of provocation (severely antagonising or tormenting the individual, or placing himself or a person for whom he cares in imminent danger). This third phase is a personal revolt against the subjugator, in which the subjugated understands that failure could result in even harsher oppression; this realisation could discourage the subjugated from acting on that violent resolution, but it could also deepen his belligerence/defiance and catalyse the subject's movement through the process of violentisation. Finally, in this third phase, if the subject succeeds, and the subject embraces the significance of that violent act, and develops a reputation/'celebrity' status as 'dangerous' or 'crazy', then the subject completes the third phase (Athens 2017c:61–68).

The fourth and final phase, *virulency*, is one in which the formerly brutalised, enjoying the advantages of his new self-image and the new deferential manner in which others treat him, becomes overly impressed with his violent performances and himself in general. The virulent individual engages in vainglorification, leading the individual to form the resolve that because of his success at performing violent acts, there is no reason why he should not engage in even more impressive violent feats in the future; the virulent individual also arrives at the hasty generalisation that he is now invincible, which others reinforce by treating him as a dangerous individual. The virulent individual, emboldened and rendered more venomous, now forms a new, even more violent resolution: to attack people physically with the serious intention of gravely harming them or even killing them, regardless of the degree (or nonexistence) of provocation. At this stage, the virulent individual is primed to become an ultraviolent individual (Athens 2017c:69–76).

Athens cautions that 'the completion of each stage is contingent upon the person fully understanding all the experiences comprising the stage, and the completion of the process as a whole is contingent upon the person undergoing all the stages' (Athens 2017c:77). Nevertheless, Athens concludes, unflinchingly, that regardless of class, race, sex, age or intelligence, once an individual completes the virulency stage, they become dangerous, violent criminals, provided they retain the physical and mental competencies necessary to perform a violent act. Athens reasons that there are fewer women who become ultraviolent individuals because they are discriminated against, in the selection and coaching of violent behaviour, and if they do progress beyond the defiance (second) phase, women are disadvantaged because in dominant engagement, the third phase, most individuals who have completed prior stages are men and possess the physical advantage of being larger and stronger, and the experiential advantages of having had access to physical contact sports, gangs and deadly weapons (Athens 2017c:111–112).

In his Introduction to the 'Transaction Edition' of *The Creation of Dangerous, Violent Criminals* (2017c), published almost 30 years after its first edition, Athens, in hindsight, holds that 'the basic principle underlying [the violentization model] is *domination*, which subsequently led [him] to reconceive [his] violentization model much more explicitly in terms of superordination and subordination' (Athens 2017c:xiv; original emphasis). Athens further refines the terminology associated with phase two, 'belligerency', with 'defiance', because it 'better captures the final condition in which the completion of this stage leaves the subject' (Athens 2017c:xiv); similarly, he alters the term for the third stage, from 'violent performances' to 'dominative encounters' to encompass three different types of encounters: (1) 'dominative tiffs', which are 'uncompleted violent dominative skirmish[es]'; (2) 'violent skirmishes', which are 'uncompleted violent dominative engagement[s]'; and (3) 'violent engagements', which are 'completed violent dominance encounter[s]' (Athens 2017c:xiv; see also Athens 2005b).

In a more significant refinement, Athens adds a fifth stage, which he labels 'violent predation', in which 'the subject's violence level becomes totally unbounded, exceeding the outer limits of humanity' (Athens 2017c:xv). Two elemental experiences comprise this stage: (1) 'acute self doubt', in which the violent predator realises that living up to his reputation as a 'monster' constitutes a great burden and ultimately forebodes a bleak future of either a premature death or a life of confinement; and (2) 'violent resoluteness', in which the violent predator realises that he has reached a point of no return as de-escalation could lead to humiliation, degradation, serious injury and possible death. Given that possibility, the violent predator may embrace infamy, and thus adopt a *boundlessly* violent resolution, which means, for his hapless victims, cooperating with him does not necessarily guarantee their survival (Athens 2017c:xv–xvi, original emphasis).

A third refinement in Athens' characterisation of the violentisation model is his parsing out of three elemental experiences during virulency, the third phase; these are (1) violent notoriety, (2) social trepidation and (3) malevolency. Of these, the most important is the third option, as it is then that the individual accepts a malevolent identity. Athens posits that it is the individuals who have low self-esteem who are most likely to accept a malevolent identity (Athens 2017c:xvi–xvii). As a fourth refinement of the original violentisation model, Athens added a 'violentisation typology', distinguishing between violent, dangerously violent, and the predatory violent type, which are differentiated from each other by 'the degree of dominative provocation needed for them to become violent' (Athens 2017c:xvii). Fifth, building from the violentisation model, Athens proposed a theory of 'dramatic self-change', based on his analysis of autobiographical subjects such as, among others, Ray Charles and Malcolm X, which is composed of five stages: (1) 'fragmentation', (2) 'provisional unity', (3) 'praxis', (4) 'consolidation' and (5) 'social segregation' (Athens 2017c:xvii; Athens 1995). Athens has also begun theorising regarding the policy implications of his model (Athens 2017a).

Athens' violentisation model appears to have successfully entered the popular cultural mainstream, as opposed to the academic communities of criminology and sociology, largely because of the influence of Rhodes' vivid biography. It was Athens' violentisation model that inspired Rhodes to seek Athens out in order to write his biography, as Rhodes, himself, had grown up in a violent family, and Athens' explanation for the creation of dangerous violent criminals struck him as consonant with his own experiences (Arbunkle 1999:3).

From Mead/Blumer to Park: RI versus SI

It should be obvious from this outlining of Athens' early work that the themes of conflict, domination and violence have been important in terms of Athens' personal life as well as of his academic development. It is also obvious that Athens throughout the years has jostled with many mainstream ideas and theories within criminology and sociology in order to carve out his own unique perspective as materialised in the 'violentisation' theory. Even though Athens' ideas originate within a symbolic interactionism framework (his 1980 book *Violent Criminal Acts and Actors* was in fact subtitled 'A Symbolic Interactionist Study'), he has gradually also started to question many key aspects of SI, which has become increasingly clear since the turn of the millennium.

Whenever the annals of interactionist sociology are written, the names that are most frequently mentioned as the 'founding fathers' are those of Charles Horton Cooley, George Herbert Mead, Erving Goffman and Herbert Blumer. However, in Athens' view, in order to fully grasp the full potential of interactionism, we need to revisit the work of Robert E. Park. As has been shown in a lot of existing literature on SI, Mead was an important intermediary between early pragmatist philosophy and later interactionist sociology (e.g., Lewis and Smith 1980). Similarly, Blumer's importance for the development of SI also expands well beyond his coining of the notion of 'symbolic interactionism' in 1937, and the impact of the publication of Blumer's *Symbolic Interactionism: Perspective and Method* in 1969 on the growing movement of so-called creative sociologies (phenomenology, ethnomethodology and symbolic interactionism) during this time (Morris 1977) cannot be underestimated. Blumer was – if not singlehandedly then at least prominently – instrumental in bringing forward the idea of a viable SI alternative to structural and functional schools of thought. According to Athens (2017b), the main reason why Mead became a much more recognised progenitor of interactionism than Park is partly due to the fact that Blumer – perhaps the main champion of SI in the mid-20th century – placed particular emphasis on and popularised the work of Mead rather than that of Park. Even though Athens was, as mentioned, mentored by Blumer, and even though he has paid due tribute to Blumer's contribution (Athens 1987), he also started to point out a number of limitations of Blumer's version of SI. In several journal articles over the past 10–15 years, Athens has explicated his critique of Mead's and Blumer's variant of SI, pointing specifically to a lacking conception of society and an underestimation of the role of conflict and domination (Athens 2002, 2005a, 2012, 2013c). This critique gradually paved the way for the more positive formulation of the idea of 'radical interactionism' (RI) to which we return later.

Under the dramatic headings of 'the rise of Mead and the fall of Park' and Park's 'fall from grace', Athens (2013d, 2017b) in detail discusses how this situation has come about and how it has had a profound impact on the way interactionism is understood and practised. Whereas the main progenitor of Park's perspective in sociology was Everett C. Hughes – who edited and was instrumental in proliferating some of Park's texts – he was not as successful as Blumer in developing the ideas of his mentor into a novel or coherent perspective. In Athens' analysis, Mead is particularly criticised for placing emphasis on the 'social act' (what Athens instead reconfigures as the 'collective act') and for failing to differentiate 'dominance' from 'domination', whereas Blumer's understanding of domination and power according to Athens is seen as too restrictive, limited – at most – only to episodic occurrences (Athens 2009). In both cases, Athens is critical, because he believes that Mead and Blumer in their work end up privileging sociality over domination rather than vice versa (Athens 2017b). Contrary to these 'traditional' or 'conventional' versions of SI, Park (and following him also Athens) was much more concerned with conflict and domination as 'the basic principle underlying the organization of human group life, from its first emergence on earth all the way to present times' (Athens 2009:406). After his investigation of these different roots of interactionism – Park, Mead and Blumer – Athens thus, perhaps unsurprisingly, concludes that Park is the only one of these three interactionists who adequately (but also not without criticism, see Athens 2013d), placed conflict (and not only race conflict) at the centre of attention. Athens quotes Hughes for saying that Park's 'inclination was towards realism' (Hughes quoted in Athens 2009:407), and this realism exactly entailed a concern with conflict, power and domination that Athens in his version of RI then develops even further. It should be stressed that even though the work of Georg Simmel is not as frequently mentioned within RI as that of Park, Simmel's (1955) concern with conflict (as well as the social form of subordination–superordination) was, in fact, an important source of inspiration for Park.

So what are the differences between RI and its, in Athens' (2013b:1) words, 'older conservative turned rival cousin' of SI? In a footnote, Athens has described RI as a 'dramatic break' with SI (Athens 2009:408), and he also insists that members of the SI community regard RI as a 'heretical frame of reference' (Athens 2013b:3). In order to show how RI diverges from SI, Athens then systematically outlines the five main points of divergence between the two perspectives. First, according to Athens, the main intellectual sources of inspiration are, as we saw, not the same: Mead and Blumer for SI and Park for RI. This difference seems to be the main reason for the following points. Second, whereas SI (meaning Mead and Blumer here) only assumes that domination and power only play a limited and 'non-essential' role for understanding social life, particularly when conflict has already erupted, RI places these topics at the very centre of attention as did also Park. Third, and following the foregoing point, whereas SI makes it merely discretionary to examine the role of power and domination in social life, RI makes this mandatory. Because SI researchers are seen as generally neglecting the topics of power and domination, according to Athens they end up, by default, supporting 'the 'status quo' of the human group or community falling under their gaze' (Athens 2013b:10). Fourth, whereas RI stresses the impact of individuals' and groups' unstated or taken-for-granted assumptions on their interactions, SI de-emphasises this aspect, because it privileges reflective, discursive and immediately visible dimensions of interaction. Fifth, and following this point, while SI thus encourages researchers to fall into the trap of so-called 'linguistic phenomenalism' (meaning to focus on what is explicitly stated), RI discourages this and instead – by focusing on verbally non-explicit dimensions – wants us to look for the unstated and thus insidious nature of power and domination in daily life (Athens 2013b:16).

Despite their obvious differences, Athens not only admits that SI and RI each in their way rely on a shared interest in the method of naturalistic observation, but also here there seem to be certain differences. Contrary to the more theoretical or speculative kind of naturalistic inquiry used by Mead (that involved, for example, the observation of children's' play and school teachers), the naturalistic approach was something Park really used comprehensively and systematically. For instance this was evident in his famous advice to his students to go out and get their 'seats of their pants dirty with real research' (Park in Lindner 1986:82), meaning that it was through the actual engagement with and observation of one's ethnographic sites – and not by doing library research – that Chicago sociology was practised. Moreover, looking at the early-day Chicago sociology, the concern with the outcasts, the 'marginal men' and all the shadowy downsides of the emerging metropolis loomed large in the empirical studies of many of Park's colleagues and students. Park's naturalistic and ethnographic approach to the study of urban life (inspired as it was by his training as a journalist) is thus by Athens contrasted with the more philosophically or theoretically informed naturalistic perspective of Mead (Athens 2013b:6–7). This idea of naturalistic inquiry also underpins RI, and, as Athens (2009) argues, here protagonists of RI may find support in Blumer's attempt through 'naturalistic inquiry' to provide sociologists – and particularly interactionists – with an alternative methodology to that of positivism (Athens 2010b). Blumer was a student and later junior colleague of Park and he developed Park's predilection for naturalistic observation into a method of obtaining knowledge about symbolic interaction as it takes place in real-life settings. Blumer believed that this method consisted of two steps: first, 'exploration' during which the researcher writes detailed descriptions of the field under study based only on a few rudimentary and initial ideas, then 'inspection' when the researcher starts analysing and developing conceptual ideas and propositions based on the initial rudimentary ideas and data collected during exploration. Besides these two important steps in naturalistic inquiry proposed by Blumer (who only developed the idea of naturalistic inquiry *in theory*), Athens adds a third component called 'confirmation' that is concerned with the testing of the propositions and conceptual ideas developed during the inspection phase. Moreover, based on his own early research on violent criminals, Athens also shows how the stages of naturalistic inquiry developed only in theory by Blumer may be put into practice in actual research (Athens 2010b).

Based on these many points of difference (and some of convergence) between SI and RI, how can the latter perspective then be defined? According to the *Blackwell Dictionary of Sociology*'s entry on 'radical interactionism', RI can be defined as 'a leading alternative to conventional symbolic interactionism (SI), integrating critiques of the theoretical and political conservatism inherent in SI with a comprehensive understanding of the foundational insights offered by this rich theoretical tradition' (Shaw 2017). As we have seen, Athens argues that interactionism (and particularly 'symbolic interactionism') needs to undertake a shift from regarding Mead as the main source of inspiration to embracing the perspective of Park as the progenitor of 'radical interactionism'. Such a shift, it is argued, will make interactionism better equipped to understand the fact that 'even in our most democratic societies, domination is still practiced' (Athens 2009:407). The specific notion of 'radical interactionism' first saw the light of day more than ten years ago (Athens 2007). As Athens has observed: '[T]he combination of the two words 'radical' and 'interactionism' … are seldom uttered in the same conversation in sociological circles, much less combined in the same sentence' (Athens 2013b:2). A question to clarify here is, therefore: Why the notion of 'radical' interactionism then? When hearing this notion, one is almost immediately propelled into thinking about the so-called radical sociology movement of the 1960s that was concerned with clearing the pathway towards human emancipation (see, e.g., Colfax and Roach 1971; Horowitz 1972). The 'radical sociology' initiative – spearheaded, for example, by activist initiatives such as Students for a Democratic Society (SDS) and civil rights movements – wanted to shake the very foundations of an orthodox consensus (consisting of functionalism, positivism, behaviourism and modernisation theories) within sociology that had persisted for too long. Even though RI does not rest on similar 'radicalist' ideas, the notion that a reconfiguration or rupture is indeed needed (especially within interactionist sociology) also underpins the ideas of RI. One might perhaps suspect that one of the most fertile and promising ways of 'radicalizing' interactionism and making it sensitive to the themes of domination, power and conflict would then be to incorporate Marxist ideas into the perspective. This would mean that the conventional Marxist and neo-Marxist preoccupation with topics such as inequality and injustice would come to the fore. However, as Athens notes, this combination has been attempted several times without much success. The reasons for this lack of success, he states, are twofold: firstly, despite attempts to synthesise Marxist and interactionist ideas, any realisation of the project has remained largely unconvincing primarily due to its apparent unfeasibility, and, secondly, that there is actually no need to seek refuge in Marxist ideas in order to radicalise interactionism (Athens 2013b:2–3). But whether the very notion of a 'radical' interactionism is, in fact, the most suitable is still a matter of discussion. For example, in a review of Athens' book *Radical Interactionism on the Rise* (2013a), Yves Laberge asked the following relevant set of questions: 'Radical interactionism is obviously seen as being 'radical' by its opponents such as the conservative tenants of symbolic interactionism; but one might ask, 'radical' compared to what? Or from which point of view can one say that this approach is radical? Is it because it is opposed to an unchanged tradition from almost one century ago?' (Laberge 2015:443). We agree with Laberge that the notion of RI (with its reliance on the 'radical' prefix) needs much more clarification and justification. In order to avoid confusion, it also needs to be stressed here that the 'radical interactionism' that Athens proposes is not to be confounded with the notion of 'radical interactionism' that relates to the study of artificial intelligence and cognitive science (see, e.g., Georgeon and Aha 2013).

Understanding domination and subjugation in everyday life

Everyday life is perhaps often – at the surface level – seen as a world characterised by smooth and unproblematic encounters among people who get along and collaborate in order to maintain a shared sense of reality. However, as Athens has proposed, everyday life is also an arena for struggles and conflict. In *Domination and Subjugation in Everyday Life* (2015), he expands principally on Park's work and focuses on the nature and dynamics of superordination and subordination, which Athens believes shapes all social interaction between human beings and groups. Athens, as he did in his earlier works, constructs a comprehensive framework and an architecture of essential terms to help analyse all forms of social conflict. Athens, for this book, expands beyond studies of violent criminals, to focus on 'dozens of first-hand accounts of criminal and non-criminal dominative encounters and lethal and non-lethal ones performed by both groups and individuals' (Athens 2015:175). For Athens, dominative encounters occur over time, rather than simultaneously, and unfold in eight stages: (1) *role claiming*, in which an aspiring superordinate, whether an individual or group, decides to take on the role of the superordinate and cast the other(s) into the role of the subordinate; (2) *role rejection*, in which ostensible subordinates decide whether to resist the aspiring superordinate's placement of them in the subordinate position, and if so, to resist actively or passively; (3) *role sparring*, in which participants in a dominative encounter 'jostle with each other' regarding who should play the superordinate and subordinate roles; (4) *role enforcement*, in which 'at least one of the two disputants must decide to use force to settle the issue of who should perform the superordinate and subordinate roles'; (5) *role determination*, in which 'the allocation of the superordinate and subordinate roles in the collective act is determined', resulting in 'a major or minor victory, a major or minor defeat, a draw, or 'no decision'; (6) *role battling*, in which combatants engage in multiple dominative engagements, when a single completed simple dominative encounter (see later) fails to determine who should perform the superordinate and subordinate roles in collective acts; these are often truncated, skipping many of the earlier stages, as the participants recognise each other as enemies; (7) *role campaigning*, in which participants engage in planned and coordinated role crusades aimed at gaining or maintaining domination; and finally (8) *role warfare*, in which combatants wage a set of coordinated role campaigns to force their opponents to assume the subordinate role (and occurs if a role campaign fails to resolve the issue of who is to perform the superordinate and subordinate roles) (Athens 2015:177–197).

As in keeping with his general method, not all that different from the way Erving Goffman also worked, Athens creates a detailed taxonomy. Simple dominative encounters are composed of stages 1–5, outlined earlier, divided into three types: (1) dominative tiffs, composed of stages 1 and 2; (2) dominative skirmishes, composed of stages 1–3; and (3) dominative engagements, composed of stages 1–5. More complex dominative encounters are composed of stages 1–8 outlined, divided into three types: (1) dominative battles, composed of stages 1–6; (2) dominative campaigns, composed of stages 1–7; and (3) dominative wars, composed of stages 1–8. Much as his aforementioned violentisation model stressed that it is completion of one phase that determines movement to the next, this eight-part model stresses that dominative engagement (stage 5) is the only completed simple dominance engagement and that dominative wars constitute the only completed complex dominance engagement (Athens 2015:176, 185).

Armed with this quite elaborate arsenal of terms, Athens aims to provide a 'common language to discuss not only wars but all other forms of human conflict' (Athens 2015:199). He cautions that dominative encounters are not only inevitable in the perpetual flow of an ongoing social process regarding the allocation of superordinate and subordinate roles, and that dominative encounters are not necessarily negative because they can be a means through which oppressed groups overthrow a regime they find tyrannical and unjust. Athens adds: 'Although the prevention of all dominative encounters is impossible, better means could be instituted to control their expression so that they take the form of nonviolent encounters rather than violent ones' (Athens 2015:199). Athens posits that combatants employ a 'calculus of escalation' in order to determine whether or not to intensify a dominative encounter through the use of force or the threat thereof (Athens 2015:204). Such a calculus of escalation involves the occurrence or non-occurrence of three events: (1) *tunnel vision*, in which acting units 'become too narrowly focused on pushing it to the next level', perhaps best colloquially summarised as 'rush[ing] to judgment'; (2) the formation of a *restraining judgment*, caused by several factors, such as the fear of an imminent or forthcoming major defeat, the possible intervention of a powerful third party, the possible loss of aid from critical allies, or the clear acquiescence of their opponents to assume the subordinate role or withdraw from the group or community; and (3) the formation of an overriding judgment, in which an acting unit initially decides to refrain from intensifying the encounter, but later re-enters it for a number of possible reasons, such as the basis for forming a restraining judgment has ceased to exist, as in when a crucial ally, formerly in favour of restraint now advocates escalation of the conflict; that a unique and advantageous opportunity to vanquish their opponents has presented itself, of which they feel compelled to exploit fully; or the acting unit, despite all the restraining factors being in place, can no longer tolerate performing the subordinate role, or being a bystander, to placate its foe (Athens 2015:204–211). Eventually, consistent with his eight-phase theory of dominative encounters, and his revised five-phase violentisation model, Athens cautions that it is possible for an acting unit to 'remain stuck' in one of the steps, and that ultimately, 'it must be underscored ... that the calculus of escalation is not only an ongoing process but an inherently precarious one that can seldom be predicted with absolute certainty over every stage of a dominative encounter's development' (Athens 2015:211–212).

Domination and Subjugation in Everyday Life ends with proposing 21 principles – some general, and others more specific – of RI. Briefly summarised, these are (1) regarding the nature of domination, human subjugation occurs during collective action; (2) regarding the agents of domination, these can be individuals or collectivities; (3) regarding 'the phylogenesis of domination', human subjugation emerged with the human acquisition of language, and with that the displacement of animal dominance with human domination; (4) regarding the 'ontogenesis of domination', 'human subjugation unfolds over a maturation process'; (5) regarding domination and the division of labour, Athens concludes that subjugation is a 'necessary evil in human group life' because it enables complex, cooperative collective interactions necessary for survival; (6) regarding domination, power and force, despite their interrelations as components of human subjugation, they can be analytically parsed apart with power and force being the means to achieve a common end: domination; (7) regarding legitimacy, institutionalisation and force, Athens sees legitimacy and institutionalisation as generally consonant with each other because the more institutionalised the exercise of force is, by an acting unit or individual, the more its exercise of power becomes accepted as legitimate, with the converse also true; thus, any 'stamp of approval' provided by institutionalisation or legitimation 'must be seen in relative rather than absolute terms'; (8) regarding the social visibility of domination, domination is usually invisible in everyday life because participants take for granted subjugation's operation; the only time the operation of subjugation erupts into visibility is when there is conflict regarding who should perform the superordinate and subordinate roles; (9) regarding the imperceptiveness of superordinates, Athens deduces that generally superordinates, being privileged, are less perceptive than subordinates during a collective act's construction; (10) regarding the omnipresence of domination in our daily lives, Athens notes its pervasiveness, even in cooperative ones, such as small talk at social events, or long-term collaborations between international corporations; (11) regarding the issue of dominance orders, Athens deduces that the long-term institutionalisation of the assignment of superordinate and subordinate roles results in the congealing of a pecking order, in which very few hold the highest positions in the dominance order; (12) all human conflicts are disputes over dominance and are therefore dominative encounters; (13) domination encounters all spring from 'status disquietude', whether personal or social; (14 and 15) dominative encounters unfold over time, comprised of a number of the eight successive but contingent stages outlined earlier, depending on whether they are simple or complex; (16) 'the size of the acting units ... does not limit the complexity and completeness of the dominative encounters' in which they can engage; (17) 'dominative engagements are the proverbial atom from which all dominative encounters (and hence conflicts) are constructed'; (18) regarding outcomes, dominative encounters can result in a 'major victory or defeat, minor victory or defeat, 'no contest,' or stalemate'; (19) an actor's or acting group's placement in the dominance order is not fixed but is determined by the outcomes discussed in number 18; (20) regarding the distinction between 'legitimate' and 'bastard' dominative encounters, 'legitimate' dominative encounters adhere to the norms of the majority, while 'bastard' dominative encounters are in consonance with the norms of the minority but contravene those of the majority; and (21) human domination is always contingent and in flux, depending upon local conditions or factors during the collective act. Nevertheless, Athens cautions that these 21 principles are provisional, and will need revision with further research. All in all, he views RI as consistent with the fundamental tenets of the Chicago School of pragmatism, which also emphasised the significance of human power and domination (Athens 2015:213–221).

The potentials and problems of RI

After this presentation of the main principles of RI and some of its antecedent ideas, we will now turn our attention to an assessment of the contribution of RI to social research. Let us first consider a few examples of the applicability and usability of RI to understand different sites of society. First of all, there is a lot of power (also in its thematic preferences) and potential in RI. RI not only recognises the importance of power, inequality, domination and subjugation (and hence also conflict) in studies of everyday life interaction. It places this concern at the centre of attention. Athens' focus on domination, power and force bears a close affinity with the theories of some sociologists or historians of science, as Antony J. Puddephat (2013:53–82) observes. Briefly summarised, to substantiate his argument, Puddephat draws from Pierre Bourdieu's work (1999, 2004), which extends concepts such as 'habitus', 'field', 'cultural capital' and 'symbolic capital' to the practices of research scientists in the natural sciences and envisages science as a competitive site of social and intellectual reproduction (Puddephat 2013:65). Bourdieu's descriptions of scientific actors, grounded in scientific hierarchies, struggling in an inherently unequal battle for upward mobility, status and esteem (as the existing hierarchies create more privileged spaces in the field, as opposed to their converse), are certainly resonant with Athens' 21 principles of RI described earlier. The work of Harry M. Collins (1992) and Collins and Trevor

Pinch (2012) as well as Ian Mitroff (1974) also intersect with Athens' observations regarding the privilege and visibility of those who occupy the superordinate position: the scientists, who do the abstract work and become first authors in any scientific article published, as opposed to the technicians, who do the practical laboratory work and are generally not acknowledged in many scientific articles. Furthermore, Collins and Pinch focus on the rhetorics of the scientific construction of facts, which entails warfare against rival camps of interpretation, with the outcome of such battles being decided principally by a camp's being able to build alliances (which are open to constant negotiation) with those who occupy the 'core set' of the relevant networks of visible scientists and financing institutions. Similarly, Caroline Joan S. Picart's early work (1994), building from Collins and Pinch (1979), Collins (1989, 1985) and G. Nigel Gilbert and Michael Mulkay's (1984) frameworks, analyses how the attempt by a French laboratory in 1988 to posit the existence of a 'ghostly imprint' (rather than the existence of molecules of triggering substances) accounting for allergic reactions led to a highly visible five-month controversy, with rhetorical battles waged both on paper and at the laboratory (Picart 1994:10–25). The case was marked by a farcical atmosphere in its initial phase, especially with *Nature* (a pre-eminent scientific journal) assembling a 'ghostbusting' team to investigate these radical claims composed of John Maddox, then-editor of *Nature*; 'The Amazing' James Randi, a professional magician (and MacArthur Foundation Fellow, Maddox was quick to stress); Walter Stewart of the National Institutes of Health in Maryland, a specialist in detecting errors and inconsistencies in scientific literature, and scientific misconduct, and Jose Alvarez, a technician whose movements remained invisible. The stakes were high: if the French laboratory could prove its claims, contemporary immunological theory, constructed from a materialistic theory of causation, would have to be displaced by a principally vitalistic theory of causation (Picart 1994:7, 12). In the second phase, probably in response to the farcical atmosphere of the first phase, the core network in the scientific community of immunologists resorted to standard rhetorical methods of 'error accounting' in order to discredit the French laboratory's alleged empirical findings as 'unscientific' (Picart 1994:20-24). As Athens (2010a) and Bourdieu (2004) has posited, in general, *ceteris paribus*, powerful groups tend to dominate weaker groups, using rhetorical and institutionalised methods, and the swift and unproblematic closure of the 'ghostly imprint' controversy is an instructive test case. Nevertheless, Athens (2002, 2007, 2010a) and Puddephat (2013) agree that 'Mead's general pragmatist epistemology ought to remain intact as a major advantage held over competing radical constructionist and postmodern positions' (Puddephat 2013:76). Similarly, Picart cautions against the 'complete reduction of the credibility of science to the merging of [Collins and Pinch's] constitutive and contingent frameworks', as doing so brings into relief unstated underlying issues regarding radical constructionists' own implicit epistemological claims to truthfulness or credibility, as well the possible danger of 'delegitimizing all scientific claims, both normative and revolutionary – that is to say, the possible creation of flat caricatures bearing the masks of three-dimensional sophistication' (Picart 1994:31).

Along a parallel path, James A. Shaw (2013) juxtaposes Richard Rorty's 'neo-pragmatism' with Athens' RI to conclude that although both begin with a 'Darwinian core', Rorty and Athens diverge 'in their positions on truth, rationality and the scientific method' (Shaw 2013:219); while Rorty's extension of 'Darwinian principles' into the relativity of language and human knowledge ends up in an ironist epistemology that makes any claim to truth problematic, Athens' application of 'Darwinian principles' is rather rooted in interpretative and lived experience, which he ultimately believes are verifiable as 'true' or 'false' (Shaw 2013:227, citing Athens 2010b), relative not to some grand notion of 'Truth', but *functionally* grounded in a particular experiential and communal context. As Shaw phrases it: 'This is not to suggest the veracity of a representational epistemology, but simply to recognize that shared interpretations of the meaning of the experience are all that is needed to provide an account of truth' (Shaw 2013:227). Nevertheless, as Puddephat urges, there is certainly potential in exploring an RI account of science, though one whose outer boundaries avoid the relativistic extremes implicit in some postmodern positions.

Moving on to the critiques of Athens' theory of, in particular, the violentisation model, we acknowledge that it would be virtually impossible to document, and do justice to, every single critique made, given their number and their diversity. Athens himself, in the 'Afterword to the Transaction Edition' of *The Creation of Dangerous, Violent Criminals* (2017b:103–153), takes it upon himself to respond systematically to what he considers the most significant of these critiques, with the hindsight of almost three decades after the book's initial publication. Roughly outlining some of these critiques and his responses (1) to those who decry his violentisation model for its 'apocalyptic' determinism (e.g., Bean 1990), Athens returns to his earlier remarks that the 'completion of all [the violentization process] is contingent rather than inevitable, far from certain' (Athens 2017c:103); (2) to those who view the violentisation model as simplistically linear (e.g., Milovanovic 1991), Athens responds that the violentisation model is circuitous, rather than linear, because the model posits 'several different routes' at each stage, allowing for an actor becoming arrested at a certain stage, regressing to a prior stage, progressing rapidly to the next stage, among other options (Athens 2017c:106–107); (3) to those who accuse Athens of completely ignoring the role victims play (e.g., O'Donnell 2003), Athens points out that the initial phase of the violentisation process, the brutalisation phase, reveals how dangerous violent criminals start out as victims, and that it is the initial victim's decision-making processes that determine whether completion of the various stages occurs (Athens 2017c:118); (4) to those who accuse Athens of not being 'scientific' in his interviewing methods, and of not allowing the subjects to speak for themselves, resulting in accounts that are 'wildly implausible' (e.g., Oates 1999), Athens responds that 'there is no such thing as *the* scientific method'; that Cambridge-trained criminologist Ian O'Donnell, despite his critique briefly outlined earlier, contrary to Oates, heaped high praise on Athens' interviewing skills (O'Donnell 2003:750–751); and then rhetorically asks: 'Should we take the opinion of a widely acclaimed writer of fiction and humanities professor or of respected criminologists and crime-beat

journalists about the 'wildly implausible' violent actions that the violent criminals in my study reported engaging in?' (Athens 2017c:139); and (5) to those
who doubt that the violentisation process can be operationalised, thus making its
usefulness for those who employ quantitative methods problematic (e.g., Glasner
2013), Athens produces an elegant and highly detailed 'Violentization Diagnostic
Checklist' (Athens 2017c:143–145).

Additionally, one of the consistent critiques that seem doggedly to follow
Athens' violentisation model is that it fails to account for why the rate of evolving into a violent, dangerous criminal is much higher for males than females,
when research on child maltreatment appears to yield the same results for both
boys and girls (see Zahn 1992; Krutschnitt 1994); adherents of these critiques are
also suspicious of Athens' claims that the 'process of creating dangerous criminals holds irrespective of age, sex and social class' (Krutschnitt 1994:334). And
similar critiques have been made in relation to social class and race (Milanovic
1991; Zahn 1992). As explained earlier, Athens points to gender bias (and general
sex differences in physical strength and stature), particularly at the brutalisation
and dominance-performance phases, as the reasons why more males than females
tend to complete the stages of violentisation (Athens 2017c:110–112). Although
Athens acknowledges that the violentisation model does not directly account for
rate differences among members of different social classes and race in their evolution into dangerous violent criminals, he argues that the larger context shows
that the model's explanatory power can be extended. Athens posits that the upper
classes' hierarchy of force usually includes enlisting the police's help in pre-
venting dominance engagements from turning violent', unlike the lower classes,
who 'perceive police intervention as less efficacious and [a] more indecorous
means of deterring violent dominance encounters, brute physical force occupies
a much higher position in the lower classes' hierarchy of force'; the end result
is that more violent, dangerous criminals generally come from the lower classes.
In relation to the issue of race, particularly in relation to the disparities in the
performance of violent crime between '*blacks and whites*' (emphasis in Athens
2017c:116–117, quoting Zahn 1992:366), Athens appears to use an intersectional
approach to explain why more blacks than whites tend to evolve into dangerous,
violent criminals:

> According to the general theory, blacks exhibit higher rates of committing
> serious violent crime than whites primarily because of two factors. First,
> blacks are more likely than whites to be not just members of the lower social
> classes, but members as well of the lowest rung of the lower classes, so that
> they usually have narrower hierarchies of force than their white counterparts.
> Second, racial segregation prevents blacks, who may be members of the
> higher social classes from moving into civil neighborhoods, which remain
> predominantly white to this day. Moreover, blacks not more often than whites
> live in turbulent neighborhoods, they also *much more often* than whites live
> in malignant neighborhoods, where their neighbors are much more likely to
> have completed the most stages of the violentization process and to have

the most compressed hierarchies of force, hierarchies which rarely [include] contacting the police because squealing on your neighbors is often regarded as taboo.

(Athens 2017c:117, original emphasis)

Picart (2013:191–214) explores how Athens' principle of domination resonates with the findings of critical race theorists, notably, those of Cheryl Harris and Kimberle Crenshaw. Briefly outlined, Picart analyses how Harris' (1993) genealogy of 'whiteness as property' tracks how whiteness, initially constructed whiteness as a racial identity, evolved into a form of property, rooted in parallel systems of domination over African American and Native American races, establishing a hierarchy built on white privilege supported by American law (Picart 2013:208, citing Harris 1993:1716, 1728–1731). Picart shows how Harris argues that after the period of slavery and conquest, whiteness became the functional basis of racialised privilege, a status that confers upward mobility and prestige, and that even when legal segregation was overturned, whiteness as status property continued to operate as an obstacle to effective change as evidenced in the *Brown I* and *Brown II* cases, and whose imprints can still be seen in jurisprudence in relation to affirmative action (Picart 2013:208–209, citing Harris 1993:1731, 1734, 1750–1756). Picart (2013) also draws from Crenshaw's (1995) 'intersectional approach', which treats factors like race, gender, nationality, class, and marital status as concrete foundations of power, which interact in a complex manner, like variables, in analysing the jurisprudence that results in various cases, such as those involving sexual harassment and domestic violence rape claims, among others (Picart 2013:209, citing Crenshaw 1995:350; see also Picart 2003). In a manner that parallels Athens' concerns, Crenshaw's focus is not on abstract identity politics, but on the experiences of violence and power differentials lived by poor African American women, institutionalised through an accretion of norms (Picart 2013:209, citing Crenshaw 1995:357–358). Although Athens does not use the word 'intersectional', the approach he utilises in responding to critiques focused on the violentisation model's apparent silence on how social class and race interact with the violentisation model bears a kinship with an intersectional approach. Similarly, in *Domination and Subjugation in Everyday Life* (2015), Athens, while discussing stage 1 (*role claiming*) of his eight-stage model outlined earlier, acknowledged that Robert E. Park's '"aggregate factors" (Park 1929/1952:179) (such as age, race, occupation, social class, nationality, religion gender, or sexual preference) can deeply affect an acting unit's views about its own standing, as well as those of other acting units in its group and community' (Athens 2015:177). Athens adds that other 'nuanced factors (such as athleticism, physical attractiveness, bravery, charm, cunningness, character, geniality, shrewdness, wittiness, and intelligence or the lack thereof), together with the time and place in which they are displayed or hidden' (Athens 2015:177), in addition to the 'aggregate factors', may serve as 'criteria' for deciding who occupy the superordinate and subordinate positions. Athens, as Picart and Crenshaw do, views these factors as involving a complex interplay, not a pre-determinative mould: 'Thus, in highly mobile and dynamic communities, the taken-for-granted assumptions that people develop about their own and other people's group or communal statuses cannot always be said to be based *exclusively* on aggregate factors' (Athens 2015:177, original emphasis).

In closing, the purpose of this subsection has been less to create a 'master narrative' of the potentials and perils in Athens' frameworks, in particular his violentisation model and less so his general notion of RI, than to capture some the dynamism and evolution of the discussions and debates surrounding his work. While there is much commentary in relation to his violentisation model, Athens' suggested notion of RI has so far not been as visible, partly because it is much more recent; and while Athens continues to develop and revise his thinking in relation to his violentisation model, as he continues to pioneer as an adherent of RI, only the passage of time will reveal how various scholarly communities (and perhaps even the broader public) will respond to his re-envisaging of his violentisation model as a microcosm grounded in the larger macrosphere of RI. Finally, we want to suggest that by RI's eagerness to stress its difference from SI, it risks overemphasising the differences between these two strands of interactionism and thus, potentially, distances itself from the intellectual community in which it was originally conceived and in which it would hopefully find a responsive audience.

Conclusion

In this chapter, we have introduced and discussed the relatively recent addition to the growing number of different strands of interactionist sociology under the heading of 'radical interactionism' (RI). We started out by showing how RI is the original outcome of one individual's efforts, namely Lonnie H. Athens. We then investigated his personal background, looking for clues as to why he later came to develop RI. Following this, we looked in some detail into his early criminological work on the so-called violentisation thesis as a backdrop for RI. Then we ventured into examining what RI is all about and how it diverges from more mainstream 'symbolic interactionism' (SI). Finally, we offered an assessment of some of the problems and potentials of RI. Admittedly, RI is neither a much-mentioned nor widespread perspective within interactionist sociology. It started out and so far remains a relatively limited perspective, predominantly promoted by Athens himself and a few colleagues. As Athens himself once stated: 'Although my hope is that my colleagues will consider radical interactionism as a viable alternative to symbolic interactionism, I am pessimistic about the chances of this happening any time soon because intellectual pursuits are no less subject to the operation of dominance orders than any other kind of human social endeavour' (Athens 2009:407). Despite this pessimism, some scholars, as we saw earlier, have in recent years in fact followed suit and have started to work within or engage with the framework of RI (see, e.g., Abermet 2012; Katovich 2011, 2013; Musolf 2013; Picart 2013; Shaw 2013). Nevertheless, this limited clout, as we have shown, does not detract from the importance of the ideas advanced by RI or its proposed principles for studying and understanding social interaction. First, RI orients our attention to the ubiquity of conflict, domination, power and subjugation in everyday life – themes that, despite their presence, still often remain at the margins of much of mainstream SI. Second, RI – with many of its main ideas stemming from violentisation theory – provides a useful (and also continuously elaborated and revised) model for understanding processes relating to some of the dark sides of social interaction, including violence, brutalisation and domination. Third, RI – by relying on the work of amongst others Robert E. Park – may prove instrumental in reviving and reactualising the ideas of some often forgotten or marginalised figures of early interactionism.

In conclusion, we want to stress that the recent rise of RI is indeed a useful and much needed addition to more mainstream SI. However, we also believe that SI in and by itself, at least in principle, can create spaces for an understanding and analysis of the themes of conflict, domination and violence without necessarily needing to resort to the specific ideas and principles of RI. Does the rise of RI then inaugurate a drastic reorientation of interactionist sociology? Hardly so based on RI's reception in the field; nonetheless, it does direct our attention, as interactionists, to some topics and themes that could beneficially be studied by getting acquainted with ideas derived from RI. In this way, in conclusion, we regard RI as a valuable supplement for a radical reorientation of interactionist sociology. To close, perhaps an analogy may clarify this point. Friedrich Nietzsche, in *The Birth of Tragedy* (1967:33), grappled with the oppositional interactions between Apollinian (reason) and Dionysian (chaos) forces at play in the generation of Hellenic art; the value of this interaction is that it excites, stimulates, rouses or irritates (*reizen*) (Picart 1999:40–41) new 'births' of art, which achieves 'greatness' only when there is a 'healthy' balance between the two forces. Perhaps RI may function as such an 'irritant/stimulant' for SI, helping enable adaptive evolutions.

References

Abermet, Viola (2012): '"And We Have Lots of Food, So We Believe it is True" – Dramatizations of Self-Change in Papua New Guinea', in Thaddeus Mueller (ed.): *Contributions from European Symbolic Interactionists: Conflict and Cooperation* (Studies in Symbolic Interaction, Volume 45). Bingley: Emerald Publishing, pp. 99–118.

Anderson, Leon and David A. Snow (2001): 'Inequality and the Self: Exploring Connections from an Interactionist Perspective'. *Symbolic Interaction*, 24 (4):395–406.

Arbunkle, Woody (1999): 'Why They Kill: Exploring the Thought Behind Violence'. *The Wag*, November 1999. Available online at: http://www.thewag.net/books/rhodes.htm.

Athens, Lonnie H. (1980): *Violent Criminal Acts and Actors: A Symbolic Interactionist Study*. London: Routledge and Kegan Paul.

Athens, Lonnie H. (1987): 'Herbert Blumer: A Tribute to Herbert Blumer: An Anomalous Figure in American Academia'. *Society for the Study of Symbolic Interaction Notes*, 14:6–7.

Athens, Lonnie H. (1989): *The Creation of Dangerous Violent Criminals*. Urbana: University of Illinois Press.

Athens, Lonnie H. (1994): 'The Self as Soliloquy'. *Sociological Quarterly*, 35 (3):521–532.

Athens, Lonnie H. (1995): 'Dramatic Self Change'. *Sociological Quarterly*, 36 (3):571–586.

Athens, Lonnie H. (1997): *Violent Criminal Acts and Actors Revisited*. Urbana: University of Illinois Press.

Athens, Lonnie H. (2002): 'Domination: The Blind Spot in Mead's Analysis of the Social Act'. *Journal of Classical Sociology*, 2 (1):25–42.

Athens, Lonnie H. (2005a): 'Mead's Lost Conception of Society'. *Symbolic Interaction*, 28:305–325.

Athens, Lonnie H. (2005b): 'Violent Encounters: Violent Engagements, Skirmishes and Tiffs'. *Journal of Contemporary Ethnography*, 34:1–48.

Athens, Lonnie H. (2007): 'Radical Interactionism: Going Beyond Mead'. *Journal for the Theory of Social Behaviour*, 37 (2):137–165.

Athens, Lonnie H. (2009): 'The Roots of 'Radical Interactionism''. *Journal for the Theory of Social Behaviour*, 39 (4):387–414.

Athens, Lonnie H. (2010a): 'Human Subordination from a Radical Interactionist's Perspective'. *Journal for the Theory of Social Behavior*, 40 (3):339–368.

Athens, Lonnie H. (2010b): 'Naturalistic Inquiry in Theory and Practice'. *Journal of Contemporary Ethnography*, 39 (1):87–125.

Athens, Lonnie H. (2012): 'Mead's Analysis of Social Conflict: A Radical Interactionist's Perspective'. *American Sociologist*, 43:428–447.

Athens, Lonnie H. (2013a): *Radical Interactionism on the Rise* (Studies in Symbolic Interaction, Volume 41). Bingley: Emerald Group Publishing.

Athens, Lonnie H. (2013b): ''Radical' and 'Symbolic' Interactionism: Demarcating Their Borders', in Lonnie H. Athens (ed.): *Radical Interactionism on the Rise* (Studies in Symbolic Interaction, Volume 41). Bingley: Emerald Group Publishing, pp. 1–24.

Athens, Lonnie H. (2013c): 'Mead's Conception of the Social Act: A Radical Interactionist's Critique', Lonnie H. Athens (ed.): *Radical Interactionism on the Rise* (Studies in Symbolic Interaction, Volume 41). Bingley: Emerald Group Publishing, pp. 25–51.

Athens, Lonnie H. (2013d): 'Park's Theory of Conflict and His Fall from Grace in Sociology'. *Cultural Studies* ↔ Critical Methodologies, 13 (2):75–87.

Athens, Lonnie H. (2015): *Domination and Subjugation in Everyday Life*. New York: Routledge.

Athens, Lonnie H. (2017a): 'Applying Violentization: From Theory to Praxis'. *Victims and Offenders: An International Journal of Evidence-Based Research, Policy and Practice*, 12 (4):497–522.

Athens, Lonnie H. (2017b): 'The Belated Appearance of 'Radical Interactionism' on the American Sociological Stage: The Rise of G. H. Mead and Fall of Robert Park'. *American Sociologist*, 48 (1):23–47.

Athens, Lonnie H. (2017c): *The Creation of Dangerous Violent Criminals* (2nd edition). New Brunswick, NJ: Transaction Publishers.

Bean, Philip (1990): 'Review of *The Creation of Dangerous Violent Criminals* by L. H. Athens'. *British Journal of Criminology*, 30 (4):528–529.

Bourdieu, Pierre (1999): 'The Specificity of the Scientific Field and the Social Conditions of the Progress of Reason', in Mario Biagioli (ed.): *The Science Studies Reader*. London: Routledge, pp. 31–50.

Bourdieu, Pierre (2004): *Science of Science and Reflexivity*. Chicago: University of Chicago Press.

Colfax, J. David and Jack L. Roach (eds.) (1971): *Radical Sociology*. New York: Basic Books.

Collins, Harry M. (1985): *Changing Order: Replication and Induction in Scientific Practice*. London: Sage Publications.

Collins, Harry M. (1989): 'The Meaning of Experiment: Replication and Reasonableness', in Hillary Lawson and Lisa Appignanesi (eds.): *Dismantling Truth: Reality in the Post-Modern World*. London: Weidenfield and Nicholson.

Collins, Harry M. (1992): *Changing Order: Replication and Induction in Scientific Practice*. Chicago: University of Chicago Press.

Collins, Harry M. and Trevor Pinch (1979): 'The Construction of the Paranormal: Nothing Unscientific is Happening', in Roy Wallis (ed.): *On the Margins of Science: The Social Construction of Rejected Knowledge*. Keele: University of Keele, pp. 237–270.

Collins, Harry M. and Trevor Pinch (2012): *The Golem: What You Should Know About Science* (2nd edition). London: Cambridge University Press.

Crenshaw, Kimberle (1995): 'Mapping the Margins: Intersectionality, Identity Politics and Violence Against Women of Color', in Kimberle Crenshaw, Neil Gotanda, Gary Peller and Kendall Thomas (eds.): *Critical Race Theory: The Key Writings that Formed the Movement*. New York: The New Press, pp. 357–383.

Dennis, Alex and Peter J. Martin (2005): 'Symbolic Interactionism and the Concept of Power'. *British Journal of Sociology*, 56 (2):191–213.

Denzin, Norman K. (1992): *Symbolic Interactionism and Cultural Studies*. Oxford: Blackwell.

Georgeon, Olivier L. and David W. Aha (2013): 'The Radical Interactionism Conceptual Commitment'. *Journal of Artificial General Intelligence*, 4 (2):31–36.

Gilbert, G. Nigel and Michael Mulkay (1984): *Opening Pandora's Box: A Sociological Analysis of Scientists' Discourse*. Cambridge: Cambridge University Press.

Glasner, Aviva Twersky (2013): 'Lonnie Athens Revisited: The Social Construction of Violence'. *Journal of Aggression and Violent Behavior*', 18 (2):281–285.

Gougherty, Matthew and Tim Hallett (2013): 'Revisiting Learning to Labor: Interaction, Domination, Resistance and the "Grind"', in Lonnie H. Athens (ed.): *Radical Interactionism on the Rise* (Studies in Symbolic Interaction, Volume 41). Bingley: Emerald Group Publishing, pp. 123–159.

Harris, Cheryl (1993): 'Whiteness as Property'. *Harvard Law Review*, 106 (8):1707–1791.

Horowitz, David (1972): *Radical Sociology: An Introduction*. New York: Canfield Press.

James, George (1999): 'In Person: Why They Kill? He Thinks He Knows'. *The New York Times*, October 10. Available online at: http://www.nytimes.com/1999/10/10/nyregion/in-person-why-they-kill-he-thinks-he-knows.html.

Katovich, Michael A. (2011): 'Death Becomes Mead: Toward a Radical Interactionist Reading of *Million Dollar Baby*', in Norman K. Denzin (ed.): *Studies in Symbolic Interaction* (Volume 36). Bingley: Emerald Group Publishing, pp. 161–181.

Katovich, Michael A. (2013): 'Dominance, Deference and Demeanor in *Mad Men*: Toward a Convergence of Radical Interactionism and Radical Dramaturgy', in Lonnie H. Athens (ed.): *Radical Interactionism on the Rise* (Studies in Symbolic Interaction, Volume 41). Bingley: Emerald Group Publishing, pp. 161–189.

Krutschnitt, Candace (1994): 'Buddy, Can You Par-a-digm? Three Predictive Models of Deviant Development'. *Journal of Research in Crime and Delinquency*, 31 (3):328–336.

Laberge, Yves (2015): 'Against the Symbolic Interactionism Dogma? Radical Inter-actionism Enters into Force'. *Symbolic Interaction*, 38 (3):442–444.

Lewis, J. David and Richard L. Smith (1980): *American Sociology and Pragmatism – Mead, Chicago Sociology and Symbolic Interaction*. Chicago: University of Chicago Press.

Lindner, Rolf (1996): *The Reportage and Urban Culture – Robert Park and the Chicago School*. Cambridge: Cambridge University Press.

McNall, Scott G. and James C. M. Johnson (1975): 'The New Conservatives: Ethno-methodologists, Phenomenologists and Symbolic Interactionists'. *Insurgent Sociologist*, 5 (4):49–65.

Milovanovic, Dragan (1991): 'Book Review: *The Creation of Dangerous Violent Criminals*'. *Criminal Justice Review*, 16 (1):110–113.

Mitroff, Ian (1974): 'Norms and Counter-Norms in a Select Group of Apollo Moon Scientists: A Case Study of the Ambivalence of Scientists'. *American Sociological Review*, 39 (4):579–595.

Morris, Monica B. (1977): *An Excursion into Creative Sociologies*. New York: Columbia University Press.

Musolf, Gil R. (1992): 'Structures, Institutions, Power and Ideology: New Directions within Symbolic Interactionism'. *Sociological Quarterly*, 33 (2):171–189.

Musolf, Gil R. (2013): 'Domination and Resistance: The Political Theory of John Dewey', in Lonnie H. Athens (ed.): *Radical Interactionism on the Rise* (Studies in Symbolic Interaction, Volume 41). Bingley: Emerald Group Publishing, pp. 83–121.

Nietzsche, Friedrich (1967): *The Birth of Tragedy and The Case of Wagner* (translated by Walter Kaufmann). New York: Random House.

Oates, Joyce Carol (1999): 'Crime and Punishment'. *The New York Times*, September 19.

O'Donnell, Ian (2003): 'A New Paradigm for Understanding Violence? – Testing the Limits of Lonnie Athens's Theory'. *British Journal of Criminology*, 43 (4):750–771.

Park, Robert E. (1929/1952): 'Sociology, Community and Society,' in Everett C. Hughes (ed.): *Human Communities*. New York: Free Press, pp. 178–209.

Park, Robert E. (1931/1950): 'Personality and Cultural Conflict', in Everett C. Hughes (ed.): *Race and Culture: Essays in the Sociology of Contemporary Man*. New York: Free Press, pp. 357–371.

Park, Robert E. (1937/1950): 'Cultural Conflict and the Marginal Man', in Everett C. Hughes (ed.): *Race and Culture: Essays in the Sociology of Contemporary Man*. New York: Free Press, pp. 372–376.

Picart, Caroline Joan S. (1994): 'Scientific Controversy as Farce: The Benveniste-Maddox Counter-Trials'. *Social Studies of Science*, 24 (1):7–37.

Picart, Caroline Joan S. (1999): *Resentment and the 'Feminine' in Nietzsche's Politico-Aesthetics*. State Park: Pennsylvania State University Press.

Picart, Caroline Joan S. (2003): 'Rhetorically Reconfiguring Victimhood and Agency: The Violence Against Women Act's Civil Rights Clause'. *Rhetoric and Public Affairs*, 6 (1):97–125.

Picart, Caroline Joan S. (2013): 'Reflections on Power and Intersectionality', in Lonnie H. Athens (ed.): *Radical Interactionism on the Rise* (Studies in Symbolic Interaction, Volume 41). Bingley: Emerald Group Publishing, pp. 191–214.

Puddephatt, Antony J. (2013): 'Toward a Radical Interactionist Account of Science', in Lonnie H. Athens (ed.): *Radical Interactionism on the Rise* (Studies in Symbolic Interaction, Volume 41). Bingley: Emerald Group Publishing, pp. 53–82.

Rhodes, Richard (2000): *Why They Kill: The Discoveries of a Maverick Criminologist*. New York: Vintage Books.

Ruiz-Junco, Natalia (2011): 'Santayana: Entering into the Drama of His Social Thought', in Norman K. Denzin (ed.): *Studies in Symbolic Interactionism*, Volume 36. Bingley: Emerald Group Publishing, pp. 137–160.

Shaw, James A. (2013): 'The Best Road for Pragmatism: Neo-Pragmatism or Radical Interactionism?', in Lonnie H. Athens (ed.): *Radical Interactionism on the Rise* (Studies in Symbolic Interaction, Volume 41). Bingley: Emerald Group Publishing, pp. 215–246.

Shaw, James A. (2017): 'Radical Interactionism', in George Ritzer (ed.): *Blackwell Encyclopedia of Sociology*. Oxford: Blackwell. Available online at: https://online library.wiley.com/doi/full/10.1002/9781405165518.wbeos0758.

Simmel, Georg (1955): *Conflict and the Web of Group Affiliations*. New York: Free Press.

Zahn, Margaret (1992): 'The Making of Violent Men'. *Contemporary Psychology: APA Review of Books*, 37 (4):365–366.

9 Symbolic interactionism and the Frankfurt School

A critical appraisal[1]

Lauren Langman

Introduction

In the early 20th century, the 'new' human sciences of sociology, anthropology and psychoanalysis each developed, with their own focus, concerns and perspectives on the relationship of culture, social structure, individual subjectivity, socialisation and personality development. For sociology, the writings of William James and Charles Horton Cooley, coupled with American pragmatism, culminated in George Herbert Mead's sociological perspective on the mind and the 'social self', which emerged through interactions with others. Exchanging nonverbal cues of facial/bodily gestures and touch enabled the subsequent use of symbols, primarily language, facilitating self-objectification and reflexivity. 'Taking the role of the other' enabled the incorporation into one's family, peer groups and eventually the 'generalized other' wherein collective values became crucial components of selfhood. Herbert Blumer (1969) would name that perspective 'symbolic interactionism' (abbreviated herein as SI). SI focused primarily on general aspects of the development of the cognitive and linguistic aspects of the 'social self', typically expressed in thought and behaviour especially in interpersonal relationships. SI became the dominant sociological approach for understanding the formation of the 'social self' through social interaction.

In Mead's perspective, the 'Me' as subject was shaped by society beginning with early play and rule-based games that would lead to learning social roles, collective attitudes and values that became part of the social self. This led to the emergence of the 'I', the volitional agent that evaluates information, initiates actions and constructs meanings. The SI perspective examined interaction and group life such as the spatial contexts of interaction (e.g., frontstage and backstage), 'teamwork', using fashions to articulate self-identity, and the use of certain 'props' to sustain various self-presentations and shape 'definitions of the situations' to accomplish certain interpersonal goals (Goffman 1959). Similarly, the social constructions of meanings, negotiations of social order, 'defining of situations' and 'framing of reality' by active agents engaged in interaction and negotiation became important realms of inquiries regarding subjectivity and interactions in a variety of settings (Strauss 1978). Closely allied to SI, one of the classical works was the *Social Construction of Reality* by Peter L. Berger and Thomas Luckmann (1966) that examined both the objective nature of reality, institutionalisation and legitima-tion, as well as the subjective aspects such as socialisation, internalisation, typi-fications, and the extent to which identity becomes tied to particular values and/or political positions. The SI concerns with the constructions of meanings and framings of issues and/or social reality became important factors in social move-ment research enabling and sustaining actions and mobilisations to realise particu-lar goals (see Benford and Snow 2000).

More recently, the social conditions of our times, riven by political–economic crises, have led to critical perspectives on subjectivity that highlight certain limitations of SI. Yet such critiques can expand and revitalise its valuable sociological traditions. In the 1960s, SI was itself a critique of the mainstreams of American sociology, namely the structural-functional view of order, consen-sus and cohesion that had become quite problematic. As Peter M. Hall noted: 'C. Wright Mills and critical theorists like Herbert Marcuse offered much less sanguine views of both sociology and American society … SI did not so much challenge the dominant views of American society as it did question the func-tionalist theory that sought to explain it' (Hall 2003:34–35). Nevertheless, a fundamental critique of SI, especially as articulated by Lonnie H. Athens, has been SI's 'value-free' and ahistorical sociology that is uncritical toward social injustice and indifferent to human suffering (see also Chapter 8 in this volume). Athens's critique of SI from within noted its limited attention to issues of domi-nation–subordination raised by Georg Simmel that also informed Robert E. Park, but this was a path not taken.

A number of contemporary circumstances have had a major impact on subjec-tivity, yet neither inequality, precarity, environmental despoliation nor authoritar-ian movements have been topics for SI theory and research. There has been little concern with (1) the political economy of neoliberal globalisation, the crises of legitimacy and growing inequality; (2) the political arena in which conservative if not reactionary forces have been ascendant; and/or (3) changing cultural pat-terns from gender roles and sexuality to Internet use. The 'social self' exists at a level of generality that little heeds *the changing nature of society and/or the class location of the socialisation of the person. As society has changed, so too have the forms and expressions of subjectivity.* Furthermore, the development of subjectivity involves desires, emotions and frustrations as much as language and cognition. Finally, the SI perspective ultimately results in a 'conformist psychol-ogy' with an 'oversocialized concept of man' mirroring the structural functional-ism that it would itself critique (Wrong 1961). Absent is a basis for resistance that disposes individuals into joining in groups and networks – topics already well studied by SI.

The Frankfurt School of Critical Theory (FS) perspective emerged in the early 20th century from a tradition rooted in G. W. F. Hegel's dialectic of his-tory, Karl Marx's critique of the alienation and suffering engendered by capital-ism, Max Weber's analysis of rationality and the entrapment within its 'iron cages', and Sigmund Freud's theory of 'unconscious desires' thwarted by civili-sation's demands for repression maintained by guilt. Following the humiliation at Versailles, with its call for drastic reparations, came a time of political and economic crisis and instability, and a weak Weimar government. Many people felt fearful, angry and aggressive towards the 'culprits' (Fromm 1941). In order to 'alleviate' these unpleasant emotions, some embraced powerful leaders who demanded deference, if not obedience, from subordinates. There was a great deal of social chaos and violent street conflicts between socialists, communists and the Nazis. Many workers voted like the highly authoritarian petty bourgeois classes, as did many elites. Adolf Hitler and the Nazi Party gained enough seats in the *Reichstag* to assume power, followed by, totalitarianism, war and genocide.

In this context, a group of Marxist philosophers, economists and sociologists came together to form the Institute for Social Research (ISR), affiliated with the University of Frankfurt from which the tradition of critical theory emerged. FS was clearly tied to traditions of German idealism. Many FS scholars were Hegelian Marxists. Moreover, influenced by Karl Korsch (1923/1970) and György Lukács (1923/2000), the FS scholars wished to revive the cultural and philosophical moments of Marxism as a normative theory with a critique of the economic conditions that lead to human suffering; they envisioned a free, rational and democratic society emancipated from ignorance, dogmatism and superstition, which enabled universal dignity and universal self-realisation. But rationality itself became a hegemonic ideology, sustaining modern capitalism and new forms of domination and dehumanisation (Adorno and Horkheimer 1947/2000).

In this chapter, it is my contention that FS can expand the SI traditions by offering many important insights. Subjectivity is not only historically variable, but the ways in which it varies and changes are consequences of an economic system, and caretakers, as agents of socialisation, raise children in ways that foster a historically specific expression of subjectivity best adapted to current realities. The 'social self' of SI, or the 'social character' of FS, is influenced by a number of macro-social factors of each era in which hegemonic ideologies sustain the domination by a particular class, the economic system, political realities, cultural factors, etc., which contextualise the development and expressions of the subjectivity ('social character') of each cohort as it flows through the life cycle. The SI perspective, focusing on cognitive and linguistic factors, has paid little attention to underlying aspects of emotions and desires below the level of awareness; these aspects of subjectivity, 'character' as the totality of the person, including conscious and unconscious moments, have been the concern of psychoanalysis with little impact on SI. But language and the realities shaped by language are not by themselves 'objective' and 'neutral', but rather shaped by cultural and political factors. Finally, the SI commitment to a 'value-free' perspective has mitigated against critical analyses of society in which norms, attitudes and understandings serve to sustain particular political or economic domination by reproducing social arrangements that generally privilege the elites. FS offers a perspective by which we can both critique SI and yet expand its perspectives, that, when informed by a normative critique of domination and suffering, makes SI more relevant to the changing times of today.

Culture, history and the rise of theory

SI first emerged at a time of growing American industrial and political development. SI was thus imbued with a degree of optimism regarding both the nation
and SI's place in the academic world. SI focused primarily on general aspects of
the self as subject and agent, emphasising the cognitive and linguistic aspects of
selfhood and volitional expressions of selfhood (Mead 1934/2015; Blumer 1969).
Self-conceptions, as well as attitudes and values, were learned through social
interaction. There were some European influences, for example, George Herbert
Mead had studied in Europe and was exposed to Hegelian philosophy in which the
'struggle for recognition' became the basis of self-consciousness. Georg Simmel
had considerable influence on early American sociology – especially his essay on
the metropolis, the centre of the monetary economy, where social interaction was
dominated by an 'objective culture' largely concerned with rationality and profit
(Simmel 1903/1950). In the metropolis, with its crowds, hustle and bustle, blar-
ing noise and multitudes of glaring lights, the modern subject, needing to defend
himself/herself from the constant overstimulation, developed a blasé attitude of
seeming indifference towards others, which enabled him/her to maintain his/her
sanity in the modern city. Simmel was among the first to point out the changing
nature of modern subjectivity and social interaction. An important development in
this tradition was the 'dramaturgical' perspective on volitional, goal-oriented selfhood articulated in region-specific 'performances' where actors wished to attain
certain goals through 'impression management' via 'face work' (Goffman 1959,
1967). SI traditions of ethnographic analyses, participant observations and studies
of small group interactions, whether at work or play, can supplement and comple-
ment the FS perspectives. For example, 'grounded theory' links actual research to
theory, while much of FS theory is more an exegesis of texts quite apart from the
lived experiences of actual actors (Glaser and Strauss 1967).

SI would become useful for studying certain patterns of deviant behaviour,
such as jack rollers, taxi hall dancers or gang members. Edwin H. Sutherland
(1924) explained deviance on the basis of 'differential association' – if a person
associates with a certain group, one learns its norms, values and perceptions of
reality, and adapts to its desirable identities and modes of interaction. Similarly,
Howard S. Becker's (1963) work on the social construction of 'deviance' as the
result of it being defined as such, has been called 'labelling theory' in which
groups with political and/or legal authority define certain actions as criminally
or morally 'deviant'. Homosexuality was once considered criminal and/or pathological as was marijuana. Labelling theory had a considerable influence in studies
of criminology and deviant behaviour in general. One of the classical studies in
the symbolic interactionist approach to collective identity was Becker's (1953)
study of marijuana users; the experience of a marijuana 'high' required socialisation into a group's norms values and identities in order to define the physiological
consequences as pleasant.

But SI was little concerned with the dominant ideologies of capitalist society and the role of ideology in legitimating the often unjust economic systems

that might colonise consciousness, subjectivity and shape political behaviour. A major concern of the FS was the critique of ideology as 'instrumental reason' had become the dominant ideology of capitalism. But FS said little about the actual production of ideology by social actors. Nevertheless, many SI scholars were concerned with the micro-social levels of ideology construction and the negotiation of the social order. At this point, it might be worthwhile to remember William I. Thomas's observation that if men defined situations as real they were real in their consequences (Thomas and Thomas 1928).

In Germany in the 1930s, as adverse economic conditions engendered fear and anger disposing mass protests, a pressing concern was to seek an understanding of the rise of fascism. Orthodox Marxism could little explain the cultural and/or psychological appeals of fascism. FS began to study Max Weber's notions of rationality, the 'disenchantment of the world' and crisis-driven charismatic leadership in order to understand the psycho-cultural appeal of Nazism. Psychoanalytic theories of sexual repression maintained by a repressive superego, along with anal sadism, group psychology and identification with the aggressor suggested an important role for authoritarian politics. Wilhelm Reich (1933) had argued that the 'mass psychology of fascism' was based on the repression of sexuality that began in early childhood, which imposed control on erotic gratification and in turn disposed authoritarianism, conformity, obedience to authority and the stifling of selfhood, thus echoing Friedrich Nietzsche's critique of the 'slave morality'. When Max Horkheimer took over the directorship of the Institute for Social Research (ISR), there was a desire to develop a wider, interdisciplinary and multilevel framework for understanding society. The FS scholars attempted to incorporate Weber's critique of 'reason' with psychoanalytic theories of the dynamics of character structure, the unconscious, desires, emotions and defences. A great deal of psychic life was unconscious and hidden from our awareness but helped understand the psycho-cultural appeal of Nazism. The ISR launched a number of large-scale studies asking questions as to how and why so many Germans, especially a significant number of union workers, supported Adolf Hitler and the Nazi party.

Erich Fromm (1941), a sociologist turned psychoanalyst, subsequently linked Freud's ideas of desires, defences and group psychology to show how authoritarianism, rooted in the sadomasochism of a repressive superego, disposed domination–submission, the desire to submit to superior authority while dominating and/or denigrating subordinates, and, at the same time, projecting aggression to out-groups. Authoritarianism was especially typical among the more right-wing, indeed reactionary, members of the working classes and/or petty bourgeoisie who supported the Nazis. The tendencies toward racism, ethnocentrism, anti-Semitism, homophobia and most of all the appeal of fascism rested upon unconscious authoritarianism, with its underlying sadomasochism expressed as anger and hostility toward 'illegitimate' elites, 'evil' subordinates, and/or 'dangerous' out-groups. Authoritarianism provided an explanation of why people, especially those who experienced strict, repressive childrearing, when faced with crises that might evoke fear, anxiety and/or humiliation, uncritically submit to charismatic authoritarians from Gabriele D'Annunzio to Benito Mussolini and most of all

Adolf Hitler. Such leaders not only served as the 'ego ideal' of the group but established connections to the leader and group which provided a sense of solidarity that alleviated anxiety in face of tenuous social bonds. Finally, party membership in such groups gave members a sense of empowerment based on their 'superiority' to out-groups who also served as blameworthy targets for aggression (see Freud 1921). Furthermore, Hitler's Minister of Propaganda, Josef Goebbels, was one of the pioneers in the use of psychologically powerful mass-mediated political spectacles. Thus, the FS scholars were among the first academics to consider the power of the mass media, especially its political impact and the psychological appeals of fascist propaganda. (Their understandings were later applied to the study of post-war consumerism.)

It is of course interesting to note that Thomas J. Scheff (1994), a leading symbolic interactionist scholar, offered a parallel and indeed complementary analysis of the rise of fascism as an expression of 'bloody revenge' against the 'enemies' of Germany following the surrender at Versailles that led to unacknowledged shame and humiliation that shattered social bonds. The pain of such emotions engendered a need for vengeance that fuelled the support for the Nazi party. Much of Scheff's analysis parallels FS and clearly anticipated many of the right-wing if not reactionary movements of today in which large numbers of people feel victimised by the policies of the elites, threatened by minorities and feel an intense *ressentiment* expressed as a need for revenge, indeed harsh punishment if not annihilation of the 'enemies' – both elites and 'outsiders'.

The historical nature of selfhood

Though Marx said little about subjectivity, Hegel's notion of the master–slave 'struggle for recognition' as the basis of consciousness informed his critique of alienated labour. Selling one's labour power for wages to produce commodities led to alienation. The worker's self was divorced from the products of his/her work, he/she was rendered powerless, without recognition, devoid of dignity, unable to realise creative self-fulfilment, bereft of community and estranged from his/her fundamental nature as a 'species being'. As Fromm put it, selfhood became alienated and thwarted; it was a monstrosity (Fromm 1961). FS, having as mentioned earlier been influenced by Marxism and psychoanalysis, was concerned with the historical contexts of socialisation and character development as well as the changes in the structure and dynamics of subjectivity from the end of the feudal era to the rise of early capitalism, the subsequent spread of Protestantism, followed by industrial capitalism, the rise of mass consumption/mass culture, and finally, today, the globalisation of neoliberalism.

The FS concern was not simply charting historical changes of capitalism and subsequent changes of subjectivity. FS remains an emancipatory critique of political–economic domination, informed by normative visions of an alternative society that might provide agency/creative self-realisation, community, recognition and meaning – in short dignity. Creative self-realisation is not the same as the radical individualisation, isolation and fragmentation of the 'self-contained individual' that is so typical in a rationalised, capitalist society based on commodity production and monetary exchange. Rather, for Marx and FS a more realised self, rich in needs rather than needing riches, who is closely connected to his or her identity granting and recognising community of shared meanings provides people with dignity (see Ashley 1985; Langman and Albanese 2015).

Freudian ideas had little impact on American sociology. The SI traditions of subjectivity and interaction placed primary emphasis on the more conscious, symbolic (linguistic) aspects of socialisation, the development of self and social interaction. The perspectives of SI and FS are not so much antagonistic as complementary – each grasps a different part of the totality of subjectivity and social relationships. A comprehensive concern with the nature of subjectivity in general, and the changing nature of contemporary subjectivity in particular, is broadened and deepened by considerations of both cognitive-/linguistic-based self-presentations and the underlying emotional, unconscious feelings and motives that impact consciousness, self-conceptions and undergird social interactions.

The SI concept of the 'social self' said little about the fundamental changes and differences in subjectivity over time. Nevertheless, the SI perspective suggested how social interactions and relationships might change over time, and in turn change the nature of parent–child interaction and socialisation practices. For FS, the historical changes in subjectivity, focusing upon a psychodynamic perspective on character, became the key to understanding the relationship between political economy of various historical epochs and the attendant suffering. What was especially important were the ways in which people attempted to ameliorate historically specific suffering through what Erich Fromm (1941) called 'mechanisms of escape' such as authoritarianism, conformity and aggression. The early studies of authoritarianism led to concerns with the historical nature of character especially in the work of Fromm and Theodor W. Adorno. Fromm traced the changes in 'social character' from feudalism to early capitalism to later industrial capitalism. Adorno's concern, on the other hand, was primarily the changing nature of authority relations that became internalised as the superego – the family was an obedience factory. That said, with the growth of modern institutions of socialisation, especially schools and the mass media, the authority of the father was undercut; notwithstanding their differences, their work illustrated the historical variations in selfhood.

Fromm (1941) integrated Marx's historical materialism with Weber's perspective on 'subjectively meaningful social action' and Freudian psychodynamics. Every society fostered a particular kind of 'social character', the character type most frequently found within a particular society with a certain kind of economic system. Parents as both role models and socialisation agents would mediate society and foster a 'social character' best adapted to the economic system. The unintended 'economic ethic' of Protestantism with work as a 'moral calling', 'this worldly asceticism', individualism and rationality fostered a 'social character' motivated to do the kinds of work demanded by a market economy. Within a short time, Protestant Northern Europe was more economically successful, industrialised and prosperous than the Catholic countries. By the 20th century, following industrialisation, mass production and bureaucratisation, came the new forms of mass media and mass consumption and a new character type was emergent: the 'marketing personality' was oriented towards selling things and indeed, selling his/her very self as part and parcel of that process. Within a few generations, a new 'social character' became typical.

For Freud, character structure was basically laid down in early childhood and more or less completed with the resolution of the Oedipus complex, which gave rise to the superego – from that point on, while intellectual abilities may continue to develop, one's character structure was more or less fixed and stable. Fromm, on the other hand, questioned that stability and indeed suggested that even past childhood, dynamic character change meant that people could adapt to changing circumstances. This notion of character change took issue with the Freudian notions of one's character being more or less established by the age of five. Fromm (1941) argued that people were capable of characterological adaptation in response to changing economic, cultural and social conditions; his analysis was primarily descriptive and he did not specify just how this took place. Robert Levine's (1982) 'social selection theory', a cultural version of Charles Darwin's theory of 'natural selection', suggested that in large societies with diverse kinds of people with a range of character structures, certain individuals, groups or classes of people, while not typical, may possess certain characterological qualities that enable them to more readily change and adapt to changing political and economic circumstances. Over time, that 'more adaptable' type becomes more numerous and these more successful 'variants' of character become more likely to be intentionally fostered by changing socialisation practices. Consequently, social norms and attitudes change and a more adaptive 'social character', that may have been present but infrequently found in the group, becomes more typical and indeed more dominant economically, socially or culturally.

When a previously rare 'social character' structure enables better adaptation to a new historical context, it becomes more likely to become more frequent and highly regarded. As each new generation moves through the life cycle, the newly emergent character type that had previously been rare and perhaps deviant is now more adaptive and becomes normative and more likely to ascend to command various resources as well as economic, cultural and political power. This control of culture includes norms of childrearing, schooling and other institutions of socialisation such as the mass media (which includes the Internet), which in turn enables a number of structural and cultural changes in values, family structures, dynamics, and socialisation practices that which cumulatively lead to changes in the frequency of the dominant 'social character' from rare and deviant to acceptable and then to the most frequent constellation. Thus, for example, the nature of the political economy, anchored within the character structures of previous generations, wanes as newer types are ascendant.

Urie Bronfenbrenner (1979) suggested that human development takes place within an ecological system that itself contains five subsystems and that the microsystem of face-to-face interactions has a considerable impact on the early development of 'social character', especially in childhood. As the person develops, he/she moves into the mesosystems of organisations such as schools and churches where interactions take place on a wider scale. (This is an extremely important moment for SI perspectives, in which interaction within peer groups becomes quite instrumental in fostering and recognising extrafamilial-based identities, often through play in which they learn rules and roles.) As the person matures, he/she is further exposed to the exosystem of the larger society, the 'generalised other', which is often mediated rather than directly experienced. Individuals live within a macro system, the organisation of cultural values customs and laws that shape interactions, cultural understandings, etc., and finally within a 'chrono' system, or the flow of both individual and social time. The important point is that the changing social–historical situation impacts all five ecological subsystems in which selfhood is developed and articulated, and thus the larger social historical events, processes and changes are ultimately mediated through these different levels and fosters historical changes in the nature of character at the deeper level, as well as the notions of selfhood, self-consciousness, forms of self-presentations, etc., at the more conscious and frequently intentional levels.

The new subjectivity

From what has been said so far, among central points for the FS approach to subjectivity has been the historical nature of selfhood, namely 'social character'. The socialisation and expressions of subjectivity have generally been shaped under conditions of political, economic and indeed cultural domination, and thus the considerations of subjectivity are not devoid of political considerations. While the role of subjectivity may be clear when expressing anger as resistance in the emergence of mass movements, it is more often evident in the more typical patterns of social reproduction that on the one hand sustains elite domination, but, in the process fosters a great deal of suffering, especially due to the truncations and distortions of an alienated subjectivity that are the consequences of living in an administered society legitimated by consumerism (Fromm 1961; Marcuse 1964).

The 'marketing personality', Fromm's term for the 'social character' that had been ascendant after World War II, is no longer adaptive or functional in a stagnating economy, while fossil fuel pollution–based global warming threatens the very existence of humanity. Considerations of the dialectical nature of social change show how new constellations of subjectivity are emerging that in many ways differ considerably from what has been the typical 'social character' of late modernity. A number of authors, some influenced by SI, have noted an emerging form of subjectivity among younger cohorts whose values and identities were clearly foreshadowed in the various progressive movements of the 1960s. Today, political, economic and cultural factors have led to a radical transformation of subjectivity with a new character type disposed to 'great refusals' of the 1960s. Between advanced technologies of communication and the general liberalisation of social values, the bearers of a 'new sensibility' show a typical character structure of our times, that while still in flux is a type of inclusive, democratic and humanistic subjectivity that is most seen in young college students and/or minority groups.

This new character type, for lack of a better label, has been termed the 'protean self' by Robert J. Lifton (1993) or the 'fluid character' by Zygmunt Bauman (2015), to which we return later. The central theme of this emerging character type is that unlike the rational, individualistic person with a stable core of fixed selfhood that was socialised by caretakers, schools, churches and the media, the older expression of subjectivity, e.g. 'Freudian Man', is now inadequate if not obsolete in face of the conditions of our time. It is hard to provide a singular term that captures the nature and qualities of this emerging form of subjectivity, which tends to be more flexible and indeed more variable, multiple and often contradictory, depending on context. Perhaps this was anticipated by William James, who was among the first to discuss the pluralities of selfhood. The multiplicity of subjectivities, or at least self-presentations, was also central for Erving Goffman (1959), whose concern was not so much the underlying nature of selfhood, but the myriad instrumental performances that were highly context-dependent.

In the 1960s, a number of social movements emerged that challenged the enduring racism of the United States, its yet repressive puritanical culture and its political system that sustained imperialist wars, and finally came the second generation of feminists critical of various forms of patriarchy, whether occupational, religious and political. While these social movements tended to be largely movements of the young, and while most people did not actively participate in the movements, certain aspects of these movements nevertheless became the context for the initial emergence of new forms of subjectivity. There were many different factions of these movements and among their central themes were seeking more democracy, inequality, inclusion, an anti-war orientation, feminism, and, perhaps the least noted but most important, humanising work and society. It is at this point that the economic, cultural and political events of the 1960s, themselves reflecting earlier changes in childrearing as well as the post-war political, economic and cultural changes, began to foster significant changes in subjectivity. Some of these themes were first articulated as the 'greening of America' or the 'coming of the counterculture', which suggested the emergence of new forms of subjectivity.

In a now classical article, Ralph Turner (1976) found that there had been a generational change in which many younger cohorts felt that one's 'real self' was to be found in one's internal feelings, desires and impulses rather than in the demands of external role performances. In 1977, as changes in college collective identities and self-definitions moved from notions of fixity and stability, Louis Zurcher argued for the coming of the 'mutable self', and the idea of self as object, as a stable entity, changed to one's self as flexible and open to change; the self was now more likely to be seen as a process and often a process of self-creation (Zurcher 1977). Such a 'mutable self' was flexible and adaptive to the emerging world of rapid change and growing uncertainty, as 'all that was solid, melts into air'. Others, often influenced by postmodern critiques of grand narratives, argued that contemporary selfhood is decentred, lacks a stable core and is without fixed identities. Indeed, there was a shift from enduring, essential qualities to inscriptions of identity, expressed not in enduring self-conceptions but through episodic performances. Kenneth J. Gergen (1991) saw that the modern 'saturated self' had gone through a dissolution into a variety of roles and identities articulated in a variety of different settings. Traditional Western ideas of a stable, enduring, individualised and indivisible self were no longer relevant. Instead, the 'saturated self' of late modernity was a collage of multiple, often contradictory self-conceptions and presentations; and many aspects of selfhood may exist largely on computers, social media, etc. The bank officer may trade his or her daytime Armani suit for studded black leather and reveal his/her tattoos when he/she plays electric guitar in a heavy metal band – while stoned. As Gergen stated:

> This syndrome may be termed multiphrenia, generally referring to the splitting of the individual into a multiplicity of self-investments. As one's potentials are expanded by the technologies, so one increasingly employs the technologies for self-expression; yet, as the technologies are further utilized, so do they add to the repertoire of potentials? It would be a mistake to view this multiphrenic condition as a form of illness, for it is often suffused with a sense of expansiveness and adventure ... So multiphrenia is the name for the condition of having many possible selves and self-representations that conflict. So, basically, everyone has multiphrenia to some degree, some just have more of it. If it becomes too overwhelming that is when people have mental breakdowns and succumb to it. I think the day of not distinguishing multiphrenia from 'normal living' has come.
>
> (Gergen 1991:74)

While Gergen questions the coherent, rational, individualistic, unified and stable self, his view has important implications for political practice/democratisation. For Lifton (1993), as people were becoming fluid and many-sided, there was an evolving sense of self that is more appropriate to the restlessness and flux of our times; he, as mentioned, called this notion of self or mode of being the 'protean self' after Proteus, the Greek sea god who took many shapes and forms. The essential quality of this Protean self is change, flexibility, discontinuity and inconsistency. But rather than seeing this as a failing or frailty, Lifton was more optimistic. At a time of fragmentation and trauma, 'Proteanism can awaken our species belonging, our species self. We can assert our organic relationship to each other and to nature ... and experience, amidst our cultural diversity, that common humanity ... of the characteristics we share as a species ... the life experiences we share' (Lifton 1993). For Zygmunt Bauman (2015), we are now at the end of the stable, solid, heavy, industrial world of late modernity and in the current era of 'liquid modernity', a more flexible, post-industrial, globalised world of rapid flows of what is light and flexible. There are fewer certainties given the rapid changes and fluidity in institutions, lifestyles, and what becomes most salient, emerging forms of subjectivity. The contemporary individual must be more flexible, think short-term and often engage in short-term relationships, so that he/she must easily be capable of dealing with changed circumstances, relationships and most of all selfhood. The constantly changing self-constructions of selfhood and identities and the variability of performances to fit changing contexts has replaced notions of a seamless, coherent lifespan as a linear process with a clear identity and consistent narrative that has been established in early life which then endures. Instead, liquid selfhood/identity is constantly constructed and reconstructed, much like one's appearance which is readily transformed though fashion, cosmetics, fitness, exercise, and, if need be, plastic surgery; all this in order to enhance the visible self and its marketability in a competitive and changing, global world. For Bauman, consumption and selfhood are closely intertwined. This has been called 'shopping mall selfhood'; whereas for Thorsten Veblen 'conspicuous consumption' displays one's self and one's economic status and aesthetic tastes; today, consumption *is* the very self. But this form of selfhood is now increasingly tied to Internet-based networks, especially social media, where one can invent a plurality of short-term selves in order to belong to a 'virtual community' as traditional forms of friendship, belonging and enduring support wane.

Is the flexible, multiple self relevant for understanding social transformation? On the one hand, contemporary selfhood as multiple, contradictory, mutable, flexible, liquid or protean would seem ideally suited for the neoliberal contemporary world without strong certainties, loyalties and/or social bonds to enduring communities. Those seeking self-realisation of some of his/her more salient selves are more committed to himself/herself, if not indeed narcissistic, and generally less committed to ideologies or loyal to traditional institutions. This typically disposes indifference to concerns with social justice and long-term struggles. But, at the same time, the psychologists who have studied and theorised the new subjectivity at a time of change in institutions, technologies and social life see this flexibility as a positive adaptation to these changes.

Most of the theorising of the mutable, liquid and/or protean self has focused on its adaptation to the conditions of bureaucratically regulated, late consumer capitalism, and while tolerance and flexibility towards a rapidly changing society may be adaptive, such qualities are not necessarily progressive or transformative. Save for the work of Richard Sennett (1998), most observers of the new mutable self have avoided addressing its political implications, especially the possibilities of progressive transformation. But academic psychology is woefully ignorant of critical theory, let alone its critical psychology. Nor does it much consider the nature of neoliberal globalisation. Thus, most of the authors of the new type of flexible selfhood were not much influenced by critical currents in philosophy, nor were the economic contradictions so blatant (especially for professors) or the culture wars so evident. But many aspects of the flexible and pluralistic selfhood dispose progressive transformation. For example, James Ogilvy (1979) suggested that authoritarian, hierarchal societies foster a unitary self that without contradictions (or ambivalence) from within accepts authoritarian social structures, much like the 'receptive character' Fromm (1941) described that never questioned feudal social arrangements. The many dimensional, liquid or protean selves tend to be more disposed toward democracy, equality and inclusion, as opposed to the more unitary self that is more typical of highly stratified, hierarchically organised societies and institutions. Such selfhood might be thought of as the polar opposite of the unitary, authoritarian character that values hierarchy; sees the world in terms of rigid and often fixed categories of black and white; and tends to be highly racist, sexist and ethnocentric. This insight has political implications for an emancipatory quest.

The multidimensionality of selfhood, while having a long history, was as mentioned evident already in the 1960s and today one could argue that many of today's youth, the millennial generation, have such a character. On the basis of a number of surveys, there are certain distinct features of the millennial generation that have been noted; they want to 'make a difference' or have a purpose, to be able to balance work with the rest of life; they are seeking fun and variety; they are likely to question the 'received wisdom' of authority and refuse to respond to authority without 'good reason'; they have unlimited ambition coupled with overly demanding, confrontational personalities, yet there is a lack of commitment in the face of unmet expectations; and they are likely to have an extreme sense of loyalty to family, friends and self. Given what has been said, the fluid or protean self seems to provide the characterological basis for political, economic and sociocultural change in a more progressive, democratic, inclusive and humanistic direction. Thus we are now seeing the emergence of the 'many dimensional character' that is more flexible, tolerant, democratic and open to change, and more likely to resist and challenge authority. Thus such folks can easily shed certain traditional ideologies seen as constrictive and/or thwarting the self. The protean self is much more predisposed towards finding meaning and authenticity in their lives, and this indeed has important social consequences. As a great deal of research has shown, most young people today would prefer a 'meaningful' life to a happy life. Happiness is more tied to the present moment, meaning to the past, present and future. Self-expression and self-realisation are important aspects of meaning, which involves stresses, strains and challenges. Happiness depends on what people give you, meaning on what you get from others. As has been said, whatever else neoliberal globalisation may provide, as a capitalist system it cannot provide meaning or dignity. Thus, young people's loyalties to capitalism have waned, struggling with massive student debts as they enter a poor job market and face precarious futures.

At this point, we might note a certain contradiction within FS theory regarding subjectivity. On the one hand, for Marx, the alienated worker was rendered powerless by the political economy that his/her wage labour had produced. This passivity of an enfeebled self was rendered docile and accepting of authority. How then might resistance be possible? For SI theory, an essential part of the 'social self' was its capacity for agency first realised in the 'play' and games of childhood, and subsequently in social relationships, in defining situations and negotiating social reality. David Ashley (1985) has indeed argued that for both Marx and the SI tradition, the empowered individual, given his/her (potential) agency, should be free to realise his/her own potential. T. R. Young's (1978) early attempt to integrate SI with FS notions of subjectivity emphasised the importance of agency and its relevance not simply for a critical theory of society, but the basis for agency, resistance and indeed progressive mobilisation.

If we consider the work of Antonio Gramsci, we might note how agency was subverted by internalised, hegemonic ideologies that produced 'willing consent' to domination, much like Franz Fanon (1961) revealed how colonialism rendered the colonised passive. For Charlotte Wolf (1986), the subaltern colluded in his/her subjugation by seeing his/her subjugation as legitimate. Nevertheless, at various times, legitimation crises that migrate into the lifeworld of emotion and identity and systems of political and cultural domination means that people withdraw their loyalty and support and hence more easily embrace alternative visions of the political economy (Habermas 1975). There follow eruptions of agency often taking the form of 'moments of madness' in which people join together, frame the issues, negotiate understandings of the current system, resist existing social arrangements, envision alternatives and develop strategies for the implementation of 'great refusals' (Langman 2017). As social actors face pressing socio-economic and personal crises of the 21st century, there has been growing support for 'great refusals' that dispose utopian visions. The crises of neoliberal capitalism have clearly impacted the subjectivities of younger, more flexible cohorts who have joined the 'great refusals' (Arab Spring/Indigandos and Occupy Wall Street) and in the support for Bernie Sanders, Jeremy Corbyn, Black Lives Matter, #MeToo and Never Again; and what is surprising, today most millennials are open to socialism. As Karl Mannheim (1952) once suggested, the major social, political and economic contexts of each generation shape the identities and worldviews of every generation, and as each cohort flows through the life cycle, they retain the worldviews and identities acquired in their youth.

Domination and 'willing assent'

For Marx, all history has been the history of class conflict, and according to him the conflicts of interests between rulers and the ruled was sustained by the power of the elites to not only own and control the economic and political spheres but its cultural realms as well. For FS, the critique of domination was a central moment of the attempt to understand and challenge the ideological factors, e.g., the dominant values, that sustained the structural domination of elite classes that was the basis of mass suffering. Domination was not simply seen within interactional processes, but as macro-structural conditions that foster the compliance of the person/group to a particular hierarchical economic system and/or social order in which most of the benefits go to a small elite that most the people accept as 'normal'. Power is the ability of one party to secure the compliance of another party to do what he/she might not ordinarily do on their own. Various intellectuals allied to elite classes, such as priests, journalists, teachers or media figures, craft hegemonic ideologies that cloak the existing social relationships of their society to sustain power. Elite literati formulate and promulgate ideologies, especially religions, that legitimate the status quo and more often than not celebrate if not sanctify its leadership.

Hegemony, the ideological control of culture, makes structural domination seem normal, natural, 'common sense' and beneficial for all (Gramsci 1971). Every society attempts to secure consent to the dominant values and norms that are mediated through its various institutions largely shaped by its elites. These hegemonic values at the collective level become internalised in the process of socialisation, yet also provide the individual with a variety of emotional gratifications, not the least of which is securing and cementing his/her relationships with other members of his/her group. Simply put, acceptance of the dominant values provides a number of social attachments. The SI focus on the interactional level does not typically address these structural factors. Nevertheless, the work of Peter M. Hall (2003) developed a so-called mesodomain analysis that

> explores social organization as recurring patterns of collective activity, linked contexts, and social conditions across space and time. It examines the intersection of historical, structural, and action contexts, showing how history and 'structure' shape action and how actions (re)produce history and 'structure'. Its conceptual framework includes collective activity, networks, power, conventions, intentions, processibility and temporality.
>
> (Hall 2003:37)

While surely Hall's perspective sheds light on the mediation of power and domination through interpersonal processes, the focus of FS is on the larger society.

Colonising subjectivity

Domination is an intrinsic part of all human societies that begins with the parent–child relationship in which the domination of the parent is an important aspect of socialisation fostering the internalisation of various norms, values and skills necessary to function in every society. Every society develops a system of values, practices of socialisation and childcare that attempt to shape the emerging subjectivity (character) of the child in such ways that he/she will become a 'well adapted' adult who functions in the society, and, to a large extent, reproduces that society. Educational institutions depend on the 'superiority' of the teacher to impart skills and knowledge that will enable one to better adapt – uncritically – to his/her society. Otherwise said, the historical shaping of selfhood is generally part of the larger moment of securing the domination of elite power. It is for this reason that the FS critiqued authority relationships within the family that secure the obedience and compliance of the child to the familial norms, which had previously shaped the parents as both role models and socialisers. This basic insight was central to Freud's (1930) view that civilisation required the repression of sexual and/or aggressive desires so that we might be able to work together in the peace and harmony necessary to build civilisation.

Repression sustained by the superego was such that sexual desires could be sublimated into the work demanded by civilisation, while the repression of aggressive desires attempted to limit the degree of interpersonal conflict that might thwart the needs for cooperation necessary for building civilisations. Nevertheless, the consequence of such repression was a sense of guilt. Wilhelm Reich (1933/1970) argued that sexual repression served to thwart desires for freedom and agency to produce loyal, dedicated, subjugated and authoritarian workers whether the proletariat of the factory or the petty bourgeois functionaries of the corporation. Max Horkheimer (1937/1972) called the family an 'obedience factory' producing a particular superego formation that would generally support the dominant norms and values and limit deviance. While this highly authoritarian superego articulated in authoritarian relationships typically well served the elite classes by 'pacifying' potential resistance from the proletariat, the contradictions within the system nevertheless often led to a variety of political and economic crises and, in turn, crises of legitimacy (Habermas 1975) that might migrate to the lifeworlds of emotion and subjectivity. But so too might resistance and challenge to authority assume progressive forms and seek social transformation. One of the most important insights of the FS is that the contexts, values and practices of socialising children are clearly political in that at an early age they create dispositions toward either democratic or authoritarian types of societies. George Lakoff (2016) suggested an isomorphism of family socialisation and society, in which the family fosters two very different types of subjectivity. The 'strict father orientation' emphasises obedience and conformity as a way of instilling the independence and toughness necessary to 'succeed' in a capitalist society. On the other hand, the 'nurturant parent orientation' emphasises caring, sharing and empathy, and disposes a more egalitarian society where people are gentle, more democratic, inclusive and generous towards the poor.

The internalisation of dominant values gives each individual a sense of collective identity that not only makes one feel part of a larger group, but membership in that group provides him or her with a sense of collective narcissism and pride in membership. The ultimate product is such that the internalisation of dominant norms becomes intertwined with individual desires, and ergo compliance with dominant norms seems appears as 'willing assent'. Power is thus most effective when compliance seems volitional and spontaneous. In other words, domination becomes internalised within the person, rendered invisible, and 'spontaneous consent' to domination appears 'freely chosen' as 'it's just common sense'. Notwithstanding, this seemingly 'willing assent' to power generally sustains levels of inequality and indeed human suffering. Thus, the 'gratifications' that accrue through 'willing assent' to domination ultimately serve to not only reproduce that domination, but also the suffering that typically accompanies systems of domination.

For Charlotte Wolf (1986), echoing Weber's concerns with 'inner justifications' to action, submission to authority is not simply determined by unconscious desires to gain love and/or alleviate anxiety, but authority in a relationship generally depends on what she calls 'reflexive legitimation' in which the subordinate accepts the legitimacy of his/her own subordination. In her research using 'grounded theory', she gathered letters and writings from three oppressed groups and found that more often than not the suppressed accepted his/her oppression as legitimate. It seems as if subordination can be looked at as based upon the psychodynamic factors explored by the FS, perhaps also noting

Franz Fanon (1961) as well as the ideologies that shape social interactions between the dominant and subordinate.

Betwixt and between social structure and the unconscious

The psychodynamic perspective of the FS placed emphasis on unconscious motivation, desire, repression and ambivalence; one of the most important aspects was authoritarianism, which has been associated with right-wing political leaders and followers alike. This was clearly evident among Germans supporting Hitler/fascism. Similarly, recently a number of studies have shown that authoritarianism was a better predictor for voting for Donald Trump in the 2016 election than was income or education. Unconscious motivation also served other functions, especially encouraging consumerism. This began when Edward Bernays, Freud's nephew, came to the United States, bringing his uncle's theories of motivation. Incorporating psycho-analytic understandings into the worlds of advertising and public relations, by linking consumption to various unconscious meanings and desires, he became a highly successful entrepreneur. In his first marketing 'success', he encouraged a number of young debutantes to suddenly begin smoking cigarettes in a parade, something that no 'proper' young woman might do in the 1920s. As the women marched down the streets of New York holding up their 'torches of liberty' as expressions of power, the cigarette indeed became a phallic symbol. Within a year, cigarette smoking became common among American women and the tobacco companies made millions of dollars. Perhaps the influence of capitalism and consumerism is most evident in the work of Herbert Marcuse (1964) and more recently Stuart Ewen (2008). With television, a great deal of advertising seemed to suggest that refrigerators, stoves, washing machines and new cars provided the owner/user with moments of intense sexual gratification. For Marcuse (1964), capitalism had succeeded in insinuating a variety of 'false needs' within the person that would inspire him/her to not only consume but also utilise that consumption to embrace an identity that might satisfy a variety of 'false needs 'for agency, recognition and self-esteem. Similarly, sexual freedom as a form of 'repressive desublimation' entrapped the person within a realm of privatised hedonism through commodity consumption that not only enhanced corporate profits but also disposed 'one-dimensional' and uncritical thought that served to reproduce social arrangements.

If social interaction within a negotiated social order was the primary concern of SI, for FS, by contrast, the fundamental concern was domination – and the initial but not final basis of that domination is, of course, the capitalist political economy, in which a historically unprecedented market society largely depends on the workers producing commodities for exchange rather than use; but insofar as they work and the products they produce remain external to their selves, workers become alienated, that is, estranged and objectified. At the same time, their work adds value that is retained by the capitalists. This tradition of FS critical theory focusing on the alienation of workers, the domination of modern capitalist society by 'instrumental reason', the colonisation of consciousness and desire, and the socialisation of 'consumer selfhood' seem to have had very little influence on the SI perspective.

Language, communication and the self

For the SI perspective, communication, from the early use of gestures and touch, smiles and frowns, between caretaker and child, followed by the acquisition and use of language and symbols, is the *sine qua non* of the basis of the social self and absolutely essential for thought qua internal conversation or social relationships and interactions. But that said, SI has little investigated the extent of the validity of the 'truth claims' of language, and the extent to which language itself may be systematically shaped by cultural factors – indeed, the normative critique of FS would go so far as to argue that language is systematically reified and distorted to serve elite ends. Perhaps we should start with the aforementioned classical statement of William I. Thomas that if people define situations as real, then they are real in their consequences. That seems like a relatively neutral statement, but definitions of situations depend on language that is always already structured by cultural factors (Lukács 1923/2000; Marcuse 1964). We simply need to recall the Sapir-Wharf hypothesis that the way people think is largely impacted by their native languages – that is, the structure of a language, its vocabulary and its syntax determine the way people view and understand the world. Thus, Aleut people and skiers might have a vocabulary, which describes snow in many ways, just as an interior decorator might suggest dozens of shades of blue or brown to a client. At this point, it is necessary to again recall the importance of Lukács's (1923/2000) critique of consciousness, recalling Marx's notion of 'commodity fetishism' in which social relationships were reified and people turned into objects, and joining reification with Weber's theory of rationalisation and Simmel's notion of 'objective culture': ergo, language was completely infused with a bourgeois logic that so distorts reality and communication as to thwart the possibility of the working classes becoming aware of themselves as the universal class with the agency to transform society. Otherwise said, language becomes the means through which class domination is simultaneously preserved and becomes 'invisible'; as a result, workers using the dominant language, which is already distorted by reification, as spoken by their parents and socialisers and learned in school, is part and parcel of mass culture. Reified language basically serves to reproduce capitalist relationships. In Lukács's words:

> The dominance of the commodity form in the economic sphere must necessarily lead to the dominance of rational calculation and formal reason in society as a whole. Because a break with the organic unity and totality of human existence is a necessary precondition for this development, the commodity form must, over time, subject all social spheres to its rule. By forcing politics and law to adapt to the demands of capitalist exchange, the commodity form consequently transforms these spheres into a mode of rational calculability (a line of thought clearly stemming from Weber's analyses) – which helps explain the rise of the bureaucratic state and the dominance of formal, positive law that continues to alienate individuals from society and encourages their passivity in the face of objectified, mechanical rules.
>
> (Lukács 1923/2000:98)

Lukács's work not only inspired the emergence of the FS, but also directly impacted both Adorno and his student Habermas, who moved the critique of domination from the alienated labour of the worker to the cultural realms, and thus moved his concerns from political economy and its legitimation crises to concerns with communication and a discursive theory of social evolution (Habermas 1984). Habermas argued that an emancipatory critical theory required 'truth speaking situations' in which people could democratically engage in 'undistorted communication' to debate various truth claims. His argument, revisiting Marx's concept of ideology, further informed by English ordinary language philosophy, distinguishes between labour and commu-nication, and compares 'undistorted communication' with systematically 'distorted communication'. Undistorted communication requires 'truth-speaking situations' in which there is a symmetry or equality between speakers so that each has the oppor-tunity to talk and listen on the basis of an egalitarian situation insofar as unequal power distorts communication and renders understanding impossible. Undistorted communication is thus emancipatory, while distorted communication, systematically distorted by the nature of power, serves to sustain that power.

The critique of the reification of consciousness articulated by Lukács (1923/2000) as a form of 'distorted communication' for Habermas points to the reproduction of the domination of the elites and to the subjugation of the subaltern classes insofar as the language available to workers makes it difficult for them to comprehend totality and gain the realisation of their power to transform the system. The same distortions of language, central for SI, are not simply a medium of communication, but for FS a means of reproducing capitalist domination; much like the alienated labour of the 19th century proletariat, which objectifies the worker, rendering him/her a stranger from himself/herself bereft of community, with thwarted self-realisation and without realisation of species being. Language, seemingly neutral, serves to create an alien-ated, distorted form of selfhood, whose self-fulfilment is thwarted and recognition denied, while his/her truncated, distorted subjectivity actively works to reproduce its own domination. Moreover, the reification of consciousness culminates in what Marcuse (1964) has called 'one-dimensional thought', which tends to be an uncritical acceptance of the status quo in which any possibility of serious critique of the system becomes impossible in the face of the mass media, mass consumption and 'repres-sive desublimation', in which the privatised hedonism of casual sexuality appears as 'sexual freedom', but serves to entrap the self into the administered society and its endless and mindless consumerism.

The normalisation of the normative

Whatever the differences between SI and most other sociological perspectives, they share the dominant normative perspective of a 'value-free' social science that seeks to establish a 'scientific truth' that eschews the embrace of any particular normative orientation. This perspective has generally well served its advocates in terms of getting jobs, promotions, publications, tenure and even offices within sociological organisations. As already Weber reminded us, classrooms were places for objective analyses not for political partisanship; the soapbox was the place for speeches and political advocacy. But when Weber was writing, there were tendencies for classrooms to increasingly become scenes of intense political debates as opposed to sites for reasoned analysis. Secondly, the demand for 'value neutrality' itself became a normative stance, implicitly sustaining the status quo and avoiding the Marxist critique of those social factors that foster exploitation, alienation, dehumanisation and suffering. Similarly, Weber's critique of rationality as entrapment within the 'iron cage' or Émile Durkheim's notions of 'egoistic suicide', 'fatalistic suicide' or 'anomie suicide' do not seem to much impact SI. The fundamental issue here is that for Marx there is an ameliorative solution – the abolition of private property, which would mean the end of the ruling bourgeois class. Surely, Weber was not so sanguine; between the authoritarian nature of the Bolshevik party and the bureaucratisation of society, he felt that a socialist society would reproduce the same form of immiseration as a capitalist society – everyone would be subjected to the dehumanisation of rationality. Also, Durkheim offered little in the way of radical reform and in fact strongly upheld the necessity of the state.

Conclusion

This chapter has sought to discuss the ideas of symbolic interactionism (SI) against those of the critical theory of the Frankfurt School (FS). Since the period when SI and FS emerged, we have seen enormous material changes in society as well as changing norms and values. With late modernity, many aspects of earlier periods of modernity have changed, and subjectivity has radically changed. My critiques in this chapter of SI have not intended to discredit as much as to update its perspectives and incorporate the critiques made to invigorate that perspective. Thus, the main points raised here:

1   *Subjectivity is historical.* One legacy of FS theory has been the historical nature of subjectivity. The social self is a product of early parent–child interaction, but these interpersonal processes take place within historically variable forms of structural, ideological and interpersonal domination, secured by the structure of a reified language that shapes a character structure psychologically disposed to reproduce the dominant class system along with the various types of suffering from inequality, alienation, dehumanisation and/or 'artificial needs' to consume (Marcuse 1964). SI has generally focused on microsocial, face-to-face, small-group interactions in what Erving Goffman (1961) called 'total institutions'. Little attention has been paid to structural/ideological factors that sustain domination and reproduce an inegalitarian social order by fostering a particular kind of subjectivity, a colonised 'social character' with insinuated desires and internalised morality that join together to sustain domination, inequality and suffering for large masses of people while the elites prosper. Moreover, hegemonic ideologies largely mask and/or legitimate the domination of ruling classes. Nevertheless, the emergence of new constellations of selfhood, conceptualised as mutable, many-dimensional, flexible, liquid or Protean, portends more inclusive social relationships and a more democratic society.

2 *Domination is ubiquitous.* One of the most fundamental differences between critical and traditional theories was the concern with values (Horkheimer 1937/1999). FS was a critique of domination wherein the capitalist class not only controls the production and distributions of wealth and of governance, but also the production of ideology that collectively sustains elite power and maintains the subjugation of workers. Further, rationality, 'instrumental reason' that might appear neutral, entrapped people within 'iron cages' of rationality erasing their fundamental humanity whilst replacing critical thought with 'one-dimensional' thought sustaining subjugation (Marcuse 1964). Language serves to frame reality while fostering the internalisation of dominant class values within the individual personality to not only maintain domination through 'willing consent' but rendering power invisible – but ideology shapes most face-to-face interactions as well.

3 *The unconscious.* A major difference between FS and SI has been the salience of unconscious processes. Whereas SI has largely focused on language, cognition and what is available to awareness and evident in behaviour, FS attempts to illuminate what is generally unseen and unconscious. But unconscious factors play little role in the face-to-face and small-group research of SI. Similarly, for FS socialisation involves emotions like separation anxiety that disposes identification as leading to the emergence of the ego, while fear of harm fosters 'identification with the aggressor' such that parental values become sedimented as conscience. An understanding of contemporary political trends needs to understand both unconscious factors as well as the more overt justifications, if not rationalisations for certain political choices.

4 *Value-free sociology is a fiction.* SI theories and research should move beyond their traditional 'comfort zone' of 'value-free'/objective sociology, which is likely to ignore values and begin to address some of the larger issues raised. As Fromm (1955) put it, a society that values death over life or weapons over a better quality of life represents a 'pathological normality' that thwarts the emergence of psychologically healthy people. FS embraces a normative stance to critique domination and suffering, yet envisions an egalitarian and inclusive society where work would be fulfilling, people free and governance democratic. Hope, rooted in unconscious wish-fulfilments, envisions alternative kinds of more humanistic social arrangements, more equitable and gratifying as well as more egalitarian forms of community life with more gratifying social interaction, meaningful social connections between people and freedom for creative self-realisation, including the production of one's own selfhood. For example, Hans Joas (2000), writing with Axel Honneth, has articulated a number of normative claims insisting that every human being is fundamentally sacred and entitled to dignity (Joas 2013).

5 *Language.* A fundamental concern of both SI and FS has been language. Today, various modes of electronic communications, such as cell phones with Facebook, can 'connect' 'friends' around the world, as does Skype or particular chat groups. For FS, language that enables the development of the self, interaction with others and exchanges of information, is not a neutral

form of communication but is shaped by its culture in general and the forces of domination within that culture; language has been systematically distorted by the logic of bourgeois rationality. Habermas (1979), incorporating ideas from SI, pragmatism and 'ordinary language philosophy', argued that domination was sustained by 'distorted communication', while realisation of the 'project of modernity' depended on the availability of 'free speech situations' where people could freely and openly discuss and critique social political issues to democratically arrive at consensus.

So, in conclusion, SI can itself also offer both valuable insights and critiques of FS, namely that it represents yet another form of ivory tower–based armchair philosophy with little empirical research to support or challenge its claims. For example, the FS approach to mass media, namely its critique of the 'culture industries', tends to give far too much attention to elite, indeed elitist, condescending interpretations of the media than attending to the actual audiences to which that culture was directed. More specifically, earlier SI research by Herbert Blumer (1933) interviewed people after they saw certain movies, and among his findings were that motion pictures are less influential among people with higher education. Movies can arouse terror and fright in children, sorrow and pathos among people in general, and excitement and passions of love among adolescents. Motion pictures provide people with schemes of life, fixed images and stereotyped conceptions of different characters and modes of conduct. It seemed that movies had the most impact on teenagers, especially concerns with beauty and romance, which adolescents seek. Movies may serve educational purposes of actually introducing teenagers to types of life, which has immediate, practical and momentous significance. More recently, critical cultural studies have shown how young people *actively interpret mass media and often reverse its many meanings, interpreting and redefining it in ways quite opposite to the interpretations offered by various 'cultural elites'* that inevitably see domination everywhere. Consider Adorno's interpretation of American jazz as proto-fascism. But American jazz, especially its modern forms, is far more concerned with freedom, innovation and experimentation than with conformity and the reproduction of the status quo. Peter M. Hall (2003) claimed that indeed SI does deal with important social issues – inequality orders, institutional analyses, collective action and spatiotemporal orders. He claims that 'dialogues with other compatible perspectives could provide the motivation and knowledge to act in ways with others, to engender more just, safe, democratic, and equitable worlds and lives' (Hall 2003:50). Many of the traditions of SI research based on direct observation of concrete interaction can be a corrective to FS theory often more based on citing abstract texts than interviewing or observing actual people. But this is not to suggest a unilateral transformation of SI, only that SI can offer micro and meso theories and research methodologies that can better substantiate some of the claims of FS scholars. While at times FS has been pessimistic, SI has generally held a more positive view of human agency in which individuals have the capacity for critiques of existing injustices, envisioning alternatives and mobilising the 'great refusals' that realise social change. A unified theory consisting of SI and FS is quite unlikely, but scholars of each framework might speak to each other, and if not closely collaborate in their research, then at least mutually enrich their research.

Note

1   The author wishes to extend his deep appreciation to both the editor of this volume, Michael Hviid Jacobsen, as well as Gary Alan Fine for comments and suggestions on this chapter. While there have been some scholars like Ashley (1985) and Goff (1980) who have indeed attempted to find certain compatibilities between Mead and Marx, the concerns with subjectivity, an essential part of this chapter, have been based on the Frankfurt School of Critical Theory that, while rooted in Marx, is equally indebted to Max Weber and Sigmund Freud. About 40 years ago, T. R. Young (1978) attempted to bridge symbolic interactionism with critical theory.

References

Adorno, Theodor W. and Max Horkheimer (1947/2000): *Dialectic of Enlightenment.* Stanford, CA: Stanford University Press.

Ashley, David (1985): 'Marx and the Category of Individuality in Communist Society'. *Symbolic Interaction*, 8 (1):63–83.

Bauman, Zygmunt (2015): *Practices of Selfhood.* Cambridge: Polity Press.

Becker, Howard S. (1953): *Becoming a Marijuana User.* Chicago: University of Chicago Press.

Becker, Howard S. (1963): *Outsiders: Studies in the Sociology of Deviance.* Glencoe, IL: Free Press.

Benford, Robert and David Snow (2000): 'Framing Processes in Social Movements'. *Annual Review of Sociology*, 26:611–639.

Berger, Peter L. and Thomas Luckmann (1966): *The Social Construction of Reality.* New York: Penguin Books.

Blumer, Herbert (1933): *Movies and Conduct.* New York: Macmillan & Company.

Blumer, Herbert (1969): *Symbolic Interactionism: Perspective and Method.* Englewood Cliffs, NJ: Prentice-Hall.

Bronfenbrenner, Urie (1979): *The Ecology of Human Development: Experiments by Nature and Design.* Cambridge, MA: Harvard University Press.

Ewen, Stuart (2008): *Captains of Consciousness: Advertising and the Social Roots of the Consumer Culture.* New York: Basic Books.

Fanon, Franz (1961): *The Wretched of the Earth.* New York: Grove Press.

Freud, Sigmund (1921): *Group Psychology and the Analysis of the Ego.* London: Hogarth Press.

Freud, Sigmund (1930): *Civilization and Its Discontents.* London: Hogarth Press.

Fromm, Erich (1941): *Escape from Freedom.* New York: Holt, Rinehart and Winston.

Fromm, Erich (1955): *The Sane Society.* New York: Holt, Rinehart and Winston.

Fromm, Erich (1961): *Marx's Concept of Man.* London: Bloomsbury Publishing.

Gergen, Kenneth J. (1991): *The Saturated Self: Dilemmas of Identity in Contemporary Life.* New York: Basic Books.

Glaser Barney G. and Anselm L. Strauss (1967): *The Discovery of Grounded Theory: Strategies for Qualitative Research.* New Brunswick: Aldine-Transaction.

Goff, Wesley Thomas (1980): *Karl Marx and George Herbert Mead: Contributions to a Sociology of Knowledge*. Boston: Routledge and Keegan Paul.

Goffman, Erving (1959): *The Presentation of Self in Everyday Life*. New York: Anchor Books.

Goffman, Erving (1961): *Asylums: Essays on the Social Situation of Mental Patients and Other Inmates*. New York: Anchor Books.

Goffman, Erving (1967): *Interaction Ritual*. New York: Pantheon Books.

Gramsci, Antonio (1971): *Selections from the Prison Notebooks*. New York: International Publishers.

Habermas, Jürgen (1975): *Legitimation Crisis*. Boston: Beacon Press.

Habermas, Jürgen (1979): *Communication and the Evolution of Society*. Boston: Beacon Press.

Habermas, Jürgen (1984): *The Theory of Communicative Action*, Volume 1: *Reason and the Rationalization of Society*. Boston: Beacon Press.

Hall, Peter M. (2003): 'Social Organization and Social Processes: Looking Back and Moving Ahead'. *Symbolic Interaction*, 26 (1):33–55.

Horkheimer, Max (1937/1972): 'Authority and the Family', in Max Horkheimer: *Critical Theory: Selected Essays.* New York: Continuum, pp. 47–128.

Horkheimer, Max (1937/1999): 'Traditional and Critical Theory', in Matthew J. O'Connell (ed.): *Critical Theory: Selected Essays*. New York: Continuum Press, pp. 188–243.

Joas, Hans (2000): *The Genesis of Values*. Chicago: University of Chicago Press.

Joas, Hans (2013): *The Sacredness of the Person: A New Genealogy of Human Rights*. Washington DC: Georgetown University Press.

Korsch, Karl (1923/1970): *Marxism and Philosophy*. New York: Monthly Review Press.

Lakoff, George (2016): *Moral Politics*. Chicago: University of Chicago Press.

Langman, Lauren (2017): 'From Great Refusals to Wars of Position: Marcuse, Gramsci and Social Mobilization', in Andrew Lamas, Todd Wolfson and Peter Funke (eds.): *The Great Refusal*. Philadelphia: Temple University Press, pp. 367–388.

Langman, Lauren and Dan Albanese (2015): 'Political Economy and the Normative: Marx on Human Nature and the Quest for Dignity', in Michael J. Thompson (ed.): *Constructing Marxist Ethics*. Leiden: Brill, pp. 59–85.

Levine, Robert (1982): *Culture, Behavior and Personality*. New Brunswick: Aldine-Transaction.

Lifton, Robert J. (1993): *The Protean Self*. Chicago: University of Chicago Press.

Lukács, György (1923/2000): *History and Class Consciousness: Studies in Marxist Dialectics*. Cambridge, MA: The MIT Press.

Mannheim, Karl (1952): 'The Problem of Generations', in Karl Mannheim: *Essays in the Sociology of Knowledge*, Volume V. New York: Routledge, pp. 276–320.

Marcuse, Herbert (1964): *One Dimensional Man: Studies in the Ideologies of Advanced Industrial Societies*. London: Routledge.

Mead, George Herbert (1934/2015): *Mind, Self and Society*. Chicago: University of Chicago Press.

Ogilvy, James (1979): *Many Dimensional Man*. New York: Harper Collins.

Reich, Wilhelm (1933/1970): *The Mass Psychology of Fascism*. New York: Farrar, Strauss and Giroux.

Sennett, Richard (1998): *The Corrosion of Character*. New York: W. W. Norton and Company.

Sutherland, Edwin H. (1924): *Principles of Criminology*. Chicago: University of Chicago Press.

Scheff, Thomas J. (1994): *Bloody Revenge: Emotions, Nationalism and War*. Boulder, CO: Westview.

Simmel George (1903/1950): 'The Metropolis and the Mental Life', in Kurt Wolff (ed.): *The Sociology of Georg Simmel*. New York: Free Press.

Strauss, Anselm L. (1978): *Negotiations – Varieties, Contexts, Processes and Social Order*. San Francisco, CA: Jossey-Bass.

Thomas, William I. and Dorothy S. Thomas (1928): *The Child in America: Behavior Problems and Programs*. New York: Knopf.

Turner, Ralph (1976): 'The Real Self: From Institution to Impulse'. *American Journal of Sociology*, 81 (5):989–1016.

Wolf, Charlotte (1986): 'Legitimation of Oppression: Response and Reflexivity'. *Symbolic Interaction*, 9 (2):217–234.

Wrong, Dennis H. (1961): 'The Over Socialized Concept of Man'. *American Sociological Review*, 26 (2):183–193.

Young, T. R. (1978): 'Some Theses on the Structure of Self'. Transforming Society Series of the Red Feather Institute. Available online at: http://critcrim.org/redfeather/archives/037thesesself.html (accessed March 28, 2018).

Zurcher, Louis (1977): *The Mutable Self: A Self-Concept for Social Change*. Thousand Oaks, CA: Sage Publications.

10 Situational analysis as a critical interactionist method

Adele E. Clarke

Introduction[1]

Over recent decades, sociologists and others have generated an array of critical interactionist approaches to the study of social life. These scholars, myself included, have woven into interactionism varied facets of feminisms, anti-racisms, political economies, anti-imperialisms, queer, decolonising, indigenous, post-colonial, postmodern and post-structural theorising and approaches to research. In the *Handbook of Symbolic Interactionism*, Kent L. Sandstrom and Gary Alan Fine (2003) viewed these as 'emerging voices'. This volume marks their transnational coalescence as critical interactionisms.

Conceptual tools useful for critical interactionist theorising and research are rooted especially in the affordances of pragmatism and its democratising tendencies (Charmaz 2017a). They include contributions by Georg Simmel, George Herbert Mead, John Dewey, Jane Addams, Robert E. Park, William I. Thomas, Dorothy Swayne Thomas, Louis Wirth, Herbert Blumer, Anselm L. Strauss, Rue Bucher, Howard S. Becker, Norman K. Denzin, David R. Maines, Lonnie H. Athens, Susan Leigh Star, Peter M. Hall, Patrick McGinty, Michael L. Schwalbe and Arlie R. Hochschild, among many others. A smaller, increasingly robust set of established critical interactionist approaches to research includes Denzin's interpretive interactionism, Kathy Charmaz's constructivist grounded theory (GT), Reiner Keller's sociology of knowledge approach to discourse (SKAD), and situational analysis (SA), an extension of GT I developed, the focus of this chapter.

In the pragmatist spirit, both John Dewey (1939) and Herbert Blumer (1969) vividly asserted the non-fungibility of theory and method. Star (1989, 1991a, 1991b, 1995, 2007) further elaborated the concept of 'theory/methods packages' as *co-constitutive,* and I draw on this concept here. My main argument is that SA is a critical interactionist theory-methods package. I sketch its theoretical and methodological foundations, describe its four analytic mapping strategies, and specify precisely why and how SA is a distinctively *critical interactionist* method.

In 2004, Bruno Latour asked: Why has critique run out of steam? With Reiner Keller (2017) and others, I find critique today is not only full of steam but also increasingly sophisticated as well as sorely needed. Critique grows in importance as the values of democracy are eroded transnationally, environmental degradation threatens multispecies survival and alternative futures with enhanced social justice must be conceptualised *in part through critique* in order to be generated. As a critical interactionist method, SA can be useful in such projects.

What is critical interactionism?

Critical interactionism rests on the fundamental assumption that *interactionism is, at heart, a conflict theory/methods package* in which differences of perspectives, commitments, allegiances, etc., not only exist but actively shape social life *individually and collectively*. Interactionism does not limit conflict to social class but expands potentially salient differences to *also include* race, ethnicity, gender, religion and sexuality – *any patterned means of marginalisation or stratification*. Collectivities are assumed to be characterised by inter- and intra-organisational contestations and conflicts over power – politics writ both small and large.

In interactionist research, power dynamics are often manifest in the capacity to establish authoritative 'definitions of the situation', which privilege some individuals and/or collectivities while disadvantaging others, including institutional situations from asylums to courts to schools. Historically, such research foregrounded negative consequences for the deviant, criminal, dropout, abused and so on. But analysis of power as dynamic and situated was relentlessly pursued (Dennis and Martin 2005:199–201). In a figure/ground gestalt switch, *critical* interactionism makes it the new focus.

As Kathy Charmaz (2017a:34) has argued, pragmatist philosophy is foundational here. George Herbert Mead (1927/1964), 'while believing in an ideal of mutual intelligibility and peaceful reconciliation, also had a keen sense of opposition and conflict between social worlds' (Cefaï 2016:178; McCarthy 1984). Dewey, too, saw conflict as inherent in social life (e.g., Rabinow 2011), hoping democracy could moderate, channelling conflict from antagonism as struggle between enemies to agonism as struggle between adversaries.

Chicago School sociology further developed the pragmatist assumption of conflict conceptually. For example, Robert E. Park and Ernest W. Burgess's (1921:574–662) chapter titled 'Conflict' in *Introduction to the Science of Sociology* asserts: 'Competition is continuous and impersonal. Conflict is intermittent and personal'. It offers excerpts from William I. Thomas's 'The Natural History of Conflict' (pp. 579–582) and Georg Simmel's 'Types of Conflict Situations' (pp. 586–592). Louis Wirth (1928:15) offered a relational ecological view of the modern metropolis as 'a mosaic of social worlds' often in conflict. Marginality and conflict also characterised Chicago urban ethnography as a so-called *sociology noir* (Salerno 2007).

Post World War II, several sustained threads of *critical interactionist theorising* emerged and furthered interactionism as a conflict approach:

- negotiated order and social worlds/arenas theories;
- ecologies of knowledge, marginalities and infrastructures;

- organisational/meta-power interactionism; and
- theories of reproduction and reinscription of power, domination and stratification.

All are lively today.

Negotiated order and *social worlds/arenas theories* are flip sides of Anselm L. Strauss's interactionist sociology – captured in the dynamic of *structural process* from GT (Glaser and Strauss 1967:239–242). While negotiated order theory emphasises processual aspects, social worlds/arenas theory centres loosely on more structural collective elements. Negotiated order theory emerged from Strauss and colleagues' (1964) empirical research on competing treatment ideologies in psychiatric hospitals. David R. Maines (e.g., 1982) was a major elaborator. There now exists 50-plus years of such research (Clarke, 2012/forthcoming).

Social worlds/arenas theory (part of SA), initiated by Strauss in the late 1970s, emphasises legitimation, intersection and segmentation processes. Significantly, arenas where social worlds meet are commonly associated with conflict and contestation. *Social worlds and arenas can serve as units of conflict analysis* and do so in SA. Conceptual elaborations include Bucher's (1962) *segments* as reform movement within worlds, Howard S. Becker's (1982) social world *entrepreneurs* and *mavericks,* Susan L. Star and James Griesemer's (1989) *boundary objects*, Joan H. Fujimura's (1988) *bandwagons*, Adele E. Clarke's (Clarke and Montini 1993; Clarke 2005:46–48) *implicated actors*, and Monica J. Casper's (1998) *work objects*.[2]

Pragmatist, feminist and antiracist, the late Susan Leigh Star's critical interactionist ecological theorising is increasingly recognised. Significant here, Star's (1995:2/2015:14) *ecologies of knowledge* draw on the pragmatist concept of 'an ecosystem, and equally important all the components that constitute the system', examining interrelationships among them and the trajectories of always contingent 'cooperation without consensus'. Star (1991a:30) listened to those at the margins, 'outsiders within' (Collins 1986), because 'voices of those suffering from abuses of ... power are among the most powerful analytically'. Her key question was '*Cui bono?*' (Who benefits?). For Star, *infrastructures* often do the 'invisible work' of imposing power under the guise of being 'mere technical innovations' (Star 1991a, 1991b; Star and Strauss 1998). *Classifications* become 'frozen policies' 'torqueing' the bodies and lives of those who do not fit, individually and/or collectively (Bowker and Star 1999, especially chapter 6 on apartheid).[3]

Another major contribution to critical interactionist theorising is *social organisational/meta-power theory as a form of mesodomain analysis,* initiated by Peter M. Hall (1987, 1997) and further developed by and with Patrick McGinty (2014; Hall and McGinty 2002) and Tom Burns (Burns and Hall 2012). Using the term social organisation in lieu of social structure, this theorising deeply integrates critical analyses of power and social organisation grounded in pragmatist interactionism. Used extensively in policy analyses, it also demonstrates an abiding understanding of history as unfolding through *contingent organisational processes*, drawing on the Straussian metaphor of 'conditional matrices' (discussed later). Fundamental here, and inspiring SA, is that 'the nature and degree of social organization must be an *empirical* question' (Hall and McGinty 2002:421, emphasis added).

Additional critical interactionist theorising in sociology includes political economic approaches in Michael L. Schwalbe's (2008, 2014, 2015) social psychology of domination, Arlie R. Hochschild's (e.g., 1983, 2012; Jacobsen and Petersen 2017) sociology of emotions, especially vis-à-vis gender, and Lonnie H. Athens' (e.g., 2013) radical interactionism (presented in another chapter in this volume). In nursing too, critical interactionist research concerns political economy (e.g., Dubbin, McLemore and Shim 2017; Martins and Burbank 2011). Momentum is growing.

There is also an array of critical interactionist *methodological approaches*: Norman K. Denzin's interpretive interactionism, Kathy Charmaz's constructivist grounded theory, Keller's SKAD and my own SA. Denzin's distinctive 'theory-methods package' of *critical interpretive interactionism* is 'emancipatory' (Denzin 1997:250) and fiercely situated/context-dependent (Denzin 1970, 1989, 2009). Aligning 'with Cornel West's prophetic pragmatism, Patricia Hill Collins's epistemology of empowerment, and Pelias's methodology of the heart, Denzin (2010:296) seeks to enhance social justice, especially but far from only for indigenous people. Denzin's (2001:143) strategies to lay bare 'biographically meaningful experiences' include analysis of epiphanies, thick description, alternative writing forms, and auto- and performative-ethnographic approaches. Denzin's (2001:xi, xii) goal is to 'situate interpretive studies in the "ethnoscapes" of daily life'. Aiding and abetting critical interactionism, Denzin has coalesced critical qualitative inquiry intellectually and institutionally.[4]

Over the half century of grounded theory (GT) in practice, major contributors have generated different emphases.[5] Glaserian GT sustains positivist functionalist traditions, while Straussian GT, always pragmatist and interactionist, also became increasingly constructionist. Straussian GT inspired most but not all of 'the second generation' of GT (Morse et al. 2009), including Charmaz and myself. Critical affordances of pragmatist interactionism were thereby imported into constructivist GTs and SA (Charmaz 2005, 2017a:37–39; Clarke, Friese and Washburn 2018, chapter 3).

Always a pragmatist interactionist, Charmaz (e.g., 2000, 2006, 2009, 2014, 2017a) became increasingly constructivist. In fact, Antony Bryant (2009:14) credits Charmaz's strong push for a fully constructivist GT with resurrecting a method too often characterised by the late 20th century as 'naively inductivist'. I agree. Notable here, Charmaz's (2005, 2017b; Charmaz, Thornberg and Keane 2018) constructivist GT has also become relentlessly *critical*. It advances social justice by 'locat[ing] the research process and product in historical, social and situational conditions', and 'excavating the structural contexts, power arrangements and collective ideologies' in the study focus (Charmaz 2017a:34–35). Justice and injustice are '*enacted processes*' (Charmaz 2005:508). The strong criticality of constructivist GT is especially salient here as SA's deepest roots lie in Straussian and constructivist GT.

A more recent addition to the critical and cultural interactionist methodological repertoire is Reiner Keller's (2005/2018, 2011) sociology of knowledge approach to discourse (SKAD). Drawing especially on Peter L. Berger and Thomas Luckmann's sociology of knowledge, pragmatist interactionism and Michel Foucault, Keller's discourse analysis investigates social practices and processes of communicative *constructions*, how discourses are stabilised, relations to symbolic orders, etc. It shares much with Joseph R. Gusfield's (1981) studies of the culture of public problems. SA too is a critical interactionist method and I turn to it next.

What is situational analysis?

Here I introduce situational analysis (SA) as a critical interactionist theory/methods package, delineating its theoretical foundations and its methodological strategies for mapping the situation of interest from multiple angles of concern. In the next section, I discuss key premises and concepts that enhance SA's critical capacities and affordances.

Theoretical foundations of SA

An extension of Straussian and constructivist GT, SA emerged at the turn of this century and reflects the altered landscapes of social theory and qualitative inquiry since the interpretive turn (Clarke 2003, 2005; Clarke, Friese and Washburn 2015; 2018, especially pp. 8–12). The theoretical foundations of SA lie deeply in pragmatism, Chicago School ecologies and interactionism, with special emphasis on Strauss's negotiated order and social worlds/arenas theories. Like Charmaz's (2014:200–204) constructivist GT, SA views the processes of data analysis as abductive as well as inductive, pursues analyses systematically, and relies on theoretical sampling for theoretical enrichment and analysing empirical conundrums.[6]

In generating SA, I sought to engage issues raised by post-structural, postmodern and interpretive turns not then engaged by GT. I therefore braided several theoretic innovations into the foundations of SA, entwining them compatibly with Chicago ecologies and pragmatist interactionism (Clarke, Friese and Washburn 2018, chapter 3). First was Foucault's (1973) work on the profound salience of discourses in power relations, the situatedness of fields of practice, and the contingency of conditions of possibility. Foucault's (1980:194–228) *dispositif*, a web of connections among seemingly disparate concepts, discourses, technologies, infrastructures, practices and institutions, was also inspirational.

From my pragmatist and science and technology studies (STS) backgrounds, I knew that *explicitly* taking the nonhuman elements in a situation – *things of all kinds* – into account was both theoretically and methodologically essential. Drawing on Mead (1938, 1972; McCarthy 1984) and STS, I argued that *nonhuman things* (living and not) are wholly worthy of our attention for posthumanist analyses, especially manifest in situational maps. As in STS, the nonhuman is very broadly construed to include natural and built environments, technologies, plants, animals, furniture – *whatever things are empirically found in the situation.*

As in Meadian pragmatism (Cefaï 2016) and Star's (1995, 2015) ecosystems, relations among elements are *ecologically* interpreted.[7]

I was also inspired by Giles Deleuze and Felix Guattari's (1987:21, emphasis added) concept of the 'rhizome', which undergirds situational maps: '[T]he rhizome pertains to a map that must be produced, constructed, a map that is always detachable, connectable, reversible, modifiable, and has multiple entryways and exits and its own lines of flight. *It is tracings that must be put on the map, not the opposite*'. Deleuze and Guattari's (1987:3–4, 8; 1983a) concept of 'assemblage' similarly draws together heterogeneous entities in dynamic, fluid relations. As an inherently unstable phenomenon, it can expand, contract, morph, etc.

Post-structural theories by and large abjure the tripartite framework of micro, meso and macro levels of social organisation as failing to grasp fundamental assumptions of relationality. SA therefore assumes that social phenomena are *co-constituted – produced through the relations of entities at all levels of organisational complexity*. Social phenomena are *non-fungibly* 'all of the above'. Hence, analytic focus should be on complexities, relationalities and ecologies explicitly situated in space and time, including geopolitically (Law 2004, 2007; Star 1995; Clarke with Keller 2014). Highly congruent with pragmatist interactionism, this expands its critical affordances.

SA also relies on and extends the inherent strength of constructivist GT in closely attending to context by 'turning away from acontextual description' (Charmaz 2006:271). To do so, SA centres analysis on the *situation* instead of context or action:

> The conditions *of* the situation are *in* the situation. There is no such thing as 'context'. The conditional elements of the situation need to be specified in the analysis of the situation itself as *they are constitutive of it,* not merely surrounding it or framing it or contributing to it. They *are* it. Regardless of whether some might construe them as local or global, internal or external, close-in or far away or whatever, the fundamental question is: 'How do these conditions appear – make themselves felt as consequential – *inside* the empirical situation under examination?'. At least some answers to that question can be found through doing situational analyses.
>
> (Clarke 2005:71–72)

In SA, the situation of interest is broadly conceived *ecologically* (Dewey 1938, chapter 4; Star 1995). Focus is on generating understandings of the *relationalities* among all the elements empirically found in the situation of interest through mapping them in various ways. These *co-constitutive* elements *together* constitute the situation as a whole (Clarke, Friese and Washburn 2018:47–49, 68–71).

Methodological strategies of SA

To analyse the situation of inquiry, doing SA involves making and analytically memoing four different kinds of maps. Inspired by Strauss, the SA method is wide open to using all kinds of empirical materials to generate these maps: interviews, ethnographic notes and/or documents collected in the situation. Moreover, SA deeply encourages the inclusion of extant discourse materials found in the situation, including narrative, visual and/or historical materials. As more empirical materials are generated and gathered, all the maps are revisited, revised and reanalysed across the life of the research project.

The first maps made are *situational maps* focused on *empirically detailing precisely what elements are in the broader situation.* These may include humans, nonhuman things, animals, technologies, organisations, institutions, natural resources, political economic elements, social and cultural events and traditions, particular visuals, cultural phenomena, spatial and temporal issues, popular and other discourses pertinent to the situation, symbolic elements, contested elements, discursive constructions of actors in the situation, etc. Preliminary situational maps are especially useful in *research design* (Clarke, Friese and Washburn 2018:110–123). Specifying precisely *how* specific elements matter, their relative power, etc., happens downstream in the research process.

Situational maps are then used to make the second kind of map, *relational maps*. Here the analyst draws lines between one element and all the other elements, working one by one, and asking: *What is the nature of the relationship between these two elements?* Gradually, and very systematically (invoking a major *empirical* strength of GT), key relationships among elements are specified and analysed in memos. Relationships in need of greater specificity are noted and further data are gathered about them through theoretical sampling, densifying the *relational analysis* (exemplary SA publications offering situational and relational maps include Barcelos 2014; Fosket 2015; Pérez and Cannella 2011, 2015; Martin, Pauly and MacDonald 2016).

The third analytic mapping strategy is the *social worlds/arenas map*, which frames the social worlds, organisational and institutional structures and their interrelations in the broader arenas of commitment in the situation of inquiry. Based in Strauss's social worlds/arenas theory, collectivities in the situation are social worlds committed to social action in one or more arenas of concern. The analyst(s) usually generates one social worlds/arenas map for the project, refining it through analysing new data. Many methods of qualitative inquiry simply do not attend to collective social, organisational and institutional aspects of the situation. They are fundamental to critical research and hence to SA (exemplary SA projects centred on social worlds/arenas maps include Alonso Yanez, Thumlert and de Castell 2016; Fosket 2015; Martin, Pauly and MacDonald 2016).

The fourth and last maps done in SA are *positional maps.* In any situation, there are a number of contested or debated issues, and positional maps analyse them. Focusing on two facets of a debate at a time, a positional map lays out the full range of positions articulated about them in the data. Moreover, positional maps also allow the analyst to specify *positions not taken* in the materials and to determine whether there are *implicated actors* in the situation, an analysis of power discussed further later. SA researchers commonly do a number of positional maps addressing all the major contested issues (exemplars of SA projects centred on positional maps include Fosket 2015; Friese 2010; Washburn 2015; Fisher 2014).

Significantly different from earlier GT, SA takes the turn to discourse analysis very seriously, urging analysis of extant narrative, visual and/or historical discourse materials in the situation, and providing distinctive resources and mapping strategies for their analysis (Clarke, Friese and Washburn 2018, chapters 10–13). Within constructivist GT, Charmaz (2014:45–54) now urges this as well.

In sum, SA extends Straussian and constructivist GT to take post-structural and interpretive turns into account, shifting the focus from action to the situation and mapping and analysing relationalities of multiple kinds in that situation.

Why and how is SA a critical interactionist method?

SA offers distinctive approaches, core concepts and angles of vision that are always already critical and interactionist. I detail the following here:

- the situation as the unit of analysis;
- attentiveness to differences and 'epistemic diversity';
- distinctive power analytics (social worlds/arenas maps; boundary objects; implicated actors);
- capacities for enhancing collaboration useful in feminist, participatory, decolonising, indigenous, (post)colonial and related research; and
- attentiveness to complexity, mess and relationalities.

The situation as the unit of analysis

SA is rooted in an *ecological conceptualisation of the situation* initially developed by pragmatist philosophers Mead (1927/1964, 1934/1962; Cefaï 2016) and Dewey (1938), elaborated through Star's (1995) ecosystems, and transformed through my own methodological engagement with Strauss and Juliet Corbin's (1990, 1998) pioneering innovation of the 'conditional matrix'. Although Barney G. Glaser and Strauss (1967) did not initially emphasise context or situatedness in GT, Strauss (e.g., 1987:77–81) later did so.

Specifically, Strauss and Corbin developed *conditional matrices* – analytic devices intended to systematically consider how various 'contextual' elements 'condition' the action that is the central analytic focus in GT. As James W. Carey (2002:202) noted, Strauss's was 'a sociology of structuration before Anthony Giddens invented the word'. While deeply appreciating Strauss and Corbin's analytic innovation and broadening of the scope of inquiry, I found the conditional matrices highly problematic in several ways: assuming that conditions are *contextual* rather than *co-constitutive*, reifying micro/meso/macro levels of interaction and geography, and lacking explicit consideration of discourses. But most inadequate was assuming inner and outer circles of influence rather than pursuing the nature of relations *empirically*. In short, while pioneering, the conditional matrices simply did not go far enough.[8]

My core methodological strategy for pushing GT around the postmodern, post-structural and interpretive turns into SA was shifting primary analytic focus from social action to the *situation of inquiry* per se. The boundaries of the situation are assumed to be porous and relations among any and all of the elements co-constitutive. Pursuing the mapping strategies described earlier generates *empirical analyses of the situation of inquiry as a whole*. Cameo portraits may also be pursued.

Theoretically, SA relies deeply here on Dewey's brilliant pragmatist framing of the concept of the situation and its ultimate import:

> What is designated by the word 'situation' is *not* a single object or event or set of objects and events. For we never experience nor form judgments about objects and events in isolation, but only *in connection with a contextual whole* ... In actual experience, there is never any such isolated singular object or event; *an object or event is always a special part, phase, or aspect, of an environing experienced world – a situation ... We live and act in connection with the existing environment, not in connection with isolated objects.*
>
> (Dewey 1938:66–68; emphases in original and added)

For Dewey – and SA – things can be interpreted and have meaning *only in relationship to the situation* in which they are found or occur. Qua method, SA makes sense of the world *through understanding its heterogeneous situations*.

Early Chicago School sociologist William I. Thomas (1927/1966) titled his presidential address to the American Sociological Society 'Situational Analysis', drawing attention to the fundamental importance of the situation in understanding human action. Extending Dewey, Mead, Wirth, Thomas, and Star, I would further assert that the world itself can be viewed as a highly fluid 'mosaic of situations', constantly shifting and morphing into new ones co-constitutively. Significantly, 'the power of the ecological model underlying the traditional Chicago approach lies in the ability to focus now on the niche and now on the ecosystem which defined it' (Dingwall 1999:217). Through these ecological roots, the capacity to shift focus within and among situations becomes a distinctive critical affordance of SA as method.

Drawing further upon pragmatism, Mead's (1927/1964) ecological orientation undergirds analytic attention to *relations among the elements* in the situation and their co-constitutiveness in a distinctive ecology. Mead argued that physical and social objects share a 'sociality' that binds them (Cefaï 2016; McCarthy 1984) in what John Law (1999:4) calls a 'relational materiality'. The social is relentlessly material, not 'merely' epiphenomenal. Daniel Cefaï (2016:174) asserts:

> This ecological dimension of social life was somewhat forgotten by the heirs of Mead, who have ... neglected a central idea in Chicago sociology in the 1920s. Social interaction does not exclusively take place between selves but between people, objects, and situations and, beyond that, between groups, cultures, and environments.

These situational ecological dimensions of life were resuscitated in interactionism by Strauss's social worlds/arenas theory and Star's (1995) 'ecologies of knowledge'. Specifically, Star extended attention to relationality by explicitly eschewing reductionism: '[B]y ecological, I mean refusing social/natural or social/technical dichotomies and inventing systematic dialectical units of analysis' (Star quoted in Timmermans 2015:3). Dichotomies disappeared when, following Dewey, she viewed such phenomena continuous (Star 1991b:277). Moreover, in analytically including the nonhuman, her goal 'was not to democratize the human/nonhuman divide but to analyze the powers of the nonhuman in reshaping the human world' (Timmermans 2015:3). In sum, centring analysis on the situation as a whole is the *critical interactionist heart of SA method.*

Attentiveness to differences, marginalities and 'epistemic diversity'

Most social science research has relentlessly sought *commonalities and simplifications* while evading and avoiding *differences and contradictions* – the 'mess' of actual social life (Law 2004). Variation is even called 'noise' or 'dirty data'. Simplifying and universalising strategies abound (e.g., Star 1983). In contrast, variation has always been more or less attended to in GT. While Glaser and Strauss (1967) wrote about difference as 'negative' cases, interactionist Strauss (1993:49) later saw grasping variation as a fundamental sociological task.

In creating SA, my goals emerged in part from feminisms, anti-racisms and related commitments to social justice. I sought to create a more explicitly critical approach that not only does not erase or paper over differences, but actively seeks to engage, name and address them. Taking Strauss very seriously, attention to variation, differences and marginalities is at the very core of SA (e.g., Clarke and Keller 2014). SA *actively resists* simplifications and *promotes* analyses of differences, seeking to make differences more legible, to help silences speak – silences in data, silences of resistance, protection, co-optation and collusion.

To engage and specify differences in SA, the GT strategy of *theoretical sampling* is directed to include the broadest range of variation within salient data sources. While studies of marginalities have a long and deep history in Chicago sociology and interactionist 'labelling theory' (e.g., Jacobsen 2017), marginalities today are more diversely inflected. Indeed, with Deleuze and Guattari (1983) we encourage beginning SA discourse analyses from the margins by pursuing 'minor' discourses that seek to present a different voice, to affirm *alternative and critical* readings of 'the situation' and, moreover, to articulate means of *changing that situation* (Clarke, Friese and Washburn 2018:225–227).

SA mapping also enhances the visibility of *epistemic diversity* (Anderson 2006) via explicit recognition that different 'ways of knowing' or 'local epistemologies' may be lively in the situation. 'Thick analysis' (Fosket 2015:196) and careful representation of epistemic diversity are fundamental for decolonising, indigenous and (post) colonial research (e.g., Battiste 2007). Again drawing on its pragmatist roots, SA uses the methodological strategy of *radical democratic empirical representation* to rupture taken-for-granted hierarchies (e.g., Becker 1967/1970). SA seeks to represent *all the actors and discourses in the situation regardless of their power*. Such thorough representational work is a key feature of SA as a critical interactionist approach.

Distinctive power analytics

Like constructivist GT, SA offers its own distinctive tools for analysing 'how power, oppression and iniquities differentially affect individuals, groups and categories of people' (Charmaz 2011:361–362). Analysing power – forms of domination, subordination and injustice – is especially important in SA, pursued through several specific strategies.

First, social worlds/arenas maps of the broader situation facilitate analysis of the collective, organisational and institutional elements in the situation and their relative power, thereby providing a 'big picture' of extant hierarchies and usually quite stratified 'conditions of possibility'. These maps detail *collective* conflict and contestation, the arenas in which it is occurring, linkages with other worlds and arenas, etc. Such structural portraits that limn social conflict *and* sites of potential social change are requisite in critical research.

Second, SA analyses seek to specify whether there are *implicated actors* in the situation under study (Clarke and Montini 1993; Clarke 2005:45–51; Clarke, Friese and Washburn 2018:76–77). Implicated actors are discursively constructed by other actors with greater power in that situation for their (the other actors') own purposes. They may be human or nonhuman, physically present but silenced, or solely discursively present. Regardless, they are *not* actively involved in self-representation, nor are they consulted. A classic example of implicated actors is constructions of women as users of contraception generated by developers of contraceptive technologies (Clarke 1998). Analysing precisely *how and for what purposes* implicated actors are discursively constructed by others, and the *consequences of those constructions for the implicated actors* as well as for those who construct them, provide SA with distinctively critical tools for grasping subtle as well as more blatant uses of power and their consequences.

Third, Star (2010; Star and Griesemer 1989) developed the concept of *boundary objects* as entities that exist at junctures where varied social worlds meet in an arena of mutual concern. Boundary objects can be treaties among countries, software programs for users in different settings, even concepts themselves as they travel across disciplines. Here the basic GT social process is 'translating' the boundary object to address the specific needs or demands placed upon it by the different worlds involved with it, while the object also retains sufficient identity to remain recognisable *across* worlds. Boundary objects are often key issues for many if not most of the worlds involved in an arena. Hence they are often sites of intense controversy and competition for the power to define and use them, making them excellent sites for analytic entrée and critical power analysis.[9]

Attentiveness to mess, complexities and relationalities

In *After Method: Mess in Social Science Research*, John Law (2004:14; emphasis in original) argued '(social) science should also be trying to make and know realities that are vague and indefinite *because much of the world is enacted in that way'*. Law (2007) objects to the tidying up of real life performed in most research as inappropriately 'hygienic' and, in the name of Deleuze and Guattari, calls for stronger *relational analyses*.

SA not only tolerates the messy complexities and relationalities of life but relishes and succeeds in describing, engaging and analysing them (e.g., Clarke with Keller 2014; Nelson 2017). Precisely because SA mapping involves *empirically specifying the elements* of the situation per se, it can be used to analyse highly heterogeneous situations. Then each of the SA maps focuses on analysing different *relationalities*. Situational and relational maps portray relations among any and all of the elements in the situation. Social worlds/arenas maps portray relations within and between social worlds and within and between arenas. Positional maps portray relations among contested issues and positions taken and not taken on those issues in the situation. Thus SA analyses conflictful processes and contingencies by focusing on complexities and relationalities.

Collaborative capacities for participatory, decolonising and related research

Critical research, especially but not only when exploring or implementing policy change, increasingly draws upon more collaborative strategies of research participation to assure more useful outcomes in 'the real world'. Both constructivist GT and SA offer excellent capacities for feminist, participatory, decolonising, indigenous, (post)colonial and related research for two primary reasons.

First, both are radically open empirically, usable in heterogeneous research settings. Rather than preconfiguring what matters, both allow the foregrounding of elements and issues salient to the situation of inquiry *as identified by researchers and participants and in extant discourse materials* (Samik-Ibrahim 2000; Charmaz 2017a, 2017b). Both are fiercely *situated* (Haraway 1991) or, as decolonising indigenous researchers term, *context-dependent* (Bainbridge, Whiteside and McCalman 2013:277). In SA, *the situation* can be featured, allowing a distinctive research setting to take centre stage.

Second, both GT coding and SA map-making and analysis can easily be undertaken collaboratively, demonstrated for many years in the 'working group' format of doing GT research (Lessor 2000; Wiener 2007), now extended to SA. Distinctively, SA maps and map-making provoke intense engagements. Maps operate as 'incitements to discourse' (Foucault 1973), pushy lift-off devices raising the level and intensity of interaction – urging people to question, discuss, clarify and keep on analysing. Students report that focusing on draft maps provokes more elaborate and productive discussions with advisors and other consultants (Clarke, Friese and Washburn 2018, chapter 8). Research teams also note the usefulness of maps in organising work sessions and deepening collaborative analysis (Clarke, Friese and Washburn 2015:234–240; 314–322; 285–291).

In sum, SA offers strong, flexible interactionist tools for critical, feminist, participatory, decolonising, (post)colonial and related research precisely because SA mapping *empirically* specifies the situation.[10] The mess, differences and complexities SA intentionally engages are everywhere with us. Such knowledge can be crucial in creating effective democratising interventions to promote social justice.

Conclusions: SA as a critical interactionist method

As this chapter has shown, the core critical interactionist methodological strategy of situational analysis (SA) is making the situation the unit of analysis. Its import cannot be overstated. *Analysing the situation is the critical interactionist heart of the SA method* – through its insistence that there is no such thing as context; that any and all elements may matter hence thick description and analysis of them is requisite (achieved through *situational maps*); that their relations need to be *empirically* determined (achieved through *relational maps*); that collective actors of all kinds and the things they struggle over (boundary objects) deserve attention in qualitative inquiry (achieved through *social worlds/arenas maps*); and that serious attention to contested issues in the situation will help reveal its power dynamics, potentially including implicated actors and silenced voices (achieved through *positional maps*). The situation is the conceptual portal to *empirical* criticality.

In analysing the situation, SA focuses intently on differences, marginalities and the heterogeneity of epistemologies, offering distinctive power analytics (e.g., social worlds/arenas mapping, implicated actors, boundary objects). SA intentionally seeks to represent *all* the major elements in the situation of inquiry, the social worlds and organisations in its arenas, and positions taken on debates in its discourses. These are radically democratic – and not undangerous – features of SA. In sum, SA demonstrates that '[b]y starting with a method rather than a theory [of power] one can come to the same conclusion as Foucault – that power is ubiquitous and that it shapes both the actor and the structures of society' (Dennis and Martin 2005:207).

SA's critical capacities are central to its having been taken up in critical, feminist, participatory, decolonising, indigenous, (post)colonial and related research. In the current qualitative landscape, SA contributes to the interpretive endeavour transdisciplinarily and transnationally. The success of SA is due in large part to its radically democratic pragmatist interactionist foundations and critical interactionist analytics. This bodes well for the future of critical interactionism.

Notes

1 For timely comments, I thank Kathy Charmaz and Reiner Keller. Citations are sparse due to space limits. For further resources, see http://study.sagepub.com/sites/default/files/Clarke2e_References.pdf.
2 On Strauss, see Strübing (2017). On 'negotiated order', see e.g., Strauss et al. (1964), Strauss (1978a, 1982a), and Clarke (2012/forthcoming). On social worlds/arenas, see Strauss (1978a, 1978b, 1982b, 1984, 1991a, 1991b, 1993; Strauss et al. 1964), Clarke (1991; 2005:39–52; Clarke and Montini 1993), and Clarke, Friese and Washburn (2018:63–77).
3 Studying with Strauss in the 1980s, Star and I were 'raised' in what Miller (1997:2) calls the 'institutional studies tradition' of interactionism. On Star, see Clarke (2010),

Timmermans (2015), Bowker et al. (2015), the Special Issue of *Mind, Culture and Activity* 22 (2) in 2015, and *Grenzarbeit und Medienforschung* at http://www.transcript-verlag.de/978-3-8376-3126-5/grenzobjekte-und-medienforschung. Rosenberg's (1979) work on ecologies of knowledge influenced Star (1989) and Clarke (1998). On 'cooperation without consensus', see Strauss (1993, especially 248–250), Star (1993), and Clarke and Star (2008).

4 See Denzin's *The Research Act* (1970, 1989a, 2009), *Interpretive Interactionism* (1989b, 2001), and *Interpretive Ethnography* (1997). Denzin (1992) framed cultural interactionism and contributed to it (2013). On critique, see, e.g., Denzin (2017), Denzin and Lincoln (1994, 2000, 2005, 2011, 2018), and Denzin and Giardina (e.g., 2016). Organisationally, see www.iiqi.org.

5 On the history of grounded theory (GT), see Bryant and Charmaz (2007, 2018), Bryant (2017), and Charmaz (2014:5–16). On the history of GT and SA, see Morse et al. (2009), Clarke, Friese and Washburn (2015:22–49), and Clarke (2019).

6 On abduction in Straussian and constructivist GT, see, e.g., Reichertz (2007), Strübing (2007) and Charmaz (2014, 2017a, 2017b); in SA, see Clarke, Friese and Washburn (2018:27–32). On theoretical sampling, see, e.g., Glaser and Strauss (1967:45–77), Strauss (1987:38–39), Strauss and Corbin (1998:201–215); and Charmaz (2014:192–212).

7 Thanks to Daniel Cefaï (2016). The term 'nonhuman' is from actor–network theory (ANT) (Latour 1987).

8 On conditional matrices, see Strauss and Corbin (1990:163; 1998:184), Strauss (1991b:455–464; 1993:57–60), and Strauss (1991a:455–463), co-authored with Corbin. For critique, see Clarke (2005:65–73), and Clarke, Friese and Washburn (2018:42–47).

9 On boundary objects, see Star (1995, 2010; Star and Griesemer 1989), Clarke and Star (2008), Bowker et al. (2015, especially pp. 171–262), and Clarke (2010).

10 Clarke (e.g., 2012/2015, 2016/in preparation) elaborates SA vis-à-vis critical feminist and decolonising inquiry. Exemplars of *critical SA projects* include Fosket (2015), French and Miller (2015), Gagnon, Jacob and Holmes (2015), Pérez and Cannella (2015), and Washburn (2015). On GT and SA, vis-à-vis decolonising research, see, e.g., Bainbridge, McCalman and Whiteside (2013), and Bainbridge, McCalman, Redman-MacLaren and Whiteside (2018). For an indigenous social worlds/arenas SA analysis, see McCalman, Bainbridge and Clarke (in preparation). For additional SA exemplars, see https://study.sagepub.com/clarke2e/student-resources/exemplars-of-situational-analysis-projects.

References

Alonso Yanez, Gabriela, Kurt Thumlert and Suzanne de Castell (2016): 'Re-Mapping Integrative Conservation: (Dis)-Coordinate Participation in a Biosphere Reserve in Mexico'. *Conservation and Society*, 14 (2):134–145.

Anderson, Elizabeth (2006): 'The Epistemology of Democracy'. *Episteme: A Journal of Social Epistemology*, 3 (1–2):8–22.

Athens, Lonnie H. (2013): ''Radical' and 'Symbolic' Interactionism: Demarcating Their Boundaries', in Lonnie H. Athens and Norman K. Denzin (eds.): *Studies in Symbolic Interaction*, 41:1–24.

Bainbridge, Roxanne, Janya McCalman and Mary Whiteside (2013): 'Being, Knowing, and Doing: A Phronetic Approach to Constructing Grounded Theory with Aboriginal Australian Partners'. *Qualitative Health Research*, 23 (2):275–288.

Bainbridge, Roxanne, Janya McCalman, Michelle Redman-MacLaren and Mary Whiteside (2018): 'Grounded Theory as Systems Science: Working with Indigenous Peoples for Social Justice', in Antony Bryant and Kathy Charmaz (eds.): *Handbook of Grounded Theory*. London: Sage Publications.

Battiste, Marie (2007): 'Research Ethics for Protecting Indigenous Knowledge and Heritage: Institutional and Researcher Responsibilities', in Norman K. Denzin and Michael D. Giardina (eds.): *Ethical Futures in Qualitative Research: Decolonizing the Politics of Knowledge*. London: Routledge, pp. 111–132.

Becker, Howard S. (1967/1970): 'Whose Side Are We On?', in Howard S. Becker (ed.): *Sociological Work: Method and Substance*. New Brunswick, NJ: Transaction Books, pp. 123–134.

Becker, Howard S. (1982): *Art Worlds*. Berkeley: University of California Press.

Blumer, Herbert (1969): *Symbolic Interactionism: Perspective and Method*. Englewood Cliffs, NJ: Prentice-Hall.

Bowker, Geoffrey, and Susan Leigh Star (1999): *Sorting Things Out: Classification and Its Consequences*. Cambridge, MA: MIT Press.

Bowker, Geoffrey, Stefan Timmermans, Adele E. Clarke and Ellen Balka (eds.) (2015): *Boundary Objects and Beyond: Working with Susan Leigh Star*. Cambridge, MA: MIT Press.

Bryant, Antony (2009). Grounded Theory and Pragmatism: The Curious Case of Anselm Strauss. *FQS Forum: Qualitative Social Research* 4(1). Online: http://www. qualitative-research.net/index.php/fqs/article/view/1358 (accessed 3/21/17).

Bryant, Antony (2017): *Grounded Theory and Grounded Theorizing: Pragmatism in Research Practice*. Oxford: Oxford University Press.

Bryant, Antony and Kathy Charmaz (eds.) (2007, 2018): *Handbook of Grounded Theory* (1st and 2nd editions). London: Sage Publications.

Bucher, R. (1962): 'Pathology: A Study of Social Movements within a Profession'. *Social Problems*, 10:40–51.

Burns, Tom R. and Peter M. Hall (eds.) (2012): *The Meta-Power Paradigm: Impacts and Transformations of Agents Institutions and Social Systems*. Frankfurt am Main: Peter Lang.

Carey, James W. (2002): 'Cultural Studies and Symbolic Interactionism: Notes in Critique and Tribute to Norman Denzin'. *Studies in Symbolic Interaction*, 25:199–209.

Casper, Monica J. (1998): 'Negotiations, Work Objects and the Unborn Patient: The Interactional Scaffolding of Fetal Surgery'. *Symbolic Interaction*, 21 (4):379–400.

Cefaï, Daniel (2016): 'Social Worlds: The Legacy of Mead's Social Ecology in Chicago Sociology', in Hans Joas and Daniel R. Huebner (eds.): *The Timeliness of George Herbert Mead*. Chicago: University of Chicago Press, pp. 164–184.

Charmaz, Kathy (2000): 'Grounded Theory: Objectivist and Constructivist Methods', in Norman Denzin and Yvonna S. Lincoln (eds.): *Handbook of Qualitative Research* (2nd edition). Thousand Oaks, CA: Sage Publications, pp. 509–536.

Charmaz, Kathy (2005): 'Grounded Theory in the 21st Century: A Qualitative Method for Advancing Social Justice Research', in Norman K. Denzin and Yvonna S. Lincoln (eds.): *Handbook of Qualitative Research*, 3rd edition). Thousand Oaks, CA: Sage Publications, pp. 507–536.

Charmaz, Kathy (2006, 2014): *Constructing Grounded Theory: A Practical Guide Through Qualitative Analysis* (1st and 2nd editions). London: Sage Publications.

Charmaz, Kathy (2009): 'Shifting the Grounds: Constructivist Grounded Theory Methods', in Jan Morse, Phyllis Stern, Julie Corbin, Kathy Charmaz, Barbara Bowers and Adele E. Clarke: *Developing Grounded Theory: The Second Generation*. London: Routledge, pp. 127–155.

Charmaz, Kathy (2011): 'Grounded Theory Methods in Social Justice Research', in Norman K. Denzin and Yvonna S. Lincoln (eds.): *The Sage Handbook of Qualitative Research* (4th edition). Thousand Oaks, CA: Sage Publications, pp. 359–380.

Charmaz, Kathy (2017a): 'The Power of Constructivist Grounded Theory for Critical Inquiry'. *Qualitative Inquiry*, 23 (1):34–45.

Charmaz, Kathy (2017b): 'Special Invited Paper: Continuities, Contradictions and Critical Inquiry in Grounded Theory'. *International Journal of Qualitative Methods*, 16:1–8.

Charmaz, Kathy, Robert Thornberg and Elaine Keane (2018): 'Evolving Grounded Theory and Social Justice Inquiry', in Norman K. Denzin and Yvonna S. Lincoln (eds.): *The Sage Handbook of Qualitative Research* (5th edition). Thousand Oaks, CA: Sage Publications, pp. 411–443.

Clarke, Adele E. (1991): 'Social Worlds Theory as Organizational Theory', in David R. Maines (ed.): *Social Organization and Social Process: Essays in Honor of Anselm Strauss*. Hawthorne, NY: Aldine de Gruyter, pp. 17–42.

Clarke, Adele E. (1998): *Disciplining Reproduction: Modernity, American Life Sciences and the 'Problem of Sex'*. Berkeley, CA: University of California Press.

Clarke, Adele E. (2003): 'Situational Analyses: Grounded Theory Mapping After the Postmodern Turn'. *Symbolic Interaction*, 26 (4):553–576.

Clarke, Adele E. (2005): *Situational Analysis: Grounded Theory After the Postmodern Turn*. Thousand Oaks, CA: Sage Publications.

Clarke, Adele E. (2010): 'In Memoriam: Susan Leigh Star (1954–2010)'. *Science, Technology & Human Values*, 35 (6):581–600.

Clarke, Adele E. (2012): 'Feminisms, Grounded Theory and Situational Analysis Revisited', in Sharlene Hesse-Biber (ed.): *Handbook of Feminist Research: Theory and Praxis* (2nd edition). Thousand Oaks, CA: Sage Publications, pp. 388–412. (Reprinted in Adele E. Clarke, Carrie Friese and Rachel Washburn (eds.) (2015): *Situational Analysis in Practice: Mapping Research with Grounded Theory*. London: Routledge, pp. 119–154.

Clarke, Adele E. (2012/Forthcoming): '"Everyone Was Negotiating About Something": Forty Years of Straussian Negotiated Order Research'. Presented at the Couch-Stone Symposium, Northwestern University. Updated version to appear in Dirk vom Lehn, Natalia Ruiz-Juno & Will Gibson (eds.): *Handbook of Interactionism*. London: Routledge.

Clarke, Adele E. (2016/in preparation): 'Situational Analysis as a Participatory, Decolonizing and (Post)colonial Approach'. Presented at the International Congress of Qualitative Inquiry, Urbana/Champaign IL.

Clarke, Adele E. (2019): 'Situating Grounded Theory and Situational Analysis in the History of Interpretive Qualitative Inquiry', in Antony Bryant and Kathy Charmaz (eds.): *Sage Handbook of Grounded Theory* (2nd edition). London: Sage Publications.

Clarke, Adele E., Carrie Friese and Rachel Washburn (eds.) (2015): *Situational Analysis in Practice: Mapping Research with Grounded Theory*. London: Routledge.

Clarke, Adele E., Carrie Friese and Rachel Washburn (2018): *Situational Analysis: Grounded Theory After the Interpretive Turn* (2nd edition). Thousand Oaks, CA: Sage Publications.

Clarke, Adele E. in Conversation with Reiner Keller (2014): 'Engaging Complexities: Working Against Simplification as an Agenda for Qualitative Research Today'. *FQS Forum: Qualitative Social Research*, 15 (2), online open access.

Clarke, Adele E. and Teresa Montini (1993): 'The Many Faces of RU486: Tales of Situated Knowledges and Technological Contestations'. *Science, Technology and Human Values*, 18 (1):42–78.

Clarke, Adele E. and Susan Leigh Star (2003): 'Symbolic Interactionist Studies of Science, Technology and Medicine', in Larry T. Reynolds and Nancy J. Herman-Kinney (eds.): *Symbolic Interactionism*. London: Routledge, pp. 539–574.

Clarke, Adele E. and Susan Leigh Star (2008): 'Social Worlds/Arenas as a Theory-Methods Package', in Edward Hackett, Olga Amsterdamska, Michael Lynch and Judy Wacjman (eds.): *Handbook of Science and Technology Studies* (3rd edition). Cambridge, MA: MIT Press, pp. 113–137.

Collins, Patricia Hill (1986): 'Learning from the Outsider Within: The Sociological Significance of Black Feminist Thought'. *Social Problems*, 33 (6):S15–S32.

Deleuze, Giles and Felix Guattari (1983): 'What is a Minor Literature?' *Mississippi Review*, 11 (3):13–33.

Deleuze, Giles and Felix Guattari (1987): 'Introduction: Rhizome', in *A Thousand Plateaus: Capitalism and Schizophrenia II*. Minneapolis: University of Minnesota Press, pp. 3–25.

Dennis, Alex and Peter J. Martin (2005): 'Symbolic Interactionism and the Concept of Power'. *British Journal of Sociology*, 56 (2):191–213.

Denzin, Norman K. (1970, 1989a, 2009): *The Research Act: A Theoretical Introduction to Sociological Methods* (1st, 2nd and 3rd editions). Chicago: Aldine (Aldine Transaction).

Denzin, Norman K. (1989b, 2001): *Interpretive Interactionism* (1st and 2nd editions). Newbury Park, CA: Sage Publications.

Denzin, Norman K. (1992): *Symbolic Interactionism and Cultural Studies: The Politics of Interpretation*. Oxford: Basil Blackwell.

Denzin, Norman K. (1997): *Interpretive Ethnography: Ethnographic Practices for the 21st Century*. Thousand Oaks, CA: Sage Publications.

Denzin, Norman K. (2013): *Indians on Display: Global Commodification of Native America in Performance, Art and Museums*. New York: Routledge.

Denzin, Norman K. (2017): 'Critical Qualitative Inquiry'. *Qualitative Inquiry*, 23 (1):8–16.

Denzin, Norman K. and Michael D. Lincoln (eds.) (2016): *Qualitative Inquiry through a Critical Lens*. New York: Routledge.

Denzin, Norman K. and Yvonna S. Lincoln (eds.) (1994, 2018): *Handbook of Qualitative Research* (1st–5th editions). Thousand Oaks, CA: Sage Publications.

Dewey, John (1938): *Logic: The Theory of Inquiry*. New York: Henry Holt and Company.

Dewey, John (1939): 'Experience, Knowledge and Value: A Rejoinder', in Jo Ann Boydston (ed.): *The Later Works of John Dewey (1925–1953): 1939–1941/Essays, Reviews, and Miscellany* (vol. 14). Carbondale, IL: Southern Illinois University Press.

Dingwall, Robert (1999): 'On the Nonnegotiable in Sociological Life', in Barry Glasner & Rosanna Hertz (eds.): *Qualitative Sociology and Everyday Life*. Thousand Oaks, CA: Sage, pp. 215–225.

Dubbin, Leslie, Monica McLemore and Janet K. Shim (2017): 'Illness Narratives of African Americans Living with Coronary Heart Disease: A Critical Interactionist Analysis'. *Qualitative Health Research*, 27 (4):497–508.

Fisher, Michael (2014): 'PTSD in the U.S. Military, and the Politics of Prevalence'. *Social Science & Medicine*, 115:1–9.

Fosket, Jennifer R. (2015): 'Situating Knowledge', in Adele E. Clarke, Carrie Friese and Rachel Washburn (eds.): *Situational Analysis in Practice: Mapping Grounded Theory*. London: Routledge, pp. 195–233.

Foucault, Michel (1973): *The Order of Things: An Archaeology of the Human Sciences*. New York: Vintage Books.

Foucault, Michel (1980): *Power/Knowledge: Selected Interviews and Other Writings 1972–1977*. New York: Pantheon.

French, Martin and Fiona A. Miller (2015): 'Leveraging the 'Living Laboratory': On the Emergence of the Entrepreneurial Hospital', in Adele E. Clarke, Carrie Friese and

Rachel Washburn (eds.): *Situational Analysis in Practice: Mapping Research with Grounded Theory.* London: Routledge, pp. 293–313.

Friese, Carrie (2010): 'Classification Conundrums: Classifying Chimeras and Enacting Species Preservation'. *Theory and Society*, 39 (2):145–172.

Fujimura, Joan H. (1988): 'The Molecular Biological Bandwagon in Cancer Research: Where Social Worlds Meet'. *Social Problems*, 35:261–283.

Gagnon, Marilou, Jean-Daniel Jacob and Dave Holmes (2015): 'Governing Through (In) Security: A Critical Analysis of a Fear-Based Public Health Campaign', in Adele E. Clarke, Carrie Friese and Rachel Washburn (eds.): *Situational Analysis in Practice: Mapping Research with Grounded Theory.* London: Routledge, pp. 270–292.

Glaser, Barney G. and Anselm L. Strauss (1967): *The Discovery of Grounded Theory: Strategies for Qualitative Research.* New York: Aldine.

Gusfield, Joseph R. (1981): *The Culture of Public Problems.* Chicago: University of Chicago Press.

Hall, Peter M. (1987): 'Interactionism and the Study of Social Organization'. *Sociological Quarterly*, 28 (1):1–22.

Hall, Peter M. (1997): 'Meta-Power, Social Organization and the Shaping of Social Action'. *Symbolic Interaction*, 20 (4):397–418.

Hall, Peter M. and Patrick J. W. McGinty (2002): 'Social Organization across Space and Time: The Policy Process, Mesodomain Analysis, and Breadth of Perspective', in Sing C. Chew and David Knottnerus (eds.): *Structure, Culture and History: Recent Issues in Social Theory.* Lanham, MD: Rowman & Littlefield, pp. 303–322.

Haraway, Donna (1991): 'Situated Knowledges: The Science Question in Feminism and the Privilege of Partial Perspectives', in *Simians, Cyborgs, and Women: The Reinvention of Nature.* New York: Routledge, pp. 183–202.

Hochschild, Arlie R. (1983): *The Managed Heart: Commercialization of Human Feeling.* Berkeley, CA: University of California Press.

Hochschild, Arlie R. (2012): *The Outsourced Self: Intimate Life in Market Times.* New York: Metropolitan Books/Macmillan Inc.

Hochschild, Arlie R. (2016): *Strangers in Their Own Land: Anger and Mourning on the American Right.* New York: The New Press.

Jacobsen, Michael Hviid (ed.) (2017): *The Interactionist Imagination: Studying Meaning, Situation, and Micro-Social Order.* London: Palgrave/Macmillan.

Jacobsen, Michael Hviid and Anders Petersen (2017): 'Arlie R. Hochschild – Interactions, Emotions and Commercialized Intimacy', in Michael Hviid Jacobsen (ed.): *The Interactionist Imagination: Studying Meaning, Situation, and Micro-Social Order.* London: Palgrave/Macmillan, pp. 375–408.

Keller, Reiner (2005/2018): *The Sociology of Knowledge Approach to Discourse (SKAD).* New York: Springer.

Keller, Reiner. (2011): 'The Sociology of Knowledge Approach to Discourse (SKAD)'. *Human Studies*, 34:43–65.

Keller, Reiner (2017): 'Has Critique Run Out of Steam? On Discourse Research as Critical Inquiry'. *Qualitative Inquiry*, 23 (1):58–68.

Latour, Bruno (1987): *Science in Action: How to Follow Scientists and Engineers Through Society.* Cambridge, MA: Harvard University Press.

Latour, Bruno (2004): 'Why Has Critique Run Out of Steam? From Matters of Fact to Matters of Concern'. *Critical Inquiry*, 30:225–248.

Law, John (1999): 'After ANT: Complexity, Naming and Topology', in John Law and John Hassard (eds.): *Actor Network Theory and After.* Oxford: Blackwell.

Law, John (2004): *After Method: Mess in Social Science Research.* London: Routledge.

Law, John (2007): 'Making a Mess with Method', in William Outhwaite and Stephen H. Turner (eds.): *Handbook of Social Science Methodology.* Thousand Oaks, CA: Sage Publications, pp. 595–606.

Lessor, Roberta (2000): 'Using the Team Approach of Anselm Strauss in Action Research: Consulting on a Project on Global Education'. *Sociological Perspectives*, 43 (4):S133–S147.

Maines, David R. (1982): 'In Search of Mesostructure: Studies in the Negotiated Order'. *Urban Life: Journal of Ethnographic Research* (special issue on Negotiated Order), 11 (3):267–279.

Martin, Wanda, Bernie Pauly and Marjorie MacDonald (2016): 'Situational Analysis for Complex Systems: Methodological Development in Public Health Research'. *AIMS Public Health*, 3 (1):94–109.

Martins, Diane C. and Patricia Burbank (2011): 'Critical Interactionism: An Upstream-Downstream Approach to Health Care Reform'. *Advances in Nursing Science*, 34 (4): 315–329.

McCalman, Janya, Roxanne Bainbridge and Adele E. Clarke (in preparation): 'Enabling the Spread of Aboriginal Australian Health Programs: A Social Worlds Analysis of the Family Wellbeing Program 1993–2017'.

McCarthy, C. Doyle (1984): 'Towards a Sociology of the Physical World: George Herbert Mead on Physical Objects'. *Studies in Symbolic Interaction*, 5:105–121.

McGinty, Patrick J. W. (2014): 'Divided and Drifting: Interactionism and the Neglect of Social Organizational Analysis in Organization Studies'. *Symbolic Interaction*, 37 (2):155–186.

Mead, George Herbert (1927/1964): 'The Objective Reality of Perspectives', in Andrew J. Reck (ed.): *Selected Writings of George Herbert Mead.* Chicago: University of Chicago Press, pp. 306–319.

Mead, George Herbert (1934, 1962): *Mind, Self and Society* (1st and 2nd editions) (C. W. Morris, ed.). Chicago: University of Chicago Press.

Mead, George Herbert (1938, 1972): *The Philosophy of the Act* (1st and 2nd editions). Chicago: University of Chicago Press.

Miller, Gale (1997): 'Introduction: Context and Method in Qualitative Research', in Gale Miller and Robert Dingwall (eds.): *Context and Method in Qualitative Research.* London: Sage Publications, pp. 1–11.

Morse, Jan, Phyllis N. Stern, Juliet Corbin, Barbara Bowers, Kathy Charmaz and Adele E. Clarke (2009): *Developing Grounded Theory: The Second Generation.* London: Routledge.

Nelson, James (2017): 'Using Conceptual Depth Criteria: Addressing the Challenge of Reaching Saturation in Qualitative Research'. *Qualitative Research*, 17:554–570.

Park, Robert E. and Ernest W. Burgess (1921): *Introduction to the Science of Sociology.* Chicago: University of Chicago Press.

Pérez, Michelle S. and Gaile S. Cannella (2015): 'Using Situational Analysis for Critical Qualitative Research Purposes', in Adele E. Clarke, Carrie Friese and Rachel Washburn (eds.): *Situational Analysis in Practice: Mapping Research with Grounded Theory.* London: Routledge, pp. 234–240.

Rabinow, Paul (2011): 'Dewey and Foucault: What's the Problem?' *Foucault Studies*, 11:11–19.

Rosenberg, Charles E. (1979): 'Toward an Ecology of Knowledge: On Discipline, Contexts and History', in Alexandra Oleson and John Voss (eds.): *The Organization of Knowledge in Modern America.* Baltimore: Johns Hopkins University Press.

Salerno, Roger A. (2007): *Sociology Noir: Studies at the University of Chicago in Loneliness, Marginality and Deviance, 1915–1935.* Jefferson, NC: McFarland & Co.

Samik-Ibrahim, Rahmat M. (2000): 'Grounded Theory Methodology as the Research Strategy for a Developing Country'. *FQS Forum: Qualitative Social Research,* 1 (1), online open access.

Sandstrom, Kent L. and Gary Alan Fine (2003): 'Triumphs, Emerging Voices, and the Future', in Larry T. Reynolds and Nancy J. Herman-Kinney (eds.): *Handbook of Symbolic Interactionism.* Walnut Creek, CA: AltaMira Press, pp. 1041–1057.

Schwalbe, Michael L. (2008, 2015): *Rigging the Game: How Inequality is Reproduced in Everyday Life* (1st and 2nd editions). New York: Oxford University Press.

Schwalbe, Michael L. (2014): *Manhood Acts: Gender and the Practices of Domination.* New York: Routledge.

Star, Susan Leigh (1983): 'Simplification in Scientific Work: An Example from Neuroscience Research'. *Social Studies of Science,* 13:208–226.

Star, Susan Leigh (1991a): 'Power, Technologies and the Phenomenology of Conventions: On Being Allergic to Onions', in John Law (ed.): *A Sociology of Monsters: Essays on Power, Technology and Domination.* New York: Routledge, pp. 25–56.

Star, Susan Leigh (1991b): 'The Sociology of the Invisible: The Primacy of Work in the Writings of Anselm Strauss', in David R. Maines (ed.): *Social Organization and Social Processes: Essays in Honor of Anselm Strauss.* Hawthorne, NY: Aldine de Gruyter, pp. 265–283.

Star, Susan Leigh (1995): 'Introduction', in Susan Leigh Star (ed.): *Ecologies of Knowledge: New Directions in the Sociology of Science and Technology.* Albany: State University of New York Press, pp. 1–35. (Reprinted in Geof Bowker, Stefan Timmermans, Adele E. Clarke and Ellen Balka (eds.) (2015): *Boundary Objects and Beyond: Working with Susan Leigh Star.* Cambridge, MA: MIT Press, pp. 14–46.)

Star, Susan Leigh (2007): 'Living Grounded Theory: Cognitive and Emotional Forms of Pragmatism', in Antony Bryant and Kathy Charmaz (eds.): *The Sage Handbook of Grounded Theory.* London: Sage Publications, pp. 75–94.

Star, Susan Leigh (2010): 'This is Not a Boundary Object: Reflections on the Origin of a Concept'. *Science, Technology & Human Values,* 35:601–617.

Star, Susan Leigh and James Griesemer (1989): 'Institutional Ecology, 'Translations' and Boundary Objects: Amateurs and Professionals in Berkeley's Museum of Vertebrate Zoology, 1907–1939'. *Social Studies of Science,* 19:387–420.

Star, Susan Leigh and Anselm L. Strauss (1998): 'Layers of Silence, Arenas of Voice: The Ecology of Visible and Invisible Work'. *Computer Supported Cooperative Work: The Journal of Collaborative Computing,* 8:9–30.

Strauss, Anselm L. (1978a): *Negotiations: Varieties, Contexts, Processes and Social Order.* San Francisco, CA: Jossey-Bass.

Strauss, Anselm L. (1978b): 'A Social Worlds Perspective'. *Studies in Symbolic Interaction,* 1:119–128.

Strauss, Anselm L. (1982a): 'Interorganizational Negotiation'. *Urban Life,* 11 (3):350–367.

Strauss, Anselm L. (1982b): 'Social Worlds and Legitimation Processes', in Norman K. Denzin (ed.): *Studies in Symbolic Interaction,* 4:171–190.

Strauss, Anselm L. (1984): 'Social Worlds and Their Segmentation Processes', in Norman K. Denzin (ed.): *Studies in Symbolic Interaction,* 5:123–139.

Strauss, Anselm L. (1987): *Qualitative Analysis for Social Scientists.* Cambridge: Cambridge University Press.

Strauss, Anselm L. (1991a): *Creating Sociological Awareness: Collective Images and Symbolic Representation.* New Brunswick, NJ: Transaction Publications.

Strauss, Anselm L. (1991b): 'A Personal History of the Development of Grounded Theory'. *Qualitative Family Research: A Newsletter of the Qualitative Family Research Network,* 5 (2). Available online at: http://dne2.ucsf.edu/public/anselmstrauss/groundedtheory.html.

Strauss, Anselm L. (1993): *Continual Permutations of Action.* New York: Aldine de Gruyter.

Strauss, Anselm L. (1995): 'Notes on the Nature and Development of General Theories'. *Qualitative Inquiry,* 1 (1):7–18.

Strauss, Anselm L. and Julie Corbin (1990, 1998): *The Basics of Qualitative Analysis: Grounded Theory Procedures and Techniques* (1st and 2nd editions). Newbury Park, CA: Sage Publications.

Strauss, Anselm L., Leonard Schatzman, Rue Bucher, Danuta Erlich and Mel Sabshin (1964): *Psychiatric Ideologies and Institutions.* Glencoe, IL: Free Press.

Strübing, Jörg (2007): 'Research as Pragmatic Problem-Solving: The Pragmatist Roots of Empirically-Grounded Theorizing', in Antony Bryant and Kathy Charmaz (eds.): *Handbook of Grounded Theory.* London: Sage Publications, pp. 580–602.

Strübing, Jörg (2017): 'Anselm L. Strauss: Action/Work as Process and Perspective', in Michael Hviid Jacobsen (ed.): *The Interactionist Imagination: Meaning, Situation and Micro-Social Order.* London: Palgrave/Macmillan, pp. 263–289.

Thomas, William I. (1927): 'Situational Analysis: The Behavior Pattern and the Situation' (Presidential Address to the American Sociological Association). (Reprinted in Morris Janowitz (ed.) (1966): *On Social Organization and Social Personality: Selected Papers (of W. I. Thomas).* Chicago: University of Chicago Press, pp. 154–167.

Timmermans, Stefan (2015): 'Introduction: Working with Leigh Star', in Geof Bowker, Stefan Timmermans, Adele E. Clarke and Ellen Balka (eds.): *Boundary Objects and Beyond: Working with Susan Leigh Star.* Cambridge, MA: MIT Press, pp. 1–9.

Washburn, Rachel (2015): 'Rethinking the Disclosure Debates: A Situational Analysis of the Multiple Meanings of Human Biomonitoring Data', in Adele E. Clarke, Carrie Friese and Rachel Washburn (eds.): *Situational Analysis in Practice: Mapping Research with Grounded Theory.* London: Routledge, pp. 241–269.

Wiener, Carolyn (2007): 'Making Teams Work in Conducting Grounded Theory', in Antony Bryant and Kathy Charmaz (eds.): *Handbook of Grounded Theory.* London: Sage Publications, pp. 293–310.

Wirth, Louis (1928): *The Ghetto.* Chicago: University of Chicago Press.

11 Cultural criminology and its incitement for symbolic interactionism

Transgression, marginalisation, resistance and media in the wider context of power and culture of late modernity

Thaddeus Müller

Introduction

The traditional strength of symbolic interactionist studies is the study of social worlds and their meanings for their members. Others see this strength as a weakness because, they argue, there is too much of a concern with describing and understanding the social life of 'small' groups, without paying sufficient attention to the wider context of power relations shaping society and larger societal transformations, such as the development of late modernity and the digital world. Though this is a stereotypical representation of symbolic interactionism, there is a grain of truth in this claim, as symbolic interactionist studies do tend to focus on the micro and meso levels and pay less or no attention to the macro level.

In this chapter, I will focus on cultural criminology as a possible inspiration for symbolic interactionism, as it has been able to focus on 'small' social worlds while relating these to a wider societal context. In doing this, it concentrates on (a) power, specifically the working of institutions of social control, and (b) culture, how people give meanings to their social world, and how this is shaped by digital communication. In its integrated critical and cultural approach, cultural criminology has been developing and interrelating a set of core concepts, such as 'transgression', 'marginalisation', 'resistance' and 'media' in late modernity, which can be an impetus for symbolic interactionism, which I will discuss comprehensively in this chapter.

Before I do this, I want to clarify how I use the two main concepts of this book: critical and cultural. I define critical research as an academic stance, which studies how inequalities in power shape social life and create social injustice. It scrutinises and exposes the ways established parties, such as elites and interest groups, use their power to defend their position, marginalise, and exclude other categories in society. It pays attention to how this is done with the support of institutions such as the media, the criminal justice system and politics. This approach also includes a focus on describing the experience of marginalised groups, thus giving them a voice which is not heard in the dominant media. Finally, it also describes the different ways these groups resist their marginalisation and how they empower themselves.

I use culture in the traditional symbolic interactionist way as a dynamic set of meanings people give to their social world, which they develop through interactions with primary and secondary others in settings, such as the media, education, work, urban space, family and other social networks. They use this dynamic set of meanings to make sense of social life and navigate through it. In this chapter, I will show how cultural criminology has implemented both elements, critical and cultural, specifically in the way it has implemented the following four central concepts, which I will clarify in this chapter: 'transgression', 'marginalisation', 'resistance' and 'media' in late modernity.

Cultural criminology is a branch of criminology with a strong focus on meaning (culture) and structural conditions, such as marginalisation and late modernity. Its critical focus is demonstrated in pointing out social injustice and marginalisation in society and more specifically in the criminal justice system. Cultural criminology expanded quickly from the 1990s and has been dominated by Anglo-Saxon scholars, such as Jock Young, Keith Hayward and Jeff Ferrell. Since the mid-2000s, academics from continental Europe have also been contributing to its development, especially from the Netherlands. Cultural criminology does not have a strict programme with a fixed set of concepts and methods. Cultural criminology is constantly developing with the influx of new scholars and social transformations. Its methods tend to be anti-positivistic and have a strong focus on ethnography and media analysis. From the outset, cultural criminology was strongly influenced by symbolic interactionism and the Chicago school ethnographic tradition. Considering this early development, we might say that cultural criminology is a branch of symbolic interactionism. Clinton Sanders was one of the editors of the first publication on cultural criminology and he is closely affiliated with symbolic interactionism, as one can see reading his work on tattoo artists and dog owners (Sanders 2003; Sanders and Vail 2009). Another clear link with symbolic interactionism is the many references to two main scholars from the symbolic interaction tradition, Howard S. Becker, especially *Outsiders* (1963), and Jack Katz, particularly *The Seduction of Crime* (1988). Jeff Ferrell, the other editor of the first cultural criminology publication, works in the ethnographic tradition of the Chicago School, as can be seen in his publication on graffiti writers (1993), scrounging (2006) and drift (2018).

Since 2000, cultural criminology has been transformed under the influence of critical and theoretical scholars from the United Kingdom. Initially, cultural criminology was criticised, as deviance studies were in the late 1960s and early 1970s, for focussing on small groups or organisations without paying attention to influences of the wider social, cultural, political and economic context. With the entrance of British scholars in cultural criminology, structural conditions, especially of marginalisation and late modernity were explicitly introduced (Hayward 2016). I believe that this development can also function as a call for the wider contextualisation of studies inspired by symbolic interactionism. The main method that I have used here is reading, rereading and analysing cultural criminology publications, which include the core publications such as *Cultural Criminology: An Invitation* (Ferrell, Hayward and Young 2015) to more current publications such as *Crime, Media, Culture*, and recent dissertations of the second generation of cultural criminologists. A crucial source has been my personal and academic involvement within cultural criminology. I have presented at cultural criminology conferences, published in the Dutch cultural criminology journal *Tijdschrift over Cultuur en Criminaliteit*, and published reports on cultural criminology, especially on the work of Ferrell. I did my master's in cultural anthropology, focused on the Chicago school ethnographic tradition during my PhD, and have been involved with the symbolic interactionism community since the early 1990s. One might say that my academic career resembles in some sense the passage of cultural criminology, a journey from a focus on the culture of small groups to including structural elements, including the processes of exclusion and marginalisation.

In order to understand the initial position of symbolic interactionism and especially deviance studies I will first focus on how deviance studies were criticised in the late 1960s and early 1970s, especially by critical scholars such as Alvin W. Gouldner (1968), Ian Taylor, Paul Walton and Jock Young (1973), and Jack D. Douglas (1971, 1976). With these critiques in mind, we can take a closer look at how cultural criminology took up this academic challenge and how it profited from doing so. Second, I will describe the development of cultural criminology since its first publication (Ferrell and Sanders 1995). Third, I will focus on its main foci in recent years. Finally, in the conclusion, I will address the ways cultural criminology can enrich symbolic interactionism by relating its thick description of small communities to four major concepts: 'transgression', 'marginalisation', 'resistance' and the 'media' in late modernity. It is difficult to find a clear definition of cultural criminology. This is even more difficult for symbolic interactionism, as it has many branches. In fact, some do focus on one or more of the major concepts of cultural criminology that I will discuss here. But this chapter does not cover the field of symbolic interactionism, which would be impossible within its word-limit constraints. The focus, therefore, is on cultural criminology and how some inspirational pathways used in cultural criminology might open new vistas in the research and writings of scholars who identify with symbolic interactionism.

Criticising deviance studies

The heyday of symbolic interactionism in the 1960s and early 1970s within sociology and criminology centres on what was then called deviance studies. One of the core publications in those years was *Outsiders* (1963) by Howard S. Becker. It was regarded as one of the most groundbreaking publications in the field of criminology. Becker coins the concepts of 'labelling', which included the way persons define themselves as members of a deviant subculture, like the jazz world, and involves how actions, such as the use of marijuana, become labelled as criminal. At the same time, deviance studies triggered critique, especially from critical (neo-Marxist) sociologists. Here I will focus on two of the most well-known examples of this type of critique, namely Alvin W. Gouldner's article 'The Sociologist as

Partisan' (1968) and *The New Criminology* (Taylor, Walton and Young 1973). I will also include the critique of Jack D. Douglas because his stance is not so much on power, but more on meaning and culture.

Here, I will not enter the debate about whether this critique is justified. That would be another publication in itself. Still, I do agree with others that some have deliberately misrepresented deviance studies, as they wanted to create a straw man for polemic purposes (Downes and Rock 1982; Plummer 1979). Gouldner was one of them. Becker (1968) agrees with Gouldner's statement that value-free sociology is not possible; when one does not make a choice, one does support the current status quo in society. Becker is clear in his opinion: the sociologist should choose the side of the underdog. But Gouldner takes a firm stance against Becker and his fellow academics, which according to Gouldner includes scholars such as John Kitsuse, David Matza and Ned Polsky, because he sees them as flâneur, pseudo-partisans. According to Gouldner, they are not truly committed to the position of the underdogs and have no deep understanding of their suffering:

> Although Becker leans toward a sympathy and special consideration for the underdog's standpoint, and although the underdog's suffering is particularly visible, it is still one further paradox in Becker's discussion that we find him displaying no such concern for suffering.
>
> (Gouldner 1968:106)

Gouldner does not reject Becker's choice to research the underdog's standpoint. He states it is justified because we do not know much of their reality and their suffering:

> This, in turn, implies that a sociology truly concerned with representing the standpoint of the underdog would most especially seek to communicate the character of his suffering, its peculiar sources and special intensity, the ways and degrees in which it is avoidable, the forces that contribute to it, and his struggle against it.
>
> (Gouldner 1968:106)

Gouldner played a crucial role in the construction of deviance studies as non-critical and oblivious to power and suffering. This polemic and imbalanced quotation is probably the most well-known in the critique on deviance studies:

> At the same time, however, Becker's school of deviance is redolent of Romanticism. It expresses the satisfaction of the Great White Hunter who has bravely risked the perils of the urban jungle to bring back an exotic specimen. It expresses the Romanticism of the zoo curator who preeningly displays his rare specimens. And like the zookeeper, he wishes to protect his collection; he does not want spectators to throw rocks at the animals behind the bars. But neither is he eager to tear down the bars and let the animals go.
>
> (Gouldner 1968:106)

Ian Taylor, Paul Walton and Jock Young (1973) focus on similar issues and share the main points of Gouldner but are more subtle and constructive in their comments:

> What is clear is that this view of deviancy deals with what we can now isolate as *the missing element of power in the creation of deviancy.* For whilst the social reaction perspective deals with power of public pressure and differential rule-enforcement in the creation of deviance, it does not deal with the larger processes which form the governing framework for the small processes and transactions.
>
> (Taylor, Walton and Young 1973:169–170)

They prefer to see deviance as a reaction against social control:

> Our contention is that much deviancy must be viewed as a struggle, or reaction, against such 'normalized repression', a breaking-through, as it were, of accepted, taken-for-granted, power invested common sense rules'.
>
> (Taylor, Walton and Young 1973:169)

Another crucial form of critique is that deviance studies have not been able to theorise their work in relation to grand sociological theory that reflects on social tensions, issues and transformation of society at large:

> Like the pragmatists before them, the social reaction theorists, operating within the confines of liberal ideologies, fail to lay bare the structured inequalities in power and interest which underpin the processes whereby the laws are created and enforced ... Our position here attempt to confront the way in which authority and interests enforce and maintain sets of law, rules and norms which in themselves are part and parcel of the creation of deviancy.
>
> (Taylor, Walton and Young 1973:169)

So far in this chapter, the emphasis in the early critique of deviance studies has centred on power. Culture has hardly played a role, as it was seen as one of the strengths of symbolic interactionism and deviance studies. Still, Jack D. Douglas (1971, 1976) criticised Becker and other deviance researchers for their simplified conception of culture and construction of meaning. Douglas had an almost what we now might call late modern perspective on American society. He saw a pluralistic society in which there was constant conflict in the construction of meaning between different societal groups, which made the construction of meaning a highly problematic process. Douglas suggests in *American Social Order: Rules in a Pluralistic Society* (1972) an all-encompassing approach, which focuses on the complexities of the construction of meaning in everyday situations in relation to conflicting perspectives on society and how these are shaped by transformations in politics, media and the criminal justice system. In *The Nude Beach* (1977), for instance, Douglas, Paul K. Rasmussen and Carol Ann Flanagan discuss the construction of meaning of public nudity from different perspectives and how this is shaped by a range of societal institutions, such as the police, the courts and the media. In the next paragraph, we will see how cultural criminology has been able to integrate the aforementioned critical and cultural critique in the use of symbolic interactionism.

The development of cultural criminology[1]

In the first publication in which the term 'cultural criminology' (Ferrell and Sanders 1995) was coined, the authors state that in order to understand crime we have to look at culture and its relation to crime. Their approach is similar to symbolic interactionism and its labelling approach, as they state that understanding criminality means foremost understanding the culture of criminals and how they perceive the social worlds in which they participate: 'Much of this subcultural meaning, action, identity and status is organized around style – that is, around the shared aesthetic of the subculture's members' (Ferrell and Sanders 1995:5). Analysing crime also means understanding the criminal justice system and how agents of control define certain acts as criminal and how they react to these acts. Cultural criminology is loosely defined in the following passage:

> To account for the culture and subcultures of crime, the criminalization of culture; and subcultural activities, and the politics of these processes, then, we must move toward an integration of cultural and criminological analysis – that is, toward a cultural criminology.
>
> (Ferrell and Sanders 1995:3–4)

Cultural criminology started as an experiment within criminology and symbolic interactionism, shaped by North American scholars who reflected on North American topics, such as the representation of crack cocaine in New York and the bluegrass murder ballads. These studies still resemble qualitative studies that have a strong internal focus, meaning they did not relate their cases systematically to the wider economic, social and cultural context, for which deviance studies were criticised in the 1970s. For instance, in the first publication, one does not see any clear statement on the possible influence of the condition of postmodernity or late modernity, nor any reference to academics who were associated with this perspective such as Jacques Derrida and Jean Baudrillard (Hayward 2016).

In its first years, cultural criminology was mainly inspired by classical qualitative studies such as *Delinquent Boys* (Cohen 1955) and *Moral Panics and Folk Devils* (Cohen 1972). Becker plays an important role in cultural criminology because of the development of concepts such as 'labelling' and 'moral entrepreneurs' in *Outsiders* (1963) with which he shows that behaviour is criminal when dominant groups in society define it as criminal. The origins of the first publication on cultural criminology located in symbolic interactionism and the (sub-)cultural approach fused with ethnography and media studies, was also visible in the two following major publications in cultural criminology – *Crimes of Style*

(Ferrell 1996) and *Ethnography at the Edge* (Ferrell and Hamm 1998). *Crimes of Style* is the urtext of the early cultural criminology and describes the subculture of graffiti writers in Denver, the criminalisation of their writing and the way they successfully resist this. Both publications celebrate the full immersion of the researcher in the field in order to reach the goal of 'Criminological Verstehen' defined as:

> A researcher's subjective understanding of crime's situational meanings and emotions – its moments of pleasure and pain, its emergent logics and excitement – within the larger process of research. It further implies that a researcher, through attentiveness and participation, can at least begin to apprehend and appreciate the specific roles and experiences of criminals, crime victims, crime control agents and others caught up in the day-to-day reality of crime.
>
> (Ferrell 1998:27)

Ethnography at the Edge (Ferrell and Hamm 1998) is a compilation of different studies on a range of topics such as drugs, shelters, and sex work in the tradition of symbolic interactionism and also contains more reflective paradigmatic and groundbreaking chapters on ethnography with a strong focus on the physical and emotional realities of full emergence in the field. In recent years, Ferrell has proposed and advanced several ethnographic forms of 'Criminological Verstehen', such as 'instant ethnography' and 'liquid ethnography', which respectively fit the momentous experience of crime and transgression, and the fluid character of social life in late modernity (Ferrell, Hayward and Young 2015:215–225). Especially, Ferrell's work radiates a strong feeling of vitalism, anarchy and resistance against the controlling forces of American society and celebrates those who resist it. He and other cultural criminologists also revolt against mainstream positivistic criminology that justifies and supports the current legal system by accepting dominant definitions of crime and by not giving voice to marginalised groups in society who are being penalised and imprisoned for trying to survive in a cutthroat neo-liberal society. This type of research disregards the human lived experience of those who are being researched:

> The 'data' from such surveys dehumanize those surveyed, draining them of their own meaningful experiences, and reducing their lives (or at least those small parts of their lives they care to report) to aggregated abstraction.
>
> (Ferrell 2013:266)

Since 2000, we have seen the entrance of Anglo-Saxon criminologists who embrace cultural criminology such as Jock Young, Keith Hayward and Mike Presdee. Their focus on crime has been more theoretical and critical. The British scholars shaped cultural criminology in two significant ways: (1) they put more emphasis on power, inspired by the European tradition of critical criminology and neo-Marxism (van Swaaningen 1997); and (2) they added a theoretical perspective in which meaning, labelling and subcultures were related to late or liquid modernity (Giddens 1991; Bauman 2000). Both elements added a new structural and theoretical component to the toolkit of cultural criminology.

With the introduction of the British contingency cultural criminology developed into a more explicit and systematic critique of the workings of the criminal justice system, seeing it as a tool of established groups in our society to maintain control and exclude and marginalise groups of outsiders. The enhanced emphasis on late modernity changed also the significance of cultural criminology as it focussed on meaning and culture in the context of the historical transformations at the end of the 20th century, in which traditional guidelines for identity such as work, family, church and neighbourhood became liquid and lost their authority.

Instead of deviance, cultural criminologists opted for the term transgression, because according to them, it puts more emphasis on empowerment and resistance. Young (2007) points out the special relevance of transgression for the identity and self-esteem of members of a (structurally defined) 'underclass'. Because of their marginal position, they have less access to social, cultural and economic resources for social recognition and status, such as income, education and social skills. For Presdee (2000), transgressive behaviour is a form of resistance to the standardisation and rationalisation of social life in late modernity that results in 'powerlessness and meaninglessness and the loosening of cultural imperatives' (Presdee 2000:18). Like Young, he relates transgression explicitly to the social world of the 'underclass'.

Inspired by the work of Jürgen Habermas, Stephen Lyng sees transgression as resistance to the colonisation of the lifeworld and the 'disembodiment that characterizes the bureaucratic-capitalist system' (Lyng 2004:372). Because of the transcendental character of edgework, those involved in it experience a sensation of autonomy and social freedom. Lyng states that edgework is especially important for people whose late modern experience is dominated by 'social over-determination', 'alienation' and 'oversocialization' (Lyng 2004:362–363). Transgression gains a different connotation in the context of late modernity and can be experienced as 'self-actualizing, self-determining, authentically real and creatively satisfying' (Lyng 2004:362).

Cultural criminology started to relate crime and transgression not only to these major cultural transformations but also put emphasis on parallel structural changes in late capitalism, such as the destruction of the welfare state, the rise of hyper neo-liberalism, disinvestment in the public sector and the globalisation of markets and industries:

> For us, that issue is clear: unchecked global capitalism must be confronted as the deep dynamic from which spring many of the ugliest examples of contemporary criminality. Tracing a particularly expansionist trajectory these days, late modern capitalism continues to contaminate one community after another, shaping social life into a series of predatory encounters and saturating everyday existence with criminogenic expectations of material convenience (Hedges, 2009). All along this global trajectory, collectivities are

converted into markets, people into consumers, and experiences and emotions into products. So steady is this seepage of consumer capitalism into social life, so pervasive are its crimes – both corporate and interpersonal – that they now seem to pervade almost every situation.

(Ferrell, Hayward and Young 2015:15)

Within these vast societal transformations, cultural criminology became sensitive to how crime and transgression were shaped by specific elements of late modernity, especially the fast-changing digitalisation/virtualisation of the mediated world where reality equals a video game, Twitter and Snapchat. The penetration of social life by new technologies confronts old world perceptions of time and space and transforms traditional crimes, such as blackmail, terrorism and human trafficking, and creates new forms of crime, such as phishing and ransomware.

Power, marginalisation and meaning come together in cultural criminology in what Ferrell calls the 'politics of meaning'. It is crucial to reconceptualise 'power in terms of meaning: meaning deployed and contested, meaning assigned and undermined, in the battle over crime and justice' (Ferrell 2013:259). Cultural criminology also has a more public active role, beyond academia:

Put differently, cultural criminology increasingly strikes me as an orientation designed especially for critical engagement with the politics of meaning surrounding crime and crime control, and for critical intervention into those politics.

(Ferrell 2013:258)

Cultural criminology has also developed beyond the United States and the United Kingdom and has been embraced in countries such as Belgium, The Netherlands, Spain and Greece (Hayward 2016). Especially in the Netherlands, cultural criminology has been thriving in universities in Amsterdam, Utrecht and Rotterdam and has resulted in a journal and regular conferences. Though critical criminology and theory did also influence the development of Dutch cultural criminology, the dominant field that shaped it was cultural anthropology. Many cultural criminologists have a degree in cultural anthropology or have been exposed to extensive training in qualitative methods.

In the following section, I will discuss the three foci within cultural criminology, which are explored with the following set of core concepts: transgression, marginalisation, resistance and media in the wider context of power and culture of late modernity.

Three foci within cultural criminology[2]

Within the overarching frame of late modernity cultural criminology detects roughly three foci which ideally should be integrated in studying crime and transgression: (1) a focus of the situation – transgression and zero tolerance; (2) a focus on subcultures – resistance to marginalisation; and (3) the media – the

construction of culture in late modernity. A more recent development is the interest in state crime and sub-state violence (terrorism) (Ferrell, Hayward and Young
2015). Though I fully agree with its vast relevance, especially in relation to the
involvement of the state in such cases as the aftermath of hurricane Katrina, the
Hillsborough disaster, the opioid crises and the housing/financial crises, this
development is too premature to include in this article as one of the central foci
of cultural criminology.

The situation: transgression and zero tolerance

Cultural criminology is clearly inspired by symbolic interactionism in its strong
focus on the construction of meaning in everyday life situations. Cultural criminology does not only pay attention to action and meaning, but also to the emotional
and sensual experience of crime and transgression. Coming from the traditions of
symbolic interaction and Chicago School ethnography, and because of its focus
on the lust and the elation of transgression and crime, Jack Katz's *Seduction of
Crime* (1988) is one of the main references in this stream trying to understand the
shaping of the actions of criminals. In his book of the morally sensual attraction
of crimes, such as cold-blooded 'senseless' murders and stickups, he argues that
it is crucial to pay attention to the 'seductive qualities of crimes: those aspects in
the foreground of criminality that make its various forms sensible, even sensually
compelling, ways of being' (Katz 1988:3).

With the concept of transgression, cultural criminologists focus on the immediate, emotional and meaningful experience of the situation. Within the concept of
transgression lies a strong focus on its empowering qualities, whereas within the
concepts of deviance and crime there is less focus on agency and the emphasis is
respectively on the labelling process, and explaining and solving criminal behaviour. Transgression is used in cultural criminology to indicate the non-rational
character of behaviour that defies the boundary between what is seen as normal
and acceptable, and what is not. Transgression focuses on symbolic and emotional
meanings, and celebrates its excitement and transcendence (Ferrell, Hayward and
Young 2015; Young 2007).

Transgression includes a wide range of risk activities, from hooliganism,
graffiti writing, skateboarding to mountain climbing and drug use. It is about the
high and the rush, which is experienced while one is involved in intense activities in which one is completely absorbed in an emotional, physical and intellectual way. Stephen Lyng's concept of 'edgework' has played a crucial formative
role in the conceptual development of transgression (Ferrell, Hayward and
Young 2015; Ferrell, Milovanovic and Lyng 2001; Young 2007). The concept
of edgework relates to voluntary licit and illicit risk-taking activities, which
explore cultural boundaries of normalcy and create transcendence experiences
of intense satisfaction.

A second concept which has shaped the usage of transgression is the 'second life'
that Mike Presdee (2000) particularly used in his book on the 'carnival of crime'.
Presdee uses this concept to point to a significant social realm where people can

escape from the strains of normal life during symbolic and expressive 'performances' (Presdee 2000:38–40). Through transgressive behaviour, individuals can express resistance to the standardisation, regulation and rationalisation of social life that result in 'powerlessness and meaninglessness and the loosening of cultural imperatives' (Presdee 2000:18). The second life is about unruly behaviour, which contradicts self-discipline and moderation, and is seen by those in power as obscene, bestial and immoral. The concepts of edgework and second life are used to open up new possibilities of meaning construction, which counter the dominant connotations of crime to be found in academia and the mainstream media.

Cultural criminology does not only pay attention to the intense or passionate aspects of crime and transgression. It also focuses on mundane situations of transgression and crime control, such as the daily experience of youth hanging around and homeless people, and how they are the object of zero-tolerance policing, urban design and the use of bylaws. It shows that interventions that seem neutral, minor and common sense, create outsiders and discriminate against groups that are already marginalised, such as 'underclass' youth and immigrant men. For example, this focus shows that the premises of the theories that support zero tolerance–type interventions are not based on in-depth research, but on fleeting observations from a top-down perspective. In contrast, cultural criminology shows that in marginalised neighbourhoods broken-windows theory is a vastly simplified perspective, infused by middle-class values, that oversees and denies the voices of the people who live in these neighbourhoods (Ferrell, Hayward and Young 2015:105–107). Such interventions are popular because they align with neo-liberal perspectives that suggest crime is caused by those who live in marginalised neighbourhoods and has no relation with the wider social economic context. Marginalised people are blamed for the position they are in and have to be held responsible for it and the resultant transgression.

An excellent example of this debunking approach of the zero-tolerance approach is a recent publication by Tom de Leeuw (2018). His fieldwork shows that the populistic right-wing rhetoric of city governments in Rotterdam and Antwerp is based on 'othering' in combination with the use of static ideas of crime, mostly supported by positivistic methods, such as the use of questionnaires and statistics on crime. These have culminated in Rotterdam in a range of neighbourhood safety scores. De Leeuw shows in a detailed way the problematic nature and the biased construction of the safety scores. He contrasts these with a range of perspectives of different stakeholders, such as neighbourhood youth, adult inhabitants, the police and civil servants. The study shows that a significant proportion of the inhabitants and professionals disagree with the safety score and the implementation of controlling interventions. They reject the populist right-wing rhetoric and try to delay or redefine social and physical interventions. This study pays extensive attention to the voices of those who are the object of the new crime policy and as a result, de Leeuw shows the complexity of day-to-day urban living in relation to safety and crime. His study shows clearly that those who suffer the most in our society are faced with a strict regime of degrading control and punishment.

In a similar vein, Thaddeus Müller (2017) contrasts the perspective of inhabitants on issues such as housing, safety and social cohesion in a marginalised neighbourhood in Utrecht, with the formal dominant negative narrative of the city and the housing corporation. This study shows that many residents have a positive view of their neighbourhood and reject the negative image attached to it, which is then used by the city and the housing co-op to defend their plans to restructure the neighbourhood and demolish over half of it.

Subcultures: creative resistance to marginalisation

Cultural criminology also continued the tradition of researching subcultural groups and how these different groups construct meaning in their interactions among each other and with those who belong to the social world around them, especially the police and other agents of control. In cultural criminology, subcultures are seen as a creative reaction and defence against the marginalising conditions of late modernity. Their reactions are shaped by what cultural criminologists call 'social bulimia', which is a mix of cultural inclusion – the exposure to the lure of high-status brands such as Apple, Adidas and Gucci – and social–economical exclusion because of limited access to vital resources, such as education and the job market:

> The problem … is not simple exclusion; rather, it is deep cultural inclusion confronting systematic exclusion from cultural and economic realization. It is a situation where inclusion and exclusion occur concurrently – a bulimic world where massive cultural inclusion is accompanied by systematic structural exclusion.
>
> (Ferrell, Hayward and Young 2015:61)

Anglo-Saxon examples, for instance, are related to graffiti writers and scroungers (Ferrell 1994, 2006). In the Netherlands, there have been several outstanding publications on minority ethnic youth groups (van Gemert 1998; de Jong 2007; Roks 2016). A crucial element in the subcultural approach is how members of these groups react to the conditions of late modernity, which consist of a fluid imagery of self, an endless amount of lifestyle choices, and stigmatising images combined with neo-liberal work conditions, such as low pay and no career jobs. Identity is inherently problematic in the swirl of images, constant ambiguity, commodification and political cynicism, which defines late modernity as a potential experience of ontological insecurity, personal failing and structural exclusion.

Jan Dirk de Jong's (2007) ethnographic study on Moroccan-Dutch young men who hang around in public places demonstrates the social psychological group dynamics and how the young men give meaning to this in relation to their definition of masculinity and their concept of 'being from the street'. De Jong does not solely focus on the group dynamics as such. He also puts it in the wider context of how Moroccan-Dutch young men who hang around are labelled in the media, by politicians and during daily interaction with police, teachers and shopkeepers. He describes the world they live in as a constant collective attack on their identity and that the only way they can create a positive sense of self is through the construction of street masculinity within their social groups.

Robert A. Roks (2016, 2017a, 2017b) describes a gang dominated by men with a Surinamese background in The Hague. He has a keen eye for their almost magical construction of being and becoming an American gang like the Crips. Just like de Jong and de Leeuw, Roks has spent years doing ethnographic fieldwork. He shows the mundane routines, such as posing with typical gang gestures and defending the neighbourhood – though there actually is no presence of an adversary gang – in order to (re)create the experience of belonging to a gang. Roks also integrates the crucial role of the media when he describes how the gang is reconstructed in the media and how the men themselves use the imagery from LA gangs to give meaning to themselves as gangsters who live the fast life. At the same time, Roks demystifies the gangster culture by showing the mundane reality, which exists of imprisonment, financial hardship, boredom and exclusion from economic, social and cultural resources. This is clearly shown in Roks' work when around twenty members leave the gang because they are disillusioned. They felt disrespected by the leader. All their hard, tedious and servant-like labour did not result in the dreams they hoped for (Roks 2017b).

The media: the construction of culture in late modernity

This focus on the media describes different narratives and representations of crime and how they intersect with 'real' life and are shaped by political, cultural and social economic forces. Such studies not only focus on the analysis of the representation of crime images (see Cohen 1972), but also include those who construct the images and those who consume them. Within this stream of cultural criminology, researchers also pay attention to the use of new media by other groups and organisations other than traditional news organisations, such as social movements, gangs, hooligans and terrorist organisations. This stream explores a crucial defining element of late modernity: the ever-expanding frontier of digital culture and how it intersects with offline social worlds, such as in the case of sexting, happy slapping and revenge porn. This focus on the virtual world shows not only how images of crime are constructed, but also how these images of crime shape the acts of criminals, as they inspire them or as they construct images that are criminal acts in themselves:

> Criminal subcultures reinvent mediated images as situated styles, but are at the same time themselves reinvented time and again as they are displayed within the daily swarm of mediated presentations. In every case, as cultural criminologists we study not only images but images of images, an infinite hall of mediated mirrors.
>
> (Ferrell and Sanders 1995:14)

Within this focus cultural criminologists have coined concepts such as 'loops' and 'spirals' (Ferrell, Hayward and Young 2015:154–164), with which they indicate that representations of crime in the media can function as an inspiration for criminals which again become represented in the media with consequences in the offline world.

Examples of this focus are abundant in the journal that closely identifies with cultural criminology: *Crime, Media, Culture*. This focus has resulted in new insights into the developing world of old and especially new media. For instance, in a recent issue of *Crime, Media, Culture*, five out of six articles were related to the media, on a range of late modern topics, such as Facebook fight pages in 'I Just Wanna See Someone Get Knocked the Fuck Out' (Wood 2018) and the consumption of female sex offenders in 'It Must be Great Being a Female Pedophile!' (Zack, Lang and Dirks 2018). Abdessamad Bouabid's (2018) study is an excellent example of how a stigmatised group, Dutch-Moroccans, show agency in reacting to the moral panic about Dutch-Moroccans in the Dutch media. Bouabid has not only analysed the moral panic in the media but also did extensive interviews with 38 respondents and discovered that they were able to resist and distance themselves from the negative portrayal of Dutch-Moroccans in the Dutch media. The overall picture is that the daily confrontation with this stigma hurts the respondents, but also that they are able to put the negative media representation in perspective and that they do not recognise themselves in this stigmatising imagery. They resist this and are able to lead their lives despite the interference of this media image.

Conclusion

In this chapter, I have given a compact overview of cultural criminology and how it has developed since the mid-1990s. During the last two decades, there has been a strong relationship with symbolic interactionism. Clinton Sanders and Jeff Ferrell both worked in the Chicago School ethnographic tradition. Some of the main references, such as Howard S. Becker (1963) and Jack Katz (1988), are rooted in symbolic interactionism. Also, the three main foci presented – situations, subcultures and the media – have a direct link with studies inspired by symbolic interactionists. Therefore, it seems not arguable to say that, in some sense, cultural criminology is a form of symbolic interactionism.

There is, however, a more important reason why cultural criminology should be of interest for symbolic interactionism. The development of cultural criminology shows a crucial transformation that can help inspire and recharge symbolic interactionism. Initially, cultural criminology was criticised for the same reasons that the deviance studies of Becker and others were criticised: there was too much focus on the researched social world and its meaning for its members, without paying structural attention to the influence of the wider context.

As shown in the chapter, Alvin W. Gouldner (1968, 1972) and Ian Taylor, Paul Walton and Jock Young (1973) both focused in their critique of deviance studies on issues of power. Gouldner accused such studies of romanticism and putting little effort in a systematic analytic and theoretical approach of the conditions shaping that suffering and those who are responsible for this. Taylor, Walton and Young (1973) also argue that deviance researchers leave out society's larger structure of inequalities in power in their social analysis. For them, deviance must be seen as a form of resistance against dominant rules and the groups that shape these.

Cultural criminology scholars took this challenge and in a systematic way integrated elements of power and social injustice in their approach. They focus on how capitalism commodifies social life and is present in almost all its features and thus contributes to, and shapes, state, corporate and interpersonal crime. Their critical stance also shows in their qualitative methods, which put an emphasis on giving a platform to voices that are normally not heard. Their stance is also present in their role as public criminologists, criticising the disempowering effect of neo-liberalism, celebrating creative resistance and proposing critical interventions.

Cultural criminology does also relate transgression and crime to late modernity, in which institutions, such as religion, family and neighbourhood, lost their imperative guiding qualities in the construction of positive self-images. Crime and transgression have become major resources for self-esteem and fulfilment, especially for the lower classes that have less access to social, capital and cultural resources for dignity and self-worth, and are confronted with the stigma and insecurity of a marginalised life.

Within this late modern frame, we can categorise three foci: (1) the situation – transgression and zero-tolerance; (2) subculture – creative resistance to marginalisation; and (3) the media – the construction of culture in late modernity. Cultural criminology pays special attention to the situation in which crime and transgression are enacted and experienced at the moment. It focuses on exciting and seducing aspects of criminal and transgressive experiences, and also studies more mundane and daily experiences, such as hanging around, and forms of crime control, such as zero-tolerance policing. Cultural criminology introduced concepts such as transgression, edgework and the second life to emphasise the empowering resistance and transcendence experience of crime and transgression. In its focus on the mundane aspects of crime and transgression, they demystify dominant representations. For instance, cultural criminology looks at the daily experience of gangbanging, its social dynamics and the disillusionment of its members. The focus on the mundane elements of crime and transgression also includes the debunking of the culture of control interventions, showing that it does not align with the complexities of living in marginalised neighbourhoods and results in increasing social injustice in these neighbourhoods.

Giving voice to marginalised groups forms a crucial element in the focus of cultural criminology on subcultures. It sees subculture as a creative reaction to the condition of late modernity, such as an endless sequence of images of commodification and stylisation of social life, and neo-liberal job conditions of low pay and no promotion. In this situation of social bulimia – cultural inclusion/social–economical exclusion – subcultures form one of the few resources that can be used to create an identity that empowers oneself and forms an antidote for ontological insecurity.

Jack D. Douglas's (1971) plea to focus on the complexities of the construction of meaning in a pluralistic society of constant conflict and change resonates in the focus of cultural criminology on (a) the 'politics of meaning' – how power shapes culture and vice versa – and (b) the complexities of culture in late modern society and especially on the fast transforming dimensions of digital culture and the intersections of the online and offline world. This focus shows how media represents crime and how crime is shaped by media and which again is represented in the media, a process that is an infinite reflection of images, described as 'loops' and 'spirals' (Ferrell, Hayward and Young 2015).

To conclude, cultural criminology has integrated many of the qualities of symbolic interactionism, its focus on the member's meanings and perspectives within 'small' social worlds, and goes beyond it. Cultural criminology scholars focus on different elements of the wider context of the social worlds they study, whilst trying to answer the following question: What is the relation of the researched social worlds with late modernity and its institutions of social control? In their search for answers, they have a keen eye for the relevance of the online world, marginalisation, and resistance through subculture and situational activities, such as edgework. The elements that define cultural criminology – transgression, marginalisation, resistance and the media in the wider context of power and culture in late modernity – can be used to formulate a challenging set of questions and foci for symbolic interactionist studies.

Notes

1 This section is inspired by Hayward (2016).
2 This section is inspired by Ferrell (2013).

References

Bauman, Zygmunt (2000): *Liquid Modernity*. Cambridge: Polity Press.
Becker, Howard S. (1963): *Outsiders: Studies in the Sociology of Deviance*. New York: Free Press.
Bouabid, Abdessamad (2018): *De Marokkanenpaniek: Een geïntegreerde morele paniekbenadering van het stigma 'Marokkaan' in Nederland*. Den Haag: Boom Criminologie.
Cohen, Albert K. (1955): *Delinquent Boys: The Culture of the Gang*. New York: Free Press.
Cohen, Stanley (1972): *Moral Panics and Folk Devils: The Creation of the Mods and the Rockers*. London: MacGibbon & Kee.
de Jong, Jan Dirk (2007): *Kapot Moeilijk: Een etnografisch onderzoek naar opvallend delinquent groepsgedrag van 'Marokkaanse' jongens*. Amsterdam: Amsterdam University Press.
de Jong, Jan Dirk (2012): 'Typically Moroccan? A Group Dynamic Explanation of Nuisance and Criminal Behavior', in Finn-Aage Esbensen and Cheryl L. Maxson (eds.): *Youth Gangs in International Perspective*. New York: Springer, pp. 225–236.
de Leeuw, Tom (2018): *Verscheidenheid in Veiligheid*. Amsterdam: Boom.
Douglas, Jack D. (1971): *American Social Order: Social Rules in a Pluralistic Society*. New York: Free Press.
Douglas, Jack D. (1976): *Investigative Social Research*. Beverly Hills, CA: Sage Publications.

Douglas, Jack D., Paul K. Rasmussen and Carol Ann Flanagan (1977): *The Nude Beach*. Beverly Hills, CA: Sage Publications.

Downes, David and Paul Rock (1982): *Understanding Deviance: A Guide to the Sociology of Crime and Rule Breaking*. Oxford: Oxford University Press.

Ferrell, Jeff (1993): *Crimes of Style: Urban Graffiti and the Politics of Criminality*. New York: Garland.

Ferrell, Jeff (1996): *Crimes of Style: Urban Graffiti and the Politics of Criminality*. Boston: Northeastern University Press.

Ferell, Jeff (1998): 'Criminal Verstehen', in Jeff Ferell and Mark Hamm (eds.): *Ethnography at the Edge. Crime, Deviance, and Field Research*. Boston: Northeastern University Press.

Ferrell, Jeff (2006): *Empire of Scrounge: Inside the Urban Underground of Dumpster Diving, Trash Picking and Street Scavenging*. New York: New York University Press.

Ferrell, Jeff (2013): 'Cultural Criminology and the Politics of Meaning'. *Critical Criminology*, 21 (3):257–271.

Ferrell, Jeff (2018): *Drift: Illicit Mobility and Uncertain Knowledge*. Oakland, CA: University of California Press.

Ferrell, Jeff and Mark Hamm (eds.) (1998): *Ethnography at the Edge: Crime, Deviance and Field Research*. Boston: Northeastern University Press.

Ferrell, Jeff, Keith Hayward and Jock Young (2015): *Cultural Criminology: An Invitation*. London: Sage Publications.

Ferrell, Jeff, Dragan Milovanovic and Stephen Lyng (2001): 'Edgework, Media Practices and the Elongation of Meaning: A Theoretical Ethnography of the Bridge Day Event'. *Theoretical Criminology*, 5 (2):177–202.

Ferell, Jeff and Clinton R. Sanders (1995): *Cultural Criminology*. Boston: Northeastern University Press.

Giddens, Anthony (1991): *Modernity and Self-Identity: Self and Society in the Late Modern Age*. Stanford, CA: Stanford University Press.

Gouldner, Alvin W. (1968): 'The Sociologist as Partisan: Sociology and the Welfare State'. *American Sociologist*, 3 (2):103–116.

Gouldner, Alvin W. (1972): *The Coming Crisis of Western Sociology*. New York: Basic Books.

Hayward, Keith (2016): 'Cultural Criminology: Script Rewrites'. *Theoretical Criminology*, 20 (3):297–321.

Katz, Jack (1988): *Seductions of Crime: Moral and Sensual Attractions in Doing Evil*. New York: Basic Books.

Lyng, Stephen (2004): 'Crime, Edgework and Corporeal Transaction'. *Theoretical Criminology*, 8 (3):359–375.

Müller, Thaddeus (2017): 'The Social Construction of the Stigma of an Inner-City Neighborhood: Conflicting Perspectives of Professionals and Residents on Social Problems and Gentrification', in Michael Dellwing, Heinz Bude, Sebastian Scheerer and Thomas Scheffer (eds.): *Jahrbuch für Soziale Interaktion 1*. Wiesbaden: Springer Fachmedien, pp. 47–67.

Plummer, Ken (1979): 'Misunderstanding Labelling Perspectives', in David Downes and Paul Rock (eds.): *Deviant Interpretations*. Oxford: Oxford University Press, pp. 85–121.

Presdee, Mike (2000): *Cultural Criminology and the Carnival of Crime*. London: Routledge.

Roks, Robert A. (2016): *In de h200d: Een eigentijdse etnografie over de inbedding van criminaliteit en identiteit* (Doctoral dissertation). Rotterdam: Erasmus School of Law.

Roks, Robert A. (2017a): 'In the 'h200d': Crips and the Intersection between Space and Identity in the Netherlands'. *Crime, Media, Culture*, doi: 1741659017729002.

Roks, Robert A. (2017b): 'Crip or Die? Gang Disengagement in the Netherlands'. *Journal of Contemporary Ethnography*, doi: 0891241617725786.

Sanders, Clinton R. (2003): 'Actions Speak Louder Than Words: Close Relationships between Humans and Nonhuman Animals'. *Symbolic Interaction*, 26 (3):405–426.

Sanders, Clinton R. and D. Angus Vail (2009): *Customizing the Body: The Art and Culture of Tattooing*. Philadelphia: Temple University Press.

Taylor, Ian, Paul Walton and Jock Young (1973): *The New Criminology: For a Social Theory of Deviance*. London: Routledge and Kegan Paul.

van Gemert, Frank (1998): *Ieder voor zich: Kansen, cultuur en criminaliteit van Marokkaanse jongens*. Amsterdam: Het Spinhuis.

van Swaaningen, Rene (1997): *Critical Criminology: Visions from Europe*. London: Sage Publications.

Wood, Mark A. (2018): 'I Just Wanna See Someone Get Knocked the Fuck Out': Spectating Affray on Facebook Fight Pages'. *Crime, Media, Culture*, 14 (1):23–40.

Young, Jock (2007): *The Vertigo of Late Modernity*. London: Sage Publications.

Zack, Emma, John T. Lang and Danielle Dirks (2018): '"It Must be Great Being a Female Pedophile!": The Nature of Public Perceptions about Female Teacher Sex Offenders'. *Crime, Media, Culture*, 14 (1):61–79.

Index

9/11 attacks 56

Abermet, Viola 158
activism 9, 45, 52–53, 57, 107; political
    14, 22; social 101
Addams, Jane (1907) 9, 99–101, 103–105,
    107–113, 189
Adorno, Theodor W. 166, 170, 182, 185
agency 13, 121, 124–127, 132, 169,
    176–177, 179–181, 219, 223; human
    185; independent 37; sexual 126
Ahmed, Sara 125
Alarid, Leanne 91
Alexander, Bryant Keith 49, 51, 55
alienation 138, 165, 169, 183, 217; human
    83; modern 17, 70; oppositional- 48, 57,
    70; of workers 180
Alonso Yanez, Gabriela 195
Althusser, Louis 83, 92
American Association for the Abolition
    of Involuntary Mental Hospitalization
    (AAAIMH) 23
American Sociological Association
    24, 111
analysis: collaborative 200; of
    communicative action 93;
    complementary 169; conflict 191;
    criminological 215; critical 8, 49, 126,
    199; cultural 51; dramaturgical 63–66,
    68; of epiphanies 192; feminist 125,
    131–132; FSI 127, 132; of ideology 88;
    interactionist 88; intersectional 120;
    media 211; mesodomain 178, 191; meta-
    122; micro- 21, 69; microsociological
    70; of power 132, 190, 195; psycho-
    164, 166, 169; reasoned 183; of
    regularity 42; relational 195; self- 25;
    situational (SA) 9, 189, 193–194, 197,
    201; sociological 19, 33

Anderson, Elizabeth 198
Anderson, Leon 92, 138
Anon 24
anthropology 61, 79, 164; cultural 212, 218
Anzaldua, Gloria 53
Arbunkle, Woody 146
Ashley, David 170, 176
Athens, Lonnie H. 9, 86, 88, 91, 138–159,
    165, 189, 192
Atkinson, Paul 3
Avishai, Orit 126, 132

Bainbridge, Roxanne 200
Baldwin, John D. 80, 85
Banerjee, Neela 128
Bartky, Sandra 123, 125, 128
Barton, Bernadette 126
Battiste, Marie 198
Bauman, Zygmunt 173–175, 217
Bean, Philip 155
Becker, Howard S. 34, 54, 119, 121, 167,
    189, 191, 198, 211–215, 223
Benard, Cheryl 122
Benford, Robert D. 71–72, 165
Bennett, Jessica 128
Berger, Bennett M. 25, 31, 69, 124,
    164, 193
Berman, Marshall 16–17
Bertrand, Sharon 82
Billig, Michael 12
Bilton, Tony 82
Bindel, Julie 126
Black Power 23
Blankertz, Laura 91
Blumer, Herbert 2, 4–6, 20, 22, 34, 45–46,
    62, 80–81, 99–100, 105, 111, 113, 119,
    121, 124, 139, 141, 146–149, 164, 167,
    185, 189
Boal, Augusto 46–48, 53

Boje, David M. 70
Boltanski Luc 19
Borreca, Art 2
Boswell, A. Ayres 122
Bouabid, Abdessamad 223
Bourdieu, Pierre (1999) 4, 16, 21, 88, 153–154
Bourne, Randolph S. 105–106
Bowker, Geof 191
Boydell, Katherine 91
Boyer, John W. 101, 105
Brecht, Bertolt 48, 53, 57
Brissett, Dennis 32, 61, 73–74
Bronfenbrenner, Urie 171
Brown, Robert E. 62
Brownfield, David 91
Brune, Jeffrey A. 26
Bryant, Antony 192
Bullingham, Liam 71
Burbank, Patricia 87–88
Burke, Kenneth 24, 63
Burns, Elizabeth 61–62
Burns, Tom 19, 21, 72, 191
Burrell, Gibson 82
Butler, Judith 4

Cabaniss, Emily 129
Cahill, Spencer E. 4
capitalism 83, 92, 105, 120, 127, 165, 169–170, 176, 180, 217, 224; consumer 175, 218; global 217; ideology of 168; industrial 169–170; modern 166, 217; monopoly 70; neo-liberal 46, 177
Carbado, Devon 129
Carey, James W. 196
Carmichael, Stokely 23
Carter, Michael J. 5
Casper, Monica J. 191
Caudill, Jonathan 92
Cavan, Sherri 24
Cefaï, Daniel 190, 194, 196–197
Charmaz, Kathy 189, 190, 192–194, 196, 199–200
Charon Joel M. 81–82
Chatfield, Charles 105
Cheal, David 19
Chomsky, Noam 84
Chou, Rosalind 123
Chriss, James J. 14
Clark, Candace 128–129
Clarke, Adele E. (1991) 191–196, 198–200
class: background 128; boundaries 130; bourgeois 166, 183; capitalist 83, 184; conflict 106, 177; -consciousness 83;

disadvantaged 14; distinction 23; domination 181, 184; elite 177, 179; hierarchies 131; inequality 9, 119; lower 156, 224; middle- 13, 24, 67, 122, 128–131, 220; privilege 130; ruling 83, 87, 92, 183; significance of 19; social 5, 86–87, 89, 128, 156–157, 190; standing 23; structure 83–84; subaltern 182; system 92, 183; theory 19; under- 92, 217, 220; universal 181; unrest 101; upper 156; working 83, 130–131, 140, 168, 181
Cleveland, Lisa M. 51, 82
Clifford, James 46
Cohen, Albert K. 215
Cohen, Stanley 222
Cohen-Cruz, Jan 53
Colfax, J. David 149
Collins, Harry M. 153–154
Collins, Randall 39
Combs, James E. 61
communication 16, 40, 48, 63, 65, 70–72, 82–84, 172, 181–182, 184–185, 210
conflict 46, 68–69, 102, 105, 112, 128, 138, 143, 146–147, 152–153, 159, 174, 190–191, 199, 214, 224; human 151, 153; of interest 69, 177; interpersonal 178; -orientated 101; perspective 138; race 147–150; resolution 111–112;street 166; theory 101, 190; violent 105; *see also* class; social
Conquergood, Dwight (1992b) 46–47, 52
Conrad, Peter 92
consciousness 70, 83, 168–170, 180–182; critical 53; false 14, 20, 85; feminist 132; self- 167, 172; shared 42; social 109, 111; true 85; world 108; *see also* class
constraint 5, 31, 34–36, 42, 45, 212; affective 36; structural 35
control: agents of 221; chain 39; conception of 20; crime 216, 218, 220, 224; of culture 171, 177; degrading 220; information 65; interventions 224; of people 20; of perceptions 20; political 70; self- 82; systems of 45; *see also* social
Cooley, Charles Horton 80–81, 146, 164
Cooper, David 22
Cooper, William 15
Copp, Martha 123
Corey, Frederick C. 53
Corradi, Consuelo 66
Coser, Lewis A. 5

Coulter, Jeff 43
Cracraft, James 109
Crenshaw, Kimberle (1991) 121, 157
criminal 190, 212, 215; actions 219;
    attorney 128; behaviour 89, 91, 215,
    219; culture of 215; dangerous 156;
    experiences of 216, 224; justice system
    210–212, 214–215, 217; subcultures
    222; violent 142, 145, 149–150,
    155–156
criminology 141, 146, 158, 167, 212, 215;
    contemporary 217; cultural 9, 210–211,
    215–225; dramaturgical 61; frameworks
    140; maverick 139, 141; positivistic
    216; professional 141; public 224;
    trained 155
criticism: astute 14; blunt 20; cultural 55;
    major 14; moral 54; points of 68; self-
    67; simple 20
cultural: approach 6, 112, 210, 215,
    221; boundaries 6, 219; capital 153;
    challenges 141; commodities 55;
    conditions 5, 171; criticism 55, 57,
    215; directions 5; domination 172,
    177; enmeshment 38; factors 166, 172,
    181; feminism 109, 120; hegemony
    92; hermeneutics 70; hierarchies 13,
    67; ideologies 39; inclusion 221,
    224; interactionism 1–3, 5–9, 192;
    microsociology 4; performances 47;
    pluralism 102; politics 45; positions
    4; psycho- 168; representations 49;
    revolution 110; studies 5, 185; theory
    5; transformations 16, 217; values 120,
    172; *see also* criminology
Cuzzort, Raymond P. 67
Cywar, Alan 106

David, Peter 16
Dearborn, Mary V. 106
Debord, Guy 71
Deegan, Mary Jo 9, 69, 99–100, 102–111,
    124
DeGloma, Thomas 3
de Jong, Jan Dirk (2007) 221–222
DeLand, Michael 41
de Leeuw, Tom 220, 222
Deleuze, Giles 194, 198, 200
democracy 23, 57, 99–100, 102–106, 109,
    112–113, 173, 175, 190; electoral 37;
    modern 51; theory of 104
Dennis, Alex 4, 86, 138, 190, 201
Denzin, Norman K. 6, 15–16, 49, 55, 88,
    138, 189, 192

desires 30, 85, 126, 165–166, 168, 173,
    179–180; aggressive 178; group's 123;
    individual's 70, 179; insinuated 183;
    sexual 178; unconscious 165, 179
deviance 6, 68–69, 86, 92, 138, 167, 179,
    213–214, 217, 219, 223–224; studies
    211–215, 223
Dewey, John 9, 80, 99–107, 109–113,
    189–190, 194, 196–198
DiCicco-Bloom, Benjamin 33
Diggins, John Patrick 105
Dillard, Courtney 62
divergence 41, 79–80, 85–86, 88, 148
Diversi, Marcelo 51
Dolan, Jill 48, 52
domination 4–5, 9, 26, 79, 83, 88, 92,
    106, 120, 123, 126, 132, 138, 140,
    145–149, 151–153, 157, 159, 165–166,
    168, 177–180, 182–185, 191–192, 199;
    economic 169; elite 172, 182; human
    152–153; impact of 88; interpersonal
    183; male 120; of power 84; social
    83–84; structural 177; *see also* class;
    cultural
Donnor, Jamel K. 52
Douglas, Jack D. 138, 212–214, 224
Downes, David 213
dramaturgy 13, 32, 47, 61–74; critical 9,
    69, 75; methodology of 73; interactionist
    69–70, 73
Dubbin, Leslie 192
Du Bois, W. E. B. 45, 51
du Gay, Paul 46
Dum, Christopher 92
Dunn, Jennifer 129
Dylan, Bob 48

Edgley, Charles 14, 61, 63, 74
ego 184; ideal 169; suicide 183; super-
    168, 170–171, 178–179; trip 25
Ehrenreich, Barbara 84
Elam, Harry J. Jr. 51
Ellis, Carolyn 49, 55–56
emotion 35–36, 48, 102–103, 107, 120–122,
    127–129, 144, 165–166, 168–170, 177,
    179, 184, 192, 216, 218–219; attraction
    106 ; damage 36; experiences 57, 219;
    expressions 127; gratification 178;
    interaction 47; labour 72, 127–129;
    management 122, 127–128, 131; politics
    of 52; realities 216; rehearsal 72; risk
    32, 41; turmoil 106; unpleasant 166;
    upheaval 106; upsets 106
Enloe, Cynthia (2017) 20, 127

Espiritu, Yen Le 131
ethnography 49, 55, 211, 215–216, 219;
    auto- 25, 48–49, 53, 55–56; feminist
    132; interactionist 46–47, 49; liquid
    216; performance 47, 49; reflexive 51;
    staged 57; urban 190
ethnomethodology 2, 15, 69, 146
Ewen, Stuart 180
Ezzell, Matthew 123, 131

Faccio, Elena 62
Fanon, Franz 177, 180
Farrugia, David 93
feminism 24, 102, 107, 109, 111, 113,
    120–121, 130, 132, 173, 189, 198
Ferrell, Jeff 211–212, 215–216,
    218–223, 225
Fields, Jessica 4
Fine, Gary Alan 88, 121–122
Fisher, Michael 196
Fitzpatrick, Suzanne 92
Forte, James A. 6
Fortini, Amanda 122
Fosket, Jennifer R. 195–196, 198
Foucault, Michel 4, 17, 20, 23, 86, 92, 193,
    200–201
fragmentation 146, 169, 174
Frankfurt School of Critical Theory (FS) 9,
    79, 83, 165–170, 172, 176–186
Free Speech Movement 22
Freire, Paulo (1970/2000) 52, 56, 79
French, Martin 50, 104, 154
Freud, Sigmund 165, 168–171, 173, 178, 180
Freudian Man 173
Friese, Carrie 196
Fromm, Erich (1941) 166, 168–172,
    175, 184
Frye, Marilyn (1983) 119–120, 126,
    129, 132
Fujimura, Joan H. 191

Gagnon, John H. 62
Gandhi, Mahatma 108, 112
Garoian, Charles R. 56
Garrison, William Lloyd 99, 108, 112
Gbowee, Leymah 111–112
gender 4, 16, 18–19, 21, 34, 51, 64, 79,
    88, 99, 101–102, 107–108, 111–112,
    120, 125, 129–130, 157, 190, 192; bias
    156; categories 120; differences 26;
    expectations 125, 129–130; hierarchy
    130; inequality 120–122; norms 122,
    124; order 122; privileges 130; relations
    14; roles 165

Georgeon, Olivier L. 150
Gergen, Kenneth J. 173–174
Giddens, Anthony 16, 19, 21, 33, 36,
    196, 217
Gilbert, G. Nigel 154
Giroux, Henry 53
Giuffre, Patti 122
Glaser Barney G. 167, 191–192, 196, 198
Glasner, Aviva Twersky 156
globalisation 17, 56, 174, 217; of crime 3;
    neoliberal 165, 169, 175–176
Goffman, Erving 8, 12–26, 31–34, 36–37,
    39, 41–42, 45–47, 61–75, 80, 128, 146,
    151, 164, 167, 173, 183
Goldmann, Lucien 22
Gonos, George 19, 24
Goodman, Paul 22
Gougherty, Matthew 139
Gouldner, Alvin W. 5, 7, 13–14, 16, 19,
    23, 25, 67, 75, 212–214, 223
Gramsci, Antonio (1971) 83, 92, 176–177
Greek, Cecil 68, 140–141
Gronbeck, Bruce E. 74
Guba, Egon 85
Gusfield, Joseph R. 3, 193

Habermas, Jürgen 16, 67, 79, 83–86, 88,
    93, 104, 113n3, 177, 182, 185, 217
Hacking, Ian 18, 20
Hall, Peter M. 5, 88, 165, 178, 185, 189,
    191–192
Hamilton, Laura 130
Haraway, Donna 123, 200
Hare, Paul A. 61. 68
Harris, Cheryl 157
Harris, Scott 126
Hayward, Keith 211, 215–216, 218
Hazzard, William R. 84
hegemony 83–84, 87, 89, 92, 177
Henslin, James M. 62
Henson, Kevin 122
Heritage, John 38
hermeneutics 70, 84
Hill Collins, Patricia (2000 & 1986)
    121–123, 132, 191–192
Hochschild, Arlie Russell 4–5, 127–128,
    138, 189, 192
Hogan, Bernie 71
Holden, Daphne 122
Hollander, Jocelyn 38
Holter, Inger 84
homelessness 80, 89, 91–93
Hondagneu-Sotelo, Pierrette 128
hooks, bell 51, 125

Hopper, Marianne 63
Horkheimer, Max 166, 168, 179, 184
Horowitz, David 149
Howlett, Charles F. 109–111
Huebner, Daniel R. 103
Hughes, Everett C. 7, 147
humanist 82, 166, 172–173, 176, 183–184

identity 6, 18, 34, 121, 127–128, 130, 138,
    165, 170, 173, 175, 177, 180, 199, 215,
    217, 221–222, 224; collective 167, 179;
    -construction 6; malevolent 145–146;
    politics 157; positive 131; preexisting
    48; professional 82; racial 157; salience
    34; self- 164
ideology 6, 35, 46, 55, 57, 79, 83–84,
    86–89, 123, 131, 166–168, 182, 184
impression management 13, 16, 46, 50,
    62–63, 65–66, 71, 138, 167
improvisation 41, 71–72
inequality 4, 9, 14, 93, 119–127, 129,
    131–132, 138, 149, 153, 165, 173, 179,
    183, 185
injustice 22, 45, 47, 52–53, 57, 127, 140,
    149, 165, 185, 192, 199, 210–211;
    racial 51
Institute for Social Research (ISR)
    166, 168
interactionism: cognitive 3; critical 1–3,
    5–9, 45, 51, 79–81, 88–89, 93–94,
    189–190, 192, 201; diffusion of 3;
    ecological 3; existential 3; feminist 3, 9,
    100, 111–112, 131; interpretive 3, 9, 45,
    88, 189, 192; intersectional 3; Marxist 3;
    neostructural 3, 8, 31, 35, 41–42; pacifist
    3, 112; phenomenological 3; politics
    of 2; postmodern 3; poststructural 3;
    pragmatist 191–194; pure 2; queer 3;
    radical (RI) 3, 9, 88, 138–139, 147–150,
    152–153, 155, 158–159, 192; semiotic
    3; structural 3, 34; symbolic (SI) 1–6,
    9, 20, 33, 45, 62, 79–82, 85–89, 91, 93,
    99–100, 102–103, 105, 108–113,
    119–122, 124, 127, 131, 138–139,
    146–150, 158–159, 164–168, 170, 172,
    176, 178, 180–186, 210–212, 214–216,
    219, 223, 225; *see also* cultural;
    dramaturgy; social; theory
intersectionality 121, 129–130
interventions 53, 84, 88–89, 93, 201,
    220, 224

Jacobsen, Michael Hviid 1, 16, 25, 65, 68,
    192, 198

James, George 141
James, William 80, 85, 100, 102, 164, 173
Jane Addams Papers (JAP) 101
Jenkins, Richard 19–21
Jensen, Robert 125
Joas, Hans 184
Johnson, Allan 120, 122, 125, 132
Jones, Stacy Holman 49
judgment 54, 142–143, 151–152, 197
justice 52, 85, 155, 192, 218; criminal
    210–211, 214–215, 217; racial 51;
    see also social

Kane, Emily 84, 122
Katovich, Michael A. 158
Katz, Jack 211, 219, 223
Keller, Reiner 189, 192–194, 198, 200
Kelley, Robin D. G. 51–52
Kemper, Theodore D. 19
Kincheloe, Joe L. 56
Kivisto, Peter 74
Kleinman, Sherryl 119, 121–122,
    124–126, 128–130
Kloppenberg, James T. 101
Knock, Thomas J. 105
Korsch, Karl 166
Krutschnitt, Candace 156
Kuhn, Manford H. 34, 80, 139

Laberge, Yves 86, 150
Laing, R. D. 22–23
Lakoff, George 179
Lan, Pei-Chia 128
Langman, Lauren 17, 70, 170, 177
Latour, Bruno 189
Law, John 194, 197–200
League of Nations 110
Ledger, Marshall 22
Lee, Jo Ann 91
Leib, Robert S. 20
Lengermann, Patricia Madoo 111
Lerner, Gerda 120
Lessor, Roberta 200
Lever, Janet 41
Levine, Robert 171
Lewis, J. David 146
Lichterman, Paul R. 6
Lifton, Robert J. 173–174
Lindemann, Danielle 126
Lindner, Rolf 148
Link, Bruce G. 26
Lipkin, Shira 126
Love, Robert 48
Luhmann, Niklas 16

Lukács, György 83, 166, 181–182
Lukes, Steven 35
Lyman, Stanford M. 67–69, 138–139
Lyndon, Audrey 82
Lyng, Stephen 217, 219

MacDonald, Richard 62
Machiavelli, Niccolò 68–69
Macomber, Kris 124
macrostructures 31, 34, 36–37, 42
Madison, D. Soyini 46–48, 52–53, 56–58
Maines, David R. 2, 40, 119, 189, 191
management: emotion 122, 127, 131;
    impression 13, 16, 46, 50, 62–63,
    65–66, 71, 138, 167; stage 64
Mannheim, Karl 177
Manning, Philip 66–68
maps 194–195, 199–200; arenas 195–196,
    199–201; draft 200; positional 195–196,
    200–201; relational 195, 200–201;
    situational 193–195, 198, 200–201;
    strategies 189, 196–197
Marcuse, Herbert 22, 165, 172, 180–184
marginalisation 9, 130, 190, 210–212, 218,
    221, 224–225
Marmot, Michael 93
Martin, Wanda 195
Martins, Diane C. 80, 83, 88–89, 91, 192
Marx, Gary T. 22–23
Marx, Karl 82, 88, 104, 165, 169–170,
    176–177, 181–183
Marxism 79, 109, 166, 169; neo- 216;
    Orthodox 168
McCall, George 2, 6
McCalman, Janya 202
McCarthy, C. Doyle 190, 193, 197
McDonald, Lynn 111
McGinty, Patrick J. W. 189, 191
McHugh, Peter 22, 81
McIntosh, Peggy 122
McKinlay, John B. 88
McNall, Scott G. 7, 138
McQueeney, Krista 130
Mead, George Herbert 34, 63, 79–81,
    85–88, 99–107, 109–113, 124, 142–143,
    146–149, 154, 164, 167, 190, 193,
    196–197
Meiers, Sonja 82
Mellinger, Wayne M. 5
Meltzer, Bernard N. 3, 80–81
Menand, Louis 25
Messinger, Sheldon L. 63
Miller, Thomas 73
Mills, C. Wright 49, 56, 165

Milovanovic, Dragan 155
Misztal, Barbara A. 111
Mitroff, Ian 154
modernity 16, 18, 183, 185;late 172, 174,
    183, 210–212, 215–219, 221–222,
    224–225; liquid 174, 217; post- 215
Morris, Charles W. 85, 87
Morris, Monica B. 2, 7, 146
Morse, Jan 192
Müller, Thaddeus 221
Mullins, Nicholas 2
Münch, Richard 65
Munoz, Jose Esteban 48, 52
Murray, Joseph 91
Musolf, Gil Richard 5, 119, 138, 158

Navarro, Vincente 84
Nazism 168
negotiation 41, 65, 110, 138, 154, 164, 168
Nelson, James 200
Nepstad, Sharon Erickson 111
Newmahr, Staci 126, 132
Nietzsche, Friedrich 159, 168
Nobel Peace Prize 110, 112

Oates, Joyce Carol 155
O'Donnell, Ian 155
Oedipus complex 171
Ogilvy, James 175
oppression 5, 48, 83, 86, 88, 92, 119–120,
    122–123, 125, 127, 129–130, 132–133,
    138, 144, 179
Orwell, George 40, 64
Overington, Michael A. 5

pacifism 99–102, 108–109, 111–113;
    feminist 110; international 101, 103,
    107–109, 113; pragmatic 111
Paolucci, Paul and Margaret
    Richardson 70
Park, Robert E. 105, 111, 138, 146–150,
    157, 159, 165, 190
Parreñas, Rhacel Salazar 128
patriarchy 120, 122, 124–125, 127, 129,
    132, 173
pedagogy 49, 51, 56
Peirce, Charles Saunders 85
Pérez, Michelle S. 195
Petras, John W. 3
Phelan, Peggy 48
phenomena 9, 15–16, 21–22, 30, 39, 66,
    82, 89, 119, 194–195, 198
phenomenology 2–3, 146, 148
Picart, Caroline Joan S. 139, 154, 157–159

Pike, Elizabeth C. J. 5
Pinar, William 49, 55
Plummer, Ken 2, 213
Polletta, Francesca 129
Pollock, Della 55
positivist 3, 141, 192, 216, 220; anti- 211; non- 3
Posner, Judith 24
Postman, Neil 61
pragmatism 80, 85, 102–103, 105–112, 124, 153, 155, 164, 185, 189, 192–194, 197
praxis 101–102, 109, 146; philosophy of 83
Presdee, Mike 216–217, 219–220
Protestantism 169–170
Prus, Robert C. 4
Psathas, George 73
Puddephatt, Antony J. 88, 139
punishment 92, 127, 169, 220
Pushkala, Prasad 63–64, 71–73
Pyke, Karen 123

Qato, Dima M. 84
Quakers 99, 103
Quinn, Beth 122

Rabinow, Paul 190
racism 9, 51, 58, 119–120, 123, 127, 131, 140, 168, 173; anti- 189, 198; reverse 130; systemic 123
Rawls, Anne Warfield 26
reality: definition of 69; mundane 121–122, 222; new 58; obdurate 119; objective 30, 64, 81, 165; perceptions of 167; physical 81; sense of 150; third 81; versions of 24; *see also* social
Reich, Wilhelm 168, 178
religion 24, 51, 82, 88, 106, 157, 177, 190, 224
resistance 9, 46, 48, 52–53, 57, 108, 122, 132, 165, 172, 176, 179, 198, 210–212, 216–218, 220–221, 224–225; non- 99, 108, 110; social 122
Reynolds, Larry T. 2, 88
Rhodes, Richard 139–142, 146
Rich, Adrienne 125
Riesman, David 16, 71
Rochelle, Anne 91
Rogers, Laura E. 122
Rogers, Mary F. 20, 74
Roks, Robert A. 221–222
Rosino, Michael L. 26
Rucker, Darnell 99
Ryan, Alan 73, 105

Saldana, Johnny 46, 57
Salerno, Roger A. 190
Samik-Ibrahim, Rahmat M. 200
Sanders, Clinton R. 211, 223
Sandstrom, Kent L. 4–5, 79, 88, 189
Sartre, Jean-Paul 23, 68
Sattel, Jack 128
Schechner, Richard 47–49, 61–62
Scheff, Thomas J. 169
Scheibe, Karl E. 61
Schneier, Bruce 40
Schott, Linda 102, 108
Schwalbe, Michael L. 4, 39–40, 88, 120, 122–125, 131, 192
Seigfried, Charlene Haddock 99
Sennett, Richard 16, 175
sexism 119, 125, 127, 129; hetero- 9, 119, 130; internalised 123
sexuality 62, 127, 131, 165, 168, 190; casual 182; hetero- 48, 125, 167; uninhibited 126
Shakespeare, William 66
Shalin, Dimitr N. 104
Sharp, Gene 111
Shaw, James A. 149, 155, 158
Shibutani, Tamotsu 87
Shott, Susan 128
Shulman, David 61
Simmel, Georg 68, 138, 147, 165, 167, 181, 190
Small, Albion W. 103, 105
Smith, Greg 24
Smith-Rosenberg, Carroll 107
Snow, David 92
social: action 15, 88–89, 170, 195, 197; arrangements 23, 74, 119, 121, 125, 166, 175, 177, 180, 184; bonds 169, 175; change 12, 14, 53, 67, 69, 86, 93, 100, 102, 108, 110, 138, 199; character 166, 170–172, 183; class 5, 86–87, 89, 128, 156–157, 190; conditions 23, 131, 165, 171, 178; conflict 12, 150, 199; control 83, 127, 210, 214, 225; injustice 165, 210–211, 224; interaction 2, 34, 45–46, 62–63, 65–66, 68, 72, 81, 102, 150, 158, 164, 167, 170, 180, 184, 197; justice 9, 45, 47, 54, 83, 92–93, 102, 108, 175, 190, 192, 198, 201; life 6, 8, 12–13, 33–34, 36, 41–42, 46, 53–54, 61–64, 66, 68–69, 71, 74, 120–121, 138, 148, 175, 189–190, 197–198, 210–211, 216–218, 220, 224; media 70–71, 174–175; network 34, 211; order 16, 18–19, 41, 65, 69, 72, 92, 164, 168, 177, 180, 183;

organisation 15, 25, 31, 119, 178, 191–192, 194–195; phenomena 9, 15, 66, 82, 119, 194; problems 9, 92; psychology 5, 61, 79, 85, 88, 101, 119, 192, 221 reality 72, 81, 120, 165, 176; relationships 19, 170, 176–177, 181, 183; self 164–166, 170, 176, 181, 183; stratification 12, 14; structure 4, 13, 15, 34, 42–43, 56, 84, 87, 138, 175, 180, 191; system 5, 12, 86; welfare 54, 106; world 12, 36, 43, 57, 67, 72, 79, 82, 86, 88, 190–191, 193, 195–196, 198–201, 210–211, 215, 217, 221–223, 225; *see also* theory

society: alternative 169; bureaucratisation of 183; capitalist 15, 71, 167, 170, 179–180, 183; civil 56; contemporary 3, 62, 69–71; democratic 53, 166, 183; egalitarian 179, 184; global 110; human 46; inclusive 184; influence 15; market 180; modern 16, 69, 225; neo-liberal 216; observations of 102; pluralistic 214, 224; polite 16; socialist 183; wider 15

Society for the Study of Symbolic Interaction (SSSI) 3

sociological: agenda 2; analysis 19, 33; approach 164; awareness 12; circles 149; concepts 2, 138; contribution 26; data 25; fields 2; imagination 56; inquiry 141; knowledge 70; landscape 2; organisations 182; perspective 164, 182; pragmatism 110; research 3, 132; scholarship 63; specification 20; task 198; thought 82; tradition 15, 165; understanding 63, 66; work 13; *see also* theory

sociology: of the absurd 68–69, 139; accepted 15; ahistorical 165; contemporary 62; creative 2; critical 70; dramaturgical 61–62, 67, 69–70; interactionist 1, 3, 6, 9, 12, 31, 61, 138–139, 146, 149, 158–159, 191; of knowledge approach to discourse (SKAD) 189, 192–193; mainstream 31; objective 184; public 111; radical 88, 149; situational micro- 16; value-free 213

Spitzer, Steven 92

Spry, Tami 45, 47–49, 52, 57

Star, Susan Leigh 189, 191, 194, 196, 198–199

Steiner, Claude M. 61–61

stereotype 55, 185; minority 123; narrow 123; negative 123; racial 130

Stevens Craig 84

Stinchcombe, Arthur L. 15

stratification 12–14, 138, 190–191

Strauss, Anselm L. 3, 40, 164, 191–196, 198

Strong, Philip M. 25

structure 5, 21, 30–31, 33–34, 36–37, 42, 46, 48, 66, 80, 83, 119–120, 169, 178, 181, 183; anti- 69; character 168, 171–172, 183; class 83–84; conception of 31, 42; of conversational interaction 15; economic 50; family 171; impermanence of 33; of inequalities 224; institutionalised 22, 195; of kinship systems 21; large-scale 34; macro- 31, 34, 36–37, 42, 83; metaphor 31; normative 64; power 86; repressive 80; *see also* social

Stryker, Sheldon 33–34, 86

subjectivity 9, 87, 125, 164–170, 172–176, 178–179, 182–183

subjugation 123, 138, 144, 150, 152–153, 159, 177, 182, 184

Sujiwade, Philip O. 62

Sundin, Deborah 86, 88

Sutherland, Edwin H. 167

Szasz, Thomas 23

Tambiah, Stanley 61

Tarrant, Shira 125

Taylor, Ian 212–214, 223

Taylor, Laurie 22, 25

theory: -building projects 16; of causation 154; critical 5, 9, 12, 25, 51, 69–70, 79, 83, 86, 88, 166, 175–176, 180, 182–183; of democracy 104; developments 79, 94; diffusion 3; dramaturgical 69; feminist 79, 100; functionalist 18, 165; influences 4; interactionist 5, 189, 191–193; inventions 2; limitations 74; modernisation 2; performance 62; perspectives 4, 12, 79–80, 83, 85–87, 89, 94, 139, 216; of power 20; pragmatist 3; schools 4; social 9, 13, 16–18, 67, 79–80, 82–89, 92, 171, 193; sociological 25, 214; understandings 61; violentisation 146; *see also* cultural

Thomas, Darwin 129

Thomas, William I. 80, 102–103, 121, 168, 181, 190, 197

Timmermans, Stefan 198

Tolstoy, Leo 108–109, 112

transgression 9, 210–212, 216–220, 224–225

truth 18, 84–85, 155, 181–182, 210
truthfulness 84–85, 154
Tseëlon, Efrat 75
Turner, Ralph 173
Turner, Ronny E. 62
Turner, Victor W. 45, 61, 69
Tylor, Imogen 19

Ulmer, Gregory 49, 56
USA Today 84

van Gemert, Frank 221
van Swaaningen, Rene 216
violence 99, 102, 104–106, 112, 124, 132,
    140, 142, 144–146, 157, 159; domestic
    92, 157; glorification of 144; non- 99,
    109–112; police 52; serious 144,
    sexual 129; state 105, 108–109, 219;
    unmitigated 143

Wade, Lisa 127
Waitzkin, Howard 83–84, 86, 88
Walby, Sylvia 120
war 56, 106–107, 151, 154, 166, 169;
    Afghanistan 56; anti- 173; Civil 112;
    culture 175[dominative 151; fever
    109–110; First World 99–105, 107–110,
    112; global 109; imperialist 173; Iraq
    56; nuclear 112; post 173; Second

World 13, 109–112, 172, 190; on terror
    56; Vietnam 22; zones 104
Washburn, Rachel 196
Waskul, Dennis 62
Welsh, John F. 70, 74
West, Candace 26, 130
whiteness 130, 157
Wiener, Carolyn 200
Wilkins, Amy 26, 130
Williams, Malcolm 89
Williams, Robin 18
Wilshire, Bruce 73
Wilson, President Woodrow 105,
    107, 110
Winkin, Yves 25
Wolf, Charlotte 177, 179
Women's International League of Peace
    and freedom (WILPF) 104, 108, 110, 112
Wood, Mark A. 223
Wrong, Dennis H. 165

Yezierska, Anzia 106
Young, Jock 211–212, 216–217, 219, 223
Young, T. R. 14, 25, 69–70, 74–75, 176

Zack, Emma 223
Zimmermann, Don H. 4
Zurcher, Louis 173
Zussman, Robert 16

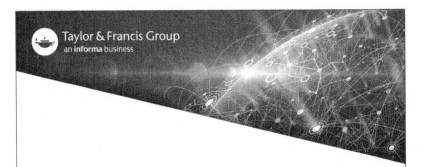

Printed in Great Britain
by Amazon